MIX & STIR

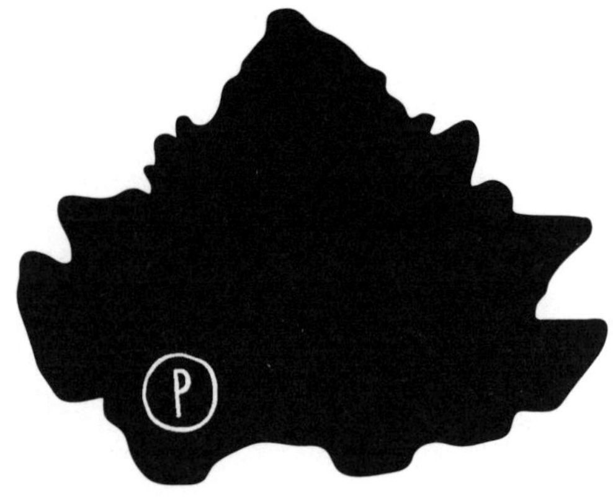

Plural
Valiz, Amsterdam

MIX & STIR
New Outlooks on Contemporary Art from Global Perspectives

Helen Westgeest and Kitty Zijlmans (eds.)

Contributors

Thomas J. Berghuis
Elisabeth de Bièvre
John Clark
Thomas DaCosta Kaufmann
Parisa Damandan
Wilfried van Damme
Sophie Ernst
Angèle Etoundi Essamba
Paul Faber
Claire Farago
Anne Gerritsen
Jacqueline Hoàng Nguyễn
Isabel Hoving
Stijn Huijts
Nancy Jouwe
Remy Jungerman
Sonja van Kerkhoff
Meta Knol
Frans-Willem Korsten
Katja Kwastek
Sybille Lammes
Charl Landvreugd
Gregor Langfeld
Chris Lee
Joo Yun Lee
Christa-Maria Lerm Hayes
Virginia MacKenny
Sarat Maharaj
Tirzo Martha
Kyveli Mavrokordopoulou
Larissa Mendoza Straffon
Ni Haifeng
Stéphanie Noach
Anja Novak
John Onians
Rob Perrée
Georges Petitjean
Rosalien van der Poel
Jennifer Pranolo
Lize van Robbroeck
Pippa Skotnes
Henk Slager
Rudi Struik
Eva-Maria Troelenberg
Leonor Veiga
Leon Wainwright
James Webb
Janneke Wesseling
Helen Westgeest
Carine Zaayman
Kitty Zijlmans
Robert Zwijnenberg

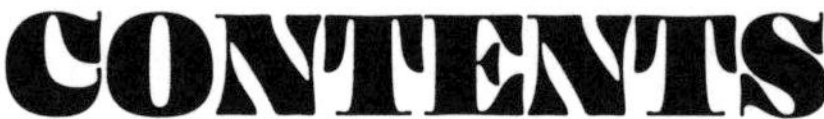

STARTERS

UNDECIDABILITY AND SPECTATORSHIP

COLLECTIVES

CIRCULATIONS

ON EXHIBITIONS

DEEP ART HISTORY

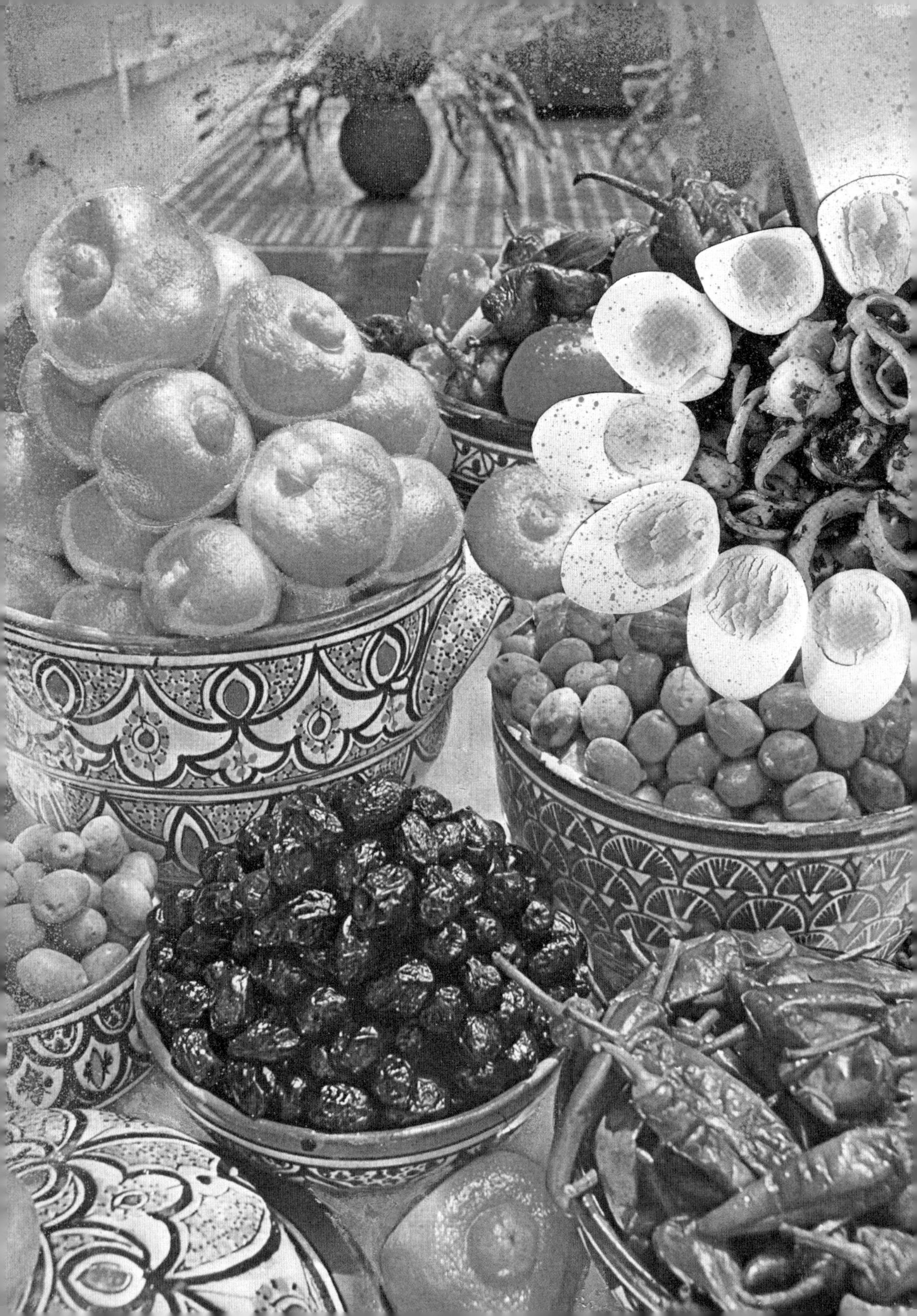

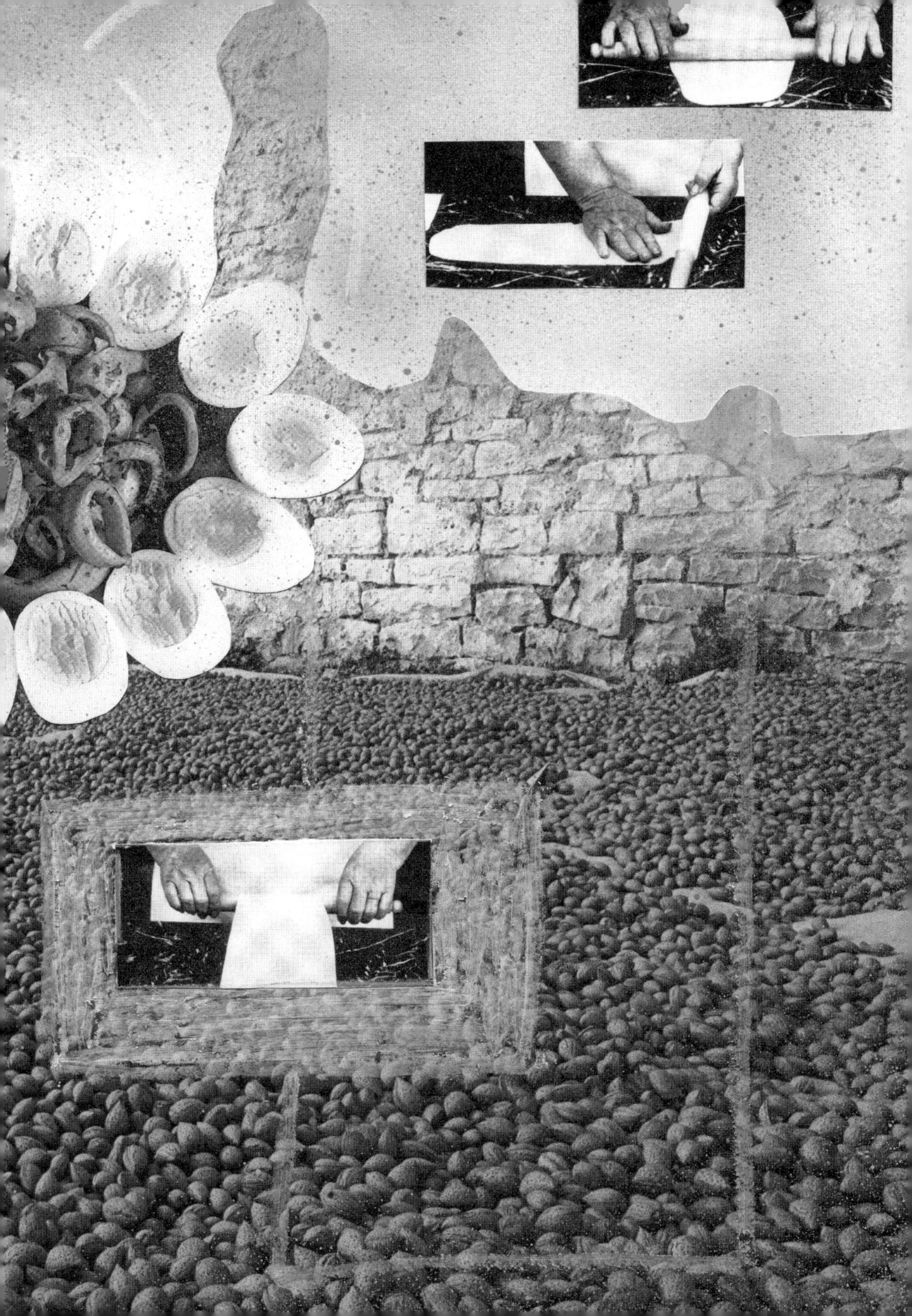

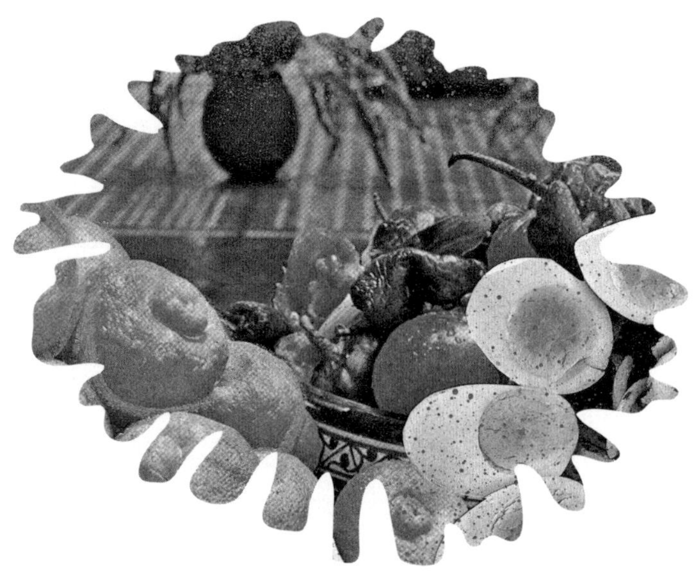

DINNER IS SERVED!

Kitty Zijlmans

Art and food are two things to enjoy most deeply. This book suggests a merging of the two, presenting approaches to contemporary art as if preparing a dish, starting from the necessary ingredients and elaborating on the mode of cooking. See it as a voyage of discovery. Cooking is fun to do. People like to eat and share meals. It is a social happening. If there is one thing that connects people around the world it is cooking. Culinary cultures are of all people and all times. We may have our taste preferences but food does not prioritize one culture over another; all cultures have distinct traditions of preparing food, passing on recipes from person to person, parents to children, chefs to apprentices, either orally or in writing. What is more pleasurable than being invited to a meal of unknown dishes and flavours? You might want to know the recipe and try it out for yourself. You may adapt it a bit, according to your own taste, or create your own variation because you do not have exactly all the right ingredients. The same applies to this volume: you may have a preference for a certain dish, but choose to add to or change the recipe following your own imagination. Dishes and recipes change, they travel with people; indeed, herbs and spices have been an incentive for worldwide exploration and trade. Leaving aside for a moment the imperialistic dark side of such endeavours, the culinary is perhaps the biggest intercultural trigger, an endless possibility of blends and flavours. In preparing this volume—which aims to grasp the study of art in its global scope because, like food, the visual arts are of all times and all places—in a flash of inspiration, co-editor Helen Westgeest suggested the format of a cookery book. I am deeply indebted to her for this marvellous idea.

Pan-human. This is a key thought in the conceptual framework of *World Art Studies*, elaborated in the 2008 volume that I edited with Wilfried van Damme: human visual expression is of all times and all cultures. So, why not art history? In his contribution to the present volume, Van Damme revisits the paths we explored in the book, the basic ingredients (interculturality and interdisciplinarity), but also their development in the transdisciplinary fields of a methodical study of the visual arts.

For over a quarter of a century, I have striven to extend the field of art history by understanding art as a panhuman phenomenon of all times and cultures, thus steering away from the persistent Eurocentric/ Western-centric viewpoint and moving towards a transcultural and transnational interconnected model that prioritizes exchange and processes of interculturalization. Contemporary art is to be found all over the planet and can be seen on countless local, national, and international platforms, but ancient, traditional art—which comes in innumerable forms—exists worldwide too. Neither in the present nor in the past were these art developments isolated phenomena; rather, art—past and present—has resulted in and from contacts and exchanges. Indeed, it is this interconnectedness and circulation of ideas, forms, and techniques that characterize the worldwide wealth of art forms.[1] The idea of intertwined histories, of shared pasts and presents, carries with it a critique of the traditional canons of art representing the grandeur of the nation state. The impact of postcolonial studies—the call to decolonize the museum, the discipline of art history, and the art world—and movements such as Black Lives Matter have led to a questioning and revising of the historiographies, methods, and theories of the discipline. Awareness of this kind of introspection is growing and it will certainly lead to a more diverse and inclusive art history and all its relevant domains, in academia, museums, and the art world at large.

We see these tendencies in the recent scholarship of the past twenty years, and, to briefly reiterate some main studies without suggesting any kind of completeness: James Elkins' 2007 volume *Is Art History Global?* questioned the extent to which the discipline of art history can be seen as globally diverse; this volume and related round table

1. Cf. *Circulations in the Global History of Art*, eds. Thomas DaCosta Kaufmann, Catherine Dossin, Béatrice Joyeux-Prunel (London/New York, 2015), with a focus on the *materialist* treatment of artifacts, a unified approach that emphasizes questions of transcultural encounters.

discussions took as their point of departure how art history is practised around the world.[2] Fourteen years later, in what he announces as his last contribution to the field of art history, the answer to this question is negative. *The End of Diversity in Art Historical Writing* is about how people write about the history of modern and contemporary art, and, according to Elkins, whereas 'the art world is becoming more diverse and inclusive, writing about art is becoming less diverse and more uniform'.[3] He sees the increasing global uniformity of scholarly and critical writing on art as 'the single most important problem in the field of art history'.[4] It is crucial that we acknowledge his analyses and suggestions, but perhaps the present volume will prove him wrong? Although Elkins raised the question in 2007, the alleged homogeneity of art-historical writing was not widely seen as a core issue at the time, the field first needed to be opened up. 2008 saw the publication of the volume *World Art Studies*, the first international study to formulate conceptual frameworks for the study of art as a panhuman global endeavour, as Van Damme expounds in his contribution. In the same year, the largest international art history conference that takes place every four years, the CIHA, was organized in Melbourne, Australia. It was the first edition of CIHA to invite both art historians and anthropologists to the five-day congress, which took the issue of crossing cultures, literally, disciplinarily, and otherwise, as its theme.[5] With a focus on contemporary art and (new) museum practices, Global Art and the Museum (GAM) was a major project led by Peter Weibel, Hans Belting and Andrea Buddensieg. It ran from 2006–2016 at the ZKM (Center for Art and Media) in Karlsruhe, Germany, and enriched the field with a series of ground-breaking volumes written by international scholars, conferences and seminars with (young) scholars from around the world, as well as exhibitions—all examining the transformation of both contemporary art production and art museums under the impact of globalization.[6] In many cases today, we are witnessing a conflation of global and contemporary art and, in Belting's view, global art can be seen as decentralizing a unified and uni-directional world.[7]

There has been some dispute over the terms 'world' and 'global'. For some, the former is seen as an old idea

2. *Is Art History Global?* ed. James Elkins (New York/London, 2007).

3. James Elkins, *The End of Diversity in Art Historical Writing: North Atlantic Art History and Its Alternatives* (Berlin/Boston, 2021), p. 7.

4. Ibid., p. 8.

5. See the 1100-page publication: *Crossing Cultures: Conflict, Migration and Convergence*, ed. Jaynie Anderson (Melbourne, 2009) (The Proceedings of the 32nd International Congress of the History of Art [CIHA], 13–18 January 2008).

6. See the website: zkm.de/en/project/gam-global-art-and-the-museum for all the publications, projects and exhibitions.

7. Hans Belting, 'Contemporary Art and the Museum in the Global Age', *Contemporary Art and the Museum*, eds. Peter Weibel, Andrea Buddensieg (Ostfildern, 2007), pp. 16–38, 22.

complementary to modernism, or as neo-colonial, while the latter is viewed as referring to post-1989 art that is truly global. In my opinion, it is a matter of explaining the terms with respect to their use and not seeing them as a new taxonomy in which 'world art' refers to all art except that of 'the West'—similar to the situation with world music—and 'global art' leaves out all art before 1989, the alleged watershed following the fall of the Berlin Wall and the year of the landmark exhibition 'Magiciens de la terre' in Paris. In 2008, we chose 'world art studies' to indicate the *study* of art through time and space, not to introduce a new category. Or as African art expert Susan Vogel and I concluded during a conversation some years ago: we do not care what it is called, as long as you do it.

Lastly, I want to mention the recently published volume *Forces of Art: Perspectives from a Changing World* because of its global scope and the way it researches art as a force for change.[8] Obviously, there are countless scholars and studies to mention that 'deal', in one way or another, with art and the global, artists from around the world, exhibitions, art worlds, museums, venues, and initiatives in their global dimensions, but this was neither our aim nor our desire. In the above, a few current historiographies of the discipline were briefly discussed, publications containing significant theoretical reflections. However, if we want to open up the field to larger groups of participants and activate them, it is time to supplement existing theory books with a format that is familiar worldwide and that does not prioritize one culture over another, one that rather includes a selection of recipes.

The present volume aims to contribute to the above mapped field of discourse by exploring and combining diverse and different angles, concepts, and practices, opening up new and unexpected perspectives in the study of art. It is our aim to take this a step further by inviting scholars and artists to present, develop, outline, and contemplate new (theoretical and artistic) frames of reference, in order to arrive at a true 'world art studies'. To use another metaphor, world art studies conceived as a landscape, not traversed by a few, major highways that deliver us quickly to a destination—the beaten tracks of theory and methodology, if you like—but rather a multitude of

8. *Forces of Art: Perspectives from a Changing World*, eds. Carin Kuoni et al. (Amsterdam, 2020). The book is the result of a three-year research project, a collaboration between the Prince Claus Fund, Hivos, and the European Culture Foundation, asking how art can weave meaningful connections between different people, their surroundings, and societal systems. Artists and scholars from around the world (that is, beyond what is considered the Euro-American realm) contributed their views on how art can be seen as a force with the ability to stimulate (societal) change.

country roads and tracks that allow for studying art beyond national constraints, cultural dominances, and hierarchies: a similar voyage to that of culinary discovery. The idea is to bring to the table new tastes and flavours, and to break new ground by allowing new, recalcitrant, queer, idiosyncratic practices and discourses, theories and topics, methods and concerns to access art in its global dimensions.

Smörgåsbord

Mix & Stir is thus conceived in the experimental format of a cookery book, filled with recipes and ways to prepare them by colleagues and artists I have worked with over the past thirty years on issues regarding the historiography, theory, and methods of world art studies, of art and the contemporary. The 'new outlooks' of the title allude to chefs' modes of preparation. The dishes reflect their insights and *modus operandi*; they reveal a particular attitude, a positioning, drawing from the inexhaustible storehouse of theory and art. We wish to bring together remarkable, exiting new flavours, unfamiliar and daring combinations from experimental chefs, who invite us to take a peek in the kitchen. We have asked the contributors to list the 'ingredients' for a particular theoretical model or mode of operation, and, on the basis of a case study, to serve a tasty, experimental dish at the table of world art studies. Much depends on the ingredients, but equally on the skills of the chef in deciding what to bring together and how to cook and season the dish. The cookery books I have at home, by chefs such as Michel Hanssen, Sergio Herman, or Yotam Ottolenghi all agree that in addition to the abundance of ingredients and methods of preparation, the secret of tasty dishes lies in the seasoning. As the proof of the pudding is in the eating, we invite you to pick and sample for yourselves. Analogous to a buffet table brimming with salads, assortments of fish, meat and vegetarian dishes, we have seven sections to choose from. Like a buffet, there is no hierarchy or order, except perhaps for starters Wilfried van Damme's world art studies revisited. The segments are interspersed with artist contributions as delicious entremets.

Undecidability and Spectatorship

What does it mean to 'comprehend' a work of art? How should we gain access to a work, to grasp what it wants from us, but at the same time appreciate that it will always slip away from a total understanding? The authors in this section all maintain an open relationship with the work, to some extent keeping alive ambiguity and undecidability in their approach. The aim is not to dissect the artwork to the bone—that would be an act of dominance and power over the artwork—but instead to work in tandem with the artwork, as an equal player in the field. Opacity, indefinability, and agonistics thus conceived as productive, non-hierarchical, pluriverse ways of operating. Freeing the approach from a restrictive methodical straitjacket to a more open and playful stance also means suspending one's (too swift) judgements and conclusions. There are many routes to insight and comprehension, all methods have flaws—intuition and heuristics are just as important.[9]

9. Cf. Paul Feyerabend, *Against Method: Outline of an Anarchistic Theory of Knowledge* (London, 1975; revised ed. 1988).

Collectives

Many-voiced in many ways, in artist collectives, as collective writing, in processes of canonization, or as a form of shared intelligence, the pluriversal continues in Section 2 of the buffet. A collective endeavour is characterized by collaboration, exchange, often also by experimentation, as in a laboratory setting, together forming a dynamic ecosystem with due respect for non-human agency. This also alludes to ideas of a planetary inclusivity of both scholarship and matter, a form of thinking *with* each other as well as with the ingredients at hand. Conceived as a swarm, intelligence does not belong to the individual but is the work of the collective and the outcome of a joint effort.

10. Karen Barad, 'Posthuman Performativity: Towards an Understanding of how Matter Comes to Matter', *Signs: Journal of Women in Culture and Society* 28, no. 3 (2003), pp. 801–831.

Circulations

Exchange implies travel, movement, and encounter, and this assembly may trigger changes in taste, fashion, styles, outlook, and manufacturing, interconnected on a global scale. Places of action are as abundant as the agents at work. This demands a new, transcultural understanding, one that upholds the dynamism of global linkages, thus relativizing Euro-American genealogies and teleology. By emphasizing 'intra-actions', as coined by feminist theorist Karen Barad, the action and meaning production erupts from *within* (intra) a context and not *between* (inter) predetermined entities of both human and non-human agency.[10] The 'intra' thus assumes equity, not hierarchy.

On Exhibitions

Exhibitions tell stories through artworks and other materials and orbit around a certain theme or topic. As simple as this may sound, every exhibition also entails concepts and strategies: how to relate the one object to another, and why? What rationale drives the selection of artworks and questions to address? How will audiences respond? And how can they be stimulated to reflect and ask questions themselves? What is their contribution to the process? It is the challenge of the curator (sometimes the artist-curator) to form alliances with the artists and the artworks, to debate, select, change, adapt, listen, and explore—the exhibition as a cocreation, on which the visitor, then, has the final say. What will be the future of museums (and exhibitions) when the visitor is empowered with (a lot) more agency?

Artists at Work

Obviously, the artist is at work in countless artistic, societal, and political domains and in many capacities, as creator, investigator, mediator, negotiator, educator, organizer, and 'wildcard', substituting any defined subset of all possible characters. There are as many and as diverse outcomes as there are artists. What constitutes a work, where does it begin and end? What influence does context have on the mindset of an artist? In their transcultural and transnational cross-connected and layered practices, artists act and make, together with humans and non-humans.[11] It is the artistic thought-processes translated into material and social discourse that speak to the percipient, to those who open up to the work.

11. Cf. Tim Ingold, *Making: Anthropology, Archeology, Art and Architecture* (London/New York, 2013).

Postcolonial Perspectives

Alongside the broader concerns of world art studies, postcolonial studies examine the impact of colonialism and Western imperialism and its aftermath on art and culture. It truly relates to the whole world, since, from the late 1970s onwards, postcolonial studies have been exploring the many cultural, historical, political, and economic aspects of the colonial encounter between 'the West' and other cultures, and how they have shaped the world. Predominantly a critical perspective—at its best, also on the scholar's own locus—it is a site of numerous investigations from many disciplines and theoretical perspectives, studying issues such as colonizing and decolonizing practices, postcolonial history, the history and impact of slavery, culture, and economy, the cultural productions of colonized societies, of marginalized people, and so forth. What will a post-postcolonial world—in particular one beyond Western dominant paradigms—look like?

Deep Art History

Human creation never ceases to amaze, not in the present but also not in the distant times of the deep past. Almost every day, new finds confirm that visual expression is of all people—all hominids actually—and dates back to over 100,000 BCE. To bring the socio-cultural and the biological-evolutionary together requires new systems of thought, a new planetary consciousness. Art, then, should be studied from every perspective and with a plurality of methods, reaching far into the deep past of human creative behaviour, which is and has been as multi-layered as it is intriguing. Understanding the earliest art may well prove to be invaluable for our understanding of the contemporary—regarding art and society alike.

Finally, when reading a book on theory and art, one is stimulated to think; when reading a cookery book, one is encouraged to dive in and try out one or more of the recipes. We hope you will feel inspired and that your taste will be awakened, but above all: *bon appétit*! And if you wish to add your own recipe or make notes, the closing section 'My Recipes' is waiting for you.

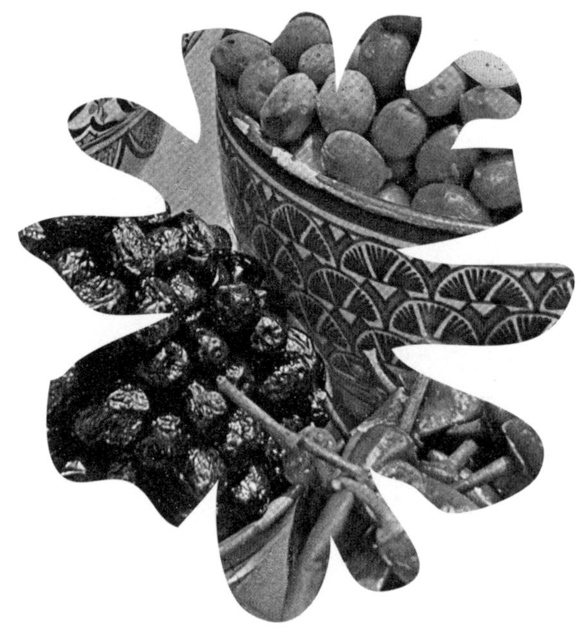

SATELLITE CUISINES The Human Sciences and the Visual Arts

Wilfried van Damme

INGREDIENTS

- World Art Studies
- Human Sciences
- Interculturality
- Interdisciplinarity
- Transdisciplines

What ingredients go into making *Homo artisticus visualis*? Which blend of what flavours of the human condition enables and incites members of our species to act as makers and users of images? These questions, formulated in the culinary metaphors this book propounds, will not be answered here—of course. Rather, for starters, I query where we might look for the beginnings of an answer to these fundamental questions concerning humans as visual artistic beings. What scholarly field—or which fields—may we turn to when we are interested in learning about the creation, experience, and deployment of visual art forms in human beings? Which domain of systematic knowledge production is concerned with addressing both foundational issues and other major research topics suggested by the human engagement in visual artistic behaviour?

In the division of labour within the human sciences—a partitioning of scholarly explorations of human nature that originates principally in nineteenth-century European academia and is in essence still current today internationally—'linguistics' has been allotted the study of human language, 'ethics' is held responsible for the investigation of humans as moral beings, and 'musicology' is assigned with studying humans as musical beings; 'literary studies' serves as a label for the systematic examination of literature, and 'religious studies' performs a similar function with respect to religion. For whatever reasons, an appellation that similarly suggests a methodical study of the visual arts—say, 'artology', or 'artistics' or 'art studies'—never gained currency in international scholarship. (There is of course the German *Kunstwissenschaft*, but unlike *Sprachwissenschaft*, *Moralwissenschaft*, *Musikwissenschaft*, *Literaturwissenschaft*, or *Religionswissenschaft*, it never spawned a commonly used equivalent label in English, nor, one may add, a corresponding international field dedicated to the systematic study of the visual artistic animal in its various dimensions.) In the absence of such an analogous label, the more descriptive designation 'art history' customarily serves—or has long served—in academia as an overarching term for those realms of study that examine the visual arts, including not only their history but their theory more generally.

Cooking Up a Plan

In the early new millennium, both Kitty Zijlmans and I felt ready and eager to try and shake up the world of 'art history'—we were motivated to have a few breaths of fresh air blow through the academic study of art. Having met through shared and complementary scholarly interests, we hoped to do so by introducing a number of thought-provoking scholarly developments that were beginning to brew at the field's fringes—when viewed from an art history-centred perspective. These new developments held the promise of opening up the field in a variety of ways, making it more up to date and intellectually more exciting. The incorporation of these new developments also seemed to have the potential to increase the level of systematicity in the study of art. In order to put some meat on the bones of these aspirations, we started thinking about publishing an edited volume that, in addition to our own views, would gather the perspectives of scholars who were considering revamping the field of art studies along lines broadly similar to ours.

What, then, were the basic ingredients that went into this edited volume, published in 2008 as *World Art Studies: Exploring Concepts and Approaches*?[1] Continuing the culinary analogy, the first question might be what this volume was in effect attempting to concoct. As editors we

1. *World Art Studies: Exploring Concepts and Approaches*, eds. Kitty Zijlmans and Wilfried van Damme (Amsterdam, 2008).

were certainly not considering the preparation of a dish, nor even thinking about providing recipes for an assortment of meals. But we could be said to have had the desire to contribute to establishing a new cuisine. In contemplating and presenting this novel approach to art studies, we merrily anticipated the emergence of a variety of original dishes, which prominently included meals we could not yet even imagine. As Kitty Zijlmans is fond of saying to students: '*You* are the scholars of the future, *you* take us to new subjects and types of analysis.' As more established scholars we did feel we might well suggest a few basic ingredients and flavours that would define the new cuisine's outline.

Basic Ingredients

The cuisine we had in mind would feature two main ingredients: interculturality and interdisciplinarity. Crucially, we conceived of these ingredients in a broad, full-scale sense. The interculturality we set out to promote was definitely not limited to the present and the recent past, even though such a more synchronic conception was emerging at the time as the most fashionable type of interculturality in the study of art. True to the idea of art *history*, interculturality in our proposal included the past, even the deep Palaeolithic past. The global or worldwide perspective we suggested, then, covered not only space but also time, from the dawn of the visual arts in human existence onwards.

Our conception of interdisciplinarity was similarly comprehensive. It went well beyond involving disciplines associated with the humanities and the social sciences in the study of art—the most common interpretation of interdisciplinarity in art history at that point. For we suggested to also incorporate the 'life sciences', which conceptualize humans first and foremost as evolved neurobiological beings. Alerting art historians to the approaches, data, and insights that such disciplines as evolutionary psychology, ethology, and neuroscience may bring to the study of the visual arts seemed as refreshing a move as the introduction of an intercultural perspective in time and space.

Interculturality and interdisciplinarity often go

together in redefining the framework for the analysis of art. The two ingredients may blend in various ways, introducing a range of interesting flavours to the new cuisine. The expression 'humanity-focused approach' may then encapsulate the two main ingredients and the flavours resulting from their fusion. The phrase references a perspective in the study of art that takes into account both the whole of humanity (interculturality in space and time) and the whole human being (interdisciplinarity from the bottom up). This encompassing approach invites us, to change metaphors, to take a 'satellite perspective' on humanity and art—it prompts us to adopt a 'view from afar' when considering *Homo sapiens* and its involvements in the visual arts. From this zoomed-out vantage point one may then zoom in, and zoom out again, in dealing with a multitude of issues in the study of visual expression.

As the title of our volume suggests—we happily borrowed John Onians' label 'world art studies',[2] reading it as *world* art studies—interculturality may in effect be considered the most basic ingredient of the new cuisine we wanted to launch with the help of like-minded scholars (contributing variously to what may be termed a fusion cuisine not only in an intercultural but in an interdisciplinary sense). From the starting point of a global perspective in time and space, the admixture of interdisciplinarity follows quite naturally. (From the two main ingredients' blending then organically flow in turn a variety of flavours, including reflection on the value of various disciplinary approaches in the study of art worldwide, consideration of issues of transcultural interpretation, and a polycentric type of intellectual history of intercultural art studies.) From the basic ingredient of interculturality also flow the three themes we proposed as initial guiding topics for the systematic study of art: the origins of visual artistic behaviour, intercultural comparison of art in its context, and interculturalization in art, meaning the uni- or bidirectional artistic exchanges between cultural traditions from across the globe.

2. John Onians, 'World Art Studies and the Need for a New Natural History of Art', *Art Bulletin* 78, no. 2 (1996), pp. 206–209.

A Satellite Cuisine

From a satellite view or planetary perspective, one cannot but notice that human beings everywhere engage in making and using visual art. This is certainly true when focusing not only on the so-called 'fine' arts but also considering such more mundane visual expressions as hairdo (which may be considered a form of sculpture) and dress (where two- and three-dimensional design may meet) or carefully shaped household objects and the symbolically rich paraphernalia of popular religious devotion. Indeed, one crucial flavour of the cuisine our volume proposed is the broad construal of subject matter in visual art studies. While the formally complex and semantically dense objects conventionally studied in art history are likely to remain at the centre of art scholars' attention, also in a global frame, the ubiquity in human life of the imaginatively visual, as highlighted by an intercultural perspective, suggests that any systematic examination would do well to take into account not only the high but also the humble in art.

Both so-called 'elite' and 'popular' art forms tend to involve expression, communication, and an impact on beholders. In these capacities, artistic behaviour and its products may become variously integrated into the fabrics of sociocultural existence. The contexts of incorporation and use may be political, religious, social, educational, economical, or recreational, including also mixtures of these and other analytical dimensions of the collective forms of life developed by our life form. In disciplinary terms, the acknowledgement of the sociocultural embeddedness of art objects worldwide may rather organically entail drawing on the expertise and analytical frames developed by scholars well versed in the contextual examination of art, notably cultural anthropologists and sociologists, but also so-called area specialists. These scholars' input may then mix with—and enrich the flavours of—the approaches already developed by social- and cultural-historically oriented students of Western art especially.

Three Sub-cuisines

From the exchanges between these related disciplines 'contextual art studies' may emerge as a major sub-cuisine in the analysis of art worldwide. Another, and overlapping sub-cuisine may be constituted by 'philosophical art studies', here conceived as a field of research examining the systematic thought that cultural traditions across the globe have developed vis-à-vis the arts, their nature, qualities, and effects. The two sub-cuisines may overlap in that a given tradition's methodical deliberations on the arts tend to be inspired by this tradition's art forms and their uses, while such systematic reflections may in turn inspire the creation, evaluation, and deployment of art forms in that tradition.

The satellite analogy introduced above is somewhat misleading in that it may result in an emphasis on the present, or the recent past. I trust, however, that anyone marvelling at the cultural diversity of art around the world today will develop an interest also in how this variety came about and what art's deep-historical roots are—an interest, that is, in the origins and developments of the human tendency to produce and use art.

Whatever one's definition of art, a humanity-focused perspective inevitably leads to the conclusion that there were times when neither visual art nor its building blocks were present among our evolutionary ancestors. The elucidation of how behaviours like applying paint to surfaces, the three-dimensional shaping of a visual medium, or the creation of geometrical patterns emerged in human evolution then requires the input of such 'naturalist' disciplines as evolutionary psychology, neuroscience, and ethology or behavioural ecology. The practitioners of these disciplines may then try to shed light on the bio-evolutionary emergence of the motor, cognitive, and affective capacities that serve as the preconditions of visual artistic behaviour. In tandem with archaeologists, art historians, and ethnographers these life scientists may also examine how such evolved neurobiological 'affordances' interacted with societal conditions to result in the adoption and retainment of the penchant to create and deploy art. The evolved capacities that contributed to the emergence of the visual arts in human existence continue to underlie the creation, responses, and sociocultural uses and effects of art. Disciplines focused on this most fundamental level of analysis may then be said to constitute the sub-cuisine of 'evolutionary art studies', encompassing today's various naturalist dealings with art.

The Human Sciences as Satellite Cuisines

The intercultural and interdisciplinary perspective briefly introduced above shows close correspondences to the approaches promoted by such transdisciplines as linguistics, religious studies, ethics, literary studies, and musicology. All these integrative fields of study share, at least in principle or ideally, both a global perspective in time and space and a reliance on the contributions various disciplines can make to understanding these fields' respective subject matters. (This reliance has in fact led to the development of a range of now established subdisciplines: neuroethics, sociomusicology, the psychology of religion, the philosophy of language, and so on.) These transdisciplines, each dedicated to dealing with one analytically singled-out dimension of being human in a coherent and encompassing manner, may then each be said to promote a 'satellite cuisine': they offer a humanity-focused approach that combines spatiotemporal interculturality with a bottom-up interdisciplinarity similar to the overall approach that the world art studies volume attempted to promote for the study of art.

The various human sciences mentioned here for comparison's sake have a head start over the comprehensive study of the visual arts in human existence. Most of them have been able to develop their integrative approaches for more than a century now, which has led to specialized journals, handbooks, and encyclopaedias covering the whole of these intercultural and interdisciplinary fields; it has also resulted in institutional homes, a variety of research programmes, and detailed intellectual histories. Most of these features are still missing for the emerging humanity-focused study of art.

Yet there are also reasons to be cheerful about the late arrival of an encompassing type of art studies. We can make a fresh start, both interdisciplinarily and, especially here, interculturally, in terms of the involvement of scholars from a wide range of cultural backgrounds. The recent initiatives to develop intercultural art studies may have been forthcoming predominantly from within Western academia, but their proponents extended invitations to colleagues across the globe to join the discussion right from the beginning—they were determined to launch the worldwide study of art as a collaborative intercultural effort from the start. (A humanity-focused satellite view readily teaches one that one's own intellectual tradition is but one among many.)

The late start of a comprehensive art studies thus offers the opportunity—absent when the other human sciences began their life—to create a *Diskussionsgemeinschaft* whose participants represent not only various disciplines but diverse cultural traditions. A forum is thus created for intercultural and interdisciplinary exchanges in formulating starting points and in envisaging future developments in the examination of the visual arts as a feature of human existence. At this forum or platform, one may ponder and debate a host of foundational issues from a range of vantage points. These issues may be of a conceptual, epistemological, and methodological nature (scrutinizing questions and terminology, examining tacit paradigms, weighing disciplinary approaches, and so on). One may also imagine such a forum to be concerned with evaluating any patterns, processes, and explanatory models that are suggested as relevant for art as a worldwide phenomenon. It may also initiate new lines of inquiry, launch collaborative projects, et cetera.

I think I may also speak for Kitty Zijlmans when I say that it was above all such an intellectual platform or meeting point that *World Art Studies: Exploring Concepts and Approaches* wished to create. As one of the opening matches of the games, the volume summoned the involvement and contributions of a new generation of scholars, hailing from diverse cultures across the globe and representing a variety of contemporary disciplines, but united in their fascination with the visual arts as a dimension of being human.

Angèle Etoundi Essamba

Jeune fille pensive, au regard fixe,
capté dans le vif
fille d'ailleurs, au regard rêveur,
qui surgit de l'ombre
absorbe la lumière et
n'en restitue que l'essence
je te regarde et tu me regardes
et me renvoie au plus profond
de mon être
Ton regard infini renferme
le champ de tous les possibles...

Pensive young girl, with a fixed gaze,
captured in the here and now
a girl from elsewhere, with a dreamy gaze,
emerging from the shadows
absorbs light and
only restores its essence
I look at you and you look at me
and send me back to the depths
of my being
Your infinite gaze encloses
the field of all possibilities ...

Angèle Etoundi Essamba, *Noire #14*, 1/20, 2000, silver gelatine print on barite paper.
Photograph taken at 'La porte du voyage sans retour' at la Maison des Esclaves, Ile de Goree.

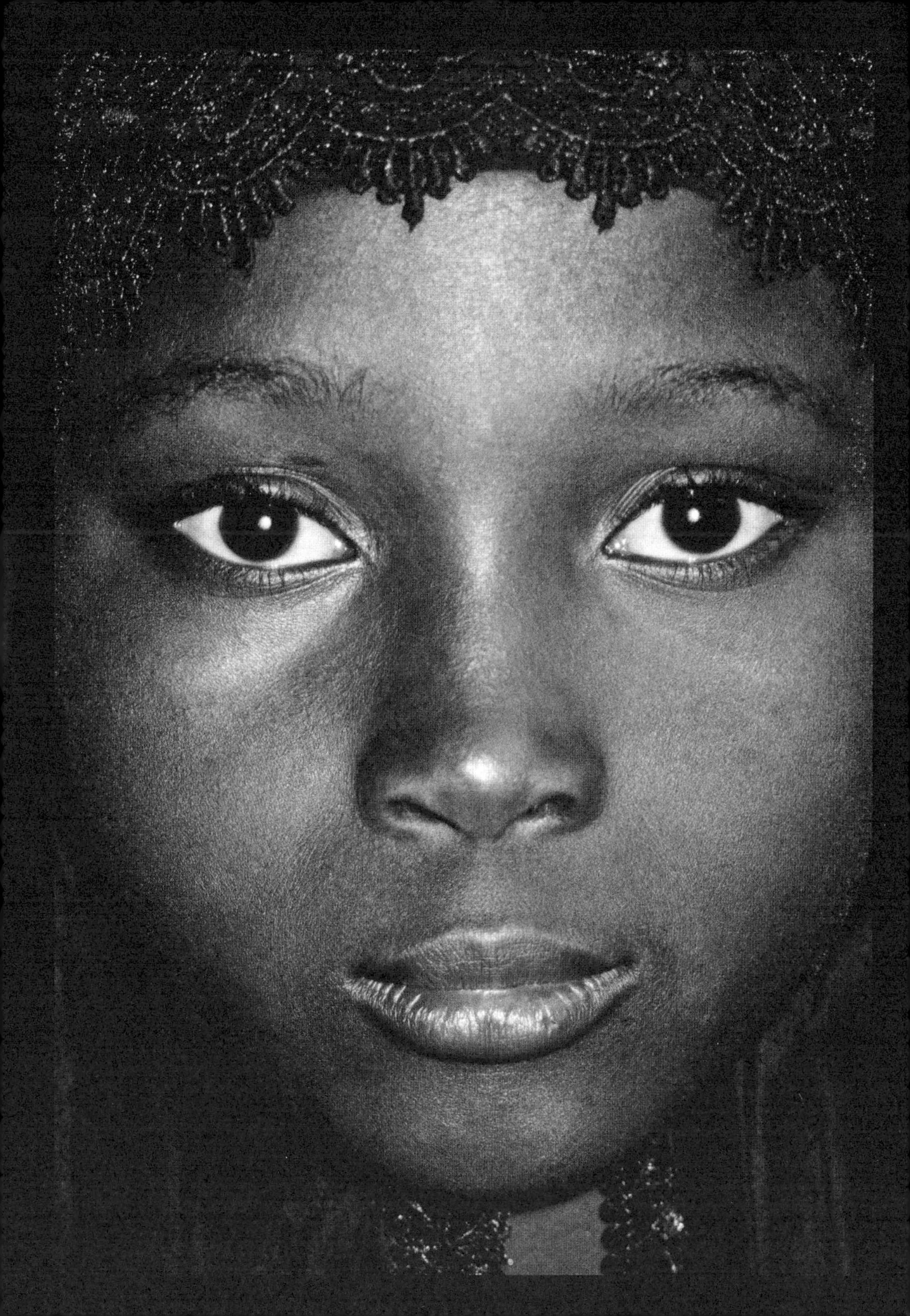

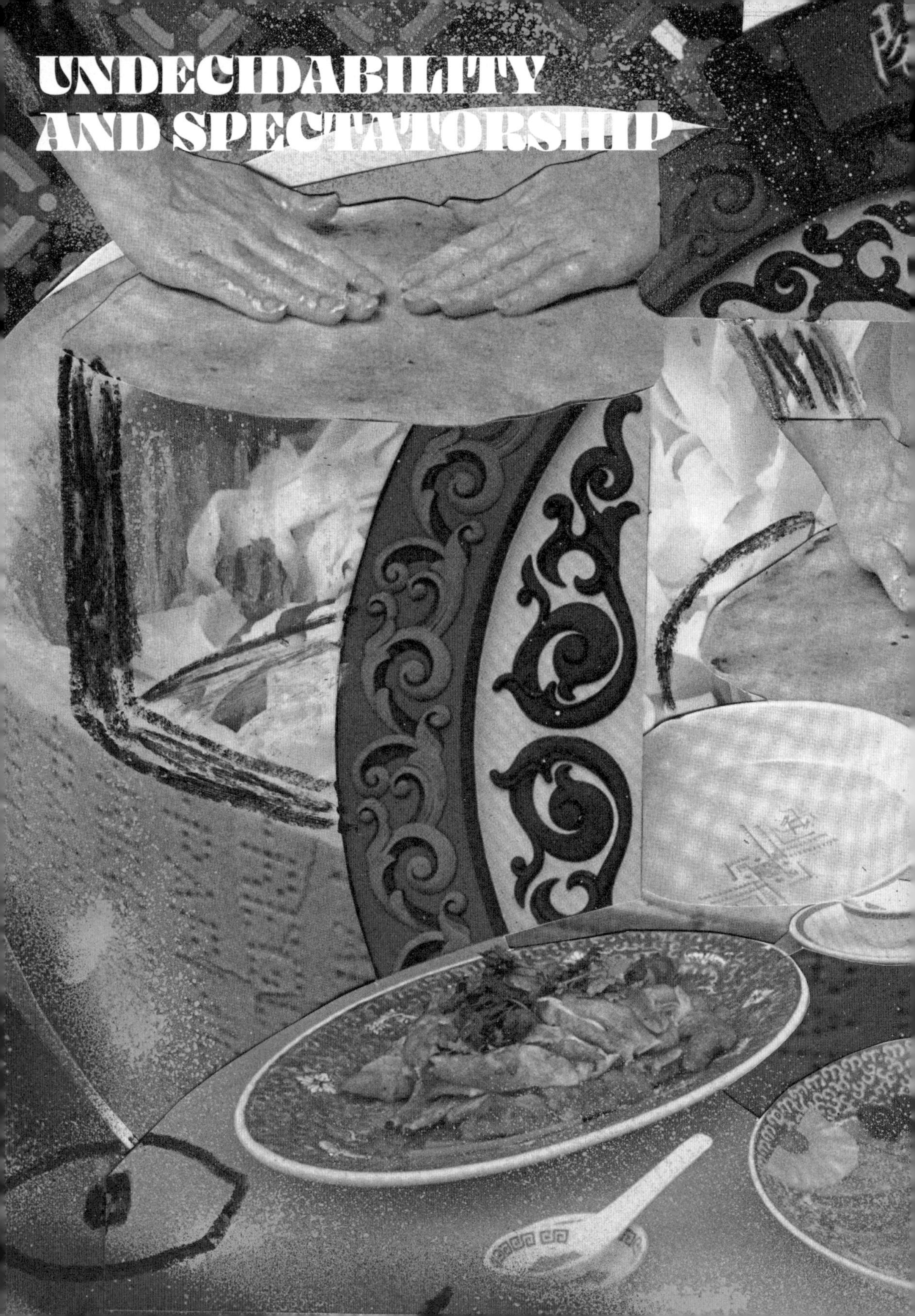

UNDECIDABILITY AND SPECTATORSHIP

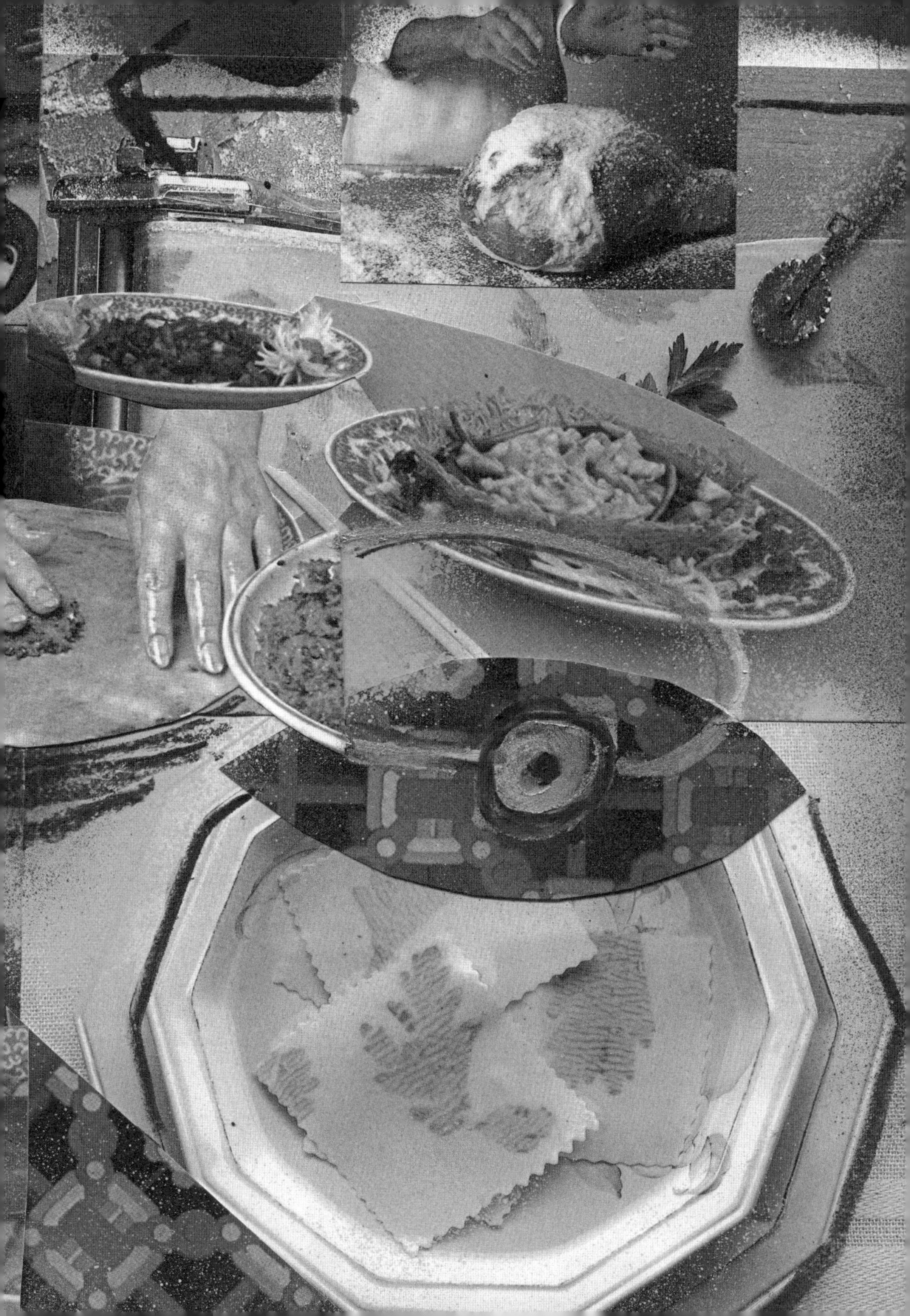

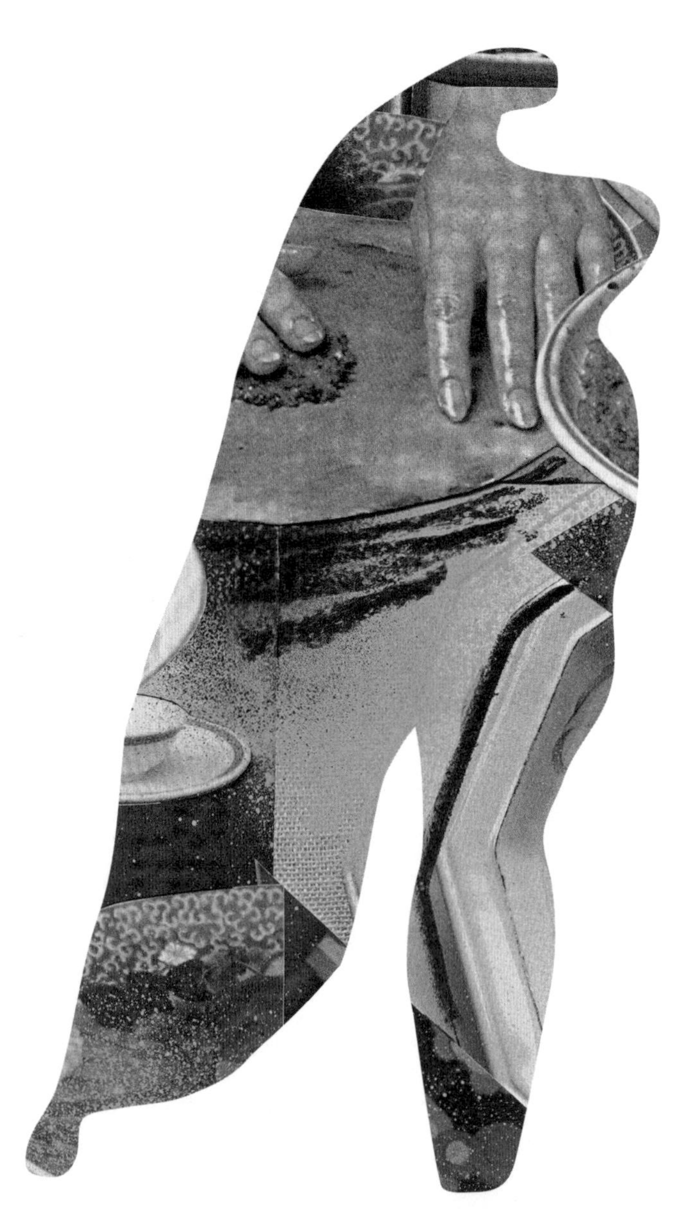

DARKNESS AS ACTOR IN THE PRINTS BY BELKIS AYÓN

Stéphanie Noach

INGREDIENTS

- Darkness
- Desire
- Black Matter
- Vitality
- The Caribbean
- Opacity

It was in the summer of 2018 that I first saw the print *Aunque vayamos al cielo siempre se acordarán de nosotros* [Even If We Go to Heaven, They Will Always Remember Us] (1990) by Cuban artist Belkis Ayón (1967–1999).[1] The largely black image of an empty-faced woman riding a goat hung in the middle of the artist's sister's house in Havana—where it ended up soon after the artist's premature death in 1999—alongside a dozen other equally dark works with similar figures. For some reason I still cannot explain, I was immediately drawn to it. It may have been because of its central location in the living room, or maybe it was something in the image itself that caught my attention. What I do know positively is that as I got closer to it, I became convinced that I was looking at a forthright representation: I had no doubt that the peculiar looking woman—with her large bare eyes, her naked body covered with fish scales and adorned with religious symbols—and the accompanying figures represented some aspect of reality. This conviction was short-lived. When turning my eye to the space around and inside the clearly delineated forms, I was overcome by darkness. From that moment onwards, there was no holding back anymore: the dark started to get to me from everywhere, swallowing up all figurative elements. Whatever I had believed about this scene no longer existed. Two thoughts imposed themselves on me: the image, which just a moment ago seemed to reveal all to me, turned out to present something ungraspable; and, related, it took me from a sense of total understanding to one of absolute, yet enjoyable confusion.

1. In this essay, I depart from one of the chapters in my dissertation *Dark Matters: Recasting Darkness Through Contemporary Latin American Art*. I presented this research in a preliminary stage at the Afro-Latin American Research Institute at Harvard University in February 2021.

In this essay, I will advance towards the proposition that only when considering *Aunque vayamos*'s darkness, equivalent to its penetrating black ink, we can come to an understanding of it. Although this term might sound paradoxical here. For, what I will argue is that comprehending this image means to be attentive to what it wants from us: that we give up on understanding. Or at least a certain kind of understanding that, as the Martinican literary scholar

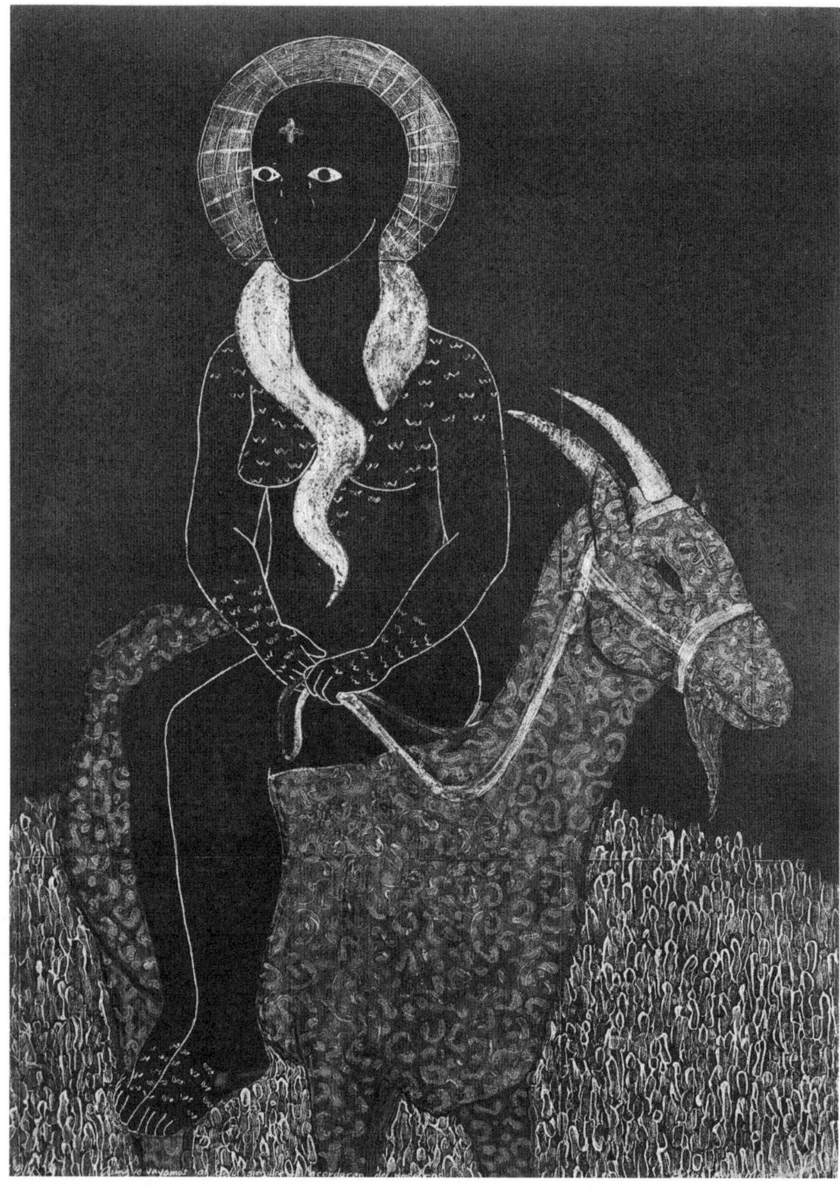

Belkis Ayón, *Aunque vayamos al cielo, siempre se acordarán de nosotros* [Even If We Go to Heaven, They Will Always Remember Us], 1990, collagraphy, 100 × 68.5 cm.

and poet Édouard Glissant considers, aims at clarification, and, hence, at objectification and appropriation. A kind of understanding which he associates with the colonizer when faced with peoples and cultures that are unknown to him. Glissant's reflections on understanding as an illuminating and objectifying exercise are vital to this essay, and so is his conceptualization of opacity. By this he means the force of people and things alike to remain unknown and thereby, to not be dominated. Drawing from this concept of opacity—which as the author writes 'is not the dark, though it is possible for it to be so and be accepted as such'—I will examine what the black ink of Ayón's image is capable of doing and provoking.[2] I am aware that it may appear naïve, absurd even, to suggest that this dark matter has the capacity to do things, that it has agency, just as much as I am aware that my previous suggestion about the desire of the image might seem so. Yet, such are exactly the premises underlying this essay. Neither of them is articulated for the first time by me. For the former, I drew from the scholarship by political theorist Jane Bennett concerning the life of non-organic matter. In her thinking, agency is not just limited to humans, but stem cells, fish oils and electricity too have the capacity to take action.[3] A sister-term of agency that appears repeatedly throughout Bennett's writing—and which I find more accurate for my purposes here—is vitality: 'the capacity of things not only to block the wills and designs of humans but also to act as quasi agents or forces with trajectories, propensities or tendencies of their own'.[4] With regard to the suggestion that *Aunque vayamos* desires, I am indebted to the art historian W.J.T. Mitchell, who was the first in the field of art history to propose that images, like people, have desires and wishes of their own.[5]

Although many of the authors who researched Ayón's work—such as Cristina Vives, Eugenio Valdés, Odette Casamayor-Cisneros, David Mateo, and Orlando Hernández—remarked that after the year 1990 her prints were predominantly black, neither of them has addressed this matter in greater depth.[6] Their eyes were fixed on the representational elements; on the sharply displayed and evidently outlined animal and human figures.

2. 'L'opaque n'est pas l'obscur, mais il peut l'être et être accepté comme tel'. Édouard Glissant, *Poétique de la Relation* (Paris, 1990), p. 205.

3. Jane Bennett, *Vibrant Matter: A Political Ecology of Things* (Durham, 2010).

4. Ibid., p. iix

5. W.J.T. Mitchell, *What Do Pictures Want? The Lives and Loves of Images* (Chicago/ London, 2005).

6. *Belkis Ayón. Arte cubano contemporáneo*, eds. Shirley Moreíra Vázquez and Patricia Martlnez Chiroles (Sevilla, 2016); *Nkamé Belkis Ayón*, ed. Alex Fleites (Madrid, 2010); Orlando Hernández, *Without Masks: Contemporary Afro-Cuban Art* (London, 2010).

As if absorbed in them, they unequivocally arrived at the same diagnosis: Ayón's prints offer the hitherto inexistent iconography of the creation myth of the Afro-Cuban brotherhood Abakuá.[7] This renowned society of occult knowledge and mutual help was established in Havana in 1836 by enslaved men transported from the Old Calabar (what is currently South East Nigeria). It was founded on a story about the sacrifice of an African princess, Sikán, after—so most versions go—she disclosed the great secret that had been told to her by a fish who reincarnated the almighty god Abasí.[8]

I have no doubt that Ayón's works have a close relationship with Abakuá. We can tell as much from the figures appearing in the print, which indeed seem to be the very same as the protagonists of the myth. It is worthwhile also to take into account the interviews with the artist and the notes she left behind. In them, she stresses that the stories surrounding the brotherhood, especially the ones related to Sikán, served as the source for her oeuvre.[9] However, I do wish to go beyond the assumption that they are iconographic. Designating them as such implies to create the illusion that the print is a visual translation of the Abakuá myth. That it is, to say this in the words of art historian and philosopher Georges Didi-Huberman, nothing more than 'an accurate mirror or a transparent window'.[10] Designating Ayón's oeuvre as iconographic also creates the illusion that we can decipher it; that we can acquire exhaustive knowledge of the black prints if only we study the stories surrounding the brotherhood in depth, and subsequently, rightly apply the iconographic tools.

I can imagine we feel attracted by the promises of knowledge, but I contend that if we want to understand *Aunque vayamos* we should not let ourselves be seduced by iconography. In fact, I want to take this one step further by suggesting that neither should we let ourselves be seduced by the representational elements which led us to the diagnosis of Ayón's work as iconographic in the first place. Inspired by Didi-Huberman's reading of the pigmentary white background as the focal point of Fra Angelico's fresco *The Annunciation* (1440-41) and not the interaction between the angel Gabriel and virgin Mary, I propose to look at *Aunque vayamos* again. Like Didi-Huberman,

7. *Nkamé Belkis Ayón*, ed. Alex Fleites (Madrid, 2010), pp. 267, 289, 297.

8. About the myth exist many different, even contradictory versions. The best-known and classic versions can be found in: Lydia Cabrera, *El Monte* (New York, 1985); Lydia Cabrera, *La sociedad secreta Abakuá narrada por viejos adeptos* (Miami, 2005); Enrique Sosa, *Los ñañigos* (Havana, 1982); Fernando Ortiz, *Los negros brujos* (Miami, 1973). An intriguing more recent revision of the myth can be found in: Patricia González Gómez-Cásseres, 'Sikanékue, Mujer Fundacional en Abakuá', *Afro-Hispanic Review* 35, no. 2 (Fall 2016).

9. Fleites 2010 (see note 7).

10. Georges Didi-Huberman, *Confronting Images: Questioning the Ends of a Certain History of Art* (Pennsylvania, 2005), p. 3.

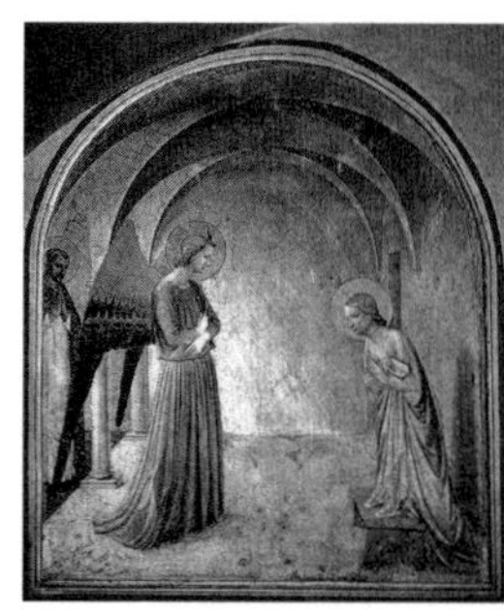

Fra Angelico, *The Annunciation*, 1440–41, fresco, Florence, Monastery of San Marco, cell 3.

I want to now turn a blind eye to 'everything that we thought we saw because we knew what to call it, and return henceforth to what our knowledge had not been able to clarify'.[11] Curiously enough, to return to those parts that I did not know what to make of, the parts that had seemed obscure to me from early on, is to return to the *Aunque vayamos*'s darkness, yet with fresh eyes. Eyes that are more sensitive to the darkness: seeing, for example, that it has a certain texture, abounds in relief, and is more translucent in some parts than in others.[12] This extreme richness regarding tone, texture, and relief, is a result of the particular printing technique Ayón worked with, collagraphy, and is so pervasive as to not leave us unaffected.[13] Once we open to the black of the image, perceive its heterogeneity and accept how it nearly takes over the entire image, we are unable to continue regarding it as secondary to the clearly displayed and outlined forms and figures. And from reducing it lightheartedly to a means used to depict the background, as well as the animal, human, and botanic figure, we begin to recognize it as an 'essential and massive component' that deserves to be regarded and named afresh.[14] But how to take on such an endeavour? Again, it is Didi-Huberman who can provide some guidance. Reflecting upon the white of Fra Angelico's painting, he writes:

> it reaches us without our being able to grasp it, and [because] it envelops us without our being able, in our turn, to catch it in the snare of a definition. It is not visible in the sense of an object that is displayed or outlined; but neither is it invisible, for it strikes our eye, and even does much more than that. It is material.[15]

What Didi-Huberman writes about the white proves to be extremely useful in my consideration of the black in Ayón's image. So much so that everything he writes about the white of *The Annunciation* can be applied to the black of *Aunque vayamos*. Like him, I recognize that the black in Ayón's images takes action: it comes ever closer to us, reaches us, envelops us, and strikes our eye. Like him, I perceive that even though the black has the capacity to engage with us in these manners, it cannot be grasped.

11. Ibid., p. 16.

12. The material qualities of Ayón's work have been discussed previously, as well as the particular technique of her prints (collagraphy), but they have not before influenced the conceptual analysis of the prints.

13. Collagraphy is a printing technique based on making a cardboard matrix which includes collaged materials of different textures, forms and levels of absorbency.

14. Didi-Huberman 2005 (see note 10), p. 17.

15. Ibid.

The suggestion that the black cannot be grasped requires special attention because, so I argue, this is the core potential of this very matter. Consequentially, only when invoking Bennett's ideas about the material powers running through nonhuman things and emphasizing that darkness is a vitality that evades being captured, we can come closer to an understanding of *Aunque vayamos*. It is Glissant who, through his reflections on opacity, can help us gain further insight into this issue. In one of his least well-known texts, 'Traité du tout-monde' (1997), some of his fundamental ideas concerning this concept are crystallized:

> I claim the right to *opacity* for everyone, which is not enclosure … I do not need to 'understand' anyone, an individual, a community, a people, to 'take them with me' at the cost of stifling them, of losing them in an amorphous totality which I would manage, in order to be willing to live alongside them, to build with them, to take risks with them.[16]

Defying standardized negative conceptualizations, Glissant evokes opacity as an enabling value which affords anybody—and anybody is understood by him in the broadest sense possible, encompassing individuals, communities, and people but also cultures, lands, and texts—the right to unknowability, to remain outside of the enclosure of comprehension. He wrote these words not as a distant scholar pretending to make so-called objective and universal claims about the world, but as a Martinican man of the twentieth century concerned with the ways in which the explorer had approached the Caribbean, and in general peoples and cultures that were not his own: as others that the explorer wanted to submit to 'the Transparent' in order to see (through) them, and thus, to understand and hold control over them.[17] According to Glissant, and I follow him here, opacity is capable of disrupting this condition; it is a 'force' that drives communities and cultures alike to, simultaneously, escape from and resist hierarchical and objectifying models of understanding installed by the explorer yet still current in our days.

16. Édouard Glissant, *Traité du Tout-Monde* (Paris, 1997), p. 29.

17. Édouard Glissant, *Poetics of Relation* (Ann Arbor, 2010), p. 189.

OPAQUENESS

18. Édouard Glissant, *Caribbean Discourse* (Charlottesville, 1992), p. 256.

Accentuating the great potential of opacity, Glissant insists on accepting the other's claim to it. This amounts to acknowledging that we do not need to understand others to be able to love them, neither to work or play with them, to suspending all efforts to objectify differences and, instead, surrender to what one cannot understand, and, ultimately, it amounts to preventing that anybody or anything, out of an objectifying and hierarchical desire for comprehension, is grabbed by the grubby hands of the other. It is in this sense also that opacity can be equated with freedom. 'Their opacity', Glissant writes, 'is nothing after all but their freedom.'[18]

In my view, the darkness of *Aunque vayamos* has a lot in common with opacity as Glissant approaches it. To start with, it is a force, or my preferred term, a vitality, that is capable of doing things. By this I mean not just any things, I consider that the black matter of Ayón's image effectively shields whatever is intended to remain secret; any occult reality of the Abakuá brotherhood or maybe something else we are even less aware of. More controversially, it prevents us from acquiring a clear comprehension of the image. It is to this degree that the actions taken by darkness are intimately bound to the desires of the image. I conclude that *Aunque vayamos* wants us to cease aiming for clarity and exhaustive knowledge in our approach to it. Instead, it wants us to open up to a way of understanding that amounts to the comprehension that it wants not to be captured, not be enclosed, and thereby, not to be understood in what Glissant has shown us is the explorer's take on this.

Ayón and Glissant, both bound to the Caribbean yet diverse in terms of discipline, age, and gender pave the way for a new outlook on art: one in which understanding ceases to be just another word for grasping and in which the unknown becomes a valuable place. At the centre of their practice lies the dark. Through the invocation of darkness, either in words or in matter, an approach to art beyond the hierarchical and objectifying approach associated with the explorer becomes imaginable.

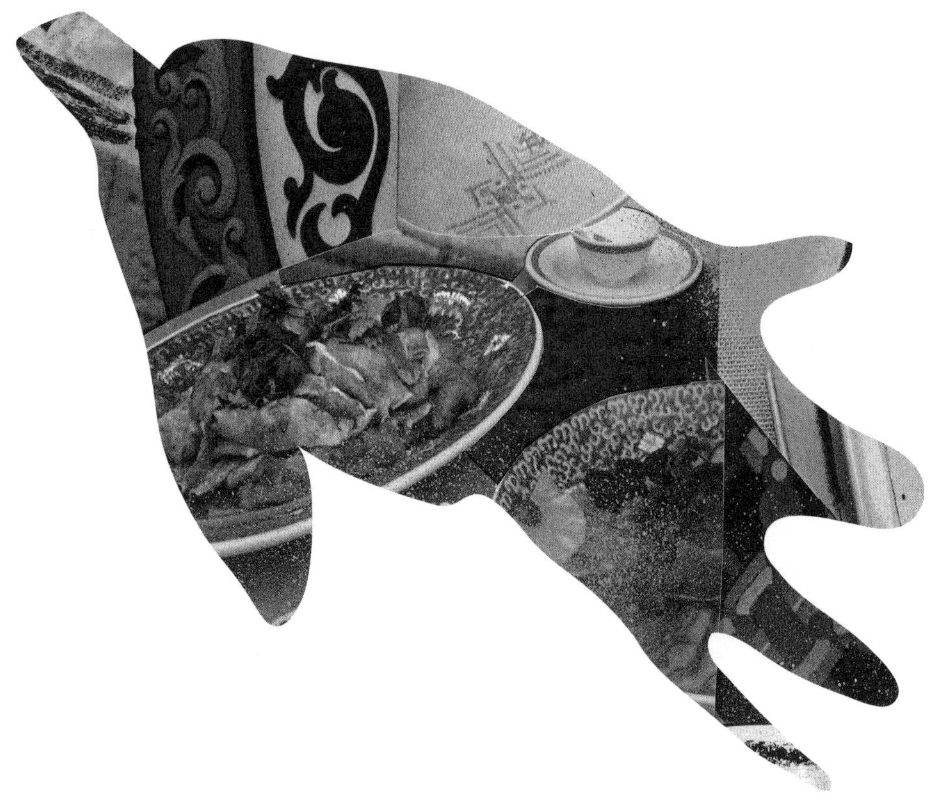

WHAT HAD HAPPENED? Reflections in Response to Melvin Edwards' *Lynch Fragments*[1]

Robert Zwijnenberg

INGREDIENTS

- Activist Art
- Archipelagic Thought
- Trembling Thinking
- Ethics
- Uncertainties

The overwhelming intellectual and sensory experience of an exceptionally prepared dish will lose momentum when we are served that dish day in and day out. After a few days, we can not just let the dish do its work, but the dish needs us to continue to excel. We ourselves—as avid eaters—have to create a very personal intellectual and sensory context over and over again in which the mix of all ingredients can fully develop. The same applies to the experience of a work of art: that too is a one-to-one experience for which we ourselves are responsible.

To put some flesh on the bones of this one-to-one relationship, I consider the work of the American artist Melvin Edwards (b. 1937). From 1963, Edwards has worked on a series of small abstract metal sculptures, using existing objects such as chains, shovels, hooks, scissors, locks, and blades. In an interview in 2015, he stated:

> I didn't want these works to be limited to formalist concerns. I called them *Lynch Fragments* because you had to consider the subjective potential. Lynching was a specific experience of

1. Thanks to Paula Kaori Nishijima; our discussions on activist art underlie this article.

> African-Americans; it was a genocide committed against our people. With that name, you had to accept that the social aspect was a basic part of the art.[2]

2. www.phaidon.com/agenda/art/articles/2015/october/15/in-conversation-with-melvin-edwards-at-frieze/, accessed on 3 May 2021.

Through the title, Edwards wanted to make it clear that the formal aesthetic quality or artistic charge of a work cannot be separated from the social context in which it is created and presented. In another interview, talking about his improvisational artistic practice in which he works on a sculpture without a clear preconceived plan, he remarks:

> Things could've gone a number of directions in that early period because the ideas led to other ideas

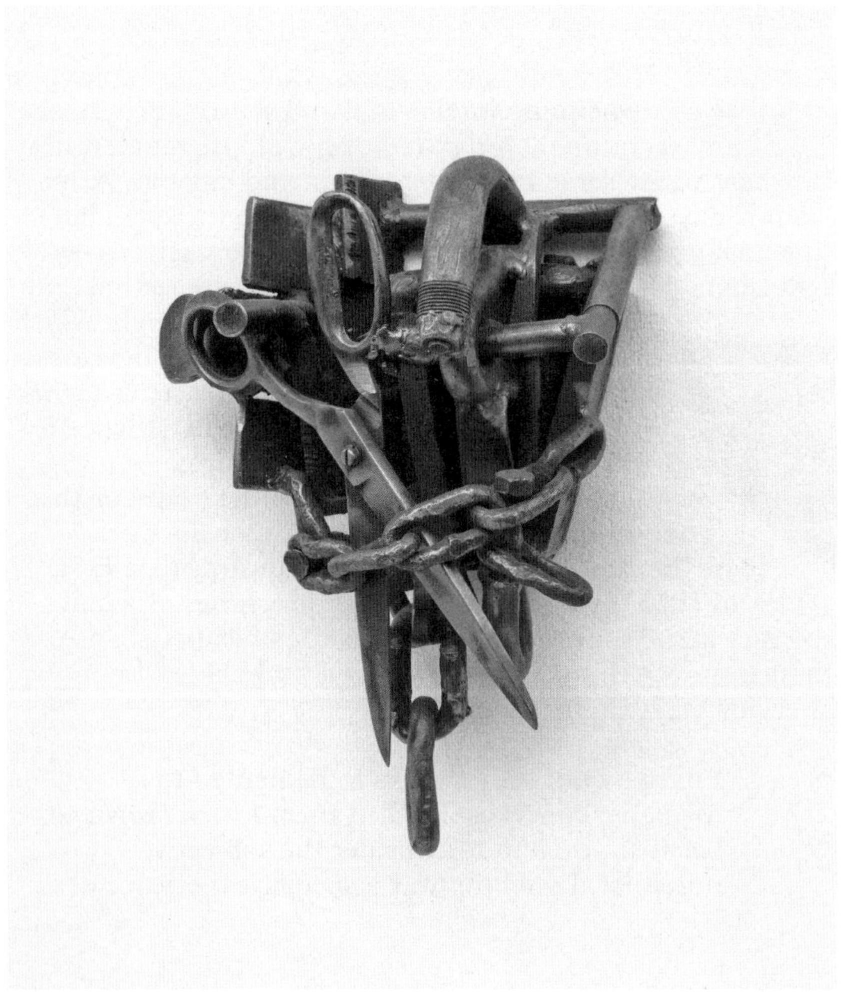

Melvin Edwards, *Sekuru Knows (Lynch Fragment)*, 1988, welded steel, MoMA New York.

3. www.nashersculpturecenter.org/art/artists/melvin-edwards-interview, accessed on 3 May 2021.

4. www.tate.org.uk/art/art-terms/a/activist-art, accessed on 3 May 2021.

5. Quoted on www.tate.org.uk/art/artworks/bruguera-tatlins-whisper-5-t12989, accessed on 3 May 2021.

> pretty quickly. Even the *Lynch Fragments* have that ability, though their loaded collective title tends to make people think more about subjective notions than the dynamic artistic process.[3]

Edwards is acutely aware that the response of the viewer is guided by the title. Today, the title undoubtedly functions as a marker for activist art, almost the only form of art that still seems to be able to claim artistic and social urgency, and relevance.

The Tate website contains some strong statements about what activist art is or should be: 'Activist art is a term used to describe art that is grounded in the act of "doing" and addresses political or social issues.' And: 'Activist art is about empowering individuals and communities and is generally situated in the public arena with artists working closely with a community to generate the art.' And: 'The aim of activist artists is to create art that is a form of political or social currency, actively addressing cultural power structures rather than representing them or simply describing them.'[4] The Tate descriptions state that activist art should not illustrate political or social views; the work of art must bring about something new or unexpected in the public domain in relation to social and political issues. On the Tate website, activist artist Tania Bruguera is quoted as saying: 'I don't want art that points to a thing. I want art that is the thing'. This raises the question of how activist art can avoid being an in-your-face picture or activity in the margins of what we already know from other sources. How can activist art avoid merely confirming what we already think? How could activist art, or art in general, actually bring about something that we have not yet experienced or already know in relation to a political or social issue? And what is the role of the viewer in activist art? If we take a closer look at the work *Tatlin's Whisper* #5 (2008) by Bruguera, referenced on the Tate website, it is striking how the description of the work exhaustively describes the meaning and experience of the work and that the function of the artwork is that 'images familiar from the news become real life experiences… by [their] placement inside a museum or a centre intended for art exhibitions'.[5] Can a work of art in and of itself be activist or does it require an effort on the part of the viewer? And if so, what effort is expected from the viewer in order for a work of art to achieve all the great goals of activist art? At least at first glance, Edwards' *Lynch Fragments* series does not seem to fall under these Tate descriptions of activist art.

When I saw some of the works in the *Lynch Fragments* series for the first time, I was immediately emotionally affected by the threat but also the pain evoked by the welded sculptures: with their hard, pointed, and fierce nature the metal objects were the solidified remains of crimes and acts of violence committed. Soon, however, I realized that my view and emotional reaction to the works was strongly guided by the title. My reactions were grounded in everything I had ever stored in my eyes and mind as knowledge and emotion about lynching: texts, photos, films, documentaries, and music. In this respect, my emotional reaction to the *Lynch Fragments* will be an experience I share with many viewers of these works. It will then seem as if the title is releasing me, as it were, to develop a more personal involvement and responsibility towards lynching or racist crimes. The title of the work becomes a coat rack for all forms of our collectively shared abhorrence and disapproval of racist crimes. We can then move on to the order of the day, without me as an individual viewer feeling that I have abandoned my responsibility on a collective level.

However, given the emphasis Edwards himself places on the fact that a specific social context ('genocide committed against our people') is part of his work, it is, I think, difficult to maintain that his work does not have an activist drive. It seems, however, that precisely because of the title we can ignore this drive, thus preventing the work from bringing about something that we have not yet experienced or do not yet know in relation to lynch practices. Is there an attitude towards the *Lynch Fragments* that does activate my responsibility towards this collective trauma and demands my agency at the collective level?

To explore such an attitude, I turn to Harun Farocki's *Serious Games* (2009–2010). This work is a video installation showing computer simulations that prepare soldiers for war and how to deal with trauma. We see footage from the game, soldiers behind a screen playing the

6. vimeo.com/370494311, accessed on 3 May 2021.

7. *Lydia Cabrera and Édouard Glissant: Trembling Thinking*, eds. Karen Marta and Gabriela Rangel, exh. cat. Americas Society (New York, 2018), p. 45.

game and instructors explaining and determining what the soldiers will see, soldiers using the game to deal with their traumas, as well as film footage of actual acts of war.[6] The title is a game genre designation that is hardly a preparation for what awaits us as viewers. However, there is no doubt about what the video actually shows: the work has an inevitable concreteness. At the same time, precisely because of that concreteness, the work has a paradoxical openness that leads—to my own surprise—to an aporia: what should I, as a viewer, do with these images? The video work offers little guidance for an unambiguous interpretation. As a spectator, I am on my own: am I on the side of the victims or on that of the perpetrator; am I a witness or a bystander; how can I know who is what and what I am? I am solely responsible for my own reaction to the artwork, i.e., for my own ethical standpoint and a possible perspective for action on a collective level.

My experience of *Serious Games*—which I consider to be of existential value—can only be described as the one-to-one experience that also characterizes the overwhelming intellectual and sensory experience of an exceptional dish. Can I make my unexpected response to *Serious Games* a more reflective position so that I can develop a contemplative attitude that could also accomplish a one-to-one experience when looking at the *Lynch Fragments*?

From October 2018 to January 2019, the Americas Society in New York hosted the exhibition 'Lydia Cabrera and Édouard Glissant: Trembling Thinking', curated by Hans Ulrich Obrist, Gabriela Rangel, and Asad Raza. The exhibition explored the intellectual impact of these two fundamental thinkers of the Caribbean, Cabrera and Glissant, on modern and contemporary art. One of the works on display was *Fin de siècle* (2000), a work from the *Lynch Fragments* series. The catalogue text states: 'Melvin Edwards had a deep relationship with Édouard Glissant and has spent significant time in Cuba and the Caribbean.'[7] Though a happy coincidence, to me the relationship between Edwards and Glissant, and Glissant's suggested influence on Edwards' work, is not that important. Rather, I intuitively suspect that Glissant's thinking can help me develop an attitude that allows for a one-to-one relationship with a work of art.

Unfortunately, within the scope of this article, it is not possible to elaborate on Glissant's thinking in detail.[8] The title of the exhibition catalogue, *Trembling Thinking*, does, however, indicate the core of his thinking: 'A thought that trembles, refuses to be definitively located, to be one. Rather, it shakes, vibrates, and stays multiple, leaving its identity undefinable.'[9] Glissant describes his thinking as 'the thought of the attempt, of the intuitive temptation'.[10] His so-called archipelagic thought, geographically based in the Caribbean, is directed against the reductive and homogenizing synthesis of Western thought. Moreover, it is a necessity for Glissant to think beyond narrow conceptions of identity. For Glissant, there is always something unknowable, something opaque, inside each person, which, rather than being what divides us, is what links us. As he wrote: 'We clamor for the right to opacity for everyone.'[11] He opposes thinking that tries to formulate a centre, a core, from which everything is determined. His thinking has no centre, just as an archipelago has no centre. Glissant refuses to systematize thinking; he wants to maintain an open and subjective relationship with the world. It is not synoptic thinking, a thinking that oversees everything from an objective point of view; it is micrological thinking. Just as you do not get to know an archipelago from a synoptic point of view but only through an unquenchable attention to details, Glissant's archipelagic thought is aligned with particularity and above all with focusing on and preserving the infinite quantity of all particularities.[12] It is thinking par excellence that can only approach what is being thought about in a very personal one-to-one relationship—in detail and from different perspectives. It requires a decentralization of focus; it is thinking that allows the imagination.

Glissant's archipelagic thought is—I cannot conceive of it any other way—a highly ethically charged attitude to thinking that goes hand in hand with a responsibility of the thinker for what is being contemplated. If I want to take this thinking as the starting point for an attitude of contemplation with regard to a work of art, which can be characterized as a one-to-one relationship, then that implies the same ethically charged attitude from a personal responsibility towards the work of art. It is a contemplation that does not look for a centre or core of the work, from

8. See for example Michael Wiedorn, *Think Like an Archipelago: Paradox in the Work of Édouard Glissant* (New York, 2017), and Stéphanie Noach's essay in this volume.

9. Marta and Rangel 2018 (see note 7), p. 36.

10. Quoted in Wiedorn 2012 (see note 8), p. 113.

11. Édouard Glissant, *Poetics of Relation*, transl. Betsy Wing (Ann Arbor, 1997), p. 194.

12. Wiedorn 2012 (see note 8), p. 113.

which it can be understood, but a contemplation in which the irreducible richness of the details demands attention. Glissant's archipelagic thought offers a metaphor for this way of viewing: my gaze is like a ship sailing through the waters of an archipelago. I may have an overview map of the area, but it cannot prepare me in any way for the experience of the trip itself: sailing through an archipelago is like sailing through a labyrinth of small sea corridors between islands that pop up here and there, and reveal an overwhelming diversity of appearances: nature, people, cultures, and identities.[13]

However, sailing through an archipelago is not without danger. The term *Trembling Thinking* indicates instability and uncertainty. At the end of Chapter 3 of Joseph Conrad's *Lord Jim* (1900) is the following passage, describing the moment when the demise of a ship is heralded by an incomprehensible event:

> What had happened? The wheezy thump of the engines went on. Had the earth been checked in her course? They could not understand; and suddenly the calm sea, the sky without a cloud, appeared formidably insecure in their immobility, as if poised on the brow of yawning destruction.... A faint noise as of thunder, of thunder infinitely remote, less than a sound, hardly more than a vibration, passed slowly, and the ship quivered in response, as if the thunder had growled deep down in the water.... The sharp hull driving on its way seemed to rise a few inches in succession through its whole length, as though it had become pliable, and settled down again rigidly to its work of cleaving the smooth surface of the sea. Its quivering stopped, and the faint noise of thunder ceased all at once, as though the ship had steamed across a narrow belt of vibrating water and of humming air.[14]

What had happened? In the light of Glissant's thinking, Conrad describes here—at least for me—what art that trembles can accomplish: your own thinking, ideas and presuppositions, wishes and desires are shipwrecked. A work of art offers an unstable open space in which I should not

13. The Caribbean archipelago comprises more than 7,000 islands and reefs divided into twenty-five parts, some of which are independent states and others dependent areas.

14. Quoted from www.gutenberg.org/files/5658/5658-h/5658-h.htm#link2HCH0003, accessed on 2 May 2021.

seek a hold on the title or established opinions. Not only is a work of art characterized by opacity, by a confounding complexity and ambiguity, but I—as a viewer of a work of art—am also opaque to myself. I am nonetheless on my own to choose an ethical position and to take appropriate responsibility vis-à-vis the work of art.

Glissant's thinking and the passage from *Lord Jim* help me in taking an attitude towards works of art such as *Lynch Fragments*, which, because of their guiding title, require more labour to achieve a one-to-one relationship with the work. Only in a one-to-one relationship can a work show itself as activist art. My reflections are thus no more than a preparation for a renewed confrontation with the *Lynch Fragments*: only in that confrontation can it become clear whether my reflections have any value.[15]

15. It sounds bland but it is true: the proof of the pudding is in the eating.

O fortes peioraque passi
mecum saepe viri, nunc vino pellite curas:
cras ingens iterabimus aequor.
(Horatius, *Carmina* I, 7, 30)

[O you brave heroes, you
who suffered worse with me often, drown your cares with wine:
tomorrow we'll sail the wide seas again]

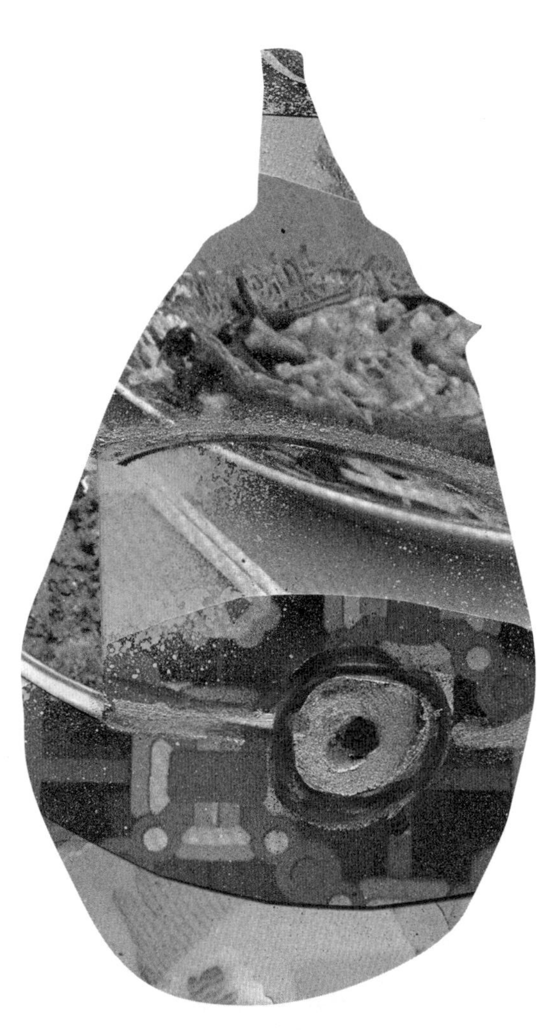

AGONISTIC RECIPES Constructive Conflicting Visual Mediation as Socio-Political Model

Helen Westgeest

INGREDIENTS

• Agonistics
• Anti-smoothness
• Collage as Medium and Culture
• Counter-visibility, Visuality, and Reverse Appropriation
• Multiple Views in Absorptive Mapping
• Undecidability

The meaningful role of mixtures of different media in contemporary artworks is often neglected in reflections on the topics addressed in such works. In some cases, the applied materials and techniques are restricted to artistic conventions, but quite a few contemporary artworks invite us to contextualize the used ingredients in various ways. Some materials literally have a 'global' character, such as earth pigments, because they are taken from the soil. Sometimes they are panhuman, such as the use of blood of the human body. Particular materials may also evoke a variety of associations, for instance gender-related connotations or references to cultural identity as linked to soap. Janine Antoni, for one, chose soap to cast a series of self-portraits (addressing the stereotypical obsession of women with cosmetics). And Mona Hatoum, in some of her installations, used olive soap produced in Nablus, the Palestine city which her parents were forced to leave at one point.[1] The current scholarly debate about 'new materialism', which addresses a multiplicity of views on the relationship of human beings with matter, including new vocabularies of materiality, will likely

1. Helen Westgeest, 'Identity and Materiality: Cultural Studies in the Artistic Practice', *The Reflexive Zone: Research into Theory in Practice*, eds. A. Coumans and H. Westgeest (Utrecht, 2004), pp. 196–198.

contribute to the development of new outlooks on aspects of materiality in contemporary art.[2]

In this essay, I focus on an even more subtle and metaphorical use of media. The keyworks in my case study are *Nyado: The Thing Around Her Neck* (2011), by the Nigerian-American artist Njideka Akunyili Crosby (b. 1983), and *Estancamiento* [Impasse] (2019) by the Spanish artist Susanna Inglada (b. 1983). Both artworks present human beings engaged in a kind of embrace. A few years

2. See, for instance, Jane Bennett, *Vibrant Matter: A Political Ecology of Things* (Durham, 2010).

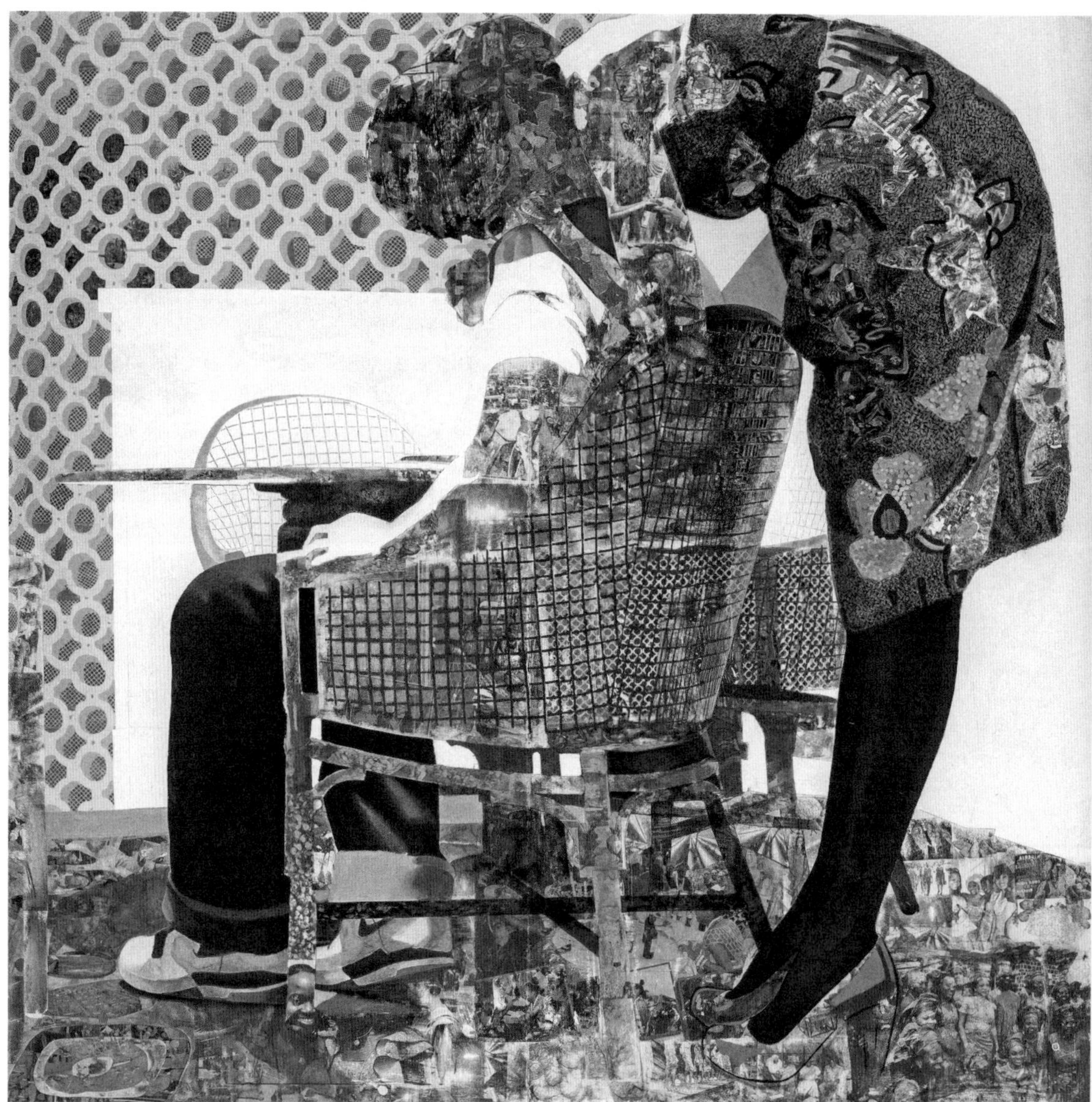

Njideka Akunyili Crosby, *Nyado: The Thing Around Her Neck*, 2011, acrylic, transfers, coloured pencil, charcoal, lace, and collage on paper, 84 × 84 in. (213.36 × 213.36 cm.). Courtesy the artist, Victoria Miro, and David Zwirner.

3. Crosby in an interview with Jason Rosenfeld. brooklynrail.org/2020/07/art/Njideka-Akunyili-Crosby-with-Jason-Rosenfeld, accessed on 2 April 2021.

4. See Helen Westgeest, *Slow Painting: Contemplation and Critique in the Digital Age* (London/New York, 2020), chapter 2 'Collage Paintings Sparring with Visual Propaganda' for a more in-depth discussion of the term 'collage painting'.

ago, these two works attracted my attention on different occasions. When I recently considered them for this essay, I momentarily wondered whether this was motivated in part by the practice of social distancing in response to the Covid-19 crisis. However, it was not the subject of the embracement that intrigued me when I saw them for the first time; rather, it was the multitude of visual conflicts in the mix and specific use of media which I saw as being more than just 'a way of creating figuration'. This essay revolves around the question of how the conflicting pluralism of visual media may act as a meaningful contribution to insights into the issues represented in these two artworks. My route to the answers is grounded in concepts that deal with constructive conflicts from various perspectives, such as agonistics as political model, collage cultures, views on counter-visibility and visuality, absorptive mapping, and anti-smoothness. More in general, this essay aims at offering a recipe for research into contemporary art from a global perspective through a focus on meaningful conflicts in the applied pluralism of visual mediation.

Njideka Akunyili Crosby's *Nyado: The Thing Around Her Neck* shows a female figure embracing a person sitting at a table. Most prominent is the presence of many fragmented photo-transfers in both figures, as well as in the chair and floor. These photo-transfers consist of cutouts from Nigerian and American magazines, as well as images from the artist's family albums.[3] These transfers are partly integrated into materials associated with drawing and painting, such as colour pencils and acrylics. As a whole, the artwork could be called a collage painting.[4] Susanna Inglada's *Estancamiento* also looks collage-like, but in a different way. This work basically shows arms of various colours embracing each other. These half-clothed body parts were executed by means of scarce traces of charcoal, ink, and acrylic and gouache paint on varying basic colours of drawing papers (subdued blue, pink, orange, yellow, and grey). After being cut out and assembled, this resulted in a collage with a slight relief and jagged contours. The most often asked questions regarding both artworks—as could be concluded from the interviews and information provided on the occasion of exhibitions—appear to concern the intentions of the artists with regard to the subject of their work. From that perspective, the applied media would merely function as a way to represent the intended subjects. If the recipe for writing this essay suggests that we should not necessarily ignore artists' statements about intentions, it also indicates that we should intend to make spectators aware that we do not only look at figurations. Human skin, cloth, and other familiar materials are actually transformed into another physicality, as well as into an obvious, non-hierarchical fragmented order. This observation brings to mind the term 'agonistics', used in literature about socio-political models of agonistic democracies focusing on positive values of pluralism and undecidable conflicts.

In *Agonistics: Thinking the World Politically*, political philosopher Chantal Mouffe advocates an agonistic approach of public space where conflicting points of view are confronted without any possibility of a final reconciliation.[5] She argues for democracy as 'agonistic pluralism', in which differences have positive connotations.[6] By accepting the contradictory tendencies set to work by social exchange, people will grasp the task of democracy, which is how to transform the potential antagonism existing in human relations into an agonism.[7] Although Mouffe proposes to reject any form of consensus in open-ended political struggles, she is aware of the importance of a thin consensus that remains conflictual, which means that undecidability continues to inhabit decisions. Any consensus should be considered as a contingent equilibrium of something essentially unstable and chaotic.[8] Is it possible to apply these views to the abovementioned characteristics of Crosby's and Inglada's works? To avoid the risk of a slippery pathway leading to a too subjective application, it is helpful to refer to Mouffe's own reflections on art and her agonistic model. According to this model, as she argued in 'Art and Democracy: Art as an Agonistic Intervention in Public Space', critical art is art that foments dissensus, that makes visible what the dominant consensus tends to obscure and obliterate, and she promotes 'artistic practices aiming at giving a voice to all those who are silenced within the framework of the existing hegemony'. Art should demonstrate that there are always other possibilities that have been repressed and that can be reactivated.[9] Although Mouffe clearly focuses on

5. Chantal Mouffe, *Agonistics: Thinking the World Politically* (London, 2013), p. 92.

6. Chantal Mouffe, *The Democratic Paradox* (London, 2000), pp. 13–14, 19, 101, 103.

7. Ibid., p. 135.

8. According to the analysis of Mouffe's view in Mark Wenman, *Agonistic Democracy: Constituent Power in the Era of Globalisation* (Cambridge, 2013), p. 195.

9. Chantal Mouffe, 'Art and Democracy: Art as an Agonistic Intervention in Public Space', *Open: Art as a Public Issue*, no. 14 (2008), p. 12.

interactive activist art projects taking place in public space, I will demonstrate below how in Crosby's and Inglada's works the conflictual pluralism of the media supports the issues addressed in the subjects of the works, be it in more subtle ways than in Mouffe's examples.

To develop this argument, it is relevant to first take a closer look at the collage-like appearance of these artworks. In both of them the collage technique obstructs a spatial illusion, common to the traditional perspective

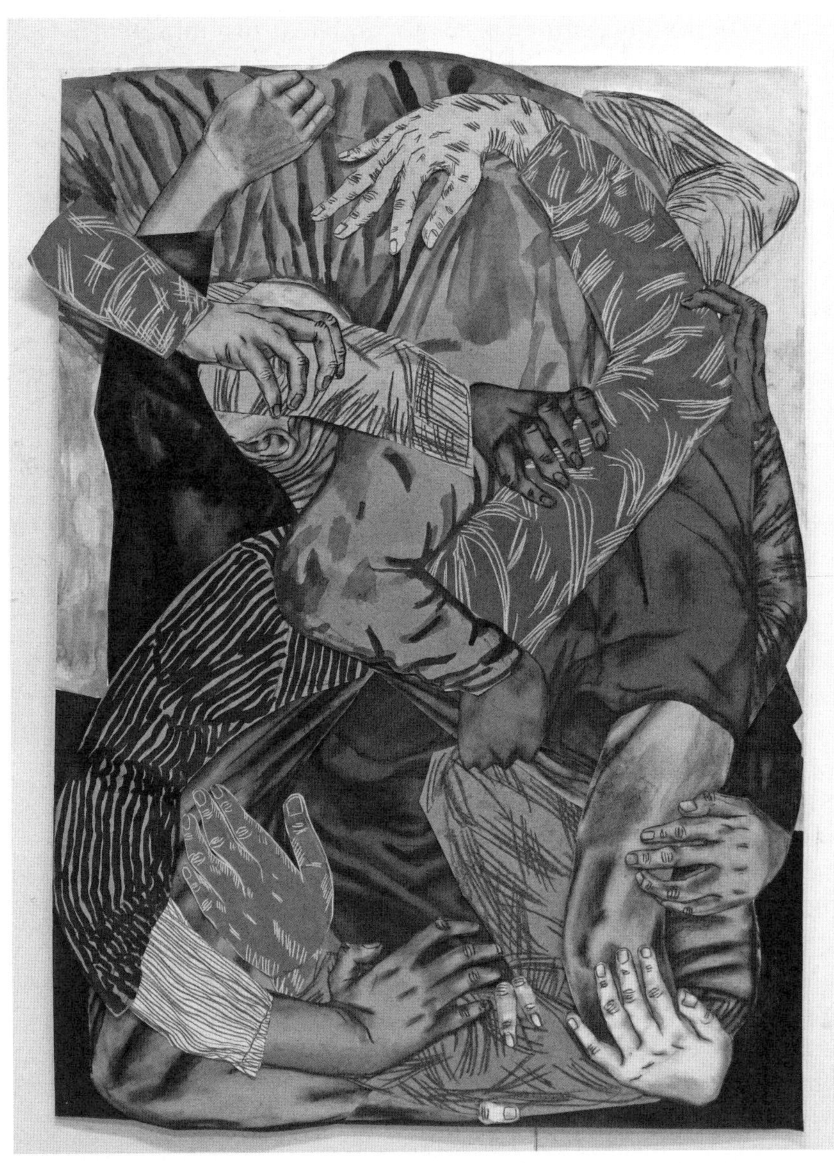

Susanna Inglada, *Estancamiento*, 2019, charcoal, acrylic, pastel on coloured, collaged paper, 132 × 92 cm. Presented in Installation *Slow Learners* Art Rotterdam 2020. Courtesy Galerie Maurits van de Laar and the artist.

in the Western-European figurative tradition. But these works also differ from Modernist paintings, which stress the flatness of the canvas and the artwork as a unity within the frame. The collage-related works by Inglada and Crosby ask for another, more fragmented mode of perception. For one thing, these fragments exist side by side, without expressing a hierarchy of importance. Mouffe's focus on undecidability and dissensus—which render visible what the dominant consensus tends to obscure and obliterate—seems to be applicable here to the experience of the spectator. Interestingly, moreover, when considering the mixtures of fragments in terms of a socio-political model, David Banash, in *Collage Culture*, proposed to look at modern society as a 'collage culture'. Banash grounds his argument in the explanation that the collage technique includes two actions, collecting and arranging, which remain recognizable, and that fragmentation and rearrangement of heterogeneous elements are main characteristics of the final result.[10] Consumers assemble new totalities out of infinite numbers of fragments, such as in shopping for identities.[11] As noted by Banash, artists have articulated two general responses to these kinds of 'collage cultures' of mass assemblage production and mass media that resulted from processes of industrialization. They either resist it, or, as in case of collage artists, they delve into it and do so in extreme ways.[12] Crosby and Inglada appear to combine both strategies. Their labour-intensive working processes counter industrial mass assemblage processes, but the collage techniques are used in such 'extreme' and obviously assembling ways that the multiplicity of fragments obstructs the becoming of a new hybrid unity (which did happen in Surrealist collages). The prominent photo-transfers in Crosby's picture consist of cutouts from contemporary Nigerian and American lifestyle magazines, alongside other kinds of vernacular images displaying local African traditions and events, as well as fragmented photographs from the artist's family albums. In their original context, all these images were part of a large corpus of images (and texts). Through selecting some of them, they gain a new individual status, but through the partly overlapping juxtaposition of fragments of images from different contexts, a pluralism full of conflict comes into being as well. When trying to

10. David Banash, *Collage Culture: Readymades, Meaning, and the Age of Consumption* (Amsterdam, 2013), pp. 14, 26, 259.

11. Ibid., p. 28.

12. Ibid., p. 13.

CONSTRUCTIVE CONFLICTS

3. susannainglada.com, ccessed on 15 April 2021; nd based on texts provided n the exhibition 'Susanna nglada: Thin Skin about to 'ear', Dordrechts Museum in)ordrecht, 15-11-2019—08-3-2020, on the occasion of he Scheffer Award.

4. Nicholas Mirzoeff, 'On 'isuality', *Journal of Visual Culture* 5, no. 1 (2006), pp. 3–54.

identify a clear narrative, the spectator is bound to be frustrated. Rather than a cliché opposition between American and Nigerian lifestyle, or between family photographs displaying African poverty and American dreams, complex and ambiguous confrontations arise, which could be called 'agonistic' in that they remain undecidable.

The term 'agonistics' appears to be also applicable to Inglada's collage technique. The jumble of arms in *Estancamiento*, which appear to have lost the contexts of their bodies, does not display an antagonism of one figure suppressing another; it is unclear who is winner or loser, or whether they are harming or rescuing each other, or, for that matter, just playing. Interviews, exhibition texts and reviews, and the artist's visual and verbal statements on her website[13] demonstrate a strong interest in social inequality and (political) power relationships. The clearly recognizable fragmentation and rearrangement of heterogeneous elements meet Banash's main characteristics of the collage. Banash mainly addresses relationships with the ideology of capitalism as political model, however. In my case study, it appears to be more interesting to relate the applied collage techniques to the pluralism and the positive and equalizing values of conflict in Mouffe's model of agonistics, in which conflicts act as a driving force, while making visible what the dominant consensus tends to obscure and obliterate.

For relating characteristics of visual media to socio-political issues that are not explicitly addressed in the artworks, Nicholas Mirzoeff's discussion of visuality as expressed through visualizations—in which sight is considered a social fact—serves as a useful additional source of inspiration. In his essay 'On Visuality', Mirzoeff, a scholar in visual culture studies, argues that visuality usually refers to representations of hegemonic systems, but that it could also be used as means of resistance through reverse appropriation.[14] In Crosby's work, the embracement of the man by the woman (identified, on the basis of interviews, as herself and her 'white' American husband) may not be viewed as a contradictory element of the picture—involving a universal expression of love and care, after all—but their different ethnicities may add a socio-political charge for some spectators. In an interview, Crosby explained that she critically addresses the acceptance in Nigeria of interethnic marriage with a white woman versus the assumption of a prostitute in the opposite case.[15] From that perspective, a common domestic event of a woman embracing her partner becomes more political than expected at first sight, if not a kind of 'reverse appropriation'. And at the point where the black skin of her neck touches his white pale face ('the thing around her neck'), the many different photo-transfers merge. Here, we touch upon a crucial issue in both artworks: the skin tones of the figures depicted. Skin tone bias, also called 'colourism', is not just about visibility of colour, but about visuality, in the meaning of sight as a social fact. Inglada's different tones of drawing paper obviously do not present any hierarchy. Crosby's photo-transfers are colourful and similarly applied in the skin of the black woman and the white man, as well as in the floor (as their joint place infused with pluriform breeding grounds).

In *The Right to Look: A Counterhistory of Visuality*, Mirzoeff offers examples of indigenous counter-visibility consisting of shifting views on reality, such as a picture of a general strike versus mapping as a pre-eminent example of hegemonic visuality and overview.[16] Looking at Crosby's and Inglada's artworks, however, will provide viewers the experience of the act of glancing over surfaces of maps, rather than consulting a map for an overview. This makes it all the more interesting to turn to philosopher Edward Casey's alternative verb of 'mapping with/in'—which he calls 'absorptive mapping'—to replace the familiar 'mapping of'. In *Earth-Mapping*, Casey rethinks art as a form of mapping, but not like conventional cartography, which is based on the 'plan' view from above.[17] In some of the abstract and landscape paintings he discusses, the views are multiple or diffuse. 'Absorptive mapping' is not about measuring exact distances, but about immersing the viewer in order to sense a certain place. But that place is not a place elsewhere, indicated by a map; the place and the map merge in the picture.[18] Additionally, Casey addresses people's basic need to become oriented. When clear borders are lacking and usual coordinates of orientation are broken, confusion will reign, but the remapping actually showcases what would otherwise be absolute disparity. This view resonates Mouffe's plea for making visible what a dominant consensus tends to obscure and obliterate. In the case of

15. Crosby in an interview with Erica Ando. bombmagazine.org/articles/njideka-akunyili-crosby, accessed on 2 April 2021.

16. Nicholas Mirzoeff, *The Right to Look: A Counterhistory of Visuality* (Durham/London, 2011), p. 45.

17. Edward S. Casey, *Earth-Mapping: Artists Reshaping Landscape* (Minneapolis/London, 2005), p. 139.

18. Ibid., pp. 149–150, 189.

19. Byung-Chul Han, *Saving Beauty*, transl. Daniel Steuer (Cambridge, 2018 [2015]), pp. 9–10.

Crosby's and Inglada's works, it is possible to think of, for instance, dissolving hierarchies related to skin tone bias, or interrogating subtle differences between caring/rescuing and suppressing/fighting in interpersonal relationships.

The fragmented and conflicting surfaces of Crosby's and Inglada's pictures are anything but smooth. If this seems to be a mere formal characteristic, it becomes more meaningful when consulting philosopher Byung-Chul Han's view on smoothness. In his *Saving Beauty*, Han notes an almost obsessive preference for smoothness, particularly in electronic devices such as smartphones and laptops, but also in some postmodern artworks and even our own bodies. In line with Mouffe's view on consensus, he claims that what is smooth does not offer any resistance. The smooth object deletes its 'against'; it lacks the negativity of opposition.[19] Returning to Crosby's and Inglada's pictures, it is interesting to note that their collage-like works, which include 'dirty dust' of charcoal and imperfect photographic transfers, are far from smooth. On the basis of Han's view, one can conclude that their anti-smoothness reinforces their agonistic nature.

Just as in the case of cooking a meal, whereby each ingredient has its own complementary role in the final dish while remaining discernible in its taste, my recipe of the 'new outlook' in this essay provided a theoretical framework with complementary roles for the used ingredients. I put in Mouffe's quite general agonistic model as a basic ingredient for reflecting on the visual conflicts in Crosby's and Inglada's works in terms of agonistic pluralism, in which differences have positive connotations, act as a driving force, and foment multiple interpretations. For dealing with the more particular differences in these artworks, Banash's more specific concept of collage appeared to be relevant, which led to the option of regarding the obvious fragmented nature of the collage-like artworks as metaphor for a socio-political model. Both Banash and Han focus on counteracting the hegemonic model of capitalism through, respectively, exaggerating the fragmented collage system and anti-smoothness, which appeared to be insightful perspectives to discover subtle agonistics in the plain subject of 'embracement'. However, because the two artworks do not seem to address a specific ideology such as capitalism in a critical fashion, Mirzoeff's notion of counter-visibility appeared to be more appropriate for analyzing how Crosby and Inglada counterbalance hegemonic visuality in the sense of hierarchical overview. In the end, the resulting identification of their non-hierarchical use of multiple visual media and fragments, which keep undecidability intact, was more specifically supported by Casey's concept of disorienting absorptive mapping, which also clarified that this kind of mapping could be considered in terms of Mirzoeff's reverse appropriation. In one way or another, and however complementary, all the concepts I relied on confirmed the important role of undecidability in the two artworks discussed. This equally applies to their topic of 'embracement', the ways their various media are combined, and the experience of the spectator. Grounded in several theoretical concepts (listed as 'ingredients'), this essay provided insights into how the particular blends of media in Crosby's and Inglada's artworks could act as socio-political agonistic models in support of the issues thematized in these works through figuration.

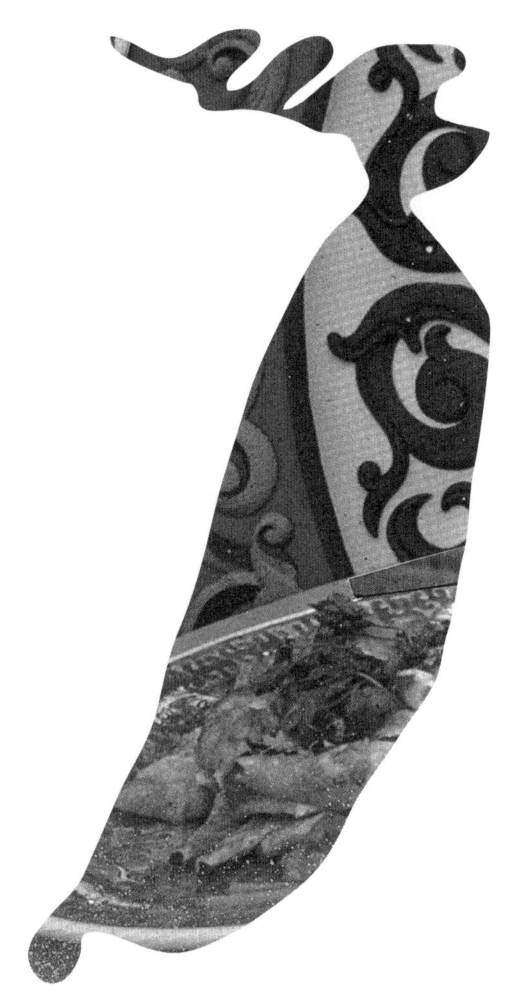

HOW NOT TO BAKE A CAKE
Playful Methods and 'Pluriversing'

Sybille Lammes

INGREDIENTS

- Two Wedges of Fun
- An Ounce of Doubt
- A Handful of Risk
- A Pinch of Salt
- A Blindfold
- A Stretch of the Imagination
- And Then Stand Back

This contribution centres around the notion of play as a creative and sometimes messy research approach that allows us to step away from the restraints of established methods. Such conventional methods surely have a function, but here I wish to critique the very functionality of such 'normalized' methods. The objective of methods to be functional, ordered, and effective leaves little space for the unexpected and the imagination. This can hinder creativity, serendipity, risk, and failure. Especially in the humanities and the social sciences, we also need methods that account for the multiplicity, complexity[1] and non-functionality of our research materials. I suggest that playful methods provide opportunities to include such perspectives. As an 'inventive method'[2] they open up possibilities to make our approach to cultures pluriverse.

The approach that I would like to present for this book has no guarantee of a satisfactory outcome. As a recipe, it will not come with glossy pictures of the end result. In this entry of the cookery book I want to stay 'with the trouble'[3] and make some suggestions for new pluriverse approaches in academia through unlearning[4] our familiar algorithms.

1. Karen Barad, *Meeting the Universe Halfway* (Durham, 2007); Donna J. Haraway, *Staying with the Trouble: Making Kin in the Chthulucene* (Durham, 2016).

2. Celia Lury and Nina Wakeford, *Inventive Methods: The Happening of the Social* (London, 2012).

3. Haraway 2016 (see note 1).

4. Paul Feyerabend, *Against Method* (London/New York, 1993).

Ubiquitous Recipes

Recipes are everywhere. They 'work' on all levels of daily life as a way to execute, prompt, and maintain complex and less complex processes. They may be singular or be comprised of an assemblage of different recipes or 'chains of actions'.[5] Furthermore, these processes are not exclusively executed directly by humans and can also be seen in other-than-human situations and interactions. The new mRNA vaccins against Covid-19 could for example be understood as dependent on a multiple recipe: the innoculated mRNA delivers a recipe (as a message) to our cells to set immunization in motion, basically being discarded as a kind of scrap paper recipe as soon as the proteine piece is made and a copying process kicks in. Likewise, taking money out of a cash dispenser involves a procedure of prescribed steps between us and the ATM as assemblages of recipes. But a phletora of practices in more mundane, everyday situations also depend on recipes: from making clothes from a pattern, brewing a cup of tea, watering the plants, to dancing a tango or baking a cake. The latter example shows how complex such processes can be. Baking a cake involves the steps of gathering ingredients (from shops, the cupboard, or neighbours), going through the steps of weighing and combining the ingredients and putting the cake in the oven at a certain temperature for a certain length of time. These steps are all executed in the hope of the right result.

What all these diverse recipes have in common is that they direct us to a particular way of doing things in order to have a certain outcome. Be it immunization, obtaining cash, a new self-made coat, a flowering plant, or a well-risen cake: these recipes are functional scripts for doing stuff methodically. They provide the steps, suggest materials, and combinations to work towards certain results.

In it simplest form, recipes in academia are rather similar: they consist of prescribed steps for (re)assembling materials in a certain way as to arrive at a certain outcome. They have a function in making methods 'work' and to guarantee an output in the form of an answer to our research question and in disentangling complex issues. In other words, they enable us to *do* methods and safeguard

5. Bruno Latour, *Reassembling the Social: An Introduction to Actor-Network-Theory*, Clarendon Lectures in Management Studies (Oxford/New York, 2005); Bruno Latour, *We Have Never Been Modern* (London, 1993).

their functionality. But what is lost when we follow such patterns religiously in the name of functionality? What remains unseen, unlearned? How can a different ingredient, an experiment with a move, a malfunction of a cash machine and a coat that does not fit, bring us different understandings?

Algorithms

Let me investigate this further by turning to a highly functional recipe, namely that of a computer algorithm. Computer algorithms meticulously, silently, and swiftly prescribe the steps in processes of sorting, deleting, gathering, or searching information. Algorithms are standardly described as having a clear input and output and as being unambiguous, finite, and independent.[6] They also remain largely unnoticed and are higly regulated in how they work and function. We only see them when they fail or when they are hacked. To refer back to the famous work of Science and Technology scholar Bruno Latour, they are black-boxed to the extent that we can only see the end results, such as the results of a google search or booking an appointment online.[7]

In their article on data and analytics, Louise Amoore and Volha Piotukh liken the workings of such algorithms to the process of sewing and making clothes.[8] Both processes are executed according to a prescribed proces of segmenting and rejoining elements as to come to an end result. What the authors want to show with this analogy is that such processes do not start with an a-priori distinction between the structured and non-structured. It is what we (as humans and other-than-humans) want to see as an output that kickstarts a process in which certain segments are chosen and recombined. Only then the rest of the material is deemed junk or residual. Amoore and Piothuk turn to Henri Bergson and Latour to further understand what happens during this ordering process. In line with Bergson they maintain that what is selected and recombined is always limited by our mindset and what we are not prepared to 'think' remains a blind spot. The authors use Latour to show that this limitation of 'vision'

6. Thomas H. Cormen, Charles E. Leiserson, Ronald L. Rivest, and Clifford Stein, *Introduction to Algorithms* (Cambridge, MA, 2009).

7. Bruno Latour, 'Opening Pandora's Black Box', *Technology, Organizations and Innovation: Theories, Concepts and Paradigms*, eds. Ian McLoughlin, David Preece and Patrick Dawson (London, 2000), pp. 679–695.

8. Louise Amoore and Volha Piotukh, 'Life beyond Big Data: Governing with Little Analytics', *Economy and Society* 44, no. 3 (2015), pp. 341-66.

is actually ruled by small devices with a lot of power. So what may seem small compared to the vast amount of data, is actually big in terms of agency. This can be likened to a magnet and a needle in a haystack. The needle is part of an unstructured vast amount of heterogeneous matter.[9] But a magnet—as a small device—allows us to seek it out. As a device it teases structure out of mess, but it also makes us unsee what the haystack is about.

9. Ibid., p. 348.

10. Ibid., p. 362.

Back to Method

These insights into how algorithms work, are important for understanding methods in academia. After all, methods are about the road we will walk, what we will bring along, the things we pick up and discard during the journey, and the output this will lead to. Concepts or theories are often strongly interwoven with this endeavour: they set the frame of mind for where and how we will travel. Taking the observation of Amoore and Piothuk a bit further, we could maybe state that concepts and theories in academia are actually akin to what Bergson had in mind: they frame what is seen and analyzed by us as researchers, but also what is not seen and discarded as unimportant.

It is of course often necessary to make selections and to follow a step-by-step procedure when it comes to academic research. But there also lies a danger in this, especially when our recipes become engrained and functional to the extent that we cannot step out of the procedure anymore to reflect on it or to do things differently. Let me link this back to baking a cake and honour the continuum that Bergson saw between academia and other kinds of perceptions in daily life.[10] We all remember those moments in the kitchen when not having the right ingredients or not knowing the right measurements made all the difference, for better or worse. Likewise, as researchers we have encountered such moments, and have been surprised by what imagination, failure, and serendipity can bring. We need methods that are open to complexity and unexpected connections and translations. Instead of walking from A to B, the unpredicted needs to be embraced so that we may wander instead of purposefully navigate to a particular point. We sometimes even need recipes for disaster.

There are different methods imaginable to account for this risky endeavour. Nina Wakeford and Celia Lury suggest Inventive Methods,[11] Donna Haraway speaks about 'staying with the trouble'[12] while Lury in her latest books proposes to understand methods as 'problem spaces'.[13] Similarly, Karen Barad speaks of diffraction as an 'apt metaphor'.[14] Such interdisciplinary methods[15] allow us to account for the complexity and heterogeneity of the socio-cultural and to not ignore the proverbial haystack.

In this essay I want to turn to play as a specification of such an alternative method.

It may feel counter-intuitive to relate play to method, as it upsets our conceptions of methods and academia as stable, unambigous, true, and objective. Furthermore, it may make academia sound frivolous. Yet we should not forget that play and academia share a desire to know and produce worlds. Or as play-scholar Brian Sutton-Smith puts it 'all forms of play are transformations of … basic modes by which we know the world'.[16] Also, as Sutton-Smith explores in his later work, play is ambiguous and it is precisely the uncertainty, ambiguity and creativity of play that makes it such a powerful approach to probe and create our approaches. As play is in a nutshell about creating multiple quixotical and capricious worldings, it allows us to see cultural practices in less instrumental ways and to focus on approaches that may not have a direct function. Or as Donna Haraway noted about play: '…. it's not a matter of direct functionality. We need to develop practices for thinking about those forms of activity that are not caught by functionality, those which propose the possible-but-not-yet, or that which is not-yet but still open.'[17] To paraphrase the situationist manifesto, playful methods enable us to find the beach under the pavement[18] and allows us to visibly engage with play and different outcomes and connections.

11. Lury and Wakeford 2021 (see note 2).

12. Haraway 2016 (see note 1).

13. Celia Lury, *Problem Spaces: How and Why Methodology Matters* (Cambridge, 2021).

14. Ibid.

15. *Handbook of Interdisciplinary Research Methods,* eds. Celia Lury, Patricia Clough, Mike Michael, Rachel Fensham, Sybille Lammes, and Angela Last (London, 2016).

16. Brian Sutton-Smith, *The Playdul Ways of Knowing* (unpublished, 1970). Retrieved from eric.ed.gov/?id=ED050806

17. Haraway 2016 (see note 1).

18. Guy Debord, A. G. Constant, H. Sturm, and M. Wyckaert, 'Situationist Manifesto', *Internationale Situationniste* 4 (1960).

Deep Play

Many of us use playful methods already in their research without framing this as such. Play can, for example, be pivotal for hatching ideas, solving problems, and making complex connections; processes that are seldomly shown in how we present our research to the outer world. More concretely, play can also be an impalpably part of many existing research methods ranging from experimental methods to data sprints, citizen science projects, practice-based research, creative methods, co-design, and—most explicitly—educational methods.[19] But also certain writing styles can be playful.

Play may be everywhere and the main 'soil' for socio-cultural practices[20] but playful methods thus often remain obscured in the end result of research. It may involve some courage and audicity to make playful methods more visible. As mentioned above, it requires sidestepping a dominant stance in academia in which play is viewed as undermining 'serious' research and as frivolous and flippant. Such prevailing assumptions do not only impede us in showing which playful methods are used already, but also hinder us in developing the potential of playful methods to its fullest. To overcome this, risks need to be taken. We have to allow space for failure, messiness, unsolved riddles and the speculative and to engage with what can be called 'deep play',[21] playful risky processes that have uncertain outcomes and put the stakes high. It does not mean that no rules apply, but that there is space for bending, probing, and countering rules: for play.

19. *Writing Academic Texts Differently: Intersectional Feminist Methodologies and the Playful Art of Writing*, ed. Nina Lykke (London, 2014); René Glas and Sybille Lammes, 'Ludo-Epistemology: Playing with the Rules in Citizen Science Games', *The Playful Citizen: Knowledge, Creativity, Power* (Amsterdam, 2019), pp. 217–234; Angela Last, 'Experimental Geographies', *Geographical Compass* 6, no. 12 (2012), pp. 706–724; Lina Higueras-Rodríguez, Marta Medina-García, and Enriqueta Molina-Ruiz, 'Analysis of Courses and Teacher Training Programs on Playful Methodology in Andalusia (Spain)'; Marjaana Kangas, *The School of the Future: Theoretical and Pedagogical Approaches for Creative and Playful Learning Environments*; M.D. Gil Llario and Consuelo Vicent Catalá, 'Comparative Analysis of the Efficacy of a Playful-Narrative Program to Teach Mathematics at Pre-School Level'; Anna Hickey-Moody, 'Affect as Method: Feelings, Aesthetics and Affective Pedagogy', eds. Rebecca Coleman and Jessica Ringrose, *Deleuze and Research Methodologies* (Edinburgh, 2013), pp. 79–94; Rita Irwin and Stephanie Springgay, 'A/r/Tography as Practice-Based Research' (London, 2017).

20. Johan Huizinga, *Homo Ludens: A Study of the Play-Element in Culture* (London, 2003).

21. Clifford Geertz, 'Deep Play: Notes on the Balinese Cockfight', *Daedalus* 101, no. 1 (1972), pp. 1–37; J. MacAloon, M. Csikszentmihalyi, J. C. Harris, and R. J. Park, 'Deep Play and the Flow Experience in Rock Climbing', *Play, Games and Sports in Cultural Contexts* (Champaign, 1983), pp. 361–384.

COLLECTIVES

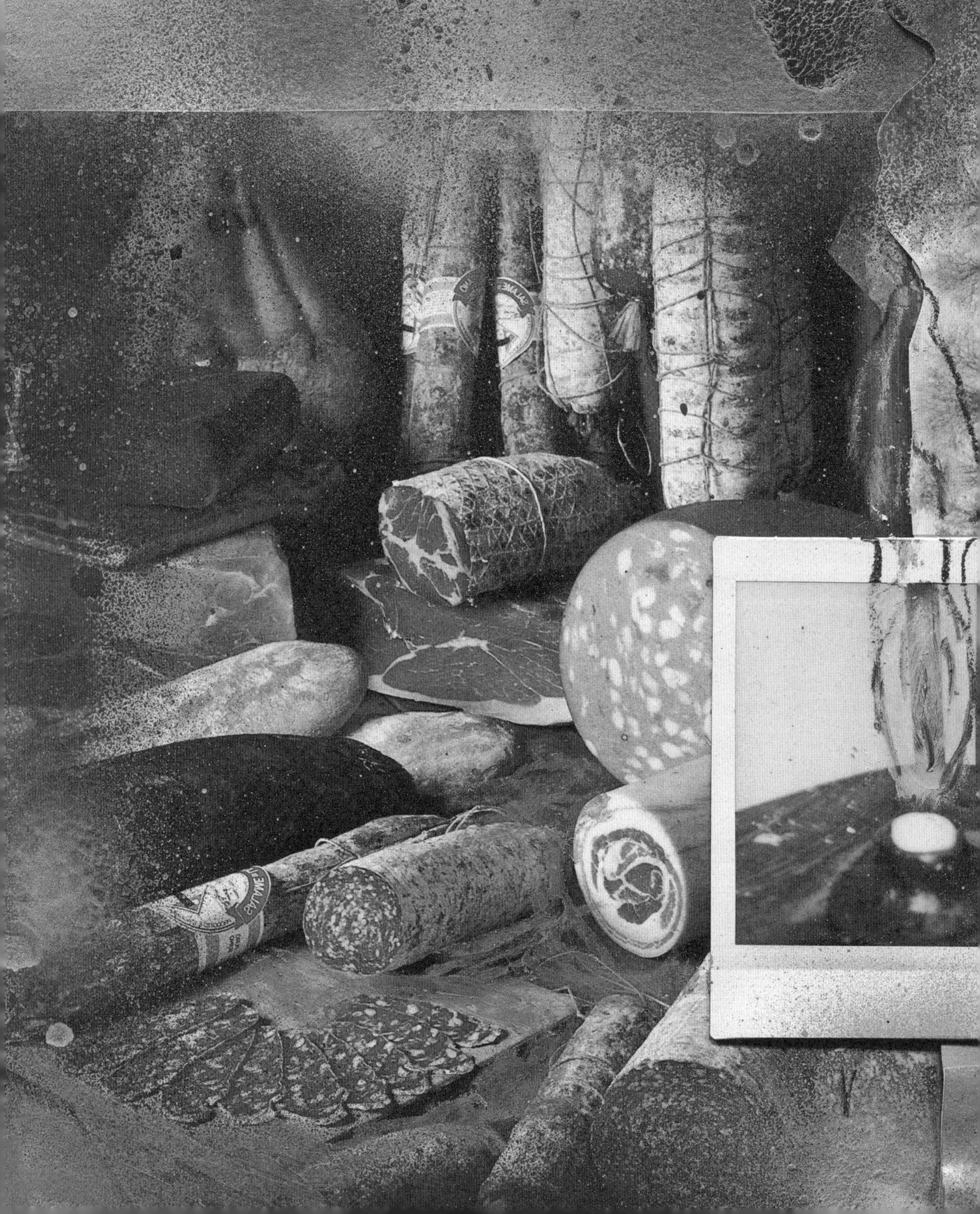

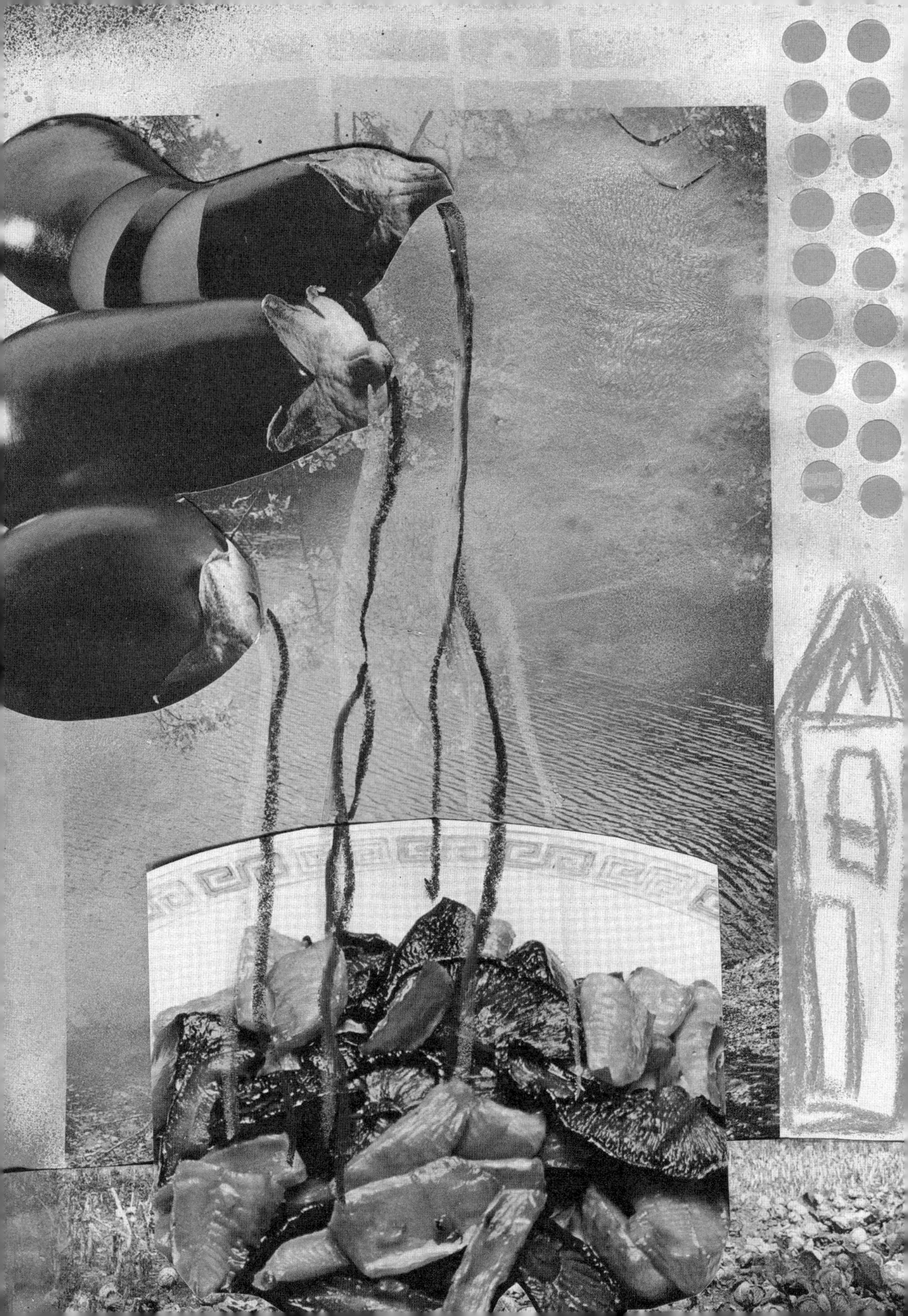

Sonja van Kerkhoff
Parisa Damandan
Rudi Struik

SET IN STONE

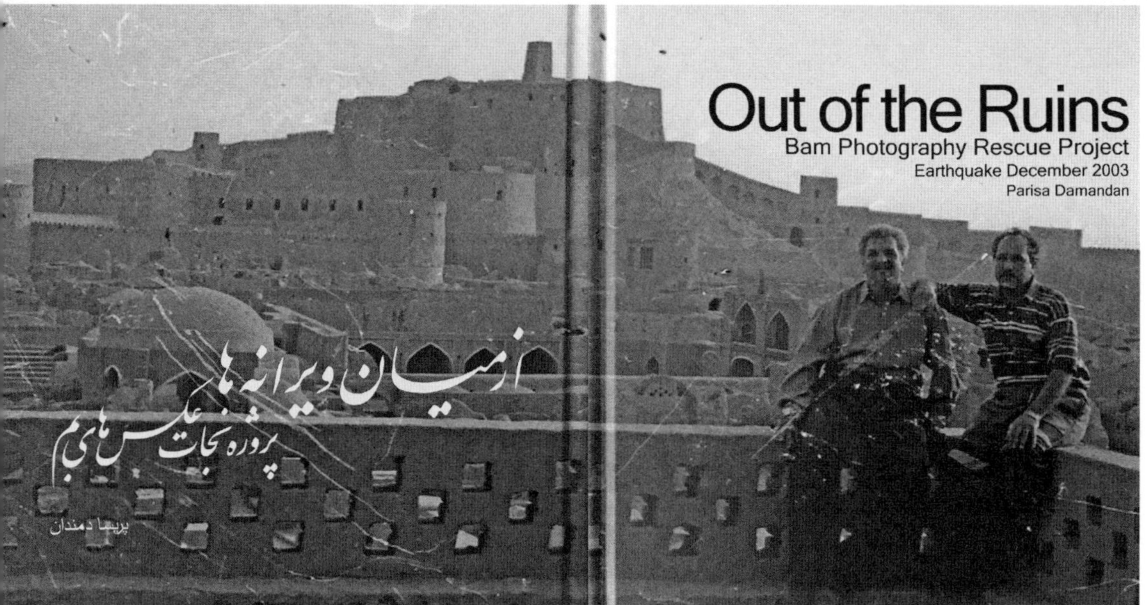

arisa Damandan, *Out of the Ruins: Bam Photography Rescue Project. Earthquake December 2003* (Gronsveld, 2013), ront and back cover.

n 2003, on 26 December, an earthquake struck the southern Iranian ity of Bam, killing over 26,000 and njuring over 30,000. The book cover hows the mud-brick citadel that was educed to rubble. Seventy percent of uildings were completely destroyed, eaving over a 100,000 homeless. here are minor earthquakes in Iran lmost daily because the edge of the rabian-Eurasian plate runs through he country. The tragedy in Bam was orse because most homes and other uildings were made of mudbricks, hich collapsed, trapping many under he rubble.

When Iranian photographer and hoto-historian Parisa Damandan eard of the tragedy she went to escue the history of the city by ollecting photographs left in the rubble. A tiny selection from the more than ten thousand photographs she collected were published in the 2013 book, *Out of the Ruins: Bam photography Rescue Project. Earthquake December 2003*, which was partly funded by Herman Divendal and the Dutch branch of AIDA (Association International de Défense des Artistes).

While Parisa Damandam was in the Netherlands in 2007 in the context of another of her photographic projects, she met Rudi Struik and was struck by the way he uses photography with plaster or concrete in his installations and she gave him more than a thousand negatives and about a hundred passport photographs to use.

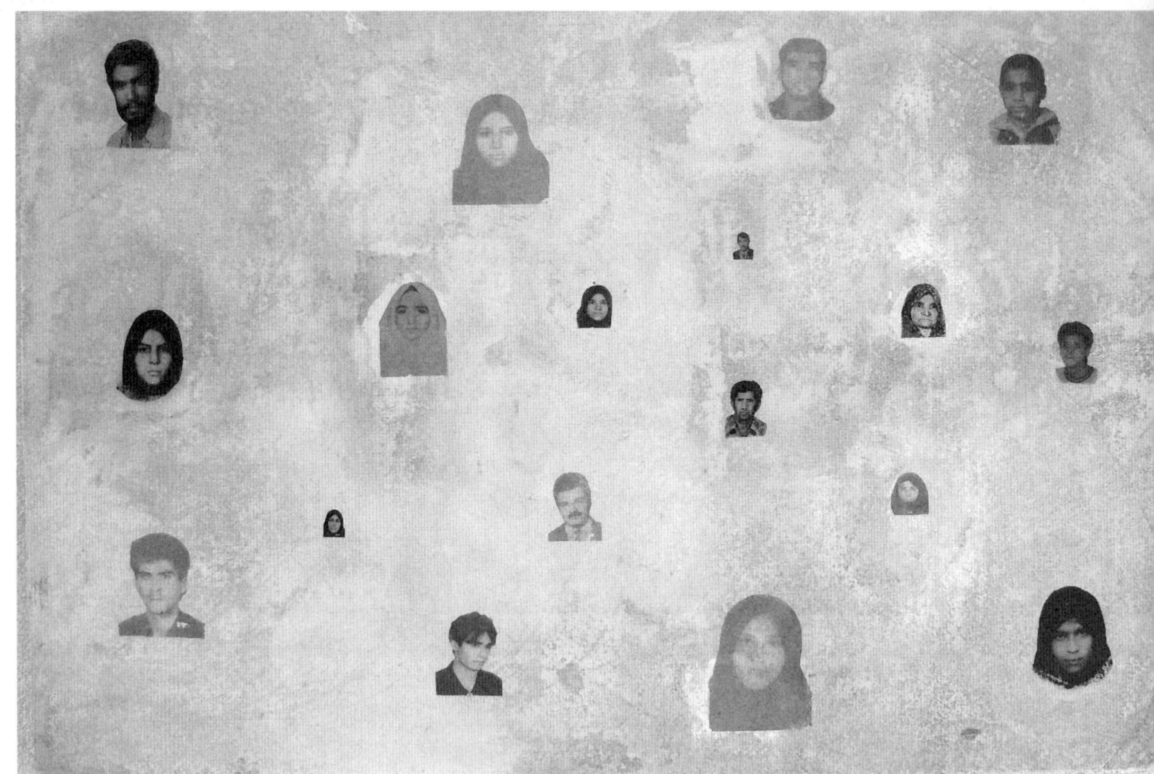

Rudi Struik, *Citizens of Bam #1*, 2007, mural, mixed media, 57 × 82 × 2 cm.

I saw two of Rudi Struik's *Citizens of Bam* photographic murals and was impressed that someone living in the Netherlands knew of the tragedy and cared enough about this to make these works. I am a Bahai and know many Iranians and so I was well aware of the tragedy. In these two works, Rudi Struik chose to keep the passport look in these photos, even though these are scans which were then printed in such a manner that they appear to sink into or come out of the fresco-like wall reliefs. Photographs, often set in frames, have transient associations, especially passport photographs. In these two works they seem to be set in stone, which is ironic given that the homes they were found in were rubble, yet being set into materials associated with permanence, these passport photographs have been elevated out of the intimacy of their former lives where they were in a drawer or folder for private viewing. In that sense they are memorials not just to the individuals whose fate is unknown, but also a platform for a frozen moment—a time in Bam, before that earthquake, when each of these photographs had been taken, and had a home.

SvK

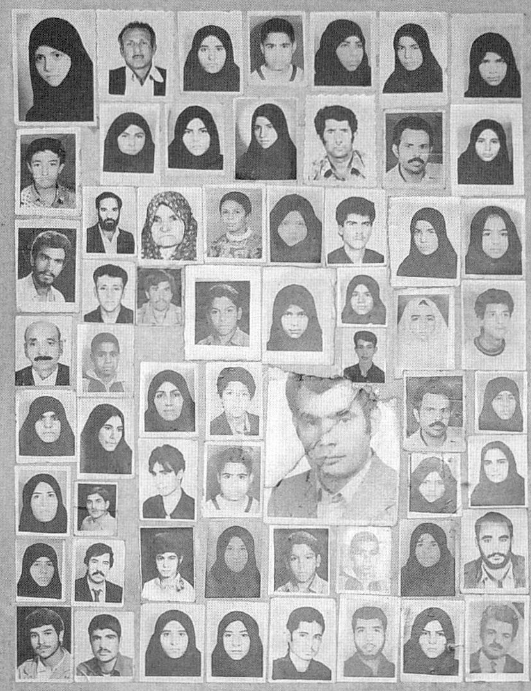
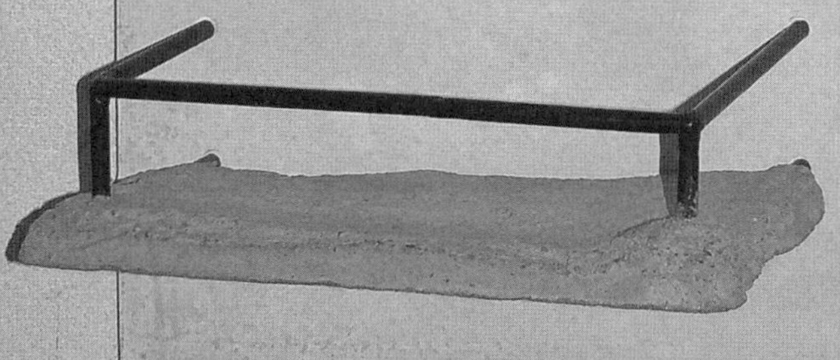

Rudi Struik, *Citizens of Bam #2*, 2007, mural, mixed media, 82 × 57 × 2 cm.

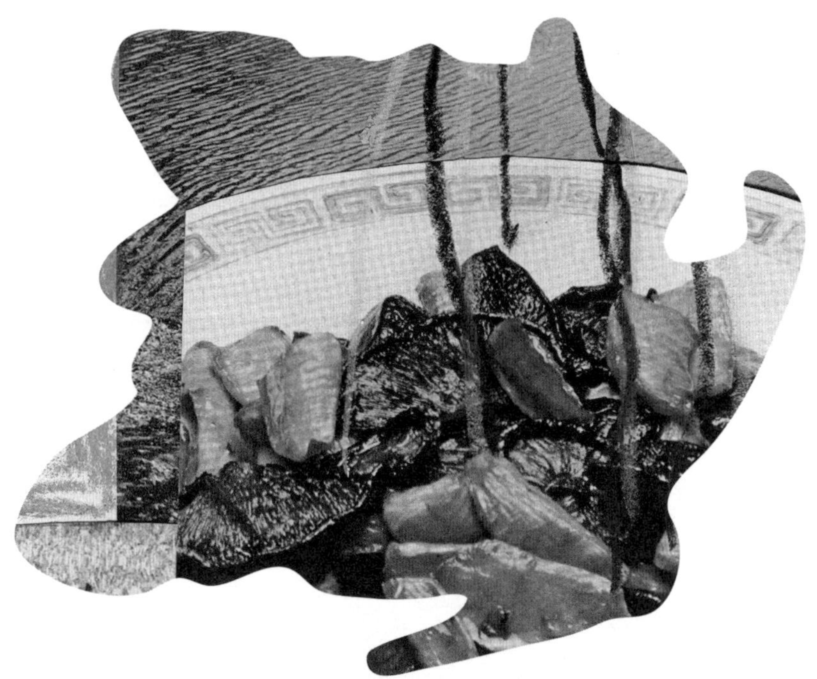

RUANGRUPA New Outlooks on Artist Collectives in Contemporary Art

Thomas J. Berghuis

INGREDIENTS

• Contemporary Art Ecosystem
• Organism without Fixed Structure (Fluidity)
• Surpassing Curatorship
• Exhibition as Counter-invitation
• *Lumbung* as Creating Assemblies (a Working Method)

In February 2019 the Jakarta-based artist collective ruangrupa[1] was selected to lead the artistic direction of one of the most prestigious contemporary art events in the world, documenta. ruangrupa will curate documenta fifteen, in Kassel, Germany in 2022.[2] Although a surprise to some, ruangrupa was in fact selected by a search committee, half of whom are familiar and close to ruangrupa and their work.[3] Therefore, selecting the search committee eight months earlier, in July 2018, already marked an important moment of change for documenta fifteen. An interview with members of ruangrupa in April 2019 by the Goethe Institute in Indonesia lists the selection of ruangrupa as part of a 'New Era of DOCUMENTA'.[4]

ruangrupa was founded in 2000 by artists Ade Darmawan, Hafiz Rancajale, Ronny Agustinus, Oky Arfie Hutabarat, Lilia Nursita and Rithmi Widanarko. Core members in charge of documenta fifteen are Reza Afisina, Ajeng Nurul Aini, Indra Ameng, Mirwan Andan, Ade Darmawan, Iswanto Hartono, Daniella Fitria Praptono, Farid Rakun and Julia Sarisetiati. ruangrupa was founded during the reform era *(era reformasi)* in Indonesia following nationwide protests that led to the resignation of President Suharto on 21 May 1998. Suharto had been

1. It is the wish of the collective that ruangrupa is always stylized without capital and abbreviated as ruru.

2. Documenta is an international art exhibition founded in 1955, that takes place every five years in the city of Kassel, Germany. Each edition is numbered and stylized differently; the 2022 edition is written as 'documenta fifteen'.

in power for thirty-two years. The reform era is marked by social and political change in Indonesia and coincides with the development of numerous artist collectives and artists run initiatives, of which ruangrupa is one.

By the time ruangrupa was selected to lead documenta fifteen it had become part of a contemporary art ecosystem known as Gudskul, comprising artists, architects, curators, designers, musicians, and writers who share a common space in South Jakarta (Gudside).[5] In an interview with the Goethe Institute in Indonesia, Farid Rakun stated that when ruangrupa was invited to submit a proposal for documenta fifteen it became clear to them that documenta should not become 'just an additional burden', but to 'broaden the scope' of what ruangrupa was already doing in Jakarta and Indonesia. Therefore, ruangrupa would continue to work as 'an organism without fixed structure' and taking into perspective the 'entire planet', since 'documenta involves the whole world'.[6]

It is this 'organism without a fixed structure' that I wish to explore in this essay, as it holds exactly what I feel that museums, exhibitions, and many contemporary art spaces today are lacking.[7] These institutions with their fixed, hierarchical structures fail to encompass what ruangrupa is succeeding in—namely creating a collective network for new exchanges in contemporary art and culture. A future history of artist collectives challenges discourses of art centred around individual artists and their patrons (curators, dealers, collectors, galleries, museums, and the art market). It is therefore also prone to criticism as it confronts the singular role of the artist and the curator as the main protagonists of contemporary art.

In 2011, I first wrote about the idea that contemporary art can be redefined in the collective, in an essay on ruangrupa published in *Third Text*.[8] In this article, I specifically addressed the role of artist collectives in surpassing the role of the curator as agents in the making of contemporary art, and that next to performance art, the work of artist collectives in Indonesia and elsewhere across Southeast Asia and the world deserved our attention. The viewpoints that artist collectives surpassed the role of the curator and could serve as an important context for expanding our understanding of contemporary art was

3. The selection committee consisted of eight members, four of whom are close to ruangrupa, namely Charles Esche, director of the Van Abbemuseum and artistic director of the Jakarta Biennial in 2015; art historian Philippe Pirotte, who was part of the curatorial team for the Jakarta Biennial in 2017; and Uta Meta Bauer, director of CCA NTU Singapore and co-curator of documenta 11 in 2002.

4. 'Interview with ruangrupa—A New Era of DOCUMENTA', Goethe-Institute Indonesien, 22 April 2019, www.youtube.com/user/goetheindonesia/featured.

5. gudskul.art.

6. Interview with ruangrupa (see note 4).

7. In a conversation with Australian cultural theorist Nikos Papastergiadis, ruangrupa stated that when it was invited for documenta fifteen it proposed a 'counter invitation', namely 'for documenta to become part of our ecosystem'. 'ruangrupa and Nikos Papastergiadis in Conversation—Living Lumbung: The Shared Spaces of Art and Life', *e-flux journal*, #118 (May 2021), www.e-flux.com/journal/118/395154/living-lumbung-the-shared-spaces-of-art-and-life/

8. Thomas Berghuis, 'ruangrupa: What Could Be "Art to Come"', *Third Text* 25, no. 4 (2011), pp. 395–407.

subsequently critiqued in an article by curator and art theorist David Teh, writing for *Afterall*. Teh pointed instead at the pivotal role of 'curatorial faculty' and 'curatorship' in shaping the role and independence of the artist collective ruangrupa.[9] In my view, the role of the artist collective surpasses the common role and 'care' of the curator, by expanding the role of the collective in shaping the space and the public for contemporary art through the collective.

Artist collectives are more fluid and open to a diversity of viewpoints, which can best be described as opening up to pluralism in art. It is surprising therefore that not more has been written on artist collectives in the history of art. The first article on 'Art as Collective Action' is by sociologist Howard S. Becker and describes the collaboration between artists and 'support personnel'.[10] In 2001, art historian Charles Green published a book examining collaborations in art in the 1960s and 1970s and what Green saw as a 'larger study: that of the shift to a new understanding of artistic identity' away from the 'single lone artistic originator and creator'.[11] In 2013, artists Gabriele Detterer and Maurizio Nannucci edited and published a volume on artist-run spaces in Europe and North America in the 1960s and 1970s.[12] Another interesting study is that of Gregory Sholette together with Blake Stimson in their edited volume, *Collectivism after Modernism: The Art of Social Imagination after 1945*, which focuses on the way 'modernist artists understood the collectivization as a way to give expression to modernity'.[13]

Until recently, no single study has been published on artist collectives in Asia, but in 2020 Indonesian art historians Agung Hutjanika and Almira Belinda Zainsjah published an essay on artist collectives in post-1998 Indonesia, listing twenty-three contemporary art collectives.[14]

Over the past decade there have been several papers and extensive conversations published on ruangrupa.[15] They include those that describe the 'fluidity' of ruangrupa as an organization, and its strategy as not having a fixed goal or objective. The concept of 'fluidity' is addressed in the 2012 article by Mirwan Andan as part of the 'flexibility of the work style in ruangrupa' and again addressed in the 2020 article by Geronimo Cristóbal, reflecting on an interview

9. David Teh, 'Who Cares a Lot? Ruangrupa as Curatorship', *Afterall: A Journal of Art, Context and Enquiry*, no. 30 (Summer 2012), pp. 108–117.

10. Howard S. Becker, 'Art as Collective Action', *American Sociological Review* 39, no. 6 (1974), pp. 767–777.

11. Charles Green, *The Third Hand: Collaboration in Art from Conceptualism to Postmodernism* (Minneapolis, 2001), p. xi.

12. *Artist-Run Spaces: Non-Profit Collective Organizations in the 1960s & 1970s*, eds. Gabriele Detterer and Maurizio Nannucci (Zurich, 2013).

13. *Collectivism after Modernism: The Art of Social Imagination after 1945*, eds. Gregory Sholette and Blake Stimson (Minneapolis, 2007).

14. Agung Hutjanika and Almira Belinda Zainsjah, 'Artist Collectives in The Post-1998 Indonesia: Resurgence, or a Turn (?)', *AESCIART: International Conference on Aesthetics and the Sciences of Art. Conference Proceedings*, (Bandung, 2020), pp. 256–263. proceedings.aesciart.itb.ac.id/publications/338617/artist-collectives-in-the-post-1998-indonesia-resurgence-or-a-turn.

15. These include Miquel Escobar Varela, 'Ruangrupa: Experimental Video Workshops and Activism in Indonesia', *Community Art: The Politics of Trespassing*, ed. Pascal Gielen (Amsterdam, 2011), pp. 287–297; Nuraini Juliastuti, 'Ruangrupa: A Conversation on Horizontal Organisation', *Afterall: A Journal of Art, Context and Enquiry*, no. 30 (Summer 2012), pp. 118–125; Mirwan Andan, 'All for Jakarta—A Note on the Tenth Anniversary of ruangrupa: Decompression #10, Expanding the Space and Public', *Inter-Asia Cultural Studies* 12, no. 4 (2011), pp. 591–602; Reinaart Vanhoe, *Also-Space, From Hot to Something Else: How Indonesian Art Initiatives Have Reinvented Networking* (Eindhoven 2016); Geronimo Cristóbal, 'Pushing against the roof of the world: ruangrupa's prospects for documenta fifteen', *Third Text Online*, 26 October 2020, www.thirdtext.org/cristobal-ruangrupa.

with ruangrupa member Farid Rakun by artist and arts professor Pedro Lasch, stating how 'we keep that fluidity on how to work and then content comes first and then structure comes later'.[16] This fluidity connects to the 'organic' nature of ruangrupa as a network, which, according to the director of ruangrupa Ade Darmawan, is 'like the idea of building a friendship. It is organic, spontaneous and open'.[17] Fluidity becomes the means for artists to work. It is both the tactic and strategy for the collective.

The 'fluidity' and 'organic' nature of artist collectives makes them interesting to study as part of the development of new networks that are being developed, linking contemporary art to contemporary activism and contemporary culture and politics in urban settings across the world. At the time of writing this essay, ruangrupa has started to collaborate with no less than fourteen artist collectives from across the world, who can also select other collectives to participate in documenta fifteen. Clearly, this is the right time to examine new perspectives on the role of artist collectives in contemporary art from a global perspective, leading to the time of documenta fifteen in 2022.

With the selection of fourteen artist collectives to join the preparations for documenta fifteen, ruangrupa has expanded their network of collaborations to encompass the entire world. They have done so using the model of the lumbung as a collective model for bringing together art and cultural practices from across the world. *Lumbung* refers to a communal 'rice barn' for shared resources (rice) that is used across Indonesia. *Lumbung* is not simply a theme for documenta but more a working method and a set of values throughout the entire working process for documenta fifteen. *Lumbung* has been used by ruangrupa since 2015, when they started working together with Serrum and Grafis Huru Hara and other collectives and organizations in a large double warehouse complex in South Jakarta, known as the Gudang Sarinah Ekosistem, which was the forerunner of the Gudskul Ekosistem that has become the current site for ruangrupa and a range of artists, creative workers, and organizations in South Jakarta to work together.[18]

Lumbung is being referred to on the documenta fifteen website as 'a kind of pooled collective resource

16. Farid Rakun interviewed by Pedro Lasch, 17 August 2015, 'Transcript, Art of the MOOC: Public Art and Pedagogy: "Ruangrupa"', Duke University, www.coursera.org/lecture/public-art-pedagogy/ruangrupa-mc2nq.

17. Ade Darmawan interviewed by Nuraini Juliastuti. 'Ruangrupa: A Conversation on Horizontal Organisation', *Afterall: A Journal of Art, Context and Enquiry*, no. 30 (Summer 2012), p. 124.

18. For a brief overview of Gudskul, see: Annie Jael Kwan, 'Gudskul: New Ecosystems for Learning', *ArtReview Asia*, 13 January 2020, artreview.com/ara-winter-2019-feature-gudskul/.

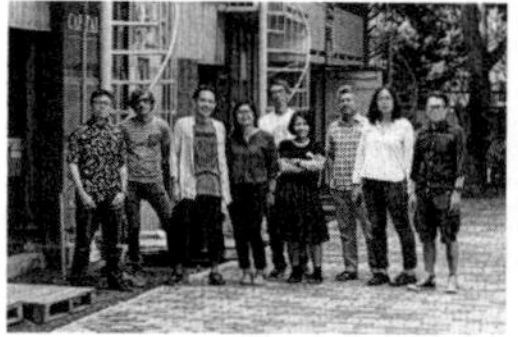

ruangrupa, team for documenta fifteen (l to r): Reza Afisina, Indra Ameng, Farid Rakun, Daniella Fitria Praptono, Iswanto Hartono, Ajeng Nurul Aini, Ade Darmawan, Julia Sarisetiati, Mirwan Andan. Courtesy of Gudskul/Jin Panji.

based in the principle of communality'. Emphasis is given to the development of the collective on the basis of 'shared resources for new sustainability and cultural practices … supported through residency programs, meetings, public activities and the development of related tools'.[19] *Lumbung* can also be seen as a working method towards self-sufficiency as outlined in a recent article on food security in Indonesia, which shows how *lumbung* in Indonesia is 'commonly used as a metaphor for food security and for storage of things of value, including knowledge and community values'.[20] During the recent Culture Summit Abu Dhabi, one of ruangrupa's founding members Ade Darmawan pointed at the role of *lumbung* as an 'ecological model' as well as an 'economic model' and a 'sustainable model for art and cultural practices'.[21] Darmawan also mentioned how *lumbung* is a model for collaboration and creating 'assemblies' between its members.[22]

It is because of this perspective of *lumbung* creating assemblies, with ruangrupa using the term *majelis* (assembly, council) that I would like to consider *lumbung* as an economic and a sociopolitical model and a model towards democratization, capable of generating citizens' assemblies. Citizens' assemblies are historically linked to participatory action research and connected to the work of the Brazilian pedagogue Paulo Freire—in particular Freire's *Pedagogy of the Oppressed* published in 1968 and translated into English in 1970.[23] Freire's P*edagogy of the Oppressed* became influential in Indonesia in the late 1980s, when artist and activist Moelyono in 1988 started to work with the NGO Association for Sociology Researchers (API) in Indonesia, introducing him to the 'participatory research and the pedagogical teachings of Paulo Freire'.[24] Moelyono took on an important role in contemporary art and activism in Indonesia next to others of his generation, including Tisna Sanjaya and Arahmaiani Feisal.[25]

The sociopolitical and democratizing model of the *lumbung* method can be examined in an early document outlining the *lumbung* method for the Vienna Secession, Union of Austrian Artists, which starts off with a reference to the 2011 Occupy Movement and moves into a discussion of the 'global dependency' on 'international funding institutions … coming from ex-colonizer countries'.[26]

19. 'Lumbung' documenta fifteen website, documenta-fifteen.de/en/lumbung/.

20. Graham MacRae and Thomas Reuter, 'Lumbung Nation: Metaphors of Food Security in Indonesia' in *Indonesia and the Malay World* 48, no. 142 (2020), pp. 338–358. Qtd. p. 345.

21. 'Reckoning with Globalism: New Realities and Possibilities Shaping Global Art museums and Biennales', panel moderated by Alexandra Munroe featuring Sheikha Hoor Al Qasimi, Gabi Ngcobo, Sunjung Kim, and Ade Darmawan and Farid Rakun for ruangrupa Culture Summit Abu Dhabi, 9 March 2021, www.youtube.com/watch?v=dru0A2xQq2M.

22. One can notice a shift towards a more collective process with nine members now being collectively brought forward as the curatorial team for documenta (instead of indicating one director) and with these assemblies generating a more collective structure for ruangrupa in its operations.

23. Paulo Freire, *Pedagogy of the Oppressed*, transl. Myra Bergman Ramos (New York/London, 2005 [1970]).

24. Ellen Kent, 'Entanglement: Individual and Participatory Art Practice in Indonesia', PhD Diss. (Canberra, 2016), p. 113.

25. Further research on Moelyono include: Juliastuti Nuraini, 'Moelyono and the Endurance of Arts for Society', *Afterall: A Journal of Art, Context and Enquiry*, no. 13 (Spring/Summer 2006), pp. 3–7; Edwin Jurriëns, 'Indonesian Artivism: Layers of Performativity and Connectivity', *Australian and New Zealand Journal of Art* 20, no. 2 (2020), pp. 231–252.

References to the Occupy Movement and to the unequal funding structures had been largely omitted in reports on ruangrupa curating documenta fifteen, as noted by Geronimo Cristóbal, who highlights the role of *lumbung* as 'the formation of a community, a Koperasi, that activates socially engaged art'. This *Koperasi* (cooperative) is particularly important for ruangrupa in making documenta fifteen, as is elaborated in the Vienna Secession:

> ....we proposed a collaboration in imagining, tinkering, experimenting and executing models of *koperasi* (closely but not exactly translatable to cooperative), a model of economy based on democratic principles of *rapat* (assembly), *mufakat* (agreement), *gotong royong* (commons), *hak mengadakan protes bersama* (right to stage collective protest) and *hak menyingkirkan diri dari kekuasaan absolut* (right to abolish absolute power). *Lumbung* as a model of resource governance will serve as the center point of this practice.[27]

Both the *gotong-royong* (commons, mutual assistance) and *musyawarah-mufakat* (agreement through deliberation) become reiterated in a conversation between ruangrupa and Nikos Papastergiadis.[28] They can be linked to former president Sukarno first replacing 'the "fifty-percent-plus-one" method of parliamentary democracy … with a system that emphasized consensus through concepts that Sukarno represented as uniquely Indonesian: mutual-help (*gotong-royong*) and consultation-consensus (*musyawarahmufakat*)'.[29] Most importantly, they are concepts of democracy distinct from Western democracy and take into consideration alternatives.

ruangrupa is capable in bringing new trans-local networks of exchanges of artist collectives to an artworld that is still largely dominated by individual artists and their patrons (curators, dealers, collectors, galleries, museums, and the art market). The coming period will see a rising interest in the role of artists collectives in shaping new perspectives and outlooks on contemporary art, also linked to trans-local networks and local indigenous practices, notions and values in providing welcome alternatives to the

TRANS-LOCAL NETWORKS

26. 'Wessen Freiheit?—ruanrupa: Lumbung' ('Whose Freedom?—ruangrupa: Lumbung'), Vereinigung Bildender KünstlerInnen Wiener Secession, www.secession.at/wp-content/uploads/2019/09/ruangrupa_lubung.pdf.

27. Cristóbal 2020 (see note 15).

28. ruangrupa and Nikos Papastergiadis 2021 (see note 7).

29. Tod Jones, *Culture, Power, and Authoritarianism in the Indonesian State Cultural Policy across the Twentieth Century to the Reform Era* (Leiden, 2013).

global art market, and discourses of global contemporary art.

One context in which the collective working structure of ruangrupa becomes clear is in the ruruHaus (ruruhouse), established in a former sports department store in the centre of Kassel. The ruruHaus serves as a collective space, 'laboratory' and 'ecosystem' for bringing people together in the practice of *nongkrong* (literally 'squatting' and 'hanging out')—an informal collective gathering in which people share their practices and ideas, which can lead to new projects or remain a conversation.[30]

How such a working structure of *nongkrong* becomes exhibited could be seen for example in the biennial exhibition 'Cosmopolis #1: Collective Intelligence', curated by Katherine Weir at Centre Pompidou in Paris in 2017.[31] For the exhibition ruangrupa created a collective resource centre for shared knowledge and ideas, consisting of several mixed-media installations that were activated by the public through listening, viewing, and live interactions and conversations.[32] It is expected that documenta fifteen will further develop and expand the collective models that were developed at Centre Pompidou and other exhibitions and events of ruangrupa in Jakarta and across the world.

30. In 2015 ruangrupa curated the five-yearly exhibition Sonsbeek in the city of Arnhem, the Netherlands (founded in 1949), which also included a 'ruru house'.

31. c1.cosmopolis.woo.cat/en/

32. See: ruangrupa.id/en/2017/10/18/ruangruparasite-cosmopolis-1-collective-intelligence/ and the interview with members of ruangrupa on the YouTube channel for *Cosmopolis* with Centre Pompidou at www.youtube.com/watch?v=jJ9hLr3p2MA

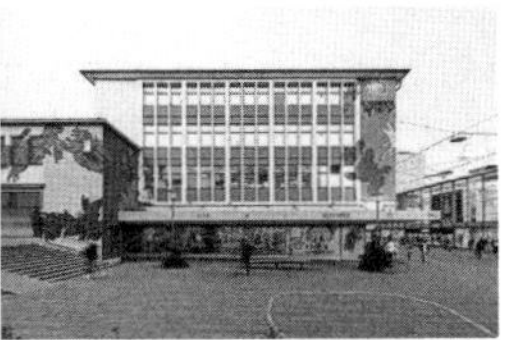

documenta fifteen, ruruHaus, Kassel, Germany. Photo Nicolas Wefers, 2020. Courtesy documenta fifteen, Kassel (Former sports department store).

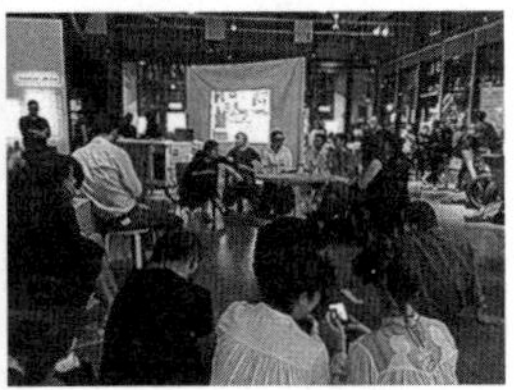

ruangrupa, installation and presentation, *Cosmopolis #1: Collective Intelligence*, curated by Katherine Weir, 18 October–18 December 2017, Centre Pompidou, Paris, France. Courtesy ruangrupa.

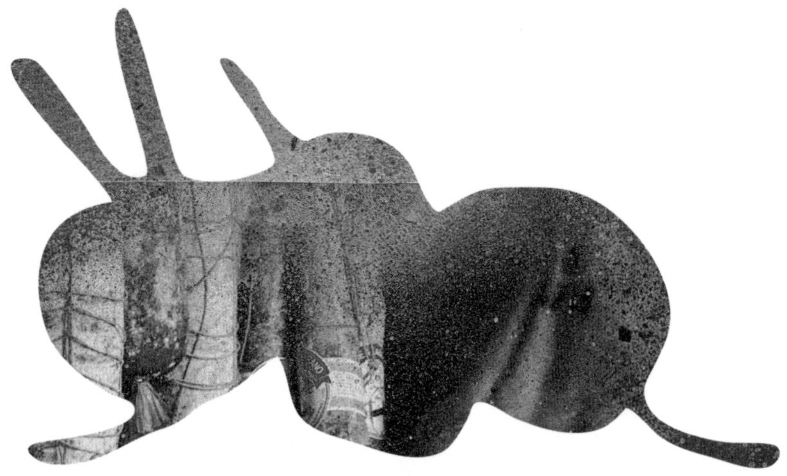

ART IS GOING UNDERGROUND

Janneke Wesseling

INGREDIENTS

- Underground Art
- Ascetic Revolution
- Collective
- Assemblage

In a lecture delivered on 20 March 1961, entitled 'Where do we go from here?', Marcel Duchamp predicted that 'the great artist of tomorrow will go underground'.[1] The reason, Duchamp argued, was that art had degenerated into a gigantic artistic production that was determined by supply and demand, degrading the art object by making it a commodity: 'The work of art is now a commonplace product, like soap and securities.' Duchamp was not alone in observing the commodification of art at the beginning of the 1960s. In 1959, on a visit to New York from Venice, Peggy Guggenheim was 'thunderstruck' by the sales of abstract expressionist paintings of, among others, Willem de Kooning and Jackson Pollock:

> The entire art movement had become an enormous business venture … Only a few persons really care for paintings. ... People only buy what is the most expensive, having no faith in anything else. Some buy merely for investment, placing pictures in storage without even seeing them, phoning their gallery every day for the latest quotation, as though they were waiting to sell stock.[2]

According to Duchamp, the commodification of art had resulted in a dilution of artistic values and in the dominance of mediocre art. Looking back on the developments in the art world over the past decades, I observe that this situation has even worsened. In every sector of the field—museum institutions, biennials, galleries, even in smaller non-profit art institutions—commercial values and economic thinking seem to determine the rules of the game.

1. invisiblecity.uarts.edu/where-do-we-go-from-here, accessed on 3 May 2021.

2. Quoted from Patricia Zohn, 'CultureZohn: Peggy Guggenheim, Art Addict', *Huffington Post* (4 November 2015) in Michael Shnayerson, *Boom: Mad Money, Mega Dealers, and the Rise of Contemporary Art* (New York, 2019).

Duchamp claimed that the response of artists to the deterioration of art would take shape as 'an ascetic revolution'. The general public would not be aware of this revolution, he added: 'Only a few initiates will develop [this revolution] on the fringe of a world blinded by economic fireworks.'[3]

3. (See note 1).

At the present moment in time, we seem to find ourselves right in the middle of Duchamp's ascetic revolution—albeit that in certain respects it differs in character from what Duchamp imagined. In the following, I will take a closer look at underground art, and at how this type of art possibly shapes the present ascetic revolution.

A short elaboration on the notion of underground, as used by Duchamp, is needed here. Two years after Duchamp's lecture, the experimental film *Flaming Creatures* by American film director Jack Smith was first shown (at the Bleecker Street Cinema, on 29 April 1963). This film, which celebrates free and unorthodox sex, marks the beginnings of the Underground Film Movement in New York, which would include artists and filmmakers such as Andy Warhol and the Kuchar brothers. The Underground Film Movement also developed ties with hippie subculture.

This is not the 'underground' that Duchamp was referring to, it seems to me, and his concept of going underground is not easily linked to hippie underground culture. In my view, Duchamp talked about going underground in the sense of a secret operation, of disappearing from public view and going into hiding beneath the surface of the earth. 'Underground' is used here in a more literal sense, and that is how I will refer to the notion of underground in this essay. An early example is the case of Dick Raaijmakers (1930-2013), Dutch avantgarde composer, performance artist, and founder of Dutch electronic music in the 1950s. Raaijmakers once described his way of operating as follows:

> I dig burrows underground and every once in a while, I stick my head above ground: hello, here I am! When I receive a blow on the head I go back into hiding, I dig further, and try again at a later point in time. If I am hit on the head once again, I withdraw again into the dark. Until finally somebody appreciates the value of my work and is

willing to collaborate with me. That is the moment I can show something above ground.[4]

Going underground enables the artist to retain a certain autonomy or freedom in carrying out the artistic practice, by severing ties with art institutions and remaining at a distance from the marketing system and from neoliberalist cultural policies. Since the early 1960s, a number of artists have performed such radical acts of disappearance or disruption. One example is the German artist Gustav Metzger (1926-2017), who produced Auto-Destructive Art (ADA). An ADA-work destroys itself, at either a fast (for example through fire or explosion) or slow pace (for example by corrosion), but never lasting longer than twenty years. In his 'Fourth Manifesto', Metzger wrote: 'The artist must destroy art galleries. Capitalist institutions. Boxes of deceit.'[5]

Even more radical is the case of Taiwanese performance artist Tehching Hsieh (b. 1950), who arrived in New York as an illegal immigrant in 1974 and literally went underground. To this day, Hsieh practices an extreme form of performance art in which art and life are indistinguishable from each other. For *One Year Performance 1980-1981*, Hsieh punched a factory-like time clock every hour, every day for 365 days, dressed in a neatly pressed uniform with his name and personnel number on the chest pocket of his shirt. He recorded the process in graphic charts and on photographs. During the *One Year Performance 1981-1982*, Hsieh lived out on the streets of Manhattan, day and night, without any protection, carrying all of his personal belongings in a small backpack. He carefully marked the routes that he was walking on Manhattan street maps.

An underground art work is ephemeral, changing, and processual; it is open and indefinite, more an open-ended assemblage than a definable object. Underground art can speak with many different voices simultaneously. Furthermore, artists are going underground by withdrawing from established institutional and commercial platforms and by rendering themselves and their art invisible as a manifestation of an individual art practice.[6]

Documenta fifteen, which will take place in 2022, is organized under the artistic direction of ruangrupa, a

4. In a conversation with his friend and colleague Frans de Ruiter (n.d.).

5. 'Manifesto World (Fourth Manifesto)', 7 October 1962. Published in *Gustav Metzger Writings 1953–2016*, ed. Mathieu Copeland (Geneva, 2019), pp. 87–88.

6. Of course, many artists continue to operate 'above ground'; and although the Covid-19 pandemic has delivered a serious blow to international art fairs and commercial galleries, the market mechanisms of the art world seem to be still firmly in place.

collective of artists and 'creatives' from Jakarta, Indonesia. Documenta fifteen is built around the notion of *lumbung*, the Indonesian word for a collectively governed rice-barn, where the gathered harvest is stored for the common good of the community. Ruangrupa's curatorial approach aims at a 'globally oriented, cooperative, interdisciplinary art and culture platform', and at 'a different kind of collaborative model of resource use—economically, but also in terms of ideas, knowledge, programs, and innovation'.[7]

Going underground may sound like a defeat to some readers, but here it means quite the opposite. Going underground is *not* an exodus from the art world and society, it is not a flight, a retreat, or a search for refuge, nor does it point to an anarcho-autonomist movement. Going underground, in the sense it is used here, entails a refusal of solitary gestures, and it aims for a re-grouping, a re-assembling, a re-connecting of forces, a re-configuring of social bonds. It is about re-affirming relations, rather than about cutting ties. It is, therefore, a political act.

Politics of Withdrawal (2020), a volume edited by the Dutch cultural theorists Joost de Bloois and Pepita Hesselberth, addresses the meaning of withdrawal as a political act. In their introduction, 'Toward a Politics of Withdrawal?', De Bloois and Hesselberth suggest that withdrawal

> is not a retreat from actuality per se, but from certain of its aspects: from our present-day 'always-on' culture, from surveillance capitalism, from neo-liberal management, and so on. … The gesture interrupts the forward motion of late-capitalism, as withdrawal is not oriented toward the future but rather invested in the possibilities of a different way of life …[8]

Indeed, underground artists resist the idea of art practice as a form of commercial entrepreneurship aimed at maximum financial profit for the individual entrepreneur; they do not produce marketable goods as financial investment for collectors and they refuse to define the value of art as economic value. Underground artists not only distance themselves from neoliberalist policies, but also from

7. universes.art/en/documenta/2022/, accessed on 3 May 2021. See also the essay by Thomas Berghuis in this volume.

8. *Politics of Withdrawal: Media, Arts, Theory*, eds. Pepita Hesselberth and Joost de Bloois (Lanham, Maryland, 2020), p. 13.

9. irational.org/cgi-bin/cv2/temp.pl, accessed on 2 June 2021.

10. status.irational.org/, accessed on 2 June 2021.

11. www.bakonline.org/program-item/trainings-for-the-not-yet/, accessed on 27 May 2021.

Western post-colonial dominance in art and culture. This happens in manifold ways, including practices that adapt late-capitalist technologies and systems (such as business models, the logistic of the warehouse and of digital distribution systems) to critically reflect on and inverse capitalist value systems.

Critiquing global capitalist logistic structures and questioning the place of technology in culture often positively embraces new technologies. In fact, a precondition for going underground seems to be an active engagement with the internet and with technical infrastructures, enabling an opening up of new zones of global collaboration and political action. Thinking with, and through, digital technology and its role in the co-existence of humans and more-than-humans is precisely what I would call one of the focal points of underground art.

A very early example of an underground artist who engages with digital technology is Heath Bunting (b. 1966), one of the first pioneers in 'Internet Art'. Bunting participated in the net.art movement during the rise of the internet, during which time he founded irational.org.[9] Bunting organizes workshops for artists, such as the Status Project, training them in resilience and survival in neoliberal times. In these workshops, Bunting teaches artists methods on how to acquire a new or alternative second identity, or to 'build new natural persons', in a way that is completely legal, allowing artists to disappear from the radar and to re-start their life and career.[10]

'Trainings for the Not-Yet' in BAK, Utrecht (2019), organized by Dutch artist Jeanne van Heeswijk (b. 1965) entailed a series of 'trainings' with people living in the neighbourhood and others 'for a future of being together otherwise', in a world where injustice and inequality of power are causing ecological and humanitarian crises.[11] The exhibition at BAK, which was changing and evolving over the course of several months, took shape as a performative presentation of a long and diverse series of workshops, meetings and dialogues, which Van Heeswijk understood as 'trainings':

> .... trainings in civic engagement, radical collectivity, and active empowerment, the project brings

together collaborators from various fields and communities to create and practice alternative imaginings of being together in the face of the pressing emergencies that shape the world today.[12]

At BAK, Van Heeswijk presented her collaborative projects within the framework of a small, public art institution. Underground artists often choose to step away from institutions altogether and to work completely outside of any pre-established frame, like Bunting and, as another example, the Dutch performance artist Ruchama Noorda (b. 1979). Noorda is interested in 'Lebensreform' philosophy and practice, and its social, ideological, and spiritual underpinnings.[13]

Recently, Noorda and several artist colleagues have engaged with the *Kabouterbeweging*, originally founded by political activist Roel van Duijn.[14] Despite its playful hippie character (*Kabouterbeweging* meaning: a movement of 'gnomes'), the movement actually existed as a leftist, ecological political party between 1969 and 1974, after which it went underground. Noorda clandestinely installs small bronze statues of gnomes (30 cm tall) on specific locations in public space, such as at the foot of the monument to Van Duijn's *Kabouterbeweging* on the Spui, right in the centre of Amsterdam. A second location is Ruigoord, a small village outside of Amsterdam that was squatted by *Kabouters* in the early seventies and still exists as an artists' colony today. It is a green oasis surrounded by the industrial landscape of Amsterdam Westpoort (the harbour area) with its huge wind turbines and gasoline tanks. In the vicinity of each bronze statue, an apple tree will be planted. A quotation on the plaquette on the plinth of one of the bronze statues reads: 'Hurried plastic man sees himself confronted with the acute danger of total catastrophe. The only solution is to bring culture into harmony with nature.'[15]

In her book *The Mushroom at the End of the World: On the Possibility of Life in Capitalist Ruins* (2015), the anthropologist Anna Lowenhaupt Tsing offers the concept of 'assemblage' as a key to understanding the world we live in. Assemblage is, in Tsing's interpretation, 'an open-ended entanglement of ways of being'. She writes: 'In an

12. Ibid.

13. In 2015, Noorda obtained a doctoral degree with research on the topic of Lebensreform and artistic practice. For more information: phdarts.eu/Dissertations/Ruchama-Noorda-E-Form

14. kabouters.nu/hoofd/kabouterbeweging, accessed on 2 June 2021.

15. 'De haastige plasticmens ziet zich voor het acute gevaar van een totale catastrofe geplaatst. De enige oplossing is de cultuur in harmonie brengen met de natuur'. Quote by Roel van Duijn in Coen Tasman, *Louter Kabouter: Kroniek van een Beweging 1969–1974* (Amsterdam, 1996), p. 54.

16. Anna Lowenhaupt Tsing, *The Mushroom at the End of the World: On the Possibility of Life in Capitalist Ruins* (Princeton, 2015), pp. 83, 157.

assemblage, varied trajectories gain a hold on each other, but indeterminacy matters. To learn about an assemblage, one unravels its knots.' And:

> ....rather than limit our analyses to one creature at a time (including humans), or even one relationship, if we want to know what makes places liveable we should be studying polyphonic assemblages, gatherings of ways of being. Assemblages are performances of liveability.[16]

The concept of assemblage, in the sense of the term as proposed by Tsing, can help in gaining a deeper understanding of post-capitalist, underground, collective art practices, of how and to what end artists collaborate and in what manner we could experience and perceive underground and collective art works. From this it might follow that art historians, in their turn, decide to shape global collaborations, in order to map the collective networks artists are building, and to participate in making these operational. I believe that this may provide an important contribution to answering the question of how to make places liveable.

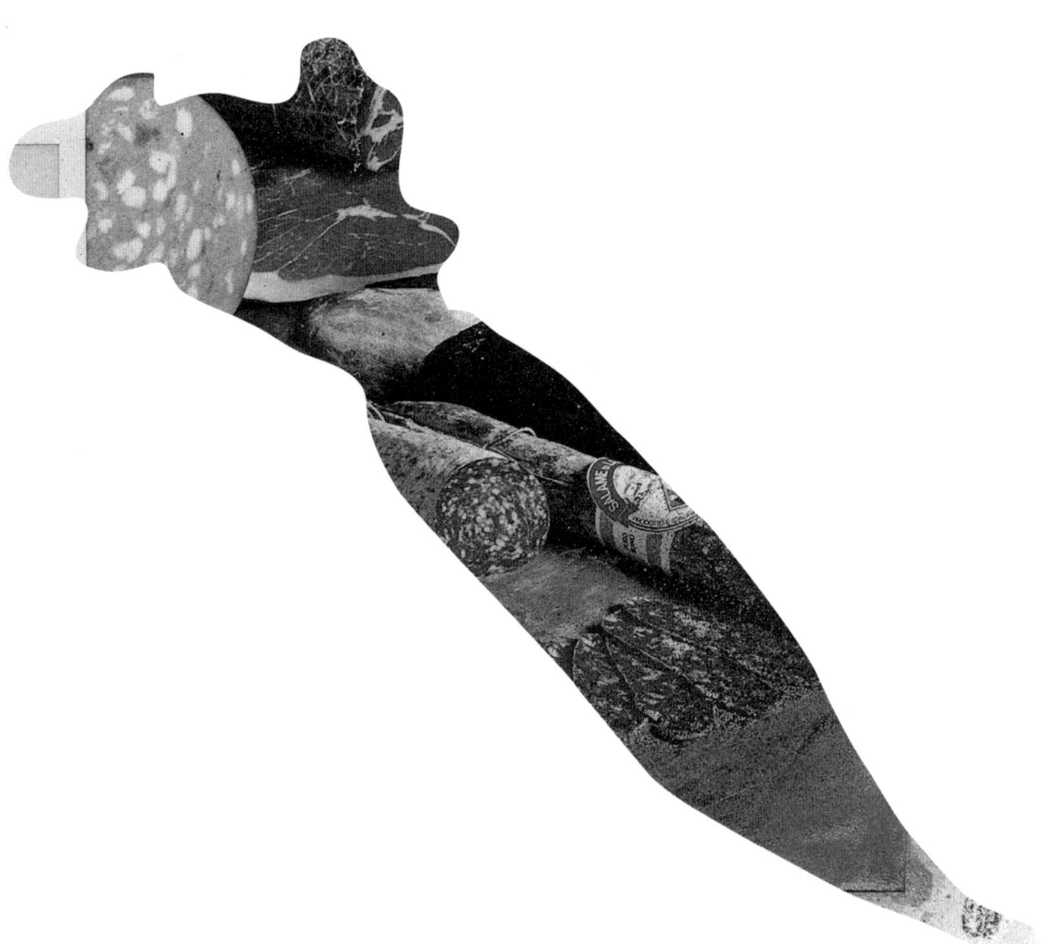
SALAME

UNANTICIPATED INTIMACIES
A Collective Writing Experiment

Joo Yun Lee, Katja Kwastek, Chris Lee, Virginia MacKenny, Kyveli Mavrokordopoulou, Jacqueline Hoàng Nguyễn, Jennifer Pranolo, Lize van Robbroeck, Pippa Skotnes, James Webb, Carine Zaayman

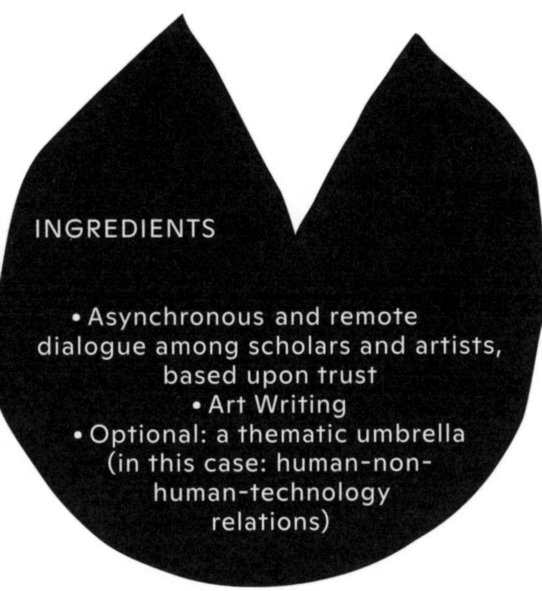

What does a recipe include? Does it start with the ingredients, or does it also question where these ingredients come from, who has access to them or can afford them, how they have been produced, and how they are entangled with our planetary ecology? If you really want an excellent dish, excellent not only aesthetically, but also ethically, you'd want to take such basic considerations into account. Before, or at least alongside creating dishes, we have to improve the 'food web', and this holds true for scholarship as well. As long as the number of people who can afford an education at an academic institution and make a living from working in the arts (as artist or scholar) is highly disproportionate across this planet, how can we ever reach a somewhat balanced 'planetary inclusivity', even just concerning humanities' scholarship? Asking for a 'recipe' to change this situation might amount to asking for a recipe for a new world order. However, as we know so well in the humanities, any change in economy or politics requires a change of minds first. Therefore, the following is a rather modest 'beginner's recipe' to work with.

Over the course of two months, we conducted a collective writing experiment. Starting with existing contacts, it aimed at broadening networks, with the goal of an exchange of ideas, and a 'thinking with' each other, based upon artistic works or practices we consider relevant. To this end, we passed on brief thoughts about works or projects to one or two further allies, hoping that they would resonate with them, if not to prepare the dish, then at least lay the table together. The instructions were straightforward: to respond to a snippet of roughly 150 words with another statement. Gradually, a chain of emails started unfolding in the mailboxes of researchers and academics who would not have found themselves working together otherwise. Somewhere between the form of a chain letter and a *cadavre exquis*, ideas centred around human and non-human technology relations bounced from author to author, generating a set of unanticipated intimacies.

Since any good recipe also contains a bit of mystery, we will not disclose which statement came first, or who contributed which section. We also consider it less relevant, as obviously this contribution does not claim to offer an in-depth scholarly argument with some clear persuasive arch or central thesis. What it does show, however, is how such a format, which we might want to address as art writing, can begin to bridge situated knowledges with planetary concerns, past and present, and make new and productive connections between artists across centuries, mediums, and continents.

Inoculate - Bird in an air pump
→ embodying technology: what are the ethical implications of science?

art science

bounded in space

The City and the City: racial ~~segregation~~ composition of everyday environments

virtual physical

Spaghetti Blockchain
material and virtual entanglements

unanticipated connections

Graft and Ash for a 3 Monitor Work Station
Algorithmic bias: what bodies count?

cyborgs

Yuy, a androide
genetically modified life: how are colonial legacies active in the present?

human, non-human-technology relations

sonic

disposable bodies

environments

eco-disaster monocultures

In Vitro/al Mukhtabar
remembering the past - imagining the future

extractive mentalities

Gold and Ivory, Elephants Charging over Quartose County: destructive modernity

nature culture

listening

indigenous perspectives

Raaswater
land occupation

Potatoe Garden Band
Data Sonification, & colonial residues

lapses of history

Calling Badger and the Symbol of the Spirit Languages
erasure of colonial memory

readjusting the past

Reading Instructions

The fragments can be read in more than one order. Next to the numbering, which is inspired by the actual chain of writing (while not actually representing it, as some texts generated more than one response), and branching out the reading process, some 'choose your own adventure style' suggestions for alternative paths through the fragments, as well as a visual intuitive rendering of the written exchange accompany the texts. Each offers a curatorial perspective, so to speak, highlighting resonances that emerged. However, the readers are of course invited to create their own path – after all, creative improvisation is at the core of our recipe…

1. I was riveted by how the work you describe casts doubt on the human as a bounded category, and regards it as a mere spectator in an alliance forged between two non-human, technologically mediated entities. What if this separation is further explored by nurturing a malleable, embodied notion of the human, for better or for worse? The premise of Ana María Gómez López's performative experiment *Inoculate* (2013-2014) is strange enough: the artist inserted a plant seed in her right tear duct. Lying indoors for days, almost fully inert, on a makeshift bed, Gómez López waited while a *Begonia semperflorens* sprouted within her body. After two weeks of mindful diligence, the plant shyly emerged from the artist's eyelid. *Inoculate* vehemently softens the boundaries between human and vegetal, opening the possibility of a symbiotic and cooperative approach to nature. Yet it also invites us to ponder the implications of transforming oneself into a scientific object.
(Next, read 2, 6, or 10)

2. This concept that you suggest of transforming—even reducing—oneself into an object of scientific experiment via a poetic symbiosis of the human and the vegetal reminds me of an arguably more 'unnatural' intimacy that is growing between the human and the computational, whose tools are increasingly treated as digital extensions of our embodied selves. In her nine-minute video installation *Graft and Ash for a Three Monitor Work Station* (2016), Sondra Perry confronts the inadequacies of this relationship by creating an ill-fitting avatar of herself. Relying solely on the pre-set parameters of an open-source 3D software programme, she discovers that neither her body type (too big) nor skin colour (too dark) can be rendered. The approximal mutation of herself that results critically deforms the very image and idea of the human. Who counts—or is instantly recognizable—as 'human', and who must labour continually to become legibly and measurably so?
(Next, read 3, 10, or 8)

1. Margot Norton, 'Not-So-Easy-Pieces', *Mika Rottenberg: Easypieces*, ed. Margot Norton, exh. cat. New Museum (New York, 2019), p. 12.

2. Winona Stevenson, 'Calling Badger and the Symbols of the Spirit Languages: The Cree Origins of the Syllabic System', *Oral History Forum*, no. 1920 (1990/2000) pp. 19–24.

3. The 'approximal mutation' in Sondra Perry's work that you describe makes the viewer critically engage in software's technical glitch with their own bodies. The artist's avatar mutating on the screen according to the viewer's peddling obfuscates the technological biases that categorize individuals based on markers such as race, gender, and sexuality. If Perry's work delves into the sensory and affective textures of algorithms and other computational methods by conjuring the (un)representable body at a micro and macro level, Mika Rottenberg's work explores data migration through the bodies, air, dirt, and optical fibre. Unveiling the 'material relationship between human and nonhuman entities'[1] through sound, Rottenberg's *Spaghetti Blockchain* (2019) juxtaposes Mongolian throat singing; the noise of giant servers at CERN; and the ASMR of jelly rolling on a hot plate. In that way, Rottenberg engages media infrastructure as global geopolitical systems and the unprecedented scope and granularity of data migrations, complicating the relation and entanglement among natural, human, or virtual borders.
(Next, read 4, 8, or 6)

4. What strikes me about Sondra Perry's work is that, through the processes of inscription by a recording device the technological limitations make clear which bodies are recordable and ought to be remembered. Artist and member of the Upper Nicola Band of the Okanagan Nation, Krista Belle Stewart revisits a wax cylinder recording of her great-grandmother, Terese Kaitmeko, singing in the Syilx language and captured by Scotland-born Canadian-based ethnographer James Alexander Teit in 1915–1918. Her audio-driven video performance and sound work *Potato Gardens Band* (2017–2020) presents Stewart playing the digital file of her great-grandmother's incantation through a public address system on their ancestral lands where her family and relatives were invited. The event is documented with a hand-held mobile phone by someone standing on the top of a nearby hill. Defying the colonial modalities of documentation and archiving, Stewart engages with the disembodied voice of her great-grandmother as a portal for accessing historical kinship and land attachment.
(Next, read 5, 7, or 11)

5. I am reminded of the origin stories of the Cree syllabary recalled by Dr. Winona Wheeler (Winona Stevenson).[2] I came across this serendipitously as I recalled a lesson from a graphic design history course where the professor narrated the inclusion of the Cree syllabary in the historiography of 'Canadian' typography. I would come

to realize that this was a problematic appropriation of an Indigenous cultural form. The Cree story holds that an elder named Calling Badger received the syllabary from the Spirit World. The colonial story attributes its 'invention' to an English missionary. One story is supported by evidentiary artifacts, protected by an institutional infrastructure of colonial memory. The other is largely transmitted orally/aurally, through a somatic infrastructure. Yet, the colonial story is mis-recognized as simply factual rather than as mythological—the myth being that colonization brings (imposes) European inventiveness, literacy, and progressive modernity.
(Next, read 6, 9, or 7)

6. The mediation/mediatization of Indigenous philosophy is also at the core of *Ywy, a androide* (2017), a short film by Pedro Neves Marques, in which we see Ywy, played by Zahy Guajajara, standing in a cornfield, addressing the viewer and, at times, the corn crops for whom Ywy acts as interpreter. We learn that both the corn and Ywy are artificially modified and designed as to not to reproduce, and that Ywy feeds on the corn, which she calls her sisters, once processed into energy (biofuel). What struck me is how this work plays out the idea of sympathy between two nonhuman entities (a genetically modified plant and a humanoid robot), while keeping the (human) viewer at a distance. We are left to wonder why it is that Indigenous concepts of plants as our sisters seem to 'naturally' align with the revelation of the artificial origin of the actors in this work.
(Next, read 7, 11, or 1)

7. What strikes me about your example is that it hinges on an unanticipated intimacy. While certain hierarchies of species, gender, and race are so naturalized that they demand conscious unlearning, technologies are presently generating spaces where accepted distinctions are proven untenable. So, alliances between presences once considered discrete come into being. By bringing an unfamiliar intimacy into view, your example reminds me of *In Vitro/al Mukhtabar* (2019), a film by Larissa Sansour and Søren Lind. Young Alia and Dunia, who is on her deathbed, debate strategies to rebuild the post-apocalyptic Bethlehem in which the film is set. Dunia pleads for rebuilding what once was. Alia is a clone, her mind a host to someone else's memories. Even as memory-made-flesh, she advocates for forgetting and starting afresh. She lives in intimacy with the ghost of a past she never experienced and knows that it seeks a different future.
(Next, read 8, 3, or 9)

8. When I read your text, my mind went to different places. In particular, I thought of the uneasy dynamics in China Miéville's *The City and the City* (2009), where two cities live side by side and residents of each have to train their eyes (their minds, more

specifically) not to see and experience the other city, its inhabitants, and all that comes with people and their transmissions. Intermingled, but segregated; routes taken to actively avoid the other. This reminds me of how during Apartheid, and countless other situations of separation, different people were forced to see the same street differently. For one person, certain spaces were available, accessible, and inviting, whereas other spaces were just not considered, not seen, rendered invisible. We do this in multiple ways, and in many aspects of our life. What unanticipated intimacies do we allow ourselves to have? And how can we be open to them?
(Next, read 9, 4, or 3)

9. What strikes me about Sansour's and Lind's work is the reflection, renewed by the global pandemic, on the possibilities presented by imagined catastrophes in which a protagonist must decide whether to fight for the recovery of old values or become the observer as new ones emerge. This reminded me of the 1768 painting by Joseph Wright in which a natural philosopher is depicted in a dramatically lit scene recreating Robert Boyle's air pump. It celebrates the experiment in which air is sucked out of a vessel, making a vacuum. Inside the vessel a bird, deprived of oxygen, is about to die. Experiments such as this—to understand the nature of air—gave rise to steam engines so instrumental in the Industrial Revolution. In the painting the dying bird stares across at the philosopher as he in turn stares out at the viewer. We are dared to accept the inevitable sacrifices progress demands.
(Next, read 10, 2, or 4)

10. Your example makes me really feel the disconnection embedded in the Western philosopher/scientist as he dispassionately inflicts death on the bird. The painting, and empathy, is notably gendered and infantilized—only two little girls indicate any emotional distress. Today, artists encourage us to feel that which we have historically neglected. Hanien Conradie, in her series *Raaswater* (2014), hears the echo of water in the agriculturally depleted dry river bed of her grandmother's farm in Worcester, Western Cape. Conradie works directly with the riverbed soil as her pigment. Mixing it with water, she lets it descend down her canvas from above and allows it to find its own way without further intervention. The resultant rivulets leave a trail of soil that evokes images of soundwaves, and the 'voice' of the river, in a synaesthetic encounter of sorts, becomes visible.
(Next, read 11, 1, or 5)

11. I find that the haunting painting you selected speaks to the pervasive sense of loss, grief, hope, and yearning that accompanies witnessing the massive environmental degradation of the Anthropocene. The tragic consequences of modern Western rapaciousness, and the instrumentalist episteme that caused it, is nowhere

more evident than in Thomas Baines' *Gold and Ivory, Elephants Charging over Quartose County* (1873). Three magnificent beasts, their trunks raised in alarm as they charge towards the viewer, are reduced to mere ivory, while the majestic mountain landscape is nothing more to the colonist-painter than quartose rock, a resource to be mined for gold. How is it that the artist could clearly see the splendour of his subjects, yet blithely embrace their imminent destruction? This work makes me wonder how our species choose material status symbols with very little innate value over the shimmer of living matter.
(Next, read 1 or 5)

BRIDGING SITUATED KNOWLEDGE

No doubt, producing a collaborative piece of writing comes with challenges. However, the exercise of letting go of authorial agency through trust in the potential of collective discourse allowed for a distinctive yet gratifying form of scholarly exchange. There is something re-animating about joy in the suspense of the unknown, which is not common in academic writing. The asynchronous and remote dialogue between unknown co-authors yielded thoughts around how art can expose the embodied dimensions of science; questions of gender and race in technology; the persistence of settler colonial mindsets and the ensuing environmental violence, and how consciousness of these ideas can offer new vocabularies for grappling with the residues of modernism's ideals of progress and hegemony.

Our recipe yielded a collection of texts that surfaces unanticipated intimacies pertaining not only to the subject matter addressed by the authors, but also to their anxieties and yearnings. As the artworks referenced in this essay and the attending commentaries make painfully clear, technological developments are never detached but rather are entangled in systems that can be as exploitative as they are nourishing. Our technology-enabled dish is thus implicated in the very polemics it explores. Hopefully, conscious reflection on the connections yielded through the work we do while simultaneously holding the damages inflicted in full view can chart ways of amplifying the former and learn to take better care of the latter.

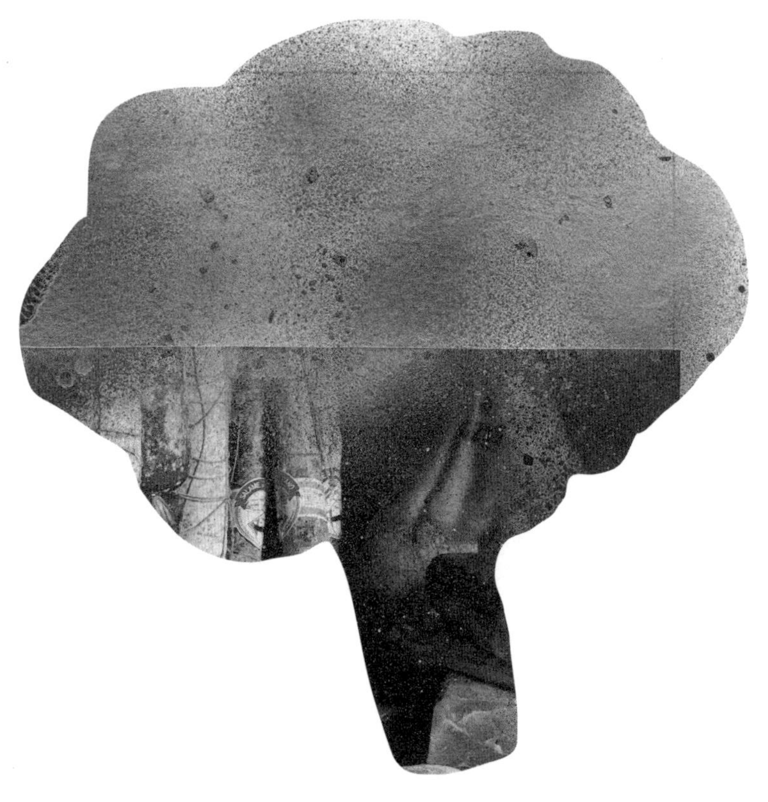

INCLUSIVE ART HISTORY AND CANON FORMATION
Contradictio in Terminis?

Gregor Langfeld

INGREDIENTS

- Canon
- Canonization
- Marginalization
- Feminism
- Aesthetics
- Social Processes

As is well known, discourses and disputes about the value of certain art movements, artists, and artworks are of all times. They have always influenced and determined ever evolving art history, resulting in specific hierarchies that find expression in art-historical textbooks by including certain artists, treating them in greater or lesser detail, or by excluding them, just to mention one example. Various actors in the art field and their associated institutions occupying specific positions in the field are actively involved in establishing certain art forms and understandings of art.

It is amazing, however, that until relatively recently art historians hardly ever tried to understand these processes, which result in the canonization or marginalization of art in all their complexity. Until the 1970s that kind of self-awareness, which ideally every discipline should possess, was virtually absent in art history. Not without reason: the art field tends to sacralize art and conceal the conditions under which art is produced and canonized.[1]

Although I am reluctant to speak of a canon, or canons, in relation to contemporary art,[2] even in this field similar structures can be identified, which have always determined the establishment of certain art forms. Especially in the contemporary art field, artists and currents are defended or fought against with great vigour.

1. Gregor Langfeld, 'The canon in art history: concepts and approaches', *Journal of Art Historiography*, no. 19 (December 2018), pp. 1–18, 5–6, arthistoriography.wordpress.com/19-dec-19/

2. The extent to which one can speak of canonization in contemporary art is debatable. It is no longer the case today that art can only be canonized post-mortem, as Bourdieu still claimed, but art always only obtains canonical status over the course of its reception within a complex process. Pierre Bourdieu, *The Rules of Art: Genesis and Structure of the Literary Field*, transl. Susan Emanuel (Stanford, CA, 1996 [1992]), p. 147.

This raises the question of whether the intentions to de-hierarchize the canon, or even to abolish it, which are frequently heard, can be successful or whether they rather confirm the system that produces these hierarchies.

A dominant approach to the canon is driven by the desire to expand the canon to marginalized groups of artists. This approach seems reasonable because the canonization of artists always entails selection and the marginalization of a much larger group. Since the early 1970s, this perspective has evolved out of Marxist and feminist art history. Later, gender, queer, and postcolonial studies developed out of this. That form of art history has done a great deal to make us increasingly aware that the canon is not timeless and fixed but represents just one possibility among others. There is always a broad spectrum of possibilities for artists, artworks, movements and so on that might enter the canon but only a few achieve this.

In particular, as a result of efforts in recent decades to realize a more global and transnational art history, questions of the canon have acquired a new dynamic. The significantly increased presence of 'non-Western' artists at documenta and other venues since the turn of the millennium[3] and in biennials organized outside the West suggests the direction in which the canon of contemporary art might evolve. However, the discipline today remains strongly rooted in a 'Western' (specifically European and North American) art historiography. As James Elkins contends, an increase in geographical inclusion should not obscure the fact that global art histories and transnational perspectives are thoroughly 'Western' constructs that are only comprehensible and persuasive to those who are already well within this vein of North Atlantic art history.[4]

This article mainly focuses on feminist approaches as one example of the kind of research that has been carried out on the exclusion of social groups, such as female, minority and 'non-Western' artists, from the canon.[5] In her influential article 'Why Have There Been No Great Women Artists?', Linda Nochlin does not dispute that in the past women created fewer masterpieces than their male colleagues did but rather explains how this inequality arose based on the institutional structure of the field of art, since

3. Lotte Philipsen, *Globalizing Contemporary Art: The Art World's New Internationalism* (Aarhus, 2010), pp. 37–38.

4. James Elkins, 'Afterword', *Circulations in the Global History of Art*, eds. Thomas DaCosta Kaufmann, Catherine Dossin, and Béatrice Joyeux-Prunel (Farnham/Burlington, 2015), pp. 203–229, 210.

5. This text was formerly published in an adapted form as a section of a more comprehensive text which covers all the different aspects and perspectives with regard to canon formation: Langfeld 2018 (see note 1).

women did not have full access to institutions, such as the academies of art.[6] This and similar studies demonstrate ways in which social history might be integrated into feminist approaches in order to understand the mechanisms that lead to the marginalization of certain social groups.[7] The focus on marginalization seems to be the most important added value of feminist and related approaches with regard to canon formation, although it must be said that it can be methodologically more challenging and harder to substantiate than research into the canonization of specific artists since discourses as they have appeared in reception documents, such as exhibition catalogues, mainly deal with artists from dominant groups and to a lesser degree with excluded or marginalized artists.

Feminists frequently called for a revision of the existing canon, aiming to expand it to female and other marginalized artists. The social marginalization of certain groups was attributed to the canon, which was accordingly regarded as unjust. The goal of revising artistic hierarchies was a reason why feminist art historians wanted to rule out the criterion of the formal quality of the work of art.[8] They distanced themselves from an aesthetic perspective, which receded to the background or was regarded as unimportant. However, more recent art historians, such as Janet Wolff, have attempted to reintroduce the aesthetic element 'without falling back on discredited notions of timeless beauty and universal values'.[9]

It cannot be denied that visual qualities are supposed to be the most innate element of fine art, and their effect is tied to their formal appearance. This distinguishes art, and more specifically the 'legitimate' Western bourgeois mode of art perception, from other areas of life, such as politics and religion. Obviously, aesthetic judgement plays an important role in art perception and therefore should be involved when engaging with canon formation. However, it must be acknowledged that even the connoisseur's or professional's eye is the product of social and historical developments. Wolff proposes that the dilemmas within aesthetic judgements that feminism is confronted with, such as gendered hierarchies and bias in museum practice, should be addressed 'in terms of the exploration of social groups and their ideological and

6. Linda Nochlin, 'Why Have There Been No Great Woman Artists?', *Art News* (January 1971), pp. 22–39, 67–71, 25, 32.

7. Since the 1990s the sometimes heavily critical tone of earlier feminist literature was tempered in surveys that explore the historical position of female artists such as: Whitney Chadwick, *Women, Art, and Society* (New York, 2012 [1990]).

8. For an analysis of 'feminism's distrust of beauty', see Janet Wolff, 'Groundless Beauty: Feminism and the Aesthetics of Uncertainty', *Feminist Theory* 7, no. 2 (August 2006), pp. 143–158.

9. Ibid., pp. 147, 153.

aesthetic interests'.[10] This concept differs from Griselda Pollock's psychoanalytical approach, which made us aware of patriarchal mechanisms and sexism, especially in relation to the work of art as such.[11] Wolff argues for an approach which is grounded more in the concrete social and historical conditions of the production and reception of art.[12]

If we want to fully understand the power struggles with regard to canon formation they should not be reduced to the hegemony of men over women, because other factors are also influential. Important processes in the field of art, such as the struggle between conservatives and progressives or innovation (phenomena that are constitutive elements of the modern era),[13] should be integrated into any true understanding of processes of canonization. In that sense, the Story of Art cannot be reduced to an illustrated Story of Man, as Pollock claimed. Later art historians, such as Whitney Chadwick and Amelia Jones, argued for a position that acknowledges differences among women conditioned by age, class, race, ethnicity, and sexual orientation, as well as social changes.[14] Queer studies have also pointed out that a binary division can be problematic and obstruct an understanding of processes of canonization. Furthermore, they do not do justice to women who played an important role in promoting and institutionalizing, for example, modern art, such as Katherine Dreier who was perhaps the most active supporter of international modern art in the United States in the 1920s and also advocated for women's rights;[15] Hilla Rebay, who assembled Solomon R. Guggenheim's art collection; the legendary Peggy Guggenheim; or Abby Aldrich Rockefeller, Lillie P. Bliss and Mary Quinn Sullivan, who established MoMA and had a considerable influence on its collecting and exhibiting strategies, to mention just a few example figures in the United States, who were not exceptional cases at all internationally in this respect despite being outnumbered by male art promoters.[16]

While, especially in the early stages, feminists had to fight against oppression and male hegemony within the patriarchal structures of art history, feminist and gender studies have since had a powerful and considerable influence on canon formation. Feminist art historians tend to be active players in the art field, and aim to change our views on art and the compilation of the canon. In their role as

10. Ibid., p. 153.

11. Griselda Pollock, *Differencing the Canon: Feminist Desire and the Writing of Art's Histories* (London, 1999).

12. Wolff 2006 (see note 8), p. 153.

13. Robert Jensen explores artistic innovation that to a large extent shapes the canon and what artworks, artists or movements are included in textbooks, for example. Jensen, 'Measuring Canons: Reflections on Innovation and the Nineteenth-century Canon of European Art', *Partisan Canons*, ed. Anna Brzyski (Durham/London, 2007), pp. 27–54.

14. Chadwick 2012 (see note 7), pp. 502, 505; Pollock 1999 (see note 11), p. 24.

15. Dreier worked for women's suffrage, advocated for social reforms in Argentina and promoted women artists. Furthermore, she headed the Manhattan Trade School for Girls, which provided young women with an education in order to open up better job opportunities for them, and she was active at the German Home for Recreation for Women and Children. Katherine S. Dreier, *Five Months in the Argentine from a Woman's Point of View, 1918 to 1919* (New York, 1920).

16. See, among other publications, Doris Wintgens, *Peggy Guggenheim and Nelly van Doesburg: Advocates of De Stijl* (Rotterdam, 2017); *The Museum of Non-Objective Painting: Hilla Rebay and the Origins of the Solomon R. Guggenheim Museum*, ed. Karole P. B. Vail (New York, 2009); *The Société Anonyme: Modernism for America*, ed. Jennifer R. Gross (New Haven, 2006); *Abby Aldrich Rockefeller and Print Collecting: An Early Mission for MoMA*, eds. Deborah Wye and Audrey Isselbacher (New York, 1999).

17. Gregory Sholette, 'Heart of Darkness: A Journey into the Dark Matter of the Art World', *Visual Worlds*, eds. John R. Hall, Blake Stimson, and Lisa Tamiris Becker (New York/London, 2005), pp. 116–138.

18. Wolff 2006 (see note 8), p. 149.

19. Ruth E. Iskin uses the terms 'counter-canons' and 'pluriversal canons' and Anna Brzyski that of 'multiple canons'. Iskin, 'Introduction: Re-envisioning the Canon: Are Pluriversal Canons Possible?', *Re-envisioning the Contemporary Art Canon*, ed. Iskin (London/New York, 2017), pp. 1–41, 13–14, 24, 28 etc.; Anna Brzyski, 'Introduction: Canons and Art History', Brzyski 2007 (see note 13), pp. 1–25, 3. Wolff problematizes the concept of multiple canons and Elkins does the same for the related concept of multiple modernities. Wolff 2006 (see note 8); Elkins 2015 (see note 4), pp. 227–229.

university teachers, they are agents of power that shape new generations of actors in the art field.

Certainly, in the past decades more female artists have been added to the canon. However, the number of these artists is relatively small and well-defined. Representatives of art institutions, such as those for the great museums of modern art, who constantly have to make choices and defend them, are largely in agreement about the selection of artists. However, the great majority of (women) artists still remain unknown or are part of 'dark matter', as has been said elsewhere.[17] For this reason, it is necessary to ask why institutions select this small group of artists and leave the vast majority unseen. The issue raised by feminist revisionism, namely that the criteria for judgement themselves are gendered, can be one way in which to answer questions pertaining to the principles of aesthetic judgement. It is the question of canon formation itself or of 'aesthetics after feminism' in the post-critical age, as Wolff phrased it.[18]

Feminist art history has hardly changed the highly selective system that has led to the canonization of specific artists; it has instead confirmed it, despite the modifications of the canon. It turns out to have been an illusion to have thought that the canon or the system in the art field that creates the canon could be eliminated. Nowadays, some art historians try to avoid the term 'canon' explicitly, but that does not mean that it disappeared or is not referred to anymore. The discipline of art history is part of a system that produces a canon. The whole art field generates and maintains the canon continuously: textbooks, prices on the art market, leading art collections and the UNESCO World Heritage List are just a few examples of institutions and media that contribute to the continual reproduction of artistic hierarchies.

Notwithstanding the importance of the societal issue of a more inclusive canon, it is doubtful whether concepts such as a counter-canon or pluriversal or multiple canons are helpful with respect to marginalized groups.[19] The concepts of pluriversal and multiple canons suggest canons that form independently of one another, although they are part of the same system and condition one another. It is not about harmonious coexistence but rather about a power struggle to acquire new positions in the field of art and in the process to consign the old (such as the Eurocentric canon) to the past as outdated. These concepts can convey a false impression of different canons of equal value existing side by side and hence they tend to conceal the objective hierarchies that actually exist in the field of art and can be very clearly demonstrated on the basis of the artists who are included in textbooks, for example. The point is rather precisely to make these hierarchies visible in order to then raise the question of why and how certain master narratives emerge and become established.[20] This does not mean, however, that there are no canons associated with subdivisions in the cultural field or no specialized canons with regard to specific media, regions, or social groups, for example. Finally, concepts such as the counter-canon and multiple canons often concern contemporary art that has not yet been canonized, which is why such concepts can likewise be misleading.

For all of their differences, both traditional and current art-historical approaches tend to contribute to giving prominence to certain artists and art forms. But what was ignored until relatively recently in art history is less concerned with the work of art as such and should be understood as being positioned at a greater distance from it, from where one can see how the canon is formed and certain works of art, artists, and movements are canonized or marginalized.

The common practice in art history of separating out aesthetic and extra-aesthetic concepts and approaches related to the canon is ultimately too absolute, since they tend instead to be characterized by complementarity and instances of overlap. If these positions are not integrated, no real understanding of the phenomenon of the canon as a whole is possible. If one ignores the formal and aesthetic aspects of the work of art, the most distinctive element of fine art is ignored. However, the aesthetic gaze can never be timeless and universal. The aesthetic and the extra-aesthetic, the political and the ideological should not be regarded separately from each other, as they are interdependent.

Although the insight that not only the historicity of the object but also that of the aesthetic experience always

20. Methodological ways on how to achieve that have been demonstrated earlier: Gregor Langfeld, *German Art in New York: The Canonization of Modern Art 1904–1957* (Amsterdam, 2015); Langfeld 2018 (see note 1).

has to be considered seems commonplace, for art historians it can be challenging to unmask such historicity because the art field covers up the conditions under which art is produced and canonized. The process from the production of the artwork up to its canonization is distinguished by mechanisms that sacralize art, resulting in these conditions being concealed. Thus, uncovering these mechanisms leads to an understanding of processes of canonization and, by extension, opens up the possibility of transforming the canon.

Canonizations are social processes that involve diverse actors, networks, institutions and discourses that collaborate and compete with each other. It is therefore necessary to guard against one-sided and simplistic attempts to explain them, for example by attributing canonization entirely to a single institution, such as the art market, which can only be one part of the overall process, or reducing power struggles in the field of art simply to the hegemony of men over women or 'Western' over 'non-Western' artists, since other factors such as innovation also influence complex processes of canonization. The struggles to strengthen the representation of certain marginalized social groups confirm a perpetual and highly selective system, despite the resulting modifications of the canon and good intentions of inclusiveness. But what has received very little attention in art history until recently is how specific master narratives emerge and become established. It is promising that in the past years concepts and approaches materialized that challenge and reconstruct the system, as well as the processes that have led to the canonization and marginalization of certain artworks and the power relations and discourses involved.

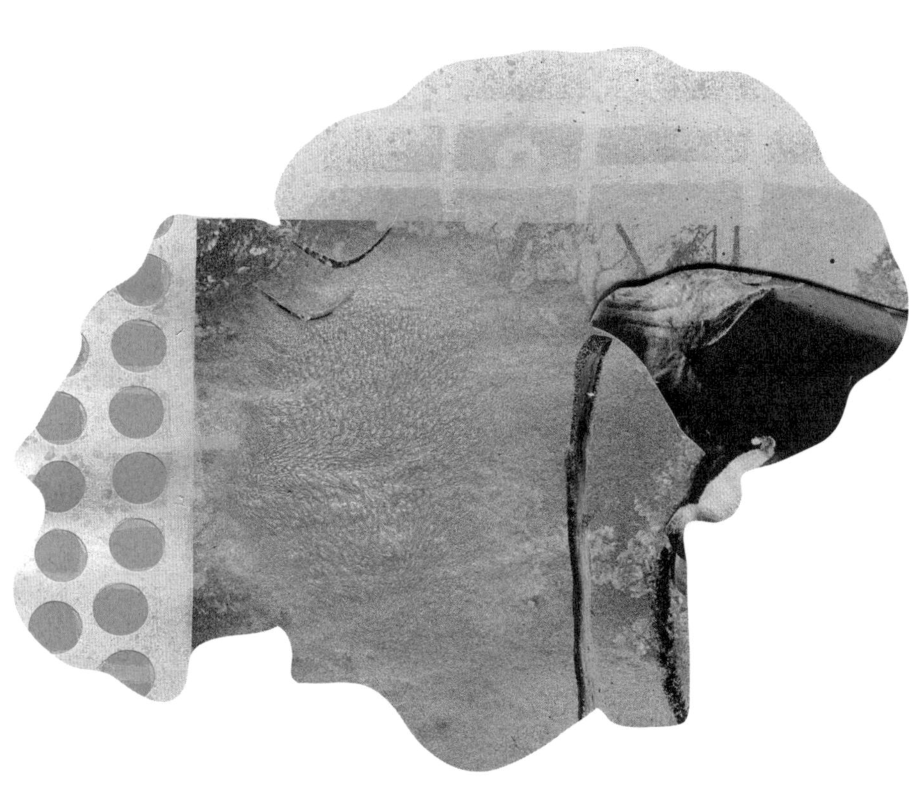

PROSTHETIC SWARM INTELLIGENCE
Of Windmills, Ships, and an Aesthetic of Brutality

Frans-Willem Korsten

INGREDIENTS

- Prosthetic Swarm Intelligence
- Colonization
- Brutality
- Human-cultural Techniques

Swarm Intelligence Traced in Art

In August 2020 a new museum opened in the north of Amsterdam that calls itself *Nxt*. It aims to disclose to a wider audience how contemporary art practices are made possible by digital techniques or digitally driven techniques. Dedicated to 'media art'—the umbrella term—the museum focuses on 'art that uses modern tools to embody modern times'. The phrase answers to the common conceptualization that art, and by implication artists, use techniques, and in using these techniques reflect on, capture, or 'embody' the times in which this art is made. Of course, in all ages, the picture is more complex because art and artists do not simply use media or techniques. Rather, the very media and techniques involved allow things to happen. Art is only one domain, here, in which the prosthetic nature of human beings, as Bernard Stiegler defined it, manifests itself. In the case of current digital media and the artists using them, it is the relation, the interaction that does the trick.[1]

This is something other than what has been called 'swarm intelligence' (SI), because such intelligence does not need a directing brain—whether human or not. The notion was introduced in 1989 in the context of collective

1. Bernard Stiegler, *Technics and Time: The Fault of Epimetheus*, transl. Richard Beardsworth (Stanford, 1998).

2. Gerardo Beni and Jing Wang, 'Swarm Intelligence in Cellular Robotic Systems'. Proceed: *NATO Advanced Workshop on Robots and Biological Systems, Tuscany, Italy, June 26–30 (1989)* (Berlin, 1993), pp. 703–712.

robotic behaviour.[2] Yet the notion has been travelling through many different disciplines since then, such as biology (for example, ants' behaviour and the flight pattern of birds), sociology, and art.[3] In all cases, whether natural or artificial, swarm intelligence consists of five factors combined: a sufficient number of entities; these entities having a form of agency; working by means of a cybernetic or algorithmic loop; as a result of which they learn, in the course of time. This is not the same as a virus logic. In current Covid-19 circumstances a recurring phrase was that the virus is 'smart'. Yet this is an anthropomorphic way of saying that a virus works by means of an enormous number of entities trying out what they can do, mostly dying in the process, with the survivors slightly altering in the process. A virus does not 'learn'. In the case of swarm intelligence there is learning involved, in its etymological origin: to follow a trace or a track. Yet the trace or track is not there beforehand, it opens up in the learning process. The intelligence involved, can be, but need not be a form of human intelligence; or that of any brain-led animal, with the capacity to reflect back, sense a present complex of factors, and project forward. Swarm intelligence is a combined sum total of collective efforts the results of which are not known to individual agents.

This essay will offer a new perspective on swarm intelligence, building on the previous definition, and in the awareness that 'human swarming' has become a separate point of study.[4] Yet in the case that we will deal with, swarm intelligence concerns the human interaction with media and techniques, as a result of which what I want to call a 'prosthetic swarm intelligence' comes to life. This type of swarm intelligence consists in the combination of two different entities, the agencies of which are intrinsically related and intertwined: human beings in their coexistence with media or cultural techniques. In all cases, such a swarm has a spiraling cybernetic loop. With two entities intertwined, they are not separately engaged in their own attempts, failures and successes, but always in combination.

I will focus on prosthetic swarms that marked a period in which economies turned global: the sixteenth and seventeenth centuries of trade and colonization, propelled by a few European states playing a dominant role in the

3. I was much helped by Marco Dorigo and Mauro Birattari, 'Swarm Intelligence', *Scholarpedia* 2, no. 9 (2007), p. 1462.

4. Louis Rosenberg, 'Human Swarms: a real-method for collective intelligence', *Conference Proceedings 07/20/2015-07/24/2015*. 27, pp. 658–659.

aggressive expansion. In many current debates the period is framed, with hindsight, by the nineteenth century of ideological colonialism and the astounding legal appropriation of two thirds of the world by a handful of European nation states. As a result, the imperial or exploitative endeavours of the sixteenth and seventeenth century have increasingly been defined as 'colonial' in terms of ideology. Yet they were only so in part and can be characterized much better in terms of a brutality, notably with regard to the Dutch Republic. As I will argue, brutality may be intrinsic to, or at least one characteristic of prosthetic swarm intelligence, whether in the seventeenth century or in the current circumstances.

At the time the prosthetic swarm intelligences at work were not explicitly dealt with as such by art, but were registered by art as a result of which they can be traced through it. Two forms dealt with here, are the cultural techniques of windmills and of ships; in massive numbers. I will first consider how, like any kind of swarm, these prosthetic swarms were difficult to represent. Especially in the case of mills, artists would opt for representing them as individualized, nameable, anthropomorphic entities; not as a swarm. I will then consider attempts to represent ships as swarms, in representations that also showed their aesthetic brutality.

Masses of Machines Individualized and Anthropomorphized

In order to be able to speak of a swarm, there needs to be mass. Of mills there were masses in the seventeenth century, although there were several types of them, with a diversity of purposes. Within the limits of just one type, say windmills, there was again a number of different types serving different purposes. With respect to consumer goods, there would be the regular grain mills, but also mustard mills, snuff mills, cocoa mills, and oil mills. Then there were mills that processed raw materials to turn them into useable goods: hemp mills, chalk mills, paint mills, paper mills, copper mills, leather mills. One specimen of the latter was immortalized by Rembrandt as 'The Little Stink Mill', on

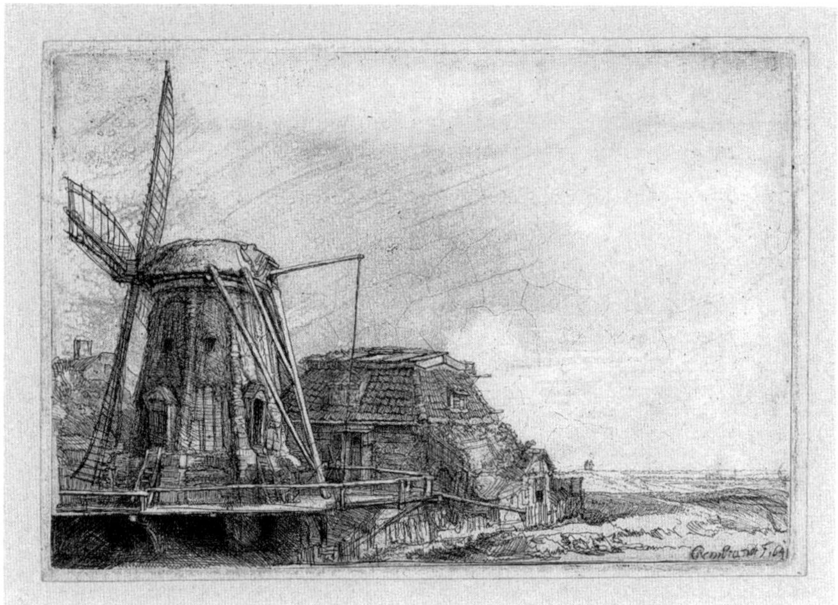

Rembrandt, *The Little Stink Mill*, 1641, etching, Rijksmuseum, Amsterdam.

the verge of Amsterdam, and called rightly so because this mill worked with cod liver oil to soften leather to produce so-called chamois leather.

The mill as a topic, in terms of representation, was not new. As Alison McNeil Kettering noticed, windmills can be found in many medieval works of art.[5] Yet the windmill as a separate object of representation, or as a separate entity of fascination, was new since the end of the sixteenth century. Rembrandt, for one, also made a drawing of the same stink mill, drew other mills, and made a painting of one.[6] He was not the only artist fascinated by windmills. Albert Cuyp or Jacob van Ruysdael, and many others as well used mills as worthy objects of depiction.

In most cases, in terms of representation, mills acquired a distinct individual quality. As Kettering noticed: 'Most mills, whatever their function, bore individual names. Just as the naming of ships granted a separate identity and enhanced status in the public mind, so did the naming of mills.'[7] Mills were also compared to human beings. For instance, Cornelis Cornelisz. van Uitgeest (1550–1607), the inventor of the sawmill, called his first prototype 'Juffertje' [The little lady]. The mill's shape resembled a woman with

5. Alison McNeil Kettering, 'Landscape with Sails: The Windmill in Netherlandish Prints', *Simiolus: Netherlands Quarterly for the History of Art* 33, no. 1/2 (2007/2008), pp. 67–80.

6. Rembrandt made a drawing of the windmill De Bok on the Bastion Blauwhoofd in Amsterdam (1650; Fondation Custodia); a drawing called 'Open Landscape with Houses and a Windmill' (ca. 1648, Albertina Museum Vienna); and he made an independent oil painting, 'The Mill' (between 1645 and 1648; National Gallery of Art, Washington).

7. McNeil Kettering 2007/2008 (see note 5), p. 69.

a tight middle and a clock-formed dress. And Rembrandt's etching may be remarkable because of how the two small windows halfway the mill are etched: it is almost as if these are eyes, with small brows and their rectangular shape tending towards becoming oval.

Mills were individualized, then; they were given names and thus anthropomorphized, which not only emphasized their independent agency but also their intrinsic connection with human beings. They came in numbers, nevertheless. First the sawmill was patented, in 1592, and after the first officially built version in 1594, others would be able to buy the rights. Amsterdam was late, here, also due to the powerful guilds that prevented the sawmill from being used—until 1630. Shortly after, no less than twenty-three were packed together in a relatively small northwestern corner of the city, close to the new wharfs where the ships for the global expansion of the Republic were built. In 1665, Amsterdam would count between seventy and eighty sawmills.[8] Throughout Holland, moreover, one polder after another would be dry-milled, not by individual mills but by whole sets of them. Mills, that is, changed an entire landscape and an economy, and the entire global explosion of the small Dutch Republic would have simply been impossible without the saw mill.

8. Ibid., p. 68.

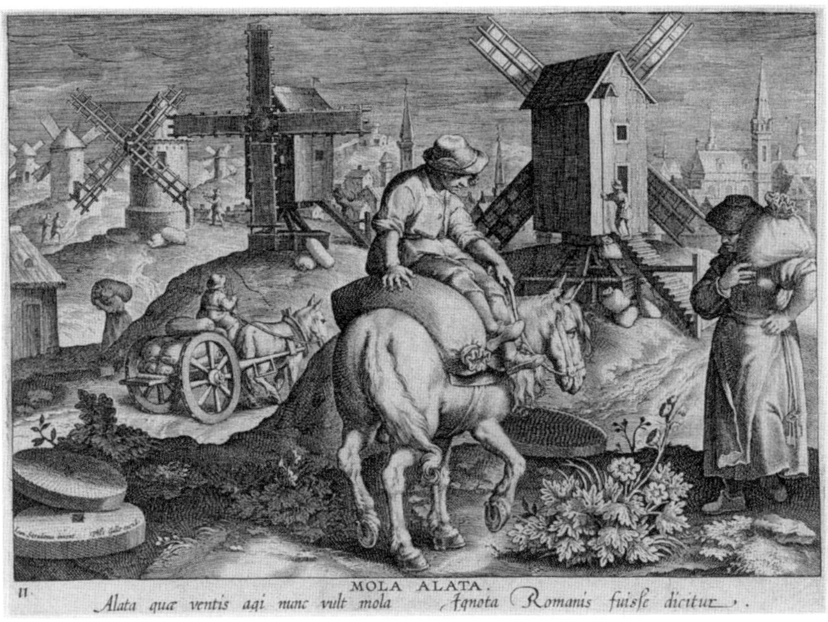

Philip Galle (workshop), after Joan Stradanus, *The Invention of the Mill* (Mola alata or Winged mill), from *Nova reperta*, 1590–95, engraving, Rijkmuseum, Rijksprentenkabinet, Amsterdam.

Whereas Rembrandt gave us an image of the mill as an individual, the swarm-like quality of mills in their connection to human beings, or the two in coexistence, is captured in an engraving made at the end of the sixteenth century. In this case the individualization of the mill has given way to a representation of mills in their mass. In this case, the mill is not a separate individualized or anthropomorphic entity with its own agency, but connotes a swarm that is prosthetically related to human beings, who appear to be working in the service of the mills as much as the mills appear to work in theirs.

As the image may illustrate, there is an aesthetic appeal to this prosthetic swarm. To assess the specific quality of this aesthetic, let me move from the 'landscape with sails' to small pieces of territory with sails: ships, and consider in more detail how intelligence is involved in their case.

Prosthetic Swarm Intelligence and Its Brutality: Ships

'Een brutaal mens heeft de halve wereld' is a Dutch proverb. It's always hard to translate proverbs properly, but let's translate it as: 'The unashamed own half of the world'. It is not coincidental that the proverb has its origin in the late sixteenth century with the Dutch author Coornhert: 'd'Onschamelen hebben de twee derdendeelen van de Werelt'.[9] Here 'onschamel' indeed meant 'unashamed', and the brutality involved was emphasized by an even bigger part than half of the world: 'twee derdendeelen' [two-thirds]. This would indeed prove to be more to the point in the heydays of colonialism. Now, etymologically, 'brutaal' falls back on Latin *brutus*: 'dull, stupid', which later came to mean 'savage' (with *brutalis*). All these meanings have their negative connotations. Tellingly, in the historical context, the Dutch word 'brutaal' not only means 'unashamed' as a shameful thing. Brutality, at least in the Dutch use of 'brutaal', also has a certain positive connotation in that one may admire the shamelessness, the savageness, the straightforwardness with which someone may act in trying to see what they can get away with, in the double sense of

9. *Maeghdekens Schole*, fol. 395 r. in D.V. Coornhert, *Het roerspel en de comedies van Coornhert*, ed. Paul van der Meulen (Leiden, 1955).

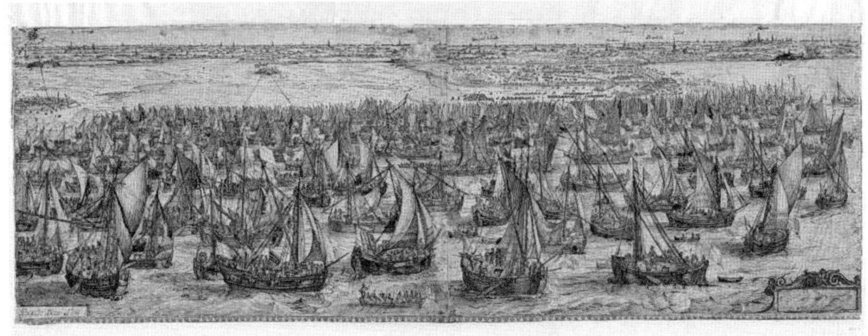

Hendrik Cornelisz. Vroom, *The Landing of the Army Fleet of Prince Maurits at Philippine*, 1600, pen and brown ink, brown wash, heightened with white, indented, Museum Boijmans Van Beuningen, Rotterdam.

the phrase: that one is not bothered with consequences, and gains a profit in the process.

The intrinsic relation between brutality and swarm intelligence consists in the fact that individual members of the mass in action have no knowledge or awareness of the larger, intelligently orchestrated picture. Just have a look at the picture that shows the landing of a fleet under Stadholder Maurits at Phillipine, in 1600, in the province of Zeeland.

Although it is still possible to distinguish individual ships in the front, this becomes impossible towards the back of the drawing, where the ships are depicted that are actually about to land or have landed. To think of this endeavor as one in which all participants knew what they were doing while having an overview, would be beside the point, or absurd. In fact, many battles are best analyzed in terms of swarm intelligence. Considered in the light of the complexity of war operations such as these, the requirement that 'agents in an SI based system have limited perception or intelligence and cannot individually carry out the task it intends to', is to the point both for all ships and their crews.[10]

10. Russel Ahmed Apu and Marina L. Gavrilova, 'Battle Swarm: An Evolutionary Approach to Complex Swarm Analysis', *31A Int. Comp. Graphics and AI*, (Limoges, 2006), p. 139.

Now, Maurits would become famous for how he managed to innovate and organize the military by means of drilling. Yet common modes of warfare in the early modern period came closer to what Gilles Deleuze and Félix Guattari defined as a war machine. Deleuze and Guattari developed the concept in the context of their nomadology, in which the war machine would be a deregulating force of violence; anti-state, flexible, and interruptive but also innovative. It is a pity that Deleuze and Guattari did not develop the commercial equivalent of this machine: a 'trade machine'. Such a term would define pretty well the commercial operations of the Dutch on a global scale under the heading and guidance of the VOC and WIC. In both cases, this can be seen as a case of prosthetic swarm intelligence too, this time joining the agency of human actors with ships.

In the picture by Hendrik Cornelisz. Vroom, one instance of the swarm is depicted. It concerned the return of four ships, with four others arriving later that year, that had sailed out under the leadership of Jacob Cornelisz. van Neck in 1598, to the East Indies. In the coming decades, the numbers would rise rapidly. The VOC alone would have around 130 ships in use in 1610, 280 in the twenties, and 330 in the fifties of the century. In fifty years' time, around 1100 ships were brought into service.[11] The ships could be built in such large numbers thanks to the invention of the sawmill. When timber still had to be sawn by hand, sixty beams or trunks would demand 120 days of work. With the sawmill, sixty beams or trunks could be dealt with in four to five work days; a difference of a factor thirty. The true father of the Dutch Republic as an imperial power may have been this relatively unknown man called Cornelis Cornelisz. van Uitgeest, the saw mill's inventor.

11. Robert Parthesius, *Dutch Ships in Tropical Waters* (Amsterdam, 2010). Also see Richard John Guy, *First Spaces of Colonialism: The Architecture of Dutch East Indian Company Ships* (Ithaca, 2012).

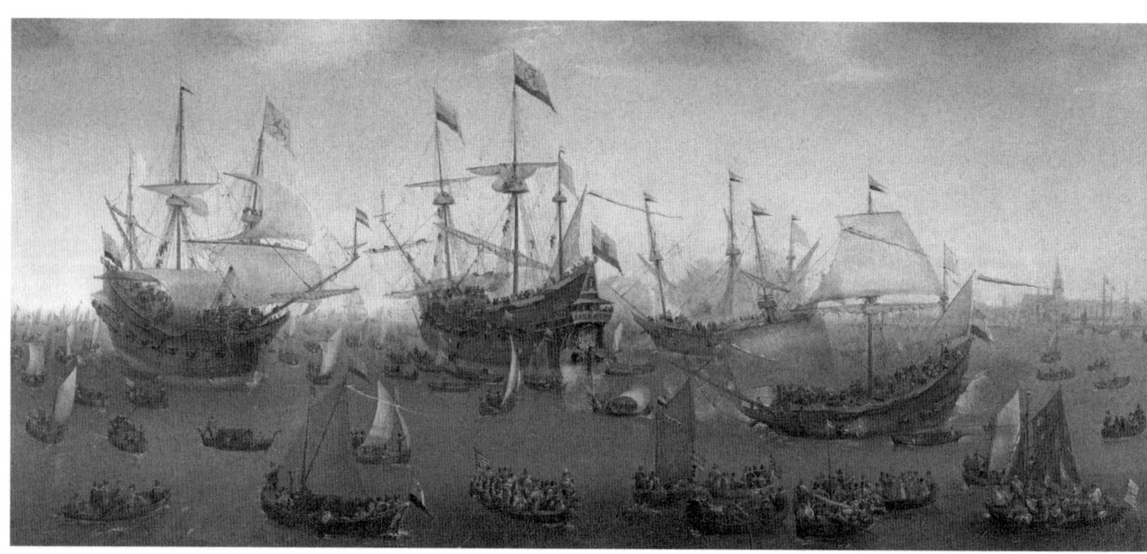

Hendrik Cornelisz. Vroom, *Return in Amsterdam of the Second Expedition to the East Indies, 19 July 1599*, 1599, oil on canvas, 102.3 × 218.4 cm. Rijksmuseum, Amsterdam.

12. Cf. Ewald Vanvugt, *Roofstaat. Wat iedere Nederlander moet weten* (Amsterdam, 2016); Reggie Baay, *Daar werd wat gruwelijks verricht: Slavernij in Nederlands-Indië* (Amsterdam, 2015); Virginia West Lunsford, *Piracy and Privateering in the Golden Age Netherlands* (New York, 2005).

The result was swarms of ships, as visualized in the painting. The scene could be any scene in the waters of the IJ, at Amsterdam. This 'any scene' would have been a common one, nevertheless, in its depicting a swarm of ships, of all sizes, filled with people, who are again as much in charge of the ships as these are in charge of human beings. The title, however, makes explicit what some first explorations of this swarm were aimed at. In this context the analysis of many scholars in recent years is that the Dutch Republic, with its quasi-sovereign bodies of the VOC and the WIC, was a pirate state or a privateer state.[12] It is not for nothing that the *Stanford Encyclopedia*, under the lemma of Territorial Rights and Territorial Justice, mentions: 'Many states have originated in deeply unjust practices: they gained territory through conquest, trickery and other forms of brutality'. Such brutality would not only be at the basis of territory, it would also be at the basis of deterritorializing the domains of others. More importantly in the context of my argument, it need not have been the brutality of individual or even groups of human actors. It may have been the brutality of prosthetic swarms.

If brutality is morally, ethically, politically, or ideologically rejectionable, aesthetically the picture is different. On the level of representation, pirates, for instance, have always been a topic of interest and fascination. As such, they are the individualized figures with whom one can identify; just as mills could be individualized and made identifiable. Swarms, however, are another matter. They fascinate precisely because no individual can be identified as the mastermind of it all, while there appears to be some kind of choreography operative. Van Neck may have been the admiral of the mentioned 'second expedition' but he is nowhere to be seen, and rightly so. This is not because in the larger picture he does not matter as an individual. The swarm logic indicates that individual agents have no awareness of what the larger picture is. No one at the time, around 1600, was aware of what the prosthetic swarms that had come to life would come to effect. Their brutality, their carelessness, had an attractive quality, though, or a frightening one, depending on the position of people and other animals, or environments. Their brutality was what made the swarms aesthetically interesting and fascinating.

This is a prominent reason why any critical reconsideration of the entire colonial endeavour might only get so far, or only solve so much, if it is not able to get to this aesthetic, double-sided, affective heart of the matter.

In terms of a new outlook on art that does not just concern the seventeenth century but any chosen period, the outlook I aimed to sketch above is one that connects to, but also moves beyond Bruno Latour's actor-network theory.[13] With this theory Latour emphasized that agency will always be distributed over different actors, human and non-human. The swarm logic indicates that individual agents have no awareness of what the larger picture is while the larger picture is organized on the basis of some sort of intelligence that because of the disconnection between collective outcome and individual unawareness has a certain brutality to it. In a sense, the seventeenth-century example only asks what types of swarm intelligence are operative today, and how they can be traced through art. A more radical question is how art, or forms of art, are part and parcel of such prosthetic swarm intelligence. It would require a rather different take on art in the sense that art can no longer be considered in terms of reflection or intervention, then, and not even in terms of responsibilities and ethics, in the classic sense of the terms. The reason is that, in the light of prosthetic swarm intelligence, art can no longer be considered as a separate entity. There are fascinating histories to be written, or new theories to be developed, in this context.

13. Bruno Latour, *Reassembling the Social: An Introduction to Actor-Network-Theory* (Oxford/New York, 2005).

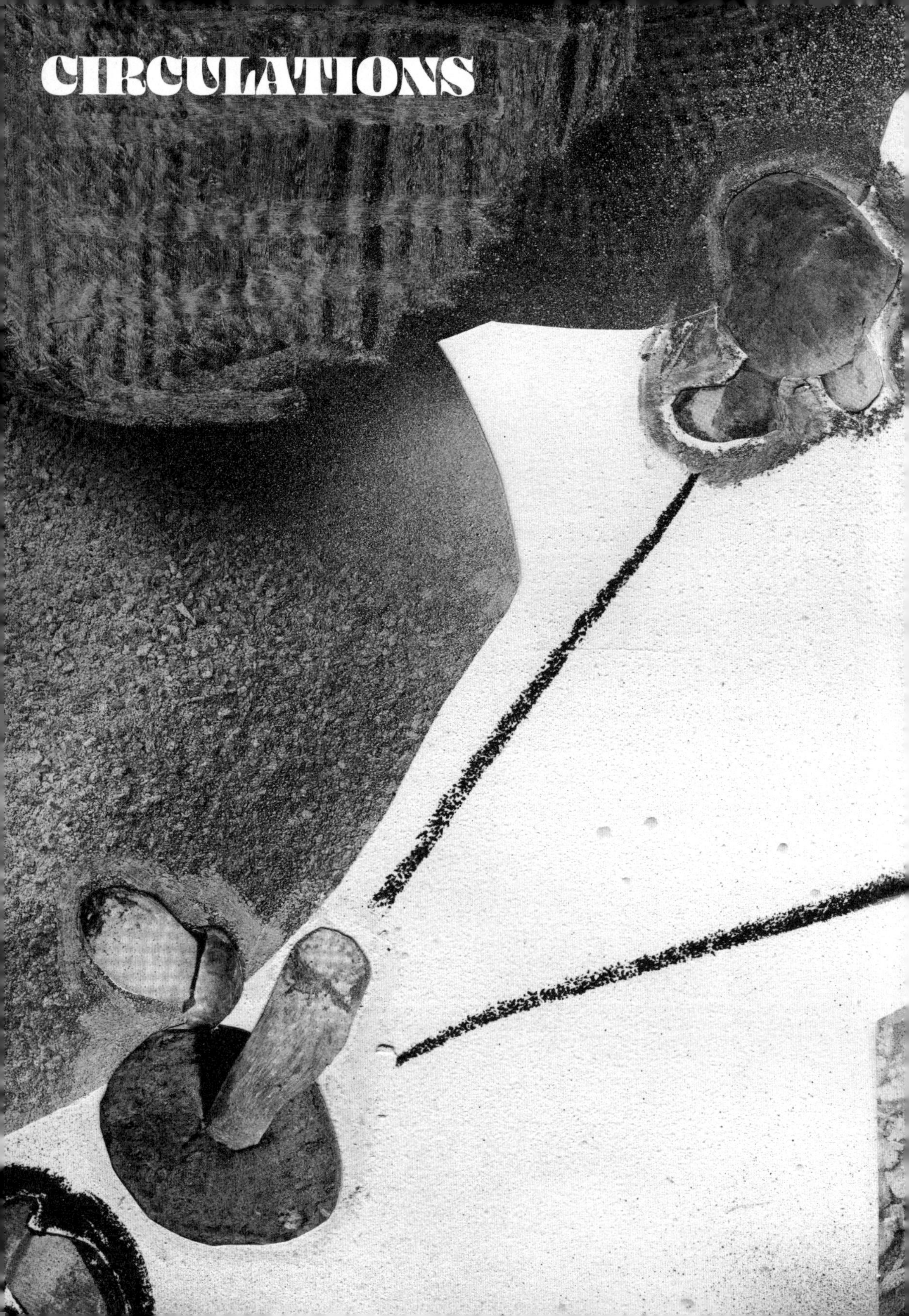
CIRCULATIONS

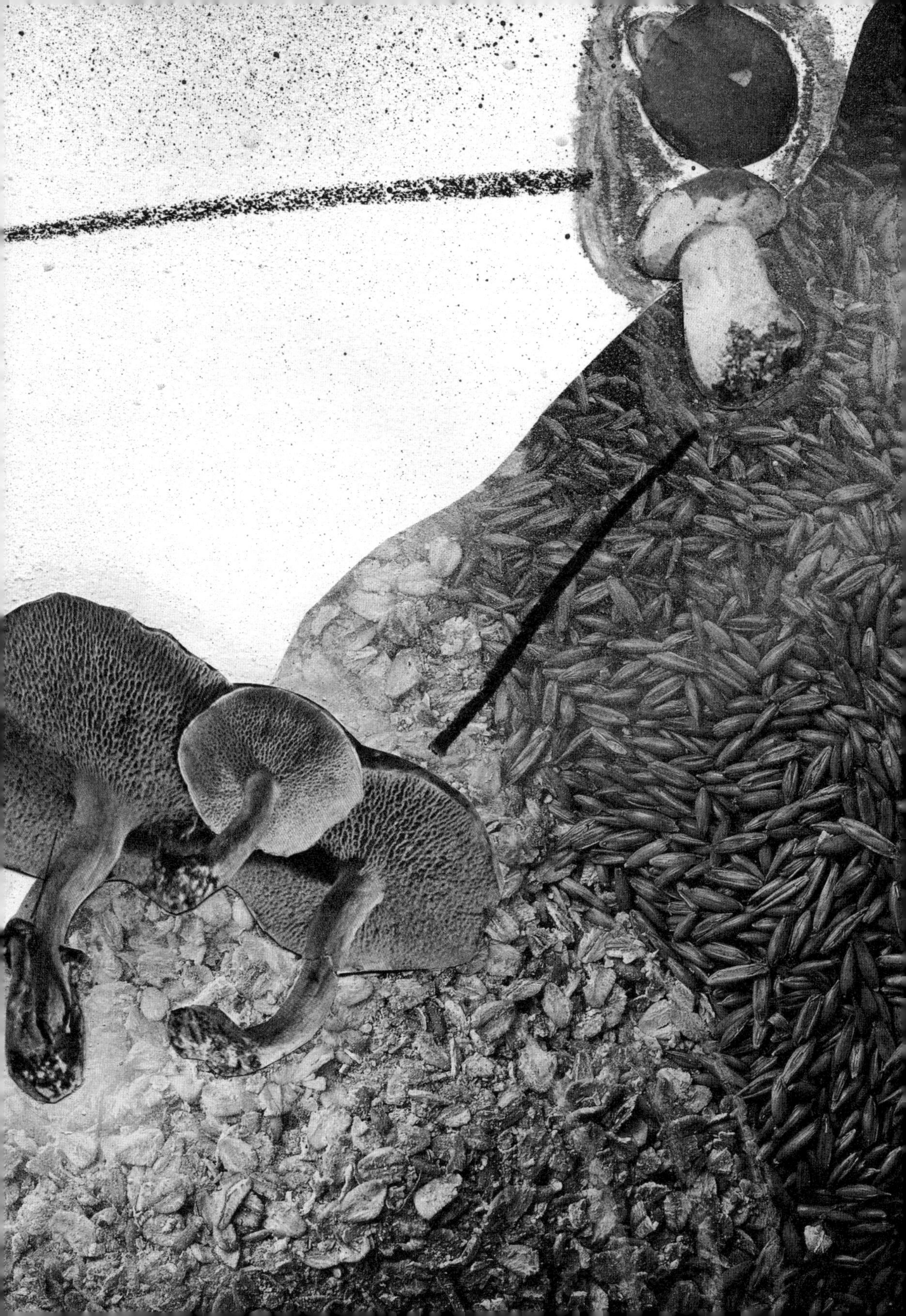

Rudi Struik

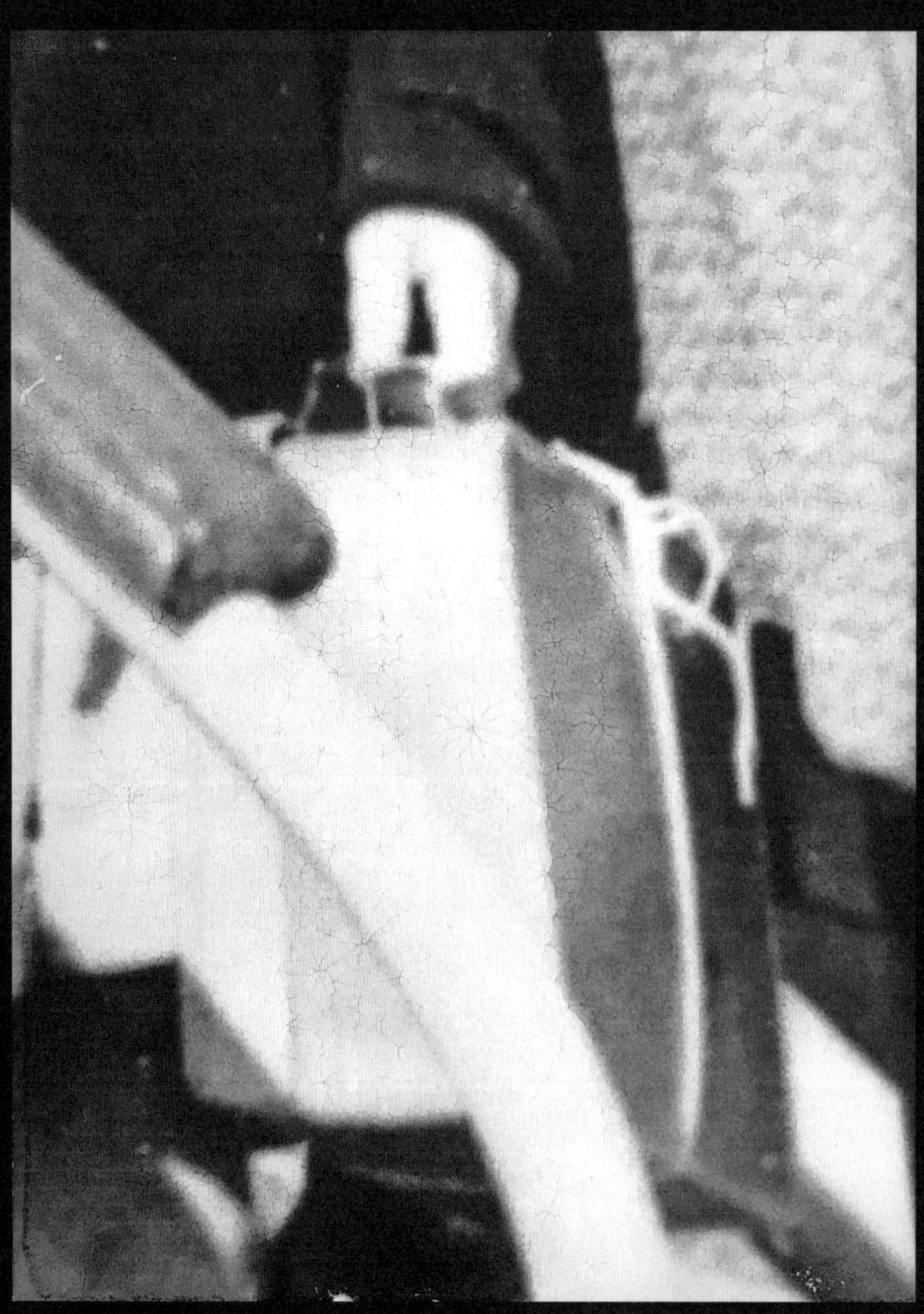

Rudi Struik, *Packed*, 2009, photo fresco on plaster, multiplex, 29 × 20 × 3 cm.

Moving

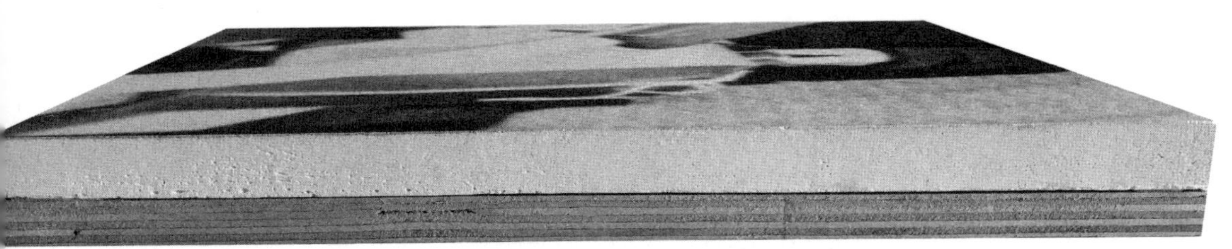

Packing
Take along
Unknowing
To
Placement
Let go
Culture
Understand
Alienate
Afraid
Longing
Thrive
Language
Loneliness
Left out
Exclude
Isolate

Home sick

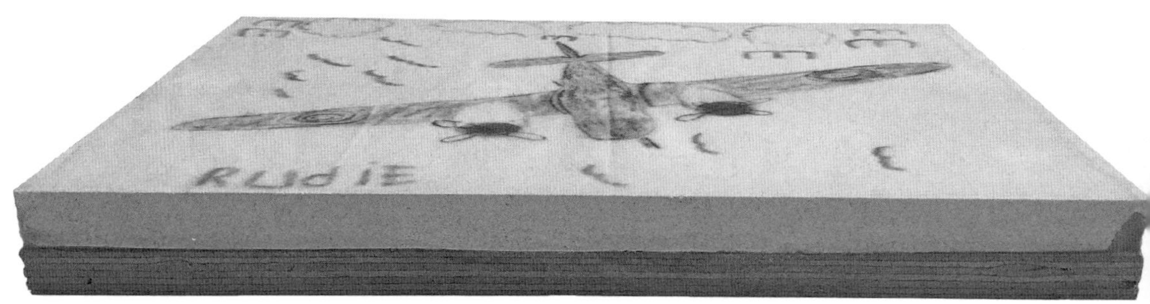

Longing

Back

WHY?

Memories

Feelings

Finding

Safety

Hanging on

Not excepting

The new

My Culture

Movement

Out of my world

To the unknown

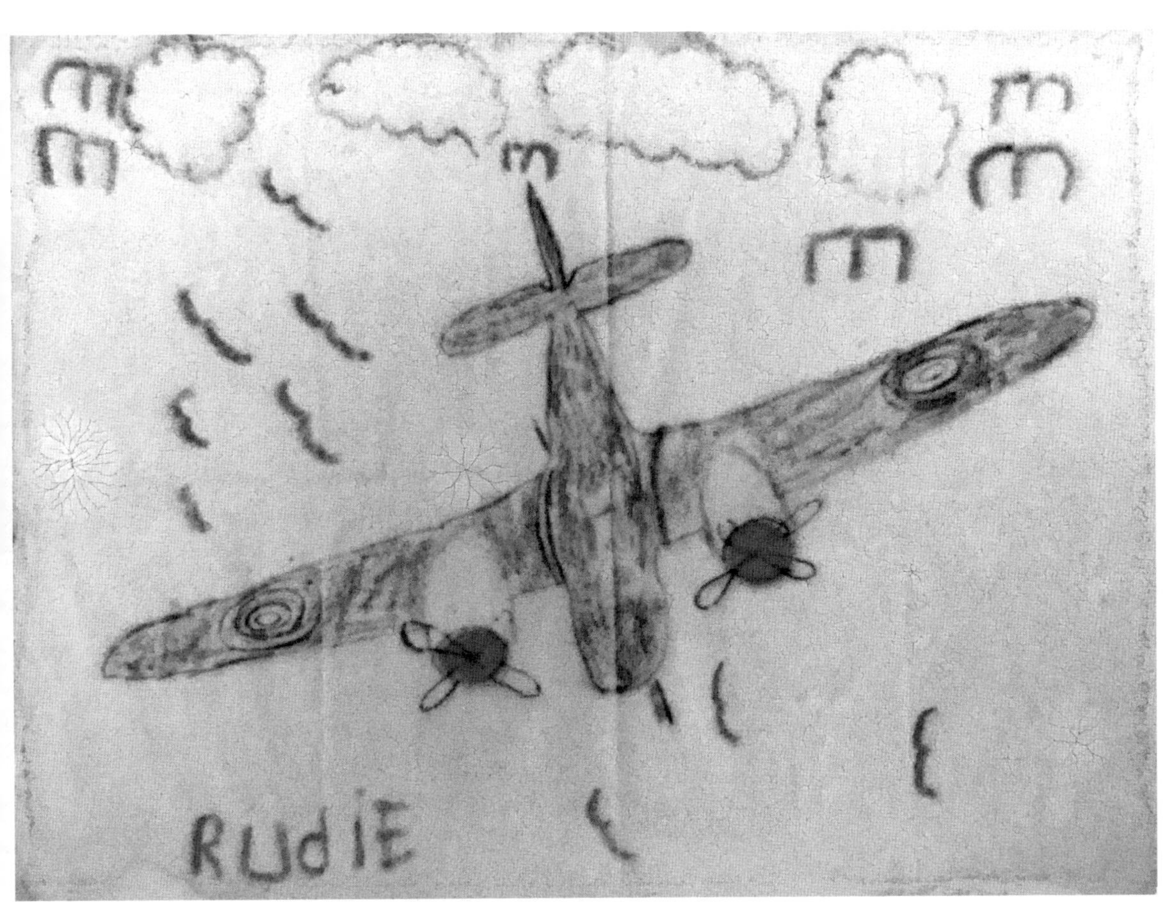

Rudi Struik, *Flight*, 2009, childhood drawing/photo fresco on plaster and multiplex, 20 × 27 × 3 cm.

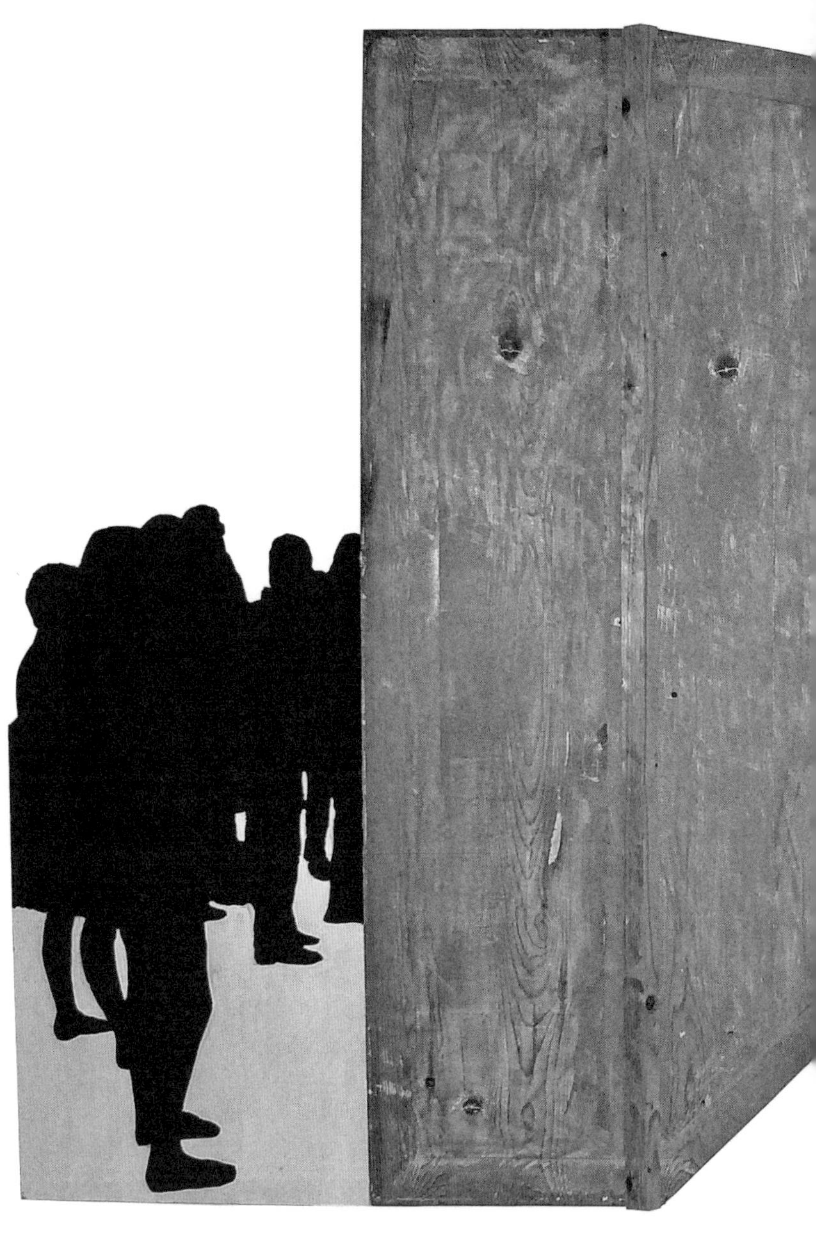

Rudi Struik, *Wall #1*, 2017, triptych, mixed media, 174 × 125 × 4.5 cm.

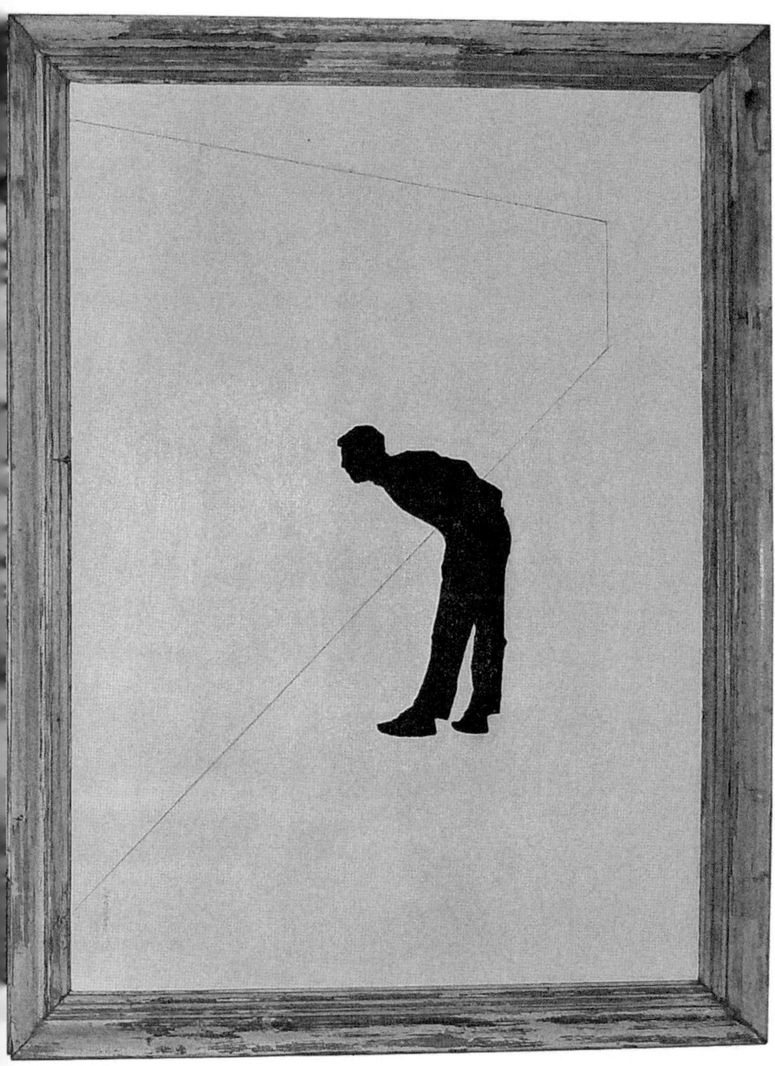

The work
above a triptych
inspired by the series
'The Wall' (VARA 2014)
Different places over the world.
Belfast. The wall separating two cultures.
Groups of kids fear the other side. Their faces say it all.
Fear of the unknown sprouts like a seed without the right food.

Exhibitions

learning

after time

forward
thinking

exploring
towards

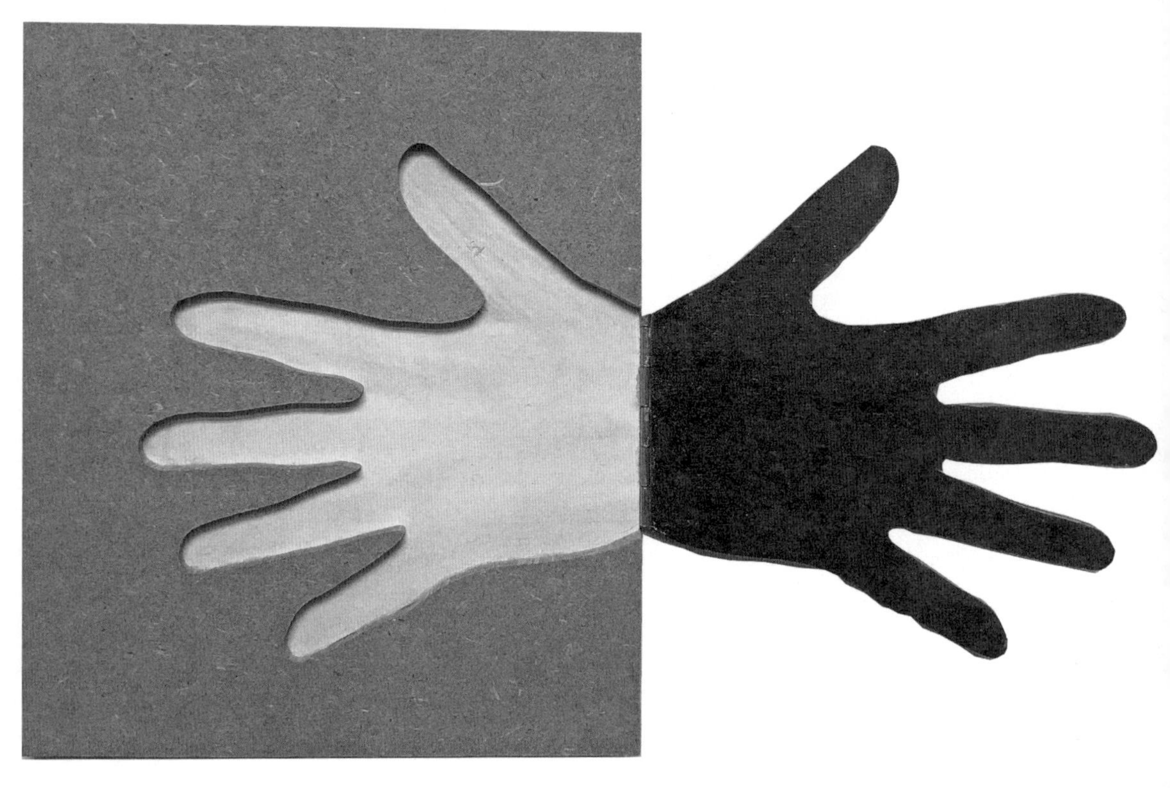

Rudi Struik, *Helping Hand*, 2020, MDF, 27 × 42 × 2 cm.

future
finding

prospect
definition
view opinion
outcome definition
culture study absorbing new
explanation meaning clarity hope
opening up for new ideas together budding

Rudi Struik

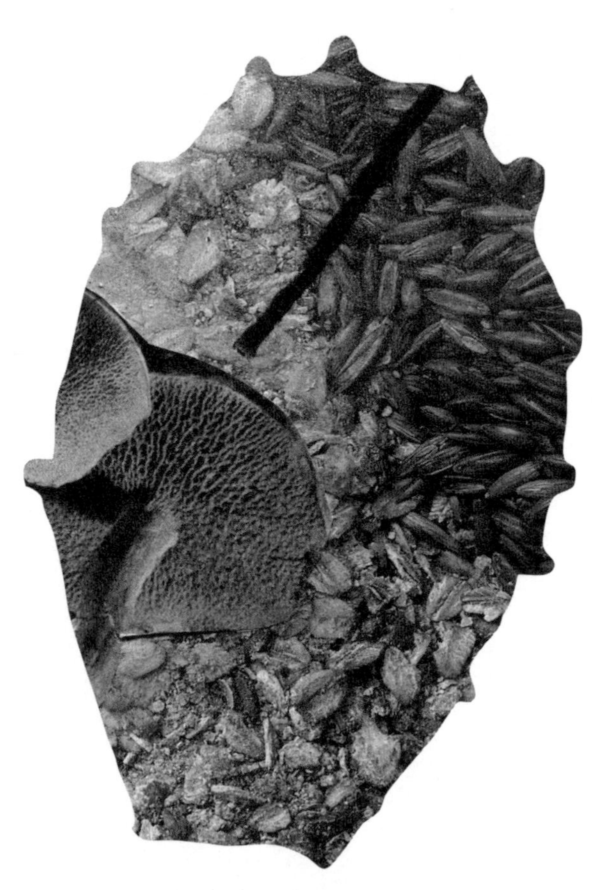

TOUCHING THE BREAK
Negotiating the World of Art by Feel

Anne Gerritsen

INGREDIENTS

- Haptic Visuality
- Fragments of Porcelain
- Illusionist Surfaces in Oil Paintings
- Transculturalism
- *Kintsugi* Technique
- Tactile Modes of Representation

'Do not touch!' is often the first message a museum visitor receives upon stepping across the gallery threshold. 'Look with your eyes, not with your hands!' Of course, we understand why most pieces of art on display cannot be touched, but that does not mean that other senses beyond sight are not engaged when we negotiate the world of art. Even when we only 'look with our eyes', we 'feel' in our hands what we see through our eyes. Take, for example, the 2019 composition by the artist Bouke de Vries (b. 1960), entitled *Guan Yin in a Cloud of Shards*. It consists of a statue of the Chinese Buddhist goddess of mercy, Guan Yin. Her head is framed by a halo, a blue and white drape hangs around her white robe, and she stands on a base with wide mouth, narrow neck, and widening lower body.

It is only upon closer inspection that the viewer becomes aware that each of the elements of the composition is in turn made up of fragmented pieces of ceramics. The halo and the drape are created by combining shards of seventeenth-century Chinese blue-and-white porcelains; the base is made up of a deep dish reconstructed from more shards, which stands on top of a Wanli bottle restored by using the so-called *kintsugi* technique, whereby broken pieces are glued together, coated with black and red lacquer, and finally sprinkled with gold powder.

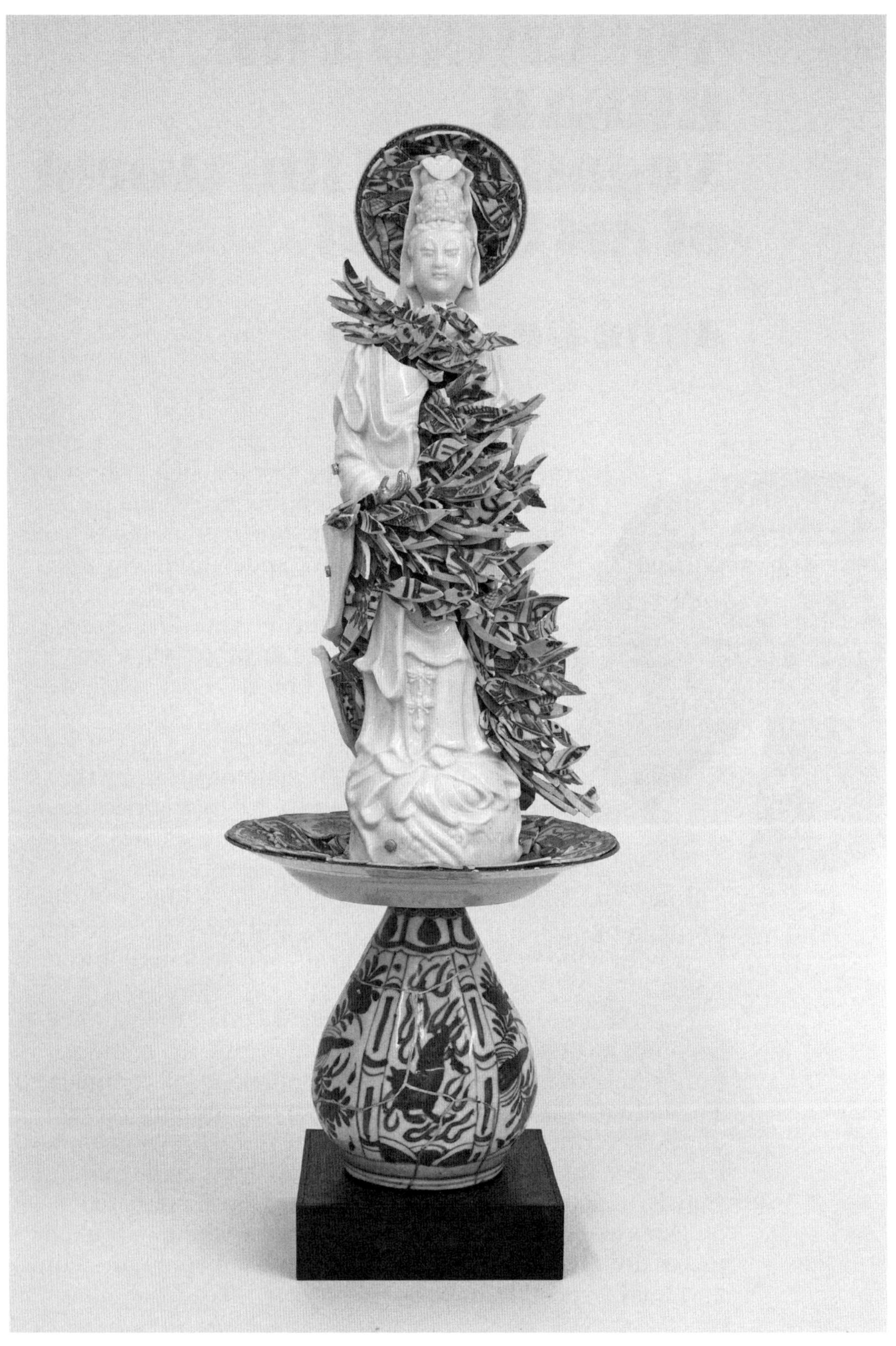

Bouke de Vries, *Guan Yin in a Cloud of Shards*, 2019, late seventeenth-century blanc-de-chine Guan Yin with seventeenth-century Chinese Wanli marine archaeology shards, 77 × 27 cm.
Courtesy Bouke de Vries.

Born and raised in the Netherlands, Bouke de Vries has been based in the United Kingdom for several decades. He trained at the Central School in London, worked first in the fashion industry and, from 1992, as a ceramics conservator. In 2009, he took the decision to stop restoring ceramics and begin creating art from broken ceramics.[1] He works with historical ceramics, including Chinese and Japanese porcelain, English, Hungarian, Dutch, and German ceramics. His materials range from the whitest blanc-de-chine Guan Yin to colourful Meissen figurines and from seventeenth-century Chinese marine archaeological pieces to twentieth-century Dutch ceramics, all broken in one way or another. Damaged pieces of historical ceramics form the basis of De Vries' creative process.[2]

Instead of repairing what was damaged or hiding from view what is broken and fragmentary, De Vries does the opposite. He deconstructs damaged pieces, giving centre stage to the fragmentary and to damage itself, allowing the viewer to reflect on the perfection of what some might see as imperfect and on the value of what others might see as valueless.[3] Historical fragments of porcelain repurposed in contemporary compositions suggest the timelessness of the material. Chronological and spatial distance as well as separate origins are all minimized in the transformative process of combining ceramic pieces—in the case of *Guan Yin in a Cloud of Shards*—made in different parts of China that were then transported to Europe, shipwrecked en route, excavated much later, and eventually assembled by a Dutch artist in a London studio. De Vries' reuse of damaged pieces might even be seen as a comment on sustainability, although De Vries himself does not see sustainability as his primary motivator: 'It was working with beautiful things that are regarded as worthless' although he acknowledges that this 'seems to be fitting in with what is going on at the moment'.[4]

In this volume's track through the landscape of world art studies, exploring new approaches to contemporary art in global perspective, themes like the crossing of boundaries of time and space and the sustainable use of materials are important. Yet, I would like to add another element to the mix. The smoothness of the blanc-de-chine

1. 'Bouke de Vries', boukedevries.com, accessed on 14 May 2021.

2. Laura Gray, 'Ceramics on Show: Domesticity, Destruction and Manifestations of Risktaking', *Contemporary Clay and Museum Culture: Ceramics in the Expanded Field*, eds. Christie Brown, Julian Stair, and Clare Twomey (London, 2016), pp. 57–65.

3. Zaneta Cheng, 'In Conversation with Ceramic Restorer and Artist Bouke de Vries', *Hashtag Legend* (blog), 1 March 2021, hashtaglegend.com/magazine/bouke-de-vries-ceramic-artist, accessed on 14 May 2021.

4. Susan Ford, *The Arresting 'Exploded' Ceramics of Artist Bouke de Vries*, 2020, www.youtube.com/watch?v=THMDZivgGYw&t=71s, accessed on 14 May 2021.

surface, the sharpness of the spikey shards in the drape, and glistening gold lines in the surface of the Wanli bottle at the base of *Guan Yin in a Cloud of Shards* all invite the viewer to contemplate reaching out and touching the surface. Even when viewing the photographed object, the eye imagines the tactility of the material. As if reading our mind, the artist has covered Guan Yin's gently curved fingers of her upturned hand with gold paint, suggestively highlighting the element of touch. Together with the gold repairs and the gold-covered nuts and bolts that hold the porcelain pieces together, the hand seemingly points to the touch of the hands of the artist who created the piece by working with broken pieces of porcelain.

Porcelain, defined in Europe as a combination of kaolin and porcelain stone fired in kiln temperatures above 1300°C, was produced exclusively in Asia until the eighteenth century, while especially Chinese blue-and-white wares were desired all over the world. And even after European porcelains began to be manufactured in the early eighteenth century, Chinese and Japanese porcelains remained popular in Europe. Even when they sustained damage, Asian porcelains continued to be treasured. We can see that in the early Japanese examples of *kintsugi*-repaired porcelain or in the descriptions of porcelain repairers in China and Europe using drilled holes and metal staples to join breaks.[5] We also see examples of this in the inventory of the Portuguese merchant-banker Emmanuel Ximenez (1564–1632).[6] Ximenez' Antwerp house had a small porcelain room ('porceleynkamerken'), in which his porcelain was stored. The room contained a collection of about fifty-three large and small bowls, dishes, boxes, and saucers. Several of these are listed as broken. We can only speculate why the Ximenez household held onto their broken pieces of porcelain: they might have been destined for being discarded; they might even have broken in the time between the death of Ximenez and the arrival of those making the inventory. It is equally possible to consider the fact that broken pieces of ceramics were kept as evidence of the high value of the material. I would like to add one final speculative reason for keeping broken pieces of porcelain. Ximenez was deeply interested in how materials were made.

5. Dawn Odell, 'Delftware and the Domestication of Chinese Porcelain', *EurAsian Matters: China, Europe, and the Transcultural Object, 1600–1800*, eds. Anna Grasskamp and Monica Juneja (Cham, 2018), p. 179.

6. ximenez.unibe.ch/inventory/reading, accessed on 13 May 2021.

7. Sven Dupré, 'Trading Luxury Glass: Picturing Collections and Consuming Objects of Knowledge in Early Seventeenth-Century Antwerp', *Intellectual History Review* 20, no. 1 (1 March 2010), p. 58.

8. Laura U. Marks, *Touch: Sensuous Theory and Multisensory Media* (Minneapolis, 2002), p. 2.

9. Ibid., p. 6.

10. Ibid.

11. Ibid., p. 163.

He worked with Antonio Neri, author of *L'Arte Vetraria* (1612) on the manufacture of glass, and even had a small alchemical studio in his house.[7] Perhaps he was also curious about the materiality of this unknown but highly valued exotic material? After all, only broken porcelain reveals the whiteness of the porcelain body and the complete fusion of glaze and body that distinguishes porcelain from the majolica that was in his collection. Only by touching the break could one feel the smoothness of the porcelain body and the sharp edge of the material. We will never know what was in Ximenez' mind, but it is a tantalizing thought that touch mattered to Ximenez in his search for understanding and recreating materials.

The objects in Ximenez' inventory were in his personal or household's possession, and he would have been free to touch these as and when he wanted. That is not the same, of course, with pieces of art that we are experiencing by way of the eye only, such as pieces of art on display or three-dimensional art depicted on a flat surface such as a painting or photograph. And yet, I would argue that here, too, the experience of seeing engages the sense of touch. This has been discussed extensively in the context of cinema. In her study of touch in media, Laura Marks develops the concept of 'haptic visuality'. In haptic visuality, also referred to as embodied spectatorship, 'the eyes themselves function like organs of touch'.[8] It refers to the physical sensations that often accompany a particular cinematic depiction, such as the lurching of the stomach when viewing a fairground ride or physically flinching when seeing a wound inflicted on the screen. She builds on earlier work on 'tactile modes of representation' by the art historian Aloïs Riegl and the theoreticians Gilles Deleuze and Félix Guattari.[9] For Riegl, this related largely to so-called 'non-Western' art, such as Islamic painting, Roman metalwork or textiles, all of which involve 'intimate, detailed images that invite a small, caressing gaze'.[10] Deleuze and Guattari developed Riegl's idea by stressing the difference between the haptic and the optical. As Marks puts it: 'While optical perception privileges the representational power of the image, haptic perception privileges the material presence of the image.'[11]

This work on cinema could also be applied to viewing certain materials and surfaces that directly engage the eye as an organ of touch. For instance, a fragment of a Wanli porcelain plate was rescued from the bottom of the seabed near St Helena, where the VOC-ship 'De Witte Leeuw' had sunk in 1613.[12]

The fact that the object has sustained serious damage, and only appears to us in this fragmented form makes us view it differently. The eye is drawn to the nearly triangular shape of the hole perfectly placed inside one of the framed niches with good-luck symbols or flowering plants. The eye leads us first through the plate to what is behind it, and then rests on the white edges of the gap, which allows us to see the inside of the body of the plate. The breaks 'feel' different to the eye; instead of reading the images—the bird in the middle, the flower, the stylized clouds—or caressing the smooth bend in the lip, the eye engages the finger and imagines the sharpness of the break on the finger. The close observer might even view the bird, and then imagine the feel of the grains of sand that became attached to the glaze in the kiln. Laura Marks calls this 'haptic looking', which 'tends to rest on the surface of its object rather than to plunge into depth … to discern texture'.[13]

12. Christine L. van der Pijl-Ketel and Johannes Bastiaan Kist, *The Ceramic Load of the 'Witte Leeuw' (1613)* (Amsterdam, 1982).

13. Marks 2002 (see note 8), p. 8.

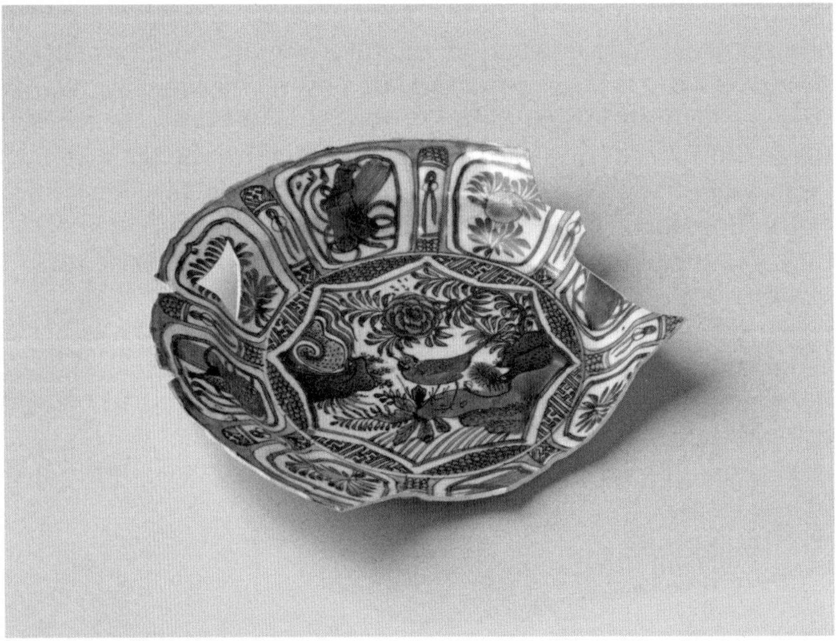

Fragment of a porcelain plate, before 1613, Jingdezhen, 5.1 × 27.5 × 27 cm. Courtesy Rijksmuseum, Amsterdam.

14. Jennifer M. Barker, *The Tactile Eye: Touch and the Cinematic Experience* (Berkeley, 2009), p. 21.

In *The Tactile Eye*, Jennifer Barker discusses cinematic perception further. She distinguishes between Marks' haptic looking, which she explores in a chapter entitled 'The Skin', the viewing experience that makes one grip the armrests or pull away from the visual experience referred to as 'prehensile vision' in a chapter entitled 'The Musculature', and finally 'The Viscera', where both continuities and discontinuities are created through the rhythms, heartbeats and pulses of the film's and the viewer's bodies.[14] In translating these cinematic experiences to the encounter with three-dimensional pieces of art, it is mostly the skin that is engaged by the eye.

The eye's engagement of the sense of touch also occurs, I would argue, when we view painted depictions of such tactile surfaces. See, for example, the seventeenth-century painting *Still Life with Ebony Chest* by Antonio de Pereda.

The still-life features a wide range of materials, which Giorgio Riello and I have argued elsewhere all suggest the global connections of the Spanish empire in the mid-seventeenth century, including chocolate-making equipment and ceramics from Mexico, porcelain from

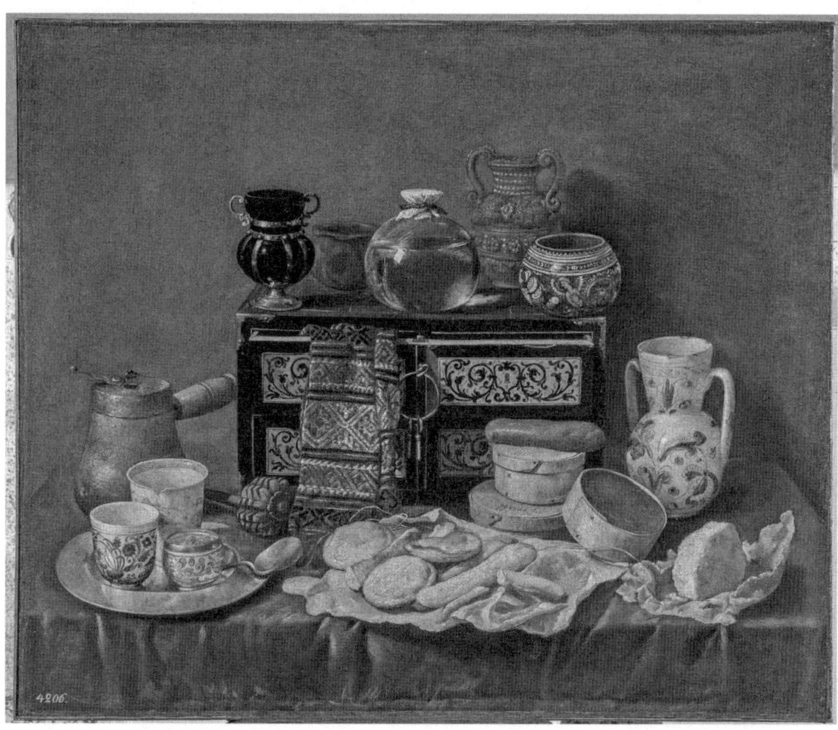

Antonio de Pereda, *Still Life with Ebony Chest*, 1652, oil on canvas, 80 × 94 cm. Hermitage. Photograph © The State Hermitage Museum. Photo Pavel Demidov.

China, and Italian majolica. The woven cloth like the one depicted may well have come from Mexico, too, and such silver-mounted gourd cups could well have come from Goa.[15] I am more interested here in the tactility of all the objects and materials depicted: the rumpled velvet, the powdery chocolate, the textured red Mexican vase, the crusty biscuits all invite the eyes to 'function like organs of touch'. Among the three vessels on the tray in front of the chocolatière, we see what looks like a Chinese porcelain cup, with an unmistakable chip leaving a wide opening in the vessel's lip. I would suggest that this damaged object enhances not only the viewer's understanding of the material by showing the whiteness of the inside of the body, but also its haptic visuality. The damage in the material shows us its essence and allows us to imagine experiencing the smoothness of the material at the same time as the acuity of the cut. Is it possible to argue that it is the tactility of the painting that allows us to imagine all these objects placed around an ebony chest but from such disparate places inhabiting a single place? Perhaps their tactility brings them closer to our own bodies, reducing their distance and making them part of our own lived experience.

If we return briefly to Bouke de Vries' *Guan Yin in a Cloud of Shards*, we see how many of the 'ingredients' come together in this recipe for negotiating the world of art. The artist works with broken pieces of ceramics to create new pieces that invite reflection on value and beauty, on the integration of materials and designs from distinct parts of the world, and on sustainability. But to navigate those ideas, we need one final ingredient: the element of touch. As our eyes touch different surfaces and dwell on the contrast between smooth surfaces and the breaks and cuts and traces of restoration that characterize De Vries' work, our sense of touch is engaged. In viewing the work, we experience it not just with our eyes, but with our whole body. As Ximenez' inventory and De Pereda's still life show, De Vries is working in a long tradition of porcelain enthusiasts who treasure the fragmentary. The ingredient of touch offers a way to navigate pieces of art from different times and spaces and making them feel familiar.

15. *The Global Lives of Things: The Material Culture of Connections in the Early Modern World*, eds. Anne Gerritsen and Giorgio Riello (London, 2016), p. 23, note 3.

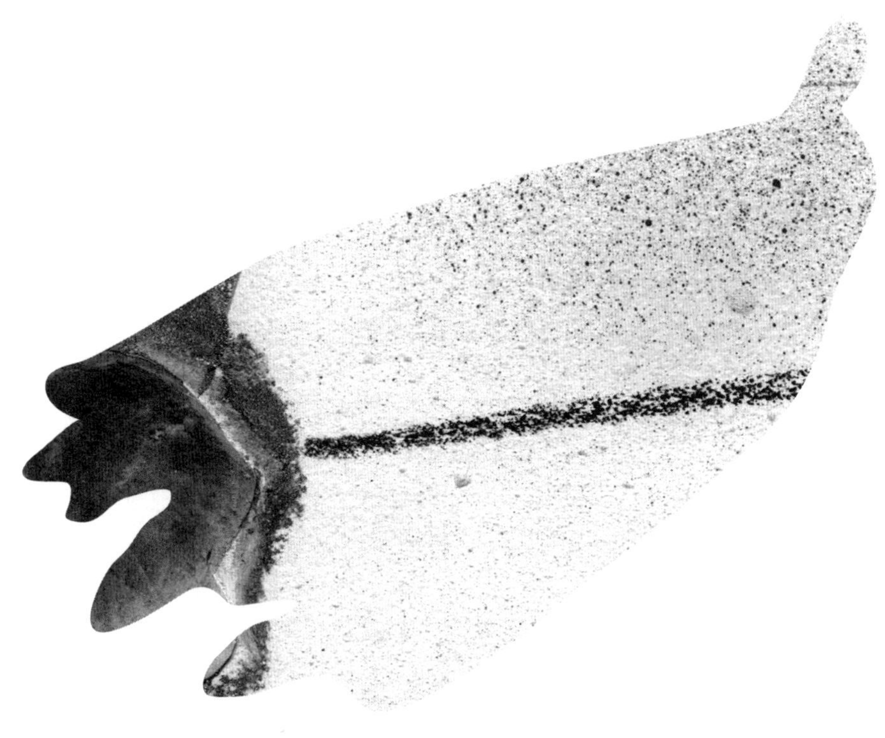

VALUE ACCRUEMENT AND DWINDLING OF AN ICONIC CHINESE EXPORT PAINTING A Journey

Rosalien van der Poel

INGREDIENTS

- Cultural Biography
- Confluence of Values: commodity/export, historical, artistic, and material values
- Interpretation related to 'layers' of use
- Revivification

In the nineteenth century, Chinese export paintings had a strong appeal to foreigners who were in China because of maritime trade. Dutch public collections comprising these kinds of paintings include a substantial number of works representing maritime topics.[1] Harbour views, such as those of Canton, are still signifiers of the historical China trade in our time. This important category of Chinese export paintings can be analysed both as representations and as commodities whose value and meaning were accrued through specific and economic forms of exchange. By mapping the 'cultural biography' of an iconic harbour view, which was in the Leiden Museum Volkenkunde and is currently in the Hong Kong Museum of Art, this essay shows that the value of this transcultural artwork lies in its movement and connected interpretations.[2] This approach of looking at the painting from a commodity perspective and treat it as an active player in the networks that connect it to human practices and current ideas and concepts, enables us to relate historical times of the Dutch China trade to present-day practices between the Netherlands and China. Even more, this case study gives us a new outlook on research into contemporary artworks from a global perspective.

1. Rosalien van der Poel, *Made for Trade—Made in China. Chinese Export Painting in Dutch Collections: Art and Commodity*. PhD diss., Leiden University, 2016.

2. Igor Kopytoff brought the notion 'cultural biography' of objects to the fore in 'The Cultural Biography of Things: Commoditization as Process', *The Social Life of Things: Commodities in Cultural Perspective*, ed. Arjun Appadurai (Cambridge, 1986), pp. 64–91.

Glorious but Overlooked Value – A Cultural Biography

From 1905 to 2018 the painting of a panoramic view of the Pearl River and the quay of Canton (ca. 1850, anonymous), central in this essay, was kept in the collection of Museum Volkenkunde in Leiden. The cultural biography of this large painting may reveal something about its function and use value over the course of time. That is to say, from the moment of purchase by its first owner, the Dutch government official, trader, and diplomat Tonco Modderman (1813–1858), in the mid-nineteenth century in China, to its current status as an educational and revealing object in the collection of the Hong Kong Museum of Art, accessible in its former glory for anyone who would like to learn about the past.

This remarkably wide panorama shows life on the Pearl River with hundreds of boats depicted in the foreground. The quay and its dwellings, as seen from the river, are depicted in the middle ground. Above this scene is a high sky, in which a light cloud cover can be discerned. The Western trading factories can be seen left of the centre. When we take a closer look at the composition of this painting it becomes clear that this constructed landscape combines different cultural conventions. On the one hand, because of its wideness and its multiple perspectives, this harbour view can be read almost like a Chinese handscroll, to be read from right to left. On the other hand, the composition of this painting is typical of seventeenth-century European landscape art, with two-thirds of the canvas used for the sky, a low horizon line and a mainly bird's-eye perspective. In this way, this representation of the thriving port city of Canton on this transcultural artwork displays the interweaving of local and global knowledge of painting conventions. Application of this integrated, shared painting style accrued value to the painting as an artwork and a commodity at the same time. Although many similar (but all slightly different) representations of this scene are known, in this case the individual authorship is recognizable and its historical and material value—the narrative makes this painting an interesting object to exhibit—gives this painting a genuine art connotation.[3]

3. Martyn Gregory, *Merchants and Mariners*. Catalogue 98 (London, 2018), pp. 98–100. Other panoramic paintings like *View on the Canton Waterfront* which can be attributed to Youqua on the strength of similarities, can be found in the collections of the National Maritime Museum in Greenwich (BHC 1785) and Guangdong Provincial Museum, to which is still attached the label of 'Youqua Painter / Old [China] Street No. 34', illustrated in Patrick Conner, *The Hongs of Canton: Western Merchants in South China 1700–1900, As Seen in Chinese Export Paintings* (London, 2009), pp. 182–83.

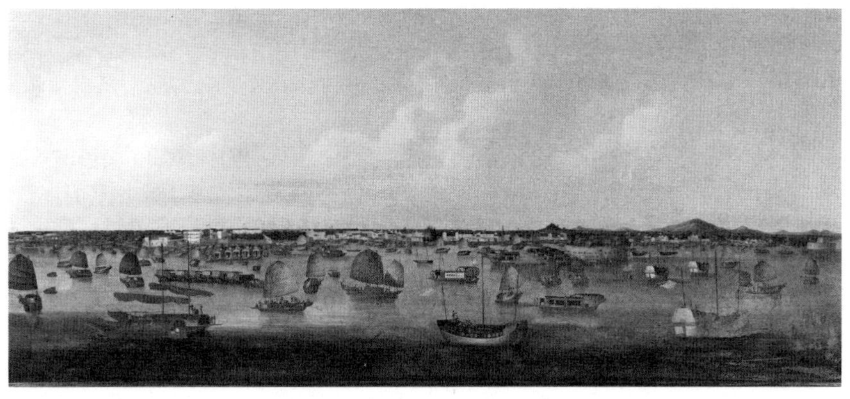

A Panoramic View of the Waterfront at Canton, anonymous, 1845–1855, oil on canvas, 87.5 × 200 cm, Hong Kong Museum of Art, inv.no. AH2018.0003.001.

Between 1843 and 1856, Tonco Modderman, the person who initially owned the work, lived alternately in Canton, Batavia, India, and Macao. In 1847 he married the Batavia-born Angelique Ardesch (1831-1852), who died in November 1852, while on board of a ship, the *Rotterdam*, bound for Holland. She left behind two children: Marie and Louise-Jacoba. Modderman's failing health forced him to leave Macao in 1856 and return to Holland, where he died in 1858.

Hypothetically, it is highly possible that Modderman obtained this Canton harbour view either in the years spanning his second Chinese and Macanese period in the 1850s, or in his Netherlands East Indies period in Batavia from 1846 to 1848, where he ran a household with his wife Angelique. Given what we do know, we can form a cultural biography with some degree of certainty. We must point out the highly attractive Chinese export art market itself, as a first meaningful and decisive cultural marker. In fact, this market was so remarkable that for this reason alone the painting was awarded a high use value as a commercial product and was judged to be of great worth. Its saleability and exchangeability were highly significant, perhaps even its main feature. In addition, it could have accomplished a commemorative and decorative function and an important means of self-fashioning and self-expression, both during Modderman's time in the East Indies trade society or in Chinese commercial circles, and when he lived in his home country again. By analysing other cultural markers in the painting's biography, we notice a major change in its use value over the course of time as a result of various sociocultural and temporal aspects.

When Modderman passed away in 1858 it is likely that his daughter Louise Modderman (1852–1875) inherited the painting, so emblematic of an elite status. In 1871, when Modderman's daughter married Cornelis Leembruggen (1838–1905), she took this heirloom with her to furnish the walls of the huge family house in Leiden, where it hung until Cornelis died, in 1905. In this year, their son, Willem Leembruggen (1871–1925), the then director of the family's Leiden textile factory, inherited the canvas. In the same year, Willem moved to another, much smaller house; he subsequently donated the painting as a long-term loan to Museum Volkenkunde. This loan to the museum clarifies something about the private valuation put upon this work of art by its owner at that time and how, consequently, this particular meaning 'evaporated' from the painting. On the one hand, to put it negatively, the work could have been too big (no wall space in the new house), too dark, or in need of a restoration. On the other hand, to put it more positively, Willem's donation was given due to the trustworthy character of Museum Volkenkunde and its curators. He might have thought that this painting would be much better off in their care, rather than keeping it himself. In all cases, the upshot was the deliberate act of renouncing the painting, which subsequently accrued new use value. Appraised as an expression of wealth and trading successes of his ancestors, the painting was assigned a different value by Willem Leembruggen. Instead of treating the painting as an ordinary and saleable commodity and putting it up for auction at the art market, it was, however, considered to be a valuable item, worth preserving for future generations. Moreover, the family must have felt that *selling* the painting was, as the cultural anthropologist, Igor Kopytoff, calls it 'trading downward'.[4] This idea springs from the idea that things called *art* or *historical objects* are superior to the world of commerce.

When looking at the total trajectory from production to consumption, this painting, for a long time languishing in the museum storeroom could be considered 'frozen' or as de-commodified.[5] There is no living or

4. Kopytoff 1986 (see note 2), p. 82.

5. I came across the term 'freezing' in *Commodification: Things, Agency, and Identities (The Social Life of Thing Revisited)*, eds. Wim van Binsbergen and Peter Geschiere (Münster, 2005), which gave me an essential insight into the Dutch collections, many of which are currently 'deep frozen', or, in other words, 'overlooked and neglected', taken out circulation. Some scholars, however, believe that a work never can be 'frozen', because even when a work of art is overlooked and neglected, it always shares a dynamic cultural context. Once a work is accessible through the internet, so I argue, it is no longer 'frozen'.

institutional memory of the painting ever having been exhibited following its donation.[6] This low status had nothing to do with identity marking or with unique, artistic, and historic value; rather, it had everything to do with priorities and strategies in collection management, whether or not motivated by valuation of Chinese export painting in general and/or by financial considerations. In turn, we can assume that these considerations were fed by ignorance of the museum management about the high use value of this artwork.

Provenance research and bringing the value of this painting and its narrative to the fore again and again since 2008 caused a turn in the cultural biography of this transcultural artwork. In 2017, when a curator from Museum Oud Amelisweerd (MOA), an eighteenth-century stately country estate near the City of Utrecht, was looking for an emblematic painting that depicted 'everything' about the historical China trade, we could not think of a better example than the piece central to this chapter. So, it happened that this painting was on show at the exhibition 'Made in China. Armando and masterworks from the Qing Dynasty'.[7] The artwork was exhibited with remarkable eighteenth- and nineteenth-century Chinese objects from the Guangdong Museum collection as they relate to the mansion's famous Chinese wallpapers.[8]

While on display at MOA, the cultural biography of the *View of the Waterfront of Canton* got another exciting turn at the end of December 2017. At this time the members of the Leembruggen family formed a new interest in the status of the painting. It seemed that the exhibition in MOA has worked as a catalyst for the family to act. In this period, the Leembruggens broke the permanent loan contract with Museum Volkenkunde, got their painting back, explored the possibilities of conservation and thought about what to do next with it. It took only a short while for them to decide to put it up for sale in the art market. In November 2018 *View of the Waterfront of Canton* had been restored and was put on display, together with a companion piece *View of Honam*, at the exhibition 'Merchants and Mariners. Historical pictures by Chinese and Western artists 1750–1970' at the Hong Kong Maritime Museum. From here it was sold to the Hong Kong Museum of Art, where *View of the Waterfront of Canton* is publicly accessible

6. Paul Van Dongen, former curator China in Museum Volkenkunde (1984–2011), informed me (July 2011) that neither he, nor his predecessor, since the 1950s to 1984, had ever displayed this painting (inv. no. RV-360-B3-1).

7. This exhibition, held from 23 September 2017 to 18 March 2018, came about as the result of close cooperation between the Guangdong Museum in Guangzhou and Museum Oud Amelisweerd (MOA). 'Made in China' included twelve works by the Dutch artist Armando, ranging from drawings in ink to landscapes in oil. Armando's view of landscape shows many similarities to the Chinese tradition. He was one of the few Western artists to create both horizontal and vertical landscapes, the latter of which display visual relationships similar to those of Chinese hanging scroll paintings. And the insignificance of mankind forms an important theme in his work, as it did for the Chinese landscape painters.

8. The walls of the two largest rooms on the ground floor are fully covered with Chinese wallpapers (1750–1770). They are unique in their size and in the fact that they have been kept in good condition at their original location.

again. Thanks to the revivification of this nineteenth-century painting, the public can now learn about the historical China trade in the Pearl River Delta and the history of Guangzhou as an important port city.[9]

This biographical approach to the understanding of this painting argues that biographies of people and things are inseparable and will indicate current and future roles for this painting. The growing knowledge about the work has led to a higher valuation of this artwork now that it is back in circulation. In short, the painting functioned as an artistic commodity at the time and place of its production, until its inheritance by the Leembruggen family, when it became a 'keepsake' and a real identity marker for the people involved. It was a neglected and overlooked item during the time it was in the depot of the Leiden museum, from where it 'escaped' and in 2017 turned into a major art piece in a Dutch national heritage exhibition on Chinese-Dutch cultural interaction. Its life story after this is known by now.

This case study also provides ingredients for a new outlook on research into contemporary artworks from a global perspective. Chinese export paintings, likewise contemporary artworks, move around the world and, when objects move, so we learn from the writings of

9. This exhibition, organized by the London-based Martyn Gregory Gallery, was held from 8 to 17 November 2018. In the Hong Kong Museum of Art, the painting got a new title: *Panoramic View of the Waterfront at Canton* and inv. no. AH2018.0003.001. In the museum collection the artwork also became part of a set with its companion piece *View on Honam*, inv.no. AH2018.0003.002.

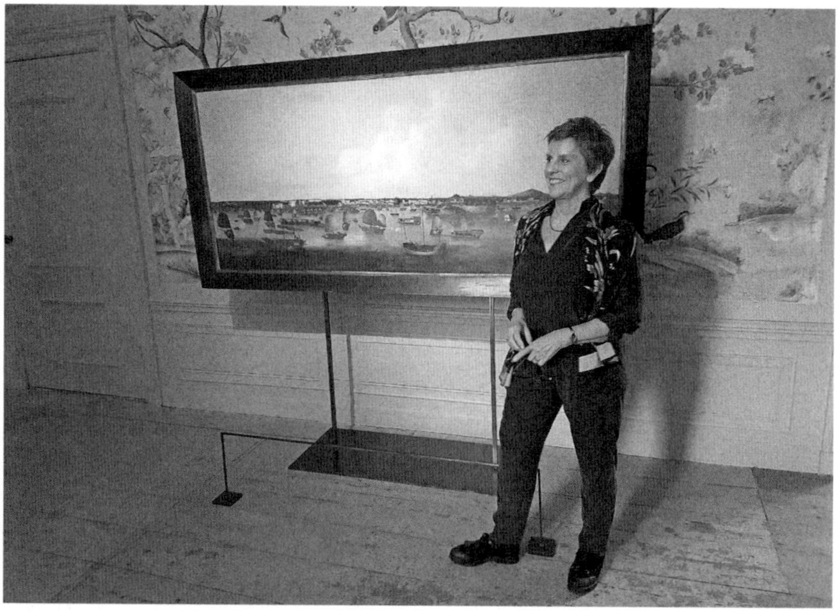

A Panoramic View of the Waterfront at Canton on display, Museum Oud Amelisweerd.

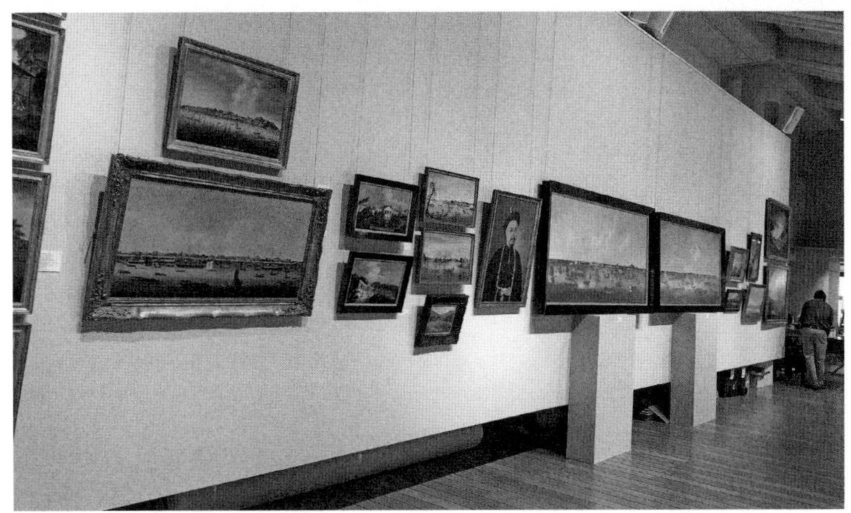

A Panoramic View of the Waterfront at Canton on display at 'Merchants and Mariners. Historical pictures by Chinese and Western artists 1750–1970', Hong Kong Maritime Museum.

Anne Gerritsen, 'they establish connections across space. … Objects articulate exchange, taste, design and cultural understanding on a global scale.'[10] The sketches of the biographical fragments of the painting and its owners show that the value of this work lies in its movement and connected interpretations. The time and place of its production and its cultural biography with some clear markers of value accruement along the journey the painting made from China to the museum in the Netherlands and back to the Chinese region again, allow the audience to become actively involved in the future shaping of this painting's meaning. Future interpretation of other worthwhile Chinese export paintings in Dutch collections for possible revivification includes awareness of the fact that these artworks are the result of different 'layers' of use, interpretation across space and restoration across time.[11] Likewise, how they are classified, archived, and labelled adds layers. The curators' responsibility to take care of and to prevent the run-down oil paintings from being further damaged, by keeping them 'frozen' on racks in the storerooms, conflicts with the curators' other social duties to valorize their research and display their collections to the public. Hopefully this essay will also be seen as a strong plea to take care of similar paintings and their otherwise dire fate.

10. *Writing Material Culture History*, eds. Anne Gerritsen and Giorgio Riello (London/New York, 2015), pp. 6–7.

11. Ibid., p. 8. Gerritsen uses this term (layers) when she writes about the presentation as well as the preservation and representation of material cultures in exhibitions, films, and museum displays.

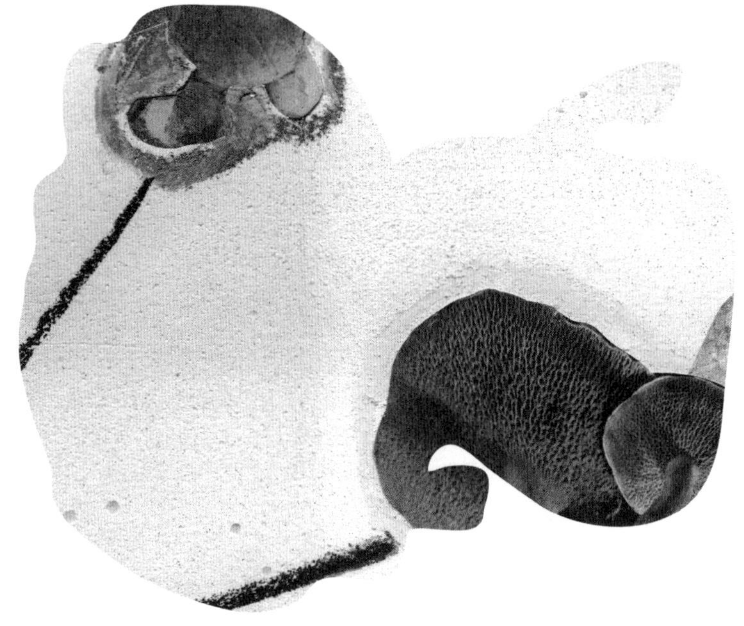

Ever Given
On Mobility, Stasis, and the Circulation of Images after the 'Global Turn'

Eva-Maria Troelenberg

INGREDIENTS

- Global history
- Mobility
- Acceleration
- Circulation of Images
- Memes
- Social Media

In the early morning hours of 23 March 2021, the container ship *Ever Given*, one of the world's largest cargo vessels, got stuck in the Suez Canal, resulting in a massive blockage of international commercial traffic. Over the following days, social media platforms quickly started trending with memes based on images of the wrecked ship and the attempts to make it afloat again. The *Ever Given* had been on its way from Yangshan to Rotterdam when it ran aground during a sandstorm, shortly after it had entered the canal coming from the southern direction. The ship turned sideways and remained diagonally wedged across the entire width of the waterway for four days before salvage work started setting things slowly in motion. None of the twenty-five Indian crew members were hurt, the cargo was undamaged. But as it remained unable to navigate either back or forth, the ship caused a traffic jam, with several hundreds of other freighters lining up, some of them carrying large numbers of life stock.

Opened in 1869, the channel links the Mediterranean and the Red Sea. It shortens the sea route between Asian and Northern European ports by circa 6,000 kilometres compared to circumnavigation of the African continent and is therefore a main traffic artery of globalized economies. Accordingly, the economic damage of the *Ever Given* blockage was considerable: it amounted to an estimated 400 million USD per hour during the week of its duration, and it affected global supply chains already under strain due to the Covid-19 crisis for a longer period.

This essay will take its cue from some of the images produced by this incident, as on the one hand they stand paradigmatically for very contemporary practices of image use and circulation. They act on the interface of social media communities, activist art, and a global, digital vernacular that is becoming an increasingly important element in new artistic practices. On the other hand, these very contemporary images are connected to a complex local history of modernization as well as to larger paradigms and possibilities of mobility that were always connected to a progressive, Eurocentric idea of modernity. These notions of mobility have been adapted affirmatively in the discourse of economic globalization, but were in reality never freely available for everyone in the colonial and post-colonial world. I will therefore also use the vantage point of the *Ever Given* incident to move towards a new outlook on the paradigm of mobility and its relation to modern and contemporary visual discourses and practices.[1]

On the surface of things, the singular accident of the *Ever Given* obviously hit the nerve of the Covid era: as an article in the German weekly *Der Spiegel* stated, the *Ever Given* wreckage provided us with a 'symbol for just about everything'.[2] Indeed, the most popular and dynamic *Ever Given* memes are based on variations of one particular motif: emphasizing the gigantic scale of the *Ever Given*, these images show a section of the ship's bow, towering against the flat desert on the eastern shore of the channel. In one iteration of this motif two workmen in safety vests stand next to a front-end loader on the bank near the accident site. In another one, a caterpillar excavator has its arm stretched out towards the area where the ship has ploughed up huge heaps of sand as it ran aground in shallow waters. The effect of such images is surreal, as the rescue vehicles and workers appear helplessly dwarfed by the literally colossal problem they are expected to solve. It is obvious that these images show only a small component of a complex salvage campaign—but this is exactly what

1. This contribution is based on an online essay published by Villa Romana's Broken Archive project: Eva-Maria Troelenberg, 'When the Machine Runs Aground, it Produces Images'. The Broken Archive, 2021, brokenarchive.org/artist/eva-maria-troelenberg.

2. Patrick Beuth, 'Die "Ever Given" ist ein Geschenk ans Internet', *Der Spiegel*, 26 March 2021, spiegel.de/netzwelt/web/ever-given-ein-geschenk-ans-internet-a-e76c06d7-ec7f-4000-a39b-0974a15a2456.

makes them strong and iconic, as they condense the mess of convoluted disaster into a simple binary: it is, as many commentators referred to implicitly or explicitly, Sisyphus against the mountain, David against Goliath.

In this sense, in many of the quickly spreading memes, the captions added by social media users spell out how the overwhelmingly large, yet immovable ship stands for a range of very different problem complexes: academic workloads, racism, climate change, the Covid crisis—all those things that have systemic foundations and often appear, literally, larger than the individual. In sharp opposition to this gigantic scale, the dredger and the front loader, dwarfed by the massive ship, embody the futility of any attempt to respond to such complex predicaments and crises. The captions attached to the seemingly hopeless instrument read: 'workload model', 'A diversity inclusion workshop', or 'business as usual', culminating in the summary juxtaposition between 'the crushing despair of everything from the past year' and 'you, doing your best'.

It is striking how a massive, global dimension of crisis suddenly appears pinpointed to one singular event and location. As long as things are literally in flow, as long as those movements that are expected, enhanced, and privileged by a progressivist economic order are running smoothly, we barely notice the complex, heavy industry that constitutes the machinery room of our time. Of course, awareness of the economic and social implications of modern consumer culture has increased over the last decades, as people have become more critical to the conditions of production both in terms of labour rights and sustainability. But how about the conditions of product circulation and transport? When we order a garment online and have it delivered to our doorstep, how often do we ask ourselves, concretely, which route the cotton used for its fabric took, and who had to work for this in the past or on the way, under what conditions, whose risk was it, whose benefit?

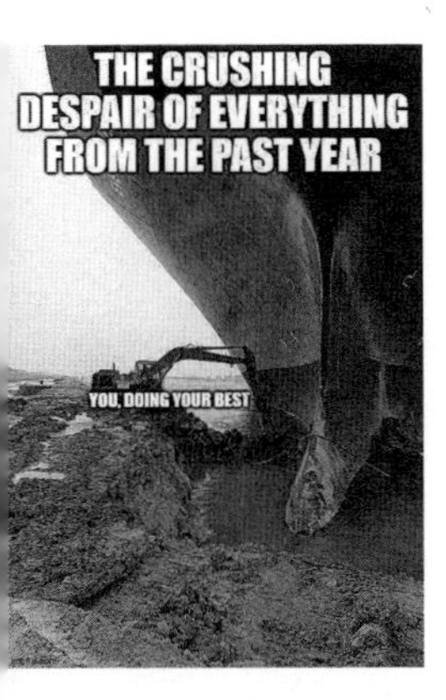

Ever Given meme created and uploaded to Twitter by Joe Streckert on 25 March 2021.

This relative invisibility, or rather disregard of the larger machineries and infrastructures of circulation contributes to the often naïve and affirmative rhetoric of globalization: as if we lived in an age of unbridled mobility, steered by the forces of goods, markets, and economic drive. As if this unbridled mobility was a given under all circumstances and for everyone.[3] This was never the case, and this illusion has been made more visible during the Covid crisis. Mobility is never a given, it is contingent upon many conditions. The *Ever Given*, down to its allusive name, is the perfect symbol of this sobering realization. It seems like particularly strong and powerful images are produced when the machinery is interrupted, when the structure is punctuated by an event that epitomizes the overwhelming complexity of … everything. Here it becomes apparent how central the role and agency of images and visual practices is. Therefore, we have moved beyond the disciplinary boundaries of art history in a traditional sense. Rather, the question is: how do we, as art and visual historians, identify, understand, and explain the works of images in relation to moments of both mobility and stasis in global circulation flows?

3. Stefanie Gänger and Jürgen Osterhammel, 'Denkpause für die Globalgeschichte', *Merkur*, no. 855, 24 July 2020. merkur-zeitschrift.de/2020/07/24/ denkpause-fuer-globalgeschichte/ #more-14759.

4. Dirk van Gehlen, *Meme* (Berlin, 2020); on meme culture see also e.g., Ryan M. Milner, *The World Made Meme: Public Conversation and Participatory Media* (Cambridge, MA/London, 2016).

MEMES AND DIALECTICS

Our first question therefore will be: what exactly is it that these images and memes are doing now? The vivid and affectionate reception that the *Ever Given* incident has found in media outlets seems propelled by a sense of relief—maybe not comic, but ironic relief. On the surface of things, what they show us is an event that is serious and disruptive enough to speak to us in a moment of collective crisis. At the same time, the captions attached to these images allow for an alternative way of communication, as they seem to signal: we are all in this place. After all, social media users from very different backgrounds obviously have very similar ideas and associations when they look at the Sisyphus constellation represented by those images.

In his recent essay on meme culture, Dirk van Gehlen describes the phenomenon of the meme as a paradigmatically dynamic, connective means of international, borderless communication. The practice of reproducing and recombining images and slogans goes beyond mere circulation. It builds a common, yet always changing and spontaneously evolving field of references, with shifting roles of recipients and creators. Participation in this game constitutes (virtual) communities.[4] Under the specific conditions of the Covid era, such a fluid practice of media use can make up for the physical stasis and disconnection—so

5. Valeska Huber, *Channelling Mobilities: Migration and Globalisation in the Suez Canal Region and Beyond, 1869–1914* (Cambridge, 2013); Darcy Grimaldo Grigsby, *Colossal: Engineering the Suez Canal, Statue of Liberty, Eiffel Tower, and Panama Canal* (Pittsburgh, 2012); Institut du Monde, *L'Epopée du Canal de Suez*, eds. Claude Mollard and Gilles Gauthier (Paris, 2018).

it is hardly surprising that meme culture responds so vividly to the case of the *Ever Given*, epitomizing both global mobility and its coming to a grinding halt. Of course, such a strong effect comes at the cost of reducing complexity, a problem also acknowledged in Van Gehlen's meme theory.

In a historical perspective, the Suez Canal stands for the highly ambivalent policies of movement and connectivity of which the costs and benefits have been and still are unevenly distributed in a capital-driven colonial and post-colonial world. Throughout its history, from its origins in the age of Empire through its nationalization up to today, the channel has been not only an infrastructural improvement, but also a site of disruption, of policed movement, and a symbol of national, regional, and global narratives and identities.[5] Along this way, it has also produced a trove of images, many of them made explicitly for global circulation, under the conditions of their time. Dredgers and devices for moving soil were for instance already a prominent photographic motif at the time of the channel's creation. Tourists would buy them on their grand tours to show that they had seen one of the most progressive engineering projects of their time. From a post-colonial point of view, these images of machinery are closely entangled with the aggressive exploitation of soil and labour.

Another typical iconographic motif that resonates with the *Ever Given* memes is the contrast between the modern, technically (hyper-)progressive shipping industry and the small scale of local practices. The Bedouin, picturesquely leading his pack-dromedary along the channel's shore, dwarfed by a steamship passing by, or just the contrast between the dynamic vessel and the seemingly timeless desert: these are familiar Orientalist tropes in the iconography of the Suez Canal. Historically, such images have often created cultural difference rather than transcultural community. Are we thus really all in one place when we look at the *Ever Given* meme? Of course, it is an interesting and dialectic echo to such an image-history when we are now looking at a moment where this celebrated machinery of progress is literally stuck.

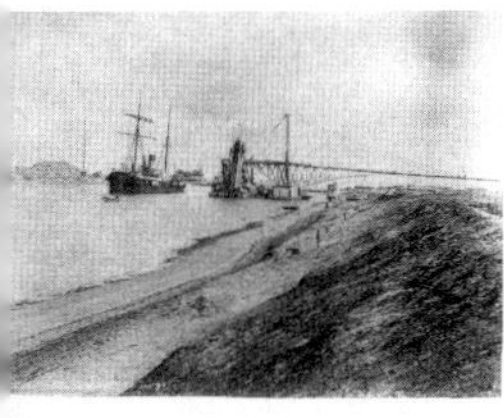

Hippolyte Arnoux, *Dredgers working on the Suez Canal*, c. 1880, Tropenmuseum—Part of the National Museum of World cultures, CC BY-SA 3.0.

Roughly two weeks after the incident, several media outlets ran stories about Abdullah Abdul-Gawad, working for a firm subcontracted by the Suez Canal Authority. He had operated the by then famous excavator at the *Ever Given*'s bow.[6] Even if it may be questionable how reliable these journalistic sources are in detail, they do give a voice to one of the workers on the ground, and thus draw attention to the labour involved: here we read, for instance, that Abdul-Gawad and his colleagues worked twenty-one-hour-shifts, and that it took a while for them to receive the overpay which was due for this task which drove them to the brink of exhaustion. At first glance, this seems like another aspect confirming the overall David-against-Goliath narrative. However, this time it is not metaphorical, but connected to a very concrete social reality on site. This reality also entails the fact that the workers were in acute danger, facing the risk that the vessel would topple and bury them. Accordingly, Abdul-Gawad explains that he did not find it funny when ironic memes started circulating while salvage work was still under way. Rather, the workers felt mocked by this kind of global attention—to the extent that it motivated them to work even harder. In this sense, the meme does have an impact here as well, the images are—now again metaphorically speaking—'at work', but their agency is ambivalently connected to the concrete labour executed at the site of the incident.

When we relate this concrete voice from the actual place where the incident happened to the free-floating images, we realize that taking the full scale and significance of global images into account today requires a concept of the image that is attached to its complex, and constantly evolving relations to space. This concept always has to start from place and space understood as a concrete, geographical location, which is connected to individual people and their conditions of life. As Marcus Filippello argues,

> .... human perceptions of space shift over time based on interactions and movements of people, goods, services, and information. In doing so, they also suggest that spatial analyses of material dimensions of things like roads, buildings, waterways, and farm fields can help us better understand

6. E.g., Mia Jankowicz, 'The guy driving the Suez Canal excavator says he got by on 3 hours of sleep a night and hasn't been paid his overtime yet', *Business Insider*, 8 April 2021, businessinsider.com/suez-excavator-driver-worked-21-hour-days-hasnt-got-overtime-2021-4?r=DE&IR=T.

'the perceptual', or how a person or group of interacting people understands spaces, and consequently, historical change. Identifying how people perceive material space can, in turn, reveal how communities and individuals affect historical change and receive or negotiate processes involving cross-cultural exchange.[7]

This provides a theoretical perspective that links to postcolonial theory[8] and follows the very basic premise that history literally 'takes place' and is to be read through spatial constellations.[9] Using the term 'constellations' with its implication of dynamic movement[10] here is deliberately meant to connect space and place to cross-cultural and often mediated encounters: in cross-cultural histories, places are not static like on a map; rather, they can be perceived differently depending on where we stand and from where we approach them.

And, one may add: those who have seen these spaces and places in images, have created images about them, have commented on images related to them. In this sense, the increasingly theoretical categories of global image histories such as geo-rhetorical space, cultural space, space for the storage and organization of knowledge, open versus closed space, accessible versus inaccessible space, liminal space, or contact zone will open up epistemic perspectives. As T.J. Demos has stated at the end of his work on 'The Migrant Image', the access to media flows, to the internet and to communication belongs to the common goods that constitute our globalized world, but which also are increasingly under threat, comparable to goods such as fresh water or public lands.[11] The uncontrolled, truly 'excessive', but at the same time often decontextualized movement of images through memes is one example of the political nature attached to this common good of (visual) communication. In order to be relevant as a field, 'global art history' will thus evolve even further into a history and theory of arts, visuality, and image practices *after* the 'global turn' as it were.[12] This is a discourse which cannot be confined to the traditional institutions and practitioners of the 'art world', but needs to relate to multiple 'meaningful places' and agents. At this moment of crisis, it becomes clear that this

7. Marcus Filippello, 'Roads of Joy, Pathways of Anger: Emotional Responses to Landscapes of Mobility', *Landscapes of Mobility. Culture, Politics and Placemaking*, eds. Arjit Sen and Jennifer Johung, pp. 165–182, quote (with reference to Allen Howard and Richard Shain) on pp. 166–167 (Burlington, 2013).

8. Stephan Günzel, *Raum: Eine kulturwissenschaftliche Einführung* (Bielefeld, 2020).

9. Karl Schlögel, *In Space We Read Time: On the History of Civilization and Geopolitics*, transl. Gerrit Jackson (New York, 2017); on the notion of 'taking place' see also Albrecht Weisker, 'K. Schlögel: Im Raume lesen wir die Zeit', Review of *Im Raume lesen wir die Zeit: Über Zivilisationsgeschichte und Geopolitik*, by Karl Schlögel. H-Soz-Kult, 13 March 2004, hsozkult.de/publicationreview/id/reb-4847.

10. Eva-Maria Troelenberg, 'Constellations', *Reading Objects in the Contact Zone*, eds. Eva-Maria Troelenberg, Kerstin Schankweiler and Anna Sophia Messner, Heidelberg Studies on Transculturality 9 (Heidelberg, 2021).

11. T.J. Demos, 'The Migrant Image', *The Art and Politics of Documentary during Global Crisis* (Durham/London, 2013), pp. 246–247.

12. Eva-Maria Troelenberg and Sria Chatterjee, 'After the Global Turn: Eco-Politics, Migration, and the Futures of Art History', *Kunstlicht* 39, no. 1 (2018), pp. 60–72.

interconnected world unfortunately has not provided more equality, fairness or, indeed, mobility which can be taken for granted: we are not all in the same place, and academic disciplines such as art history today therefore bear heavy responsibilities when it comes to the 'works' and circulations of so-called global images. The main precondition will be to place these agents and institutions—and ultimately our discipline itself—in relation to the social realities of an interconnected world.

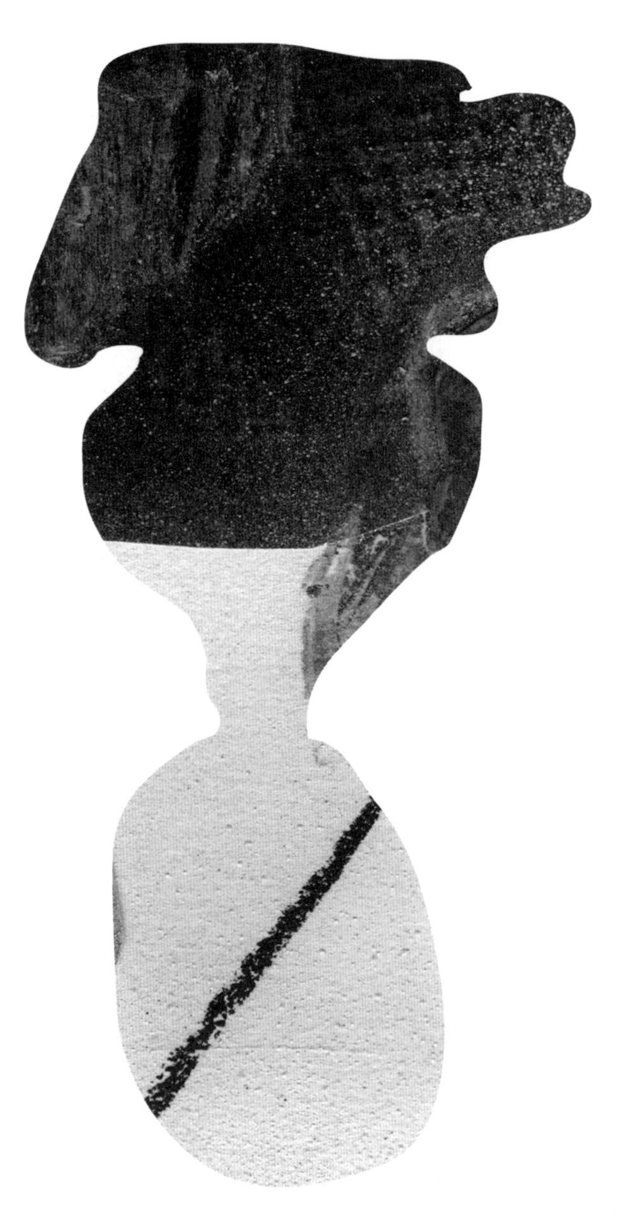

NEW APPROACHES TO ASIAN MODERNITY

John Clark

INGREDIENTS

- Australasia
- Inter-Asian Comparison
- Endogenous/Exogenous Identification
- Focus on Single Artists

Asian modernity is neither a single set of historical realities, nor is modern Asian art a monodirectional development towards a restricted set of formal and expressive outcomes. This multi-layered lack of singularity is the principal reason why it is very difficult to map, let alone describe the local Asian causations of modern art separate from those in Euramerica—what used to be called 'The West'. It is particularly so since most of Asia has only recently left behind the colonial inter-positions and institutional structures which had dominated since the late eighteenth century. There are various paths towards other modernities specific to particular geographical and cultural zones and they criss-cross in different and often unobserved places. Some set of interlinked and parallel phenomena has been developing since the mid-nineteenth century to form a grouping of modernities which serve as a counter-part to those in Euramerica, and also provide a counter-definitional possibility or generizable way of talking about modernity in art, other than, say, describing the genealogy from Degas to Duchamp. And, since the observation and historical theorization of modernity in art has hitherto largely been from Euramerica, then seeing modernity in art elsewhere necessitates leaving Euramerica to see it. It should go without saying that it preferably requires reading of at least two Asian languages to make inter-Asian comparison possible.

As to the domains of the in-between so produced, hybridity and post-coloniality are slippery fields arguing from which may re-establish precisely the intellectual and real world order they were hoped to overcome, after the end of any possible notion of art relations between single mono-cultural states or englobing one-state dominated colonial empires. These are more dangerous slippages that anyone interested in other modernities has to encounter and circumvent.

One way out, which requires stepping away from Euramerican material as prior case, is to simply ask how now, long after the 1850s in Asia, can we track the inception of that modernity? In doing so, does it make any sense to see what this distancing defines as the pre-modern, as in position at its base? Is tradition something against which modernity is opposed or does it go hand in hand, back and front, with modernity? Of course, these are questions which some modern art discourses in Asia with continuous links to their pre-modern art could long have been able to reply to, as in the Philippines from Simon Flores y de la Rosa or Japan from Takahashi Yuichi, or even Indonesia going back to Raden Saleh with a caesura to the Persagi era of the late 1930s. It really depends on what historical material remains—or has been re-constituted by modern museum-like institutions—to establish the discourse. Certainly, the notion of 'national art' or 'our-style art' as in *nihonga*, or *guohua*, or 'beautiful Philippines', signifies that 'our' art was there before the modern and could be re-formulated by it.

The formation of 'tradition' and 'modernity' must be positioned endogenously inside local historical structures rather than exogenously through and in mere perpetuation of others. Such a lot of stylistic transfer or translocation took place once 'French' salon and anti-salon art became available as a reference model in the 1900s to 1920s, that the illusion of borrowing can be conveniently argued between Euramerican positions and those arrived at in Asia. The whole phenomenon of modernity seems just like or lazily appears to be another kind of cultural borrowing. In fact, as the practice of numerous artists attests, it only appears as a borrowing when the artist starts out with local materials and often endogenously developed art discourses which he or she relativizes and renders other.

To the endogenous/exogenous identification issue the last twenty years have added the unspoken domination of the transnational and its specially authorized units and agents. These appear as: curators, collectors, exhibition sites, and even transnational artists. Often the last-named have an apparently local or regional identity but move between different domains of the international art system without owing much beyond inherited visual or material discourses to any one culture. This is a complex phenomenon mediated by various forces such as ease of inter-state physical transport or rapidity and density of non-physical transmission systems such as digital media. The cultural relativization of past art discourses thus appears as a sort of miasma, where cultural affiliation can be claimed and then projected beyond any possible domain of origin and sometimes beyond any actual physical origin of the artist.

Identifying and then validating transnational art tendencies is a false solution to the important task of leaving behind the old binaries of Modern and Contemporary, Europe and Asia, Japan and America, China and the West. The problematic of two, and binarily mutually interdependent, monovocal interpretations can be avoided by either a focus on art as produced by a nameless or relatively insignificantly nameable mass—where virtually anonymous local populations are asked to fabricate multiples in series directed by a master artist—or by a multi-levelled interrogation of the discourse and work of single artists. This needs to be abstemious of genius-centred, nationalistic, or transnational meshing, as the emphasis of understanding and appreciation.

This is quite difficult because of the slippery presentational ease of single-artist spectacle works to galleries, museums, and art media, even before works have become the subject of economic speculation or competitive political affiliation. Art history has to deploy the artist, biography, oeuvre, and discursive context as a kind of index for other phenomena beyond them, or at least one which analyzes the foregoing with this collateral problematization in mind.

Concentration on the artist removes the need to generalize about whole art worlds and their vertical relationships with economic and political systems. Many art-historical analyses are little more than a readout of institutional practices into non-art systems, and the fact that art works and artists are usually so positioned forces them to perform as a kind of reflex of other ideological debates. Important as they are for art, these are only background noise, often white noise, which impedes looking at the art and its maker.

But the artist does not exist in a solitary and solipsistic domain. The selection and comparison of artists is critical to strategies for avoiding binarism in its various guises even if the artists compared exist in quite distant and uncommunicating cultures. Artists have to be capable of creating and in an art-historical sense bearing the weight and depth of multi-layered interpretations. Selection of prominent artists should therefore not be confused with the spectacularization of artists' lives and the explosive prominence given to singular works, even master works. The artists talk to the world, especially to other artists, if sometimes reactively against other tendencies, or actively in seeking solutions to artistic problems beyond their own individual domain.

Artists can be an endangered species who do not easily find a niche where they can survive. They might not exist as separate entities anymore by critical re-situation of the audience as a semiotic co-author of a 'work'. Or they can have their position usurped by cultural mediators such as curators and critics who claim to operate the artist-function, and may even mount exhibitions with the claim that they are artworks in themselves. Artists are particularly endangered by repetitions in the mode of international spectacle exhibitions which are now iterated as Biennales and Triennales.

These exhibitions display an inbuilt compulsion to repeat by selection of the same or similar artists against very similar and up-to-the-moment notional themes. However, laudable, that is politically valuable some of these are, they are not artistic themes as such. The use of material from life, and for life, can also often mean absorption into life, and an evisceration of art qualities in the work or in the maker.

Biennales, including those in Asia, frequently make a larger claim to historical understanding whether of a place or a problematic, rather than follow or reflect history.

1. See John Clark, 'Time Processes in the History of the Asian Modern', *Time in the History of Art: Temporality Chronology and Anachrony*, eds. Dan Karlhom and Keith Moxey (New York, 2018).

It may be that 'history' is too fast and too large now to wait for and allow post-facto reflection. This future-anticipating drive means that many temporary exhibitions, sites, or artworks that deal with ephemerality are already institutionalized when they happen even though they appear to be physically held in a non-permanent place. Indeed, many Asian Biennales have now run through ten or more editions over from twenty to forty years. Despite their temporal iteration and sometimes radical conceptual plans they cannot be considered as temporary or counter-institutional. The attraction to China, Korea, or Thailand in having a temporary exhibition iterate has meant that these exhibitions have substituted for inter-regional exchanges and in fact, if not entirely in intention, functioned to integrate local art worlds upwards into a world art system. This goes against carrying out local exchanges and artistic conversations, which have greater depth and would not necessarily be in the interest of 'independent' international art curators. 'Avoid local, regional, provincial, or ethnic!' associations, seems to be the implicit curatorial mantra in an attitude which can be termed 'superheated cosmopolitanism'.

The geographical extension of such curators and their global field of operation has meant the absorption of art history into the rhetoric of public spectacles often in public museums, and also in commercial galleries, which fold lecture presentations and pod-casts into their PR strategies. In these cases, art has to be 'important' and function largely through physical size. The transnational does not readily tolerate 'minor' art unless under a rubric of ethnic decorativism. A little consideration also indicates that not all the time scales and temporal concepts are the same between differently constituted art cultures,[1] blended into the same transnational cultural soup as all the others, since languages, cultures, art discourses all survive by self-discrimination and these discriminations have a lineage and are being perpetuated. One can think of analogous situations of the contemporary, and these situations may be structurally, or as flows, similar because of a cognate, linked network. These all have cultural origins and tend to be culturally characterized, even so far that the notion of a transnational evaporates. What may be there across cultural boundaries are relations of affinity and sometimes direct imbrication in the same sub-set of art discourses. These we may term art 'regional' such as in the 'Asian', and these, as historical fact, have built on extensive pre-histories of pre-modern linkages whether through religion, art forms, or even analogies in the types of patronage class. The contemporary may include or relativize these pre-histories as it wishes, or as certain kinds of artistic intentions about the future may require.

Whatever the formal properties of the contemporary or common set of practices distancing art from other now nation-centred discourses, in addition, cultural or geographical re-siting of the contemporary is required either as a descriptive mapping or as a formal hermeneutic technique. The discourses of contemporaneity that appear everywhere, are actually specifically sited or placed where their operators are situated, and the list of places, operators, and agents is not very long. Perhaps the grand and in some ways admirable prolepsis of the Asian Biennales has been their promise of an expansion of the sites of contemporaneity to what the transnational systems deem to be periphery or borderlands, mired in discourses of the past which do not add up to 'now'. To understand these Biennales, art history is given an unacceptably and ultimately fruitless task to remain both distanced from *and* intimate with the local or regional or provincial, at the same time. If it can do that then art as a practice, and art history as a special form of time-based knowledge which transcends the ancient barriers or demarcations of inter-cultural fault lines can truly be said to be contemporary.

These difficult changes of attitude and practice require the abandonment of old rigidities, which do not correspond to the way artists are in the world. This was evidenced probably best in early modern times by the flows between Mughal painting and Europe around the 1580s to 1650s. We can easily identify by historical comparison even then that the structures of art are not so different between cultures, and may be more neutral than usually considered by art history at the cultural boundaries, or in the culturally identified flows which announce them.[2] Art history, like art, is a discourse of socially based disciplines or practices and we should not blindly expect art history to overcome the limitations of their times, and to always be able to shine

2. See the review of 'Comparativism in Art History', *Journal of Art Historiography*, ed. Jaś Elsner (London/New York, 2017), online, June 2017.

light through the long shadows of the nineteenth century which both in Europe and Asia still overshadow them.

All the modernities everywhere now relativize any notion of modernity between them. Modernity is not established by one cultural domain but mapped across all of them that claim these modernities. Thus, the content of traditional becomes not a reverse or reflexive criterion for establishing any kind of modernity but functions as a store of values that can be selectively adopted and varied to find a cultural modernity. Insofar as there are many similarities and sometimes causal links between different modernities, they may be regionally grouped, such as in Asian Modernity and Euramerican Modernity and other regional groupings. This means that some modernities belong in regional sets other than those where history and political prejudice has placed them: Australia or the Russian Far East now really should be grouped as Asian and not placed unthinkingly in the Euramerican. Here the parenthetic power of separating away from the old notion of 'West' should be clear.

Structure of distancing from Euramerica means the historical, discursive, and broader cultural relativization of Euramerican linear genealogies of association, and the subversion of their self-privileging teleology. And if the ends of a discourse—the perpetual re-invention of the 'new'—are called into question then the canon of artworks worthy of knowledge or of providing stylistic exemplars or models has to be re-formulated. Modern transportation and information transmission technology has also both undermined and reinforced the geographical specificity of Asia since what flows can be fed back into its culture of origin and those flows can be reinforced.

The nature and extent of inter-Asian linkages in art need to be re-examined, given the inclusion of 'strange' inceptors and receptors such as Australasia, the Pacific, and Russian Pacific. If 'Asian' modernity is re-defined as part of this re-examination, then the 'modern' as such will also be changed.

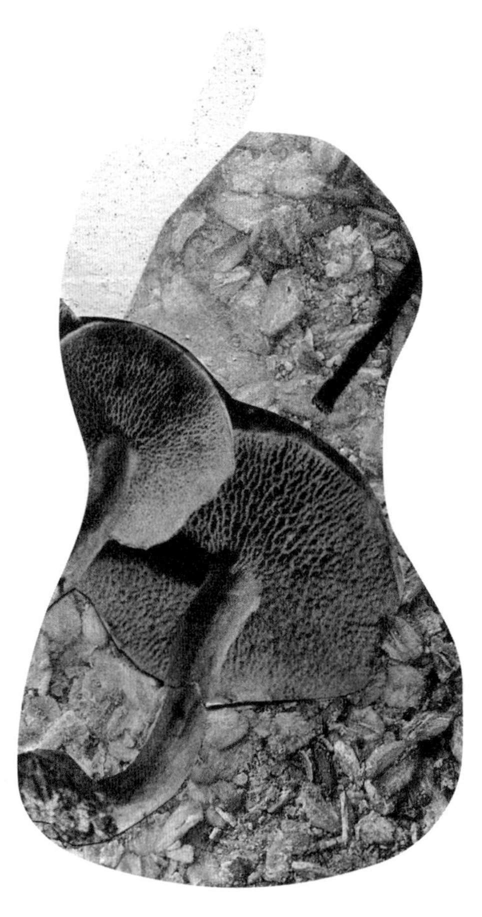

ART IN JADE
Or, How to Identify a 'Cultural Avant-Garde' Work

Leonor Veiga

INGREDIENTS

- Contemporary Art from Elsewhere
- Materiality Rooted in Timeless Cultural Traditions
- Art/Culture Divide
- Cultural Avant-garde
- Jade

An installation made of 102 engraved jade pieces, each measuring 8 x 3 x 1.5 cm, rests against the wall. The work depicts a vista formed by a long line of mountains followed by a series of skyscrapers. The composition can be read from left to right either as a narrative or as a landscape. If read as a narrative, it transports the viewer to a natural landscape that gave place to a human-made environment; if read as a landscape, it shows the coexistence of the natural world with human-made structures. The image is conveyed through miniscule wedge-shaped cuneiform strokes that were incised onto the jade stone. The different directions of the engraving produce an impression of depth, movement, and form while providing the final composition.

The work *Invariable Mountain* was first made by artist Ho Weng Chi (b. 1991, Macau SAR), on the occasion of her artistic residency at the Hong Kong Jockey Club Creative Arts Centre, in 2015. Born from her imagination, the landscape has no relationship with the loss of nature in Hong Kong, where she attended the residency, or in Macau, where she lives.[1] Instead, it represents the problems of the world through a *mountain*. While identical to the first version, *Invariable Mountain II*, made in 2019 and showcased at 'Natura' (the second edition of 'ARTFEM, Women International Biennial of Art of Macau SAR' in

1. Ho Weng Chi, 'Invariable Mountain', interview by Leonor Veiga, transl. Hui Winston, 20 March 2021.

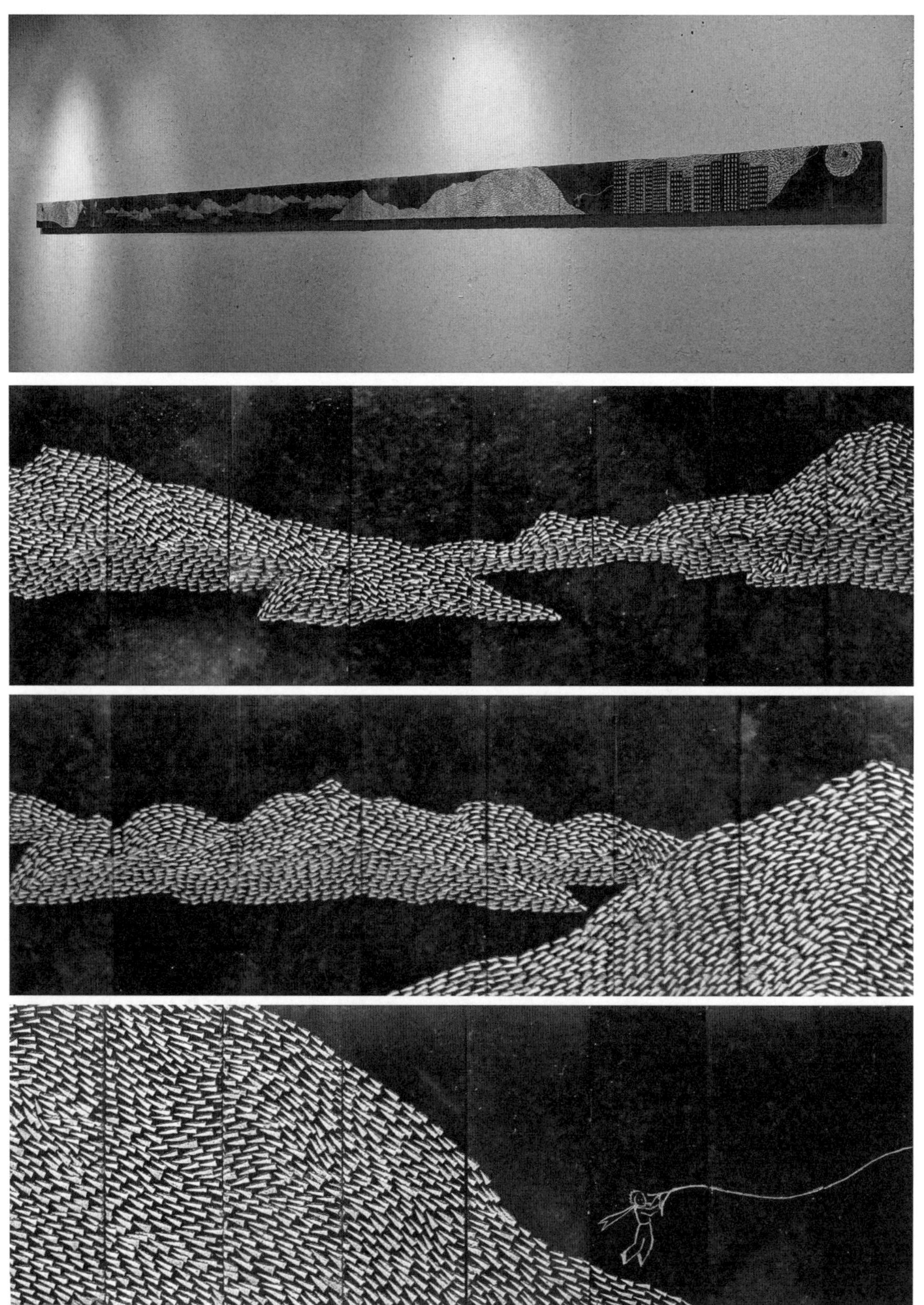

Ho Weng Chi, *Invariable Mountain II*, 2019, lithoglyph, 309 × 8 × 1.5 cm. Images courtesy of the artist.

2. Ibid.

3. Email correspondence with the artist, 20 March 2021.

4. Jensen Chung, 'Cultural Impacts on Non-Assertiveness of East Asian Subordinates', *Management Development Forum* 1, no. 2 (1998); Ray Friedman, Chi Shu-Cheng, and Anne Liu Leigh, 'An Expectancy Model of Chinese-American Differences in Conflict-Avoiding', *Journal of International Business Studies*, no. 37 (2006), p 78.

Fall 2020), differs from the first version, due to the natural stone's intrinsic properties, which allow for variations. Ho explains that every stone has its character, which she analyzes prior to her graphic interventions. As such, the resulting composition incorporates the stones' natural colour changes which, in the case of *Invariable Mountain II*, contribute to an added sense of perspective (darker tones, which seem closer to the viewer, were integrated in the mountains, lighter tones, which provide a sense of distance, were matched with the sky); veins caused by different mineral concentrations became lines; and defects such as holes (that may appear in the cut) became the centre of the sun. Made in rectangular, vertical pieces to allude to the visual interruptions of the metallic windows of her room in Hong Kong,[2] *Invariable Mountain* (from here on referring to both version *I* and *II*) represents how humans experience environmental loss: as a gradual succession of events. This is also an intrinsic aspect of the works, as the stone used is sourced in the mountains she wishes to protect. So, the work reflects this tension: the need for material to make an artwork versus the need to preserve the environment.

Through *Invariable Mountain*, Ho accuses humanity of careless intervention in the environment–'In the future, the natural landscape will gradually shrink and be replaced by cement and towering buildings filled with windows'.[3] She advances an unorthodox art register that borrows elements from her cultural background (the Chinese art of engraving jade), that is discouraged by the local art community, who values 'skill' over 'reflection'. Despite the double-critique (toward humankind and the artist community), the work's agency is non-confrontational, an approach which is highly prized in East Asia and stems from the value of harmony and 'face' originating in Confucianist, Buddhist and Taoist influences.[4]

Ho's work discursively promotes a classical and reputed material while communicating with an audience frequently distant from art through familiar cultural signs (such as jade). This, I argue, has been a major contribution of contemporary artists 'from elsewhere', an expression I borrow from Nigerian curator Okwui Enwezor. This procedure has had its foundational moment on postmodernism, but its characteristics vary according to location and culture of emergence.

Currently a PhD-candidate in Chinese Seal Carving and Chinese Calligraphy at the China Academy of Art in Hangzhou, Ho initially explored these two art forms from the standpoint of technical perfection. Through this learning process, 'writing' in jade—nephrite, in this case[5]—became her preferred medium. After years of practice, she understood the appealing aspect of stone carving: once 'written', the stone acquires perpetual 'life'.

As she started reflecting on how to use the stone more conceptually, *Invariable Mountain* emerged. It remains one among the few contemporary expressions employing the craft, which even today tends to adopt traditional registers. Ho suggests that there are two main factors behind this state of affairs: one, the educational system, which focuses exclusively on 'how to craft', as a repetitive process reliant on imitation, and two, the national awards system, which values technical expertise. These academic and professional constraints make young generations feel discouraged to try the art. Furthermore, practitioners and public regard jade as a 'decorative material', devoid of agency. This current disinterest contrasts with the paramount position that jade has enjoyed in Chinese art and culture for centuries. Yet, she recognizes that this form of teaching and valuing the practice enabled her to master the technique and later break with these conventions. I suggest that her move is disruptive and constitutes a form of 'cultural avant-garde', as defined by Peter Bürger: first, it integrates cultural forms alien to the Euro-American standard of art making (which have been present in former avant-garde manifestations). Second, it breaks with laws imposed by the local and global academic communities, and third, through its message, it approximates art with life.[6]

Jade is so central to Chinese culture that it came to be a generic name given to all gem stones. The Chinese call jade the 'stone of heaven' because it is believed to connect the earth with the sky (as a mountain does). At a human level, it is believed that jade is a living stone that heals and protects its user. This understanding is corroborated by Ho: 'When I write a line, I give it energy.'[7] Used in China since the Neolithic period in jewellery, sculpture, and amulets, throughout history, jade acquired a symbolic and cultural

5. Jade is the generic designation given to both gems, jadeite and nephrite. Jadeite, the green gem, is a distinctively different mineral from Chinese jade and is used in China since the seventeenth century where it became a very highly priced commodity. Sourced in Northern Myanmar, from where it is exported to China, jadeite is easier to embellish, having become the preferred gem for Chinese artisans. Chinese jade, or nephrite, has been used since the Neolithic period and has traditionally been sourced in the mountains of the western regions of China. Its colours range from dark green to red, white, and orange (various colours can occur simultaneously in one single piece of stone). Scientifically, the Chinese did not distinguish jadeite and nephrite, and the tradition of carving the stones encompasses both. See James C.Y. Watt, *Chinese Jades from Han to Ch'ing* (New York, 1980), pp. 26–29.

6. Peter Bürger, *Theory of the Avant-Garde*, transl. Michael Shaw (13th ed., Vol. 4, Theory and History of Literature) (Minneapolis, 1984).

7. Ho 2021 (see note 1).

. Jessica Rawson, *Chinese ade: From the Neolithic to he Qing* (London, 1995); Vatt 1980 (see note 5), p. 26.

. Watt 1980 (see note 5), . 13.

0. Ibid., p. 25.

1. Ping-ti Ho, 'The ignificance of the Ch'ing eriod in Chinese History', *he Journal of Asian Studies* 6, no. 2 (1967), pp. 189–191.

2. Ho 2021 (see note 1).

3. Stephen Greenblatt, Culture', *Critical Terms for iterary Study*, eds. Frank entricchia and Thomas McLaughlin (Chicago, 1995, nd ed.), p. 229.

4. Ibid., p. 229; Watt 1980 see note 5), p. 25.

5. Anna Brzyski, ntroduction: Canons nd Art History', *Partisan Canons*, ed. Anna Brzyski Durham, 2007), p. 6; James Clifford, *Museum Realisms: What Does Realism Mean in Museum Contexts, Especially Those Concerned with Cross Cultural Translation?* (Leiden, 016), www.youtube.com/ vatch?v=eQL09kUTUes.

value that relates to the mountains and the rivers where it is sourced.[8]

'The history of jade in many ways reflects the evolution of Chinese culture', says Hong Kong-born Chinese curator of Asian art James C.Y. Watt.[9] To him, not only is jade present in the entire history and all the regions that constitute present-day China, it is equally important for all the cultural traditions associated with it. His affirmation would make one expect jade to remain important today, but it remains confined to traditional registers. So, Ho's use of nephrite expands its artistic possibilities, while her carving reassesses the large naturalistic patterns that emerged during the Ch'ing dynasty (1644-1911).[10] This period is, according to American-Chinese historian Ping-ti Ho, apt 'to analyze the heritage of present-day China' and the acculturation processes that have led to 'the inherent strength of traditional Chinese institutions and culture', where jade craft is found.[11]

'Jade is the best stone for the Chinese', posits Ho.[12] Her incursion into jade is relevant for she works at the interstices of her evolving culture while negotiating what to retain and what to change. This procedure is described by American literary critic Stephen Greenblatt as the nature of all cultural processes, while noting that artists work on 'variations upon received themes'.[13] He argues that this negotiation signals that all given cultures are mobile (including landscape representations in jade, as Watt equally posits).[14] This mobility results from one's confrontation with other cultures, the event that enables an exchange process. Herein resides the origin of Ho's approach: as her education equally covered Western art, she borrowed the critical thinking it favours, and transposed it into this century-old art. Hence, she started to intervene in her own culture.

When referring to cultures outside of the Euro-American axis, the term 'culture' has come to be opposed to the term 'art'. This has been recognized by scholars including American art historian Anna Brzyski and American anthropologist James Clifford, who mention that the initial segregation is felt as 'two avenues [that] are still separate zones of valuation and display'.[15] These divisions have meant that artists from elsewhere have remained constrained to two possible scenarios: first, to repeat the tradition as it is transmitted, and second, to adopt the Western art paradigm. As *Invariable Mountain* combines both approaches, it advances novel ways of making and receiving art. Its reference to 'cultural forms' is exemplary of 'historically situated canonical formations ... produced at different times and in different geographical locations', while conveying distinct hierarchic orders that embody cultural meanings, confer value and produce knowledge relating to a particular tradition.[16]

American-Chinese cultural theorist Jane Chu reminds that 'The Chinese have been writing about art for over two thousand years', and accordingly developed a canonical narrative of Chinese culture.[17] However, the term 'art' 'began to be used only during the republican period'—since 1911—and was borrowed from the Japanese translation of the European meaning.[18] Since then, the concept of art is debated alongside notions of 'Chineseness', of a perceived distinctive character of Chinese cultural forms to 'set them apart from Western culture and from the traditional culture appropriated by the Manchu of the recently toppled Qing dynasty'.[19] This theoretical approach leaves practices such as jade art in a limbo because its authenticity appears associated to the *literati* canon rejected by Marxist theorists, who consider folk art and culture as the true representation of the Chinese people. Ho's unorthodox approach, adequately, integrates the rejected high art tradition into the canon. In doing so, she meets one of the most significant Western avant-garde's traits, something equally identified by Bürger: the accommodation of objects and values considered alien to art's realm into its classification.[20] And because art history has remained firmly rooted in Western cultural history—thus distinguishing, validating, and interpreting art produced predominantly in the West—it has not fully included avant-garde gestures from elsewhere.[21] This neglect is discussed since the mid-1990s, when Indian curator Geeta Kapur announced the condition for the event of an avant-garde in Asia and Africa: the double-dismantle against national and Western forces, including the avant-garde.[22] Kapur equally accused American art historian Hal Foster of opening the avant-garde spectrum to Western postmodern artists, while

16. Brzyski 2007 (see note 15), p. 3.

17. Jane C. Chu, 'Chinese Art, the National Palace Museum, and Cold War Politics', Brzyski 2007 (see note 15), p. 115.

18. Ibid., p. 116.

19. Ibid. The unevenness of the spelling 'Ch'ing' and 'Qing' to refer to the imperial dynasty that ruled China between 1644 and 191 relates to Chinese internal divisions that the author of this text chose to respect. The first spelling—Ch'ing—refers to the form employed within the Cantonese-speaking Southern regions of Mainland China, especially in Guangzhou, Macau SAR and Hong Kong SAR. Meanwhile, Qing refers to the Mandarin-speaking regions of Northern China, the form that has been adopted worldwide. The exception is Taiwan; in Western script, Taiwanese write Qing, whereas in Chinese script Taiwanese write in traditional Chinese calligraphy which remains in use in the aforementioned Southern Chinese regions.

20. Examples abound. In the early decades of the twentieth century, African masks and industrial objects were appropriated, respectively, by heroic and anarchic avant-garde artists, ultimately leading to their accommodation into art's domain. These events accelerated their integration.

21. I have argued for the recognition of an avant-garde from the so-called 'non-Western' world, rooted in traditional arts (which remain, to this day, the subject of study by the discipline of anthropology). With this text, I suggest that all 'non-Western' art forms remain outside of art history's scope. See Leonor Veiga, *The Third Avant-Garde: Contemporary Art from Southeast Asia Recalling Tradition* (PhD-thesis Leiden University, 2018), openaccess.leidenuniv.nl/handle/1887/62200.

22. Geeta Kapur, 'Dismantled Norms: Apropos Other Avantgardes', *Art and Social Change: Contemporary Art in Asia and the Pacific*, ed. Caroline Turner (Canberra, 2005), p. 58.

23. Ibid., p. 57.

24. Ibid.

25. Anna Brzyski, 'By Whose Rules? Contemporary Art and Geography of Art Historic Significance', *Artl@s Bulletin* 2, no. 1 (2013), pp. 47–50.

26. Kitty Zijlmans, 'Recalcitrant Geographies: National Claims, Transnationalism, and the Institutionalization of Contemporary Art', *Stedelijk Studies Journal*, no. 1 (2014), stedelijkstudies.com/journal/recalcitrant-geographies/.

showing indifference towards so-called 'non-Western' ones.[23] She argued that the fact that the avant-garde remained an unfinished project and its historically conditioned character meant that it would 'appear in various forms in different parts of the world at different times.'[24]

I have argued that if art historians, when analyzing an artwork, prioritize what they see—the artworks' *materiality*, which is often rooted in traditional arts—the Asian avant-garde that Kapur announced would have already been identified. My argument stems from the fact that much art—including Cultural Avant-garde artworks—is frequently supported and described through contextual conditions (e.g., the political situation) which may be concealed within the work (due to the adoption of non-confrontational expressions). By including cultural elements, artists actively show *how* their reality is shaped and convey the complexity of their locus of production, while providing a comment on history. Works such as *Invariable Mountain* also make known that canons (including the Chinese, which cornered its high art on the assumption that it does not contribute to the revolution) are in need of revision. This allows me to suggest that they contribute, in their own terms, to the unfinished avant-garde project while expanding it to include 'non-Western' art.

Today, practicing artists originating from elsewhere have come to contradict the predominance of the Euro-American tradition of art making, while disputing the exclusionary hierarchization of contemporary art.[25] As Dutch art historian Kitty Zijlmans proposes, the abundant art from elsewhere 'cannot simply be added to the existing canons or inserted into prevalent discourses'.[26] Her observation implies that the avant-garde, as the art-historical category that has enabled the extension of art's realm, must be called upon. Not only it is necessary to integrate (re)presentations beyond those that fill exhibitions and museums, it is mandatory that art history accommodates artworks rooted in their own cultural tradition, whatever tradition that may be. Such works, including *Invariable Mountain*, show that while cultural forms contain a passive and an immutable side, they equally comprise a contemporary vitality. This is also observed by Chinese artist Mio

Pang Fei who says that 'change transforms tradition into a relevant entity'.[27] While he reassessed Chinese classical texts to reflect on issues of brotherhood, feminism, and beauty, Ho employs the classical art of jade to comment on environment destruction. Her work meets Kapur's conditions while making known the cosmopolitan artist of today—an individual who is articulate in more than one tradition of making. Through Ho's work, jade is elevated to an 'art' status, thus gaining a place within the field of World Art Studies proposed by Zijlmans and Van Damme.[28] The avant-garde is, as they advanced for art, a pan-human phenomenon that needs to be identified. As such, each Cultural Avant-garde artist must choose which norm(s) to dismantle, so that (cultural) constructs regarded as devoid of critical agency, become relevant again.

With this text, I hope to have enabled a viewer facing a Cultural Avant-garde work to identify it. This means, first, to look for the materiality of the work (which is often rooted in a cultural tradition), second, to consider whether it dismantles totalizing norms, and third, to grasp its inherent critical message of global relevance.

27. Mio Pang Fei, 'Neo-Orientalism', *Review of Culture*, no. 30 (1997), p. 178.

28. *World Art Studies. Exploring Concepts and Approaches*, eds. Kitty Zijlmans and Wilfried van Damme (Amsterdam, 2008).

This work is financed by national funds through the FCT – Foundation for Science and Technology, I.P., under the project CEECIND/01949/2018.

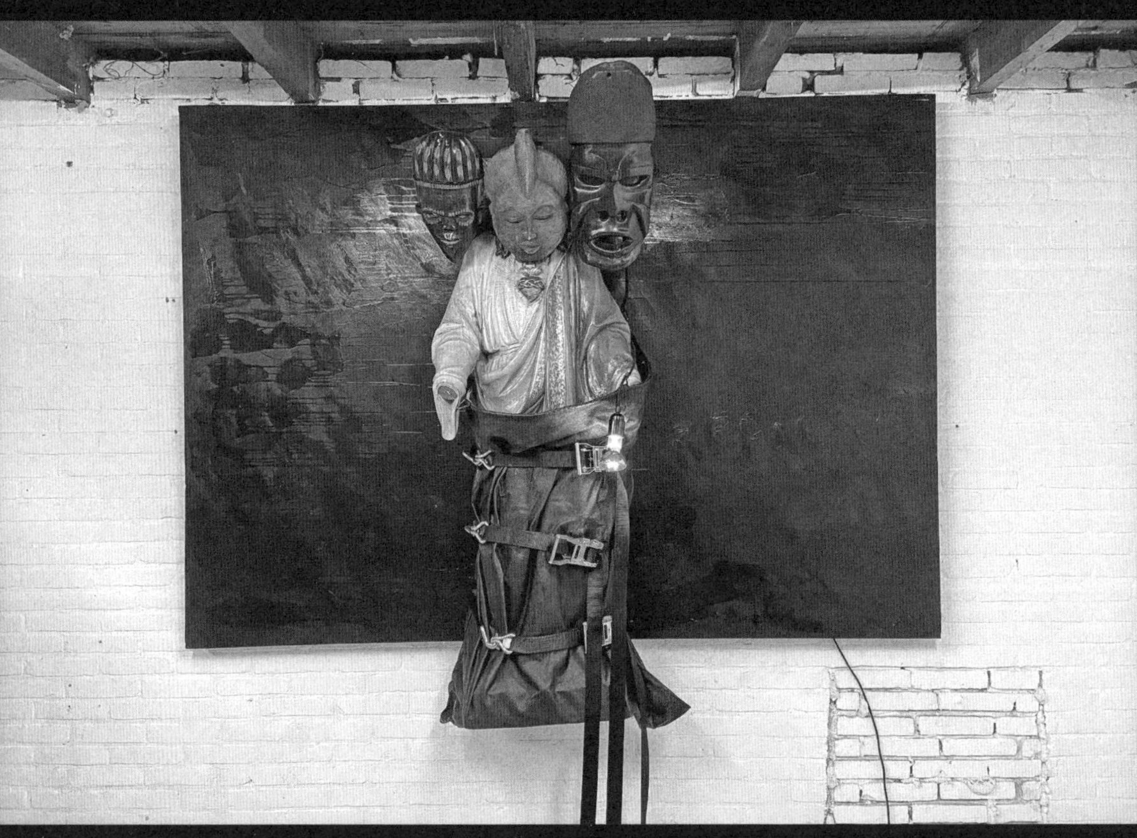

Tirzo Martha, *Represent*, 2020, mixed media.
Photo Tirzo Martha.

EMPTY WORDS TRYING TO OVERCOME A POWERFUL SCULPTURE

Intellectual.
Thinking 3 dimensional.
History, the theater of war and provocation. Only it's a 2 dimensional thought, not enough.
Empathy.
The environment in which history is happening.
Checking out my diary to see if I've missed something out of my own personal history and my interpretation of it.
These last decades people have become obsessed with history. It has become the big reason to justify a lot that's going wrong in our contemporary societies. This incredible, sometimes exaggerated, awareness has led to a broad variety of justifications of this consciousness.
As base, argument and justification of this alertness many quotes by well-known figures in history are being quoted and referred to.
Quotes like: 'Those that fail to learn from history are doomed to repeat it' are very popular. Nowadays the popular one is 'together we write history.'
Is it my objective to define or write my history together with others?
Do I want to write history or do I want to make my present work?
Like who am I or where am I going?
I don't want to fill my existence with words but with deeds.

Where to start.

identity

/ʌɪˈdɛntɪti/

Leren uitspreken

noun

1. the fact of being who or what a person or thing is. 'he knows the identity of the bombers'

2. a close similarity or affinity. 'an identity between the company's own interests and those of the local community'

civil

/ˈsɪv(ə)l/

Leren uitspreken

adjective

1. relating to ordinary citizens and their concerns, as distinct from military or ecclesiastical matters. 'civil aviation'

2. courteous and polite .'they were comparatively *civil to* their daughter'

visual

/ˈvɪʒ(j)ʊəl,ˈvɪzjʊəl/

Leren uitspreken

adjective

1. relating to seeing or sight. 'visual perception'

disobedience

/dɪsəˈbiːdɪəns/

Leren uitspreken

noun

1. failure or refusal to obey rules or someone in authority. 'disobedience to law is sometimes justified'

Title: study for an artwork for art, the artist, art history and the art world

……suddenly art turned into a research based practice.
……suddenly art needs to match the colour of your skin like your curtain matches your sofa.
Art needs to be defined.
In search of the definition of art
Art is…..
Art is…..
Art is…… blah blah blah blah
I can't explain, express or translate it
It's too deep, it's like therapy
Words aren't enough to justify the strength and depth in art
...but I'm an artist
Is that title enough??
Painter
Sculptor
Installations
Video
Performance
Am I one of these disciplines mentioned above? I'm confused and lost in these terms
Lost in translation
Victim.
Minder bedeeld, kans arm, niet bevoorrecht.
Kansen creëren
The ambitions to turn art into science, the ambitions to be able to answer the why? in this once called autonomous practice.
The need to explain and understand.
Mijn zoon van 6 kan het ook!
Ja, maar jij kan het niet papa.
Need.
Urgency.
Relax.
Play.
Critical.
Reflection.
Analyze

Instagram joined Facebook when
Whatsapp died.
Art for art sake.
Contemporary art
World art
Folk art
Museum for modern art
Museum for contemporary art
Museum for folk art
The curator
The art critic

The art historian
The gallery
The collector
Encyclopedia of art
Sounds like a known melody
Does this music match the colour of
my skin,
My background,
Or is my taste misplaced
What's the difference between André
Hazes, de Jeugd van Tegenwoordig,
Jay-Z, 50 Cent, Sex Pistols, Dead
Kennedys, Mozart, Bach, Beethoven,
Wagner, Holst, Wilbrandt, Philip
Glass, Arvo Pärt, Miles Davis, Butch
Morris, Edith Piaf, Compay Segundo,
Bob Marley, Celia Cruz, Kassav,
Molotov and Doble R?

Tirzo Martha, *Represent*, 2020, mixed media.
Photo Tirzo Martha.

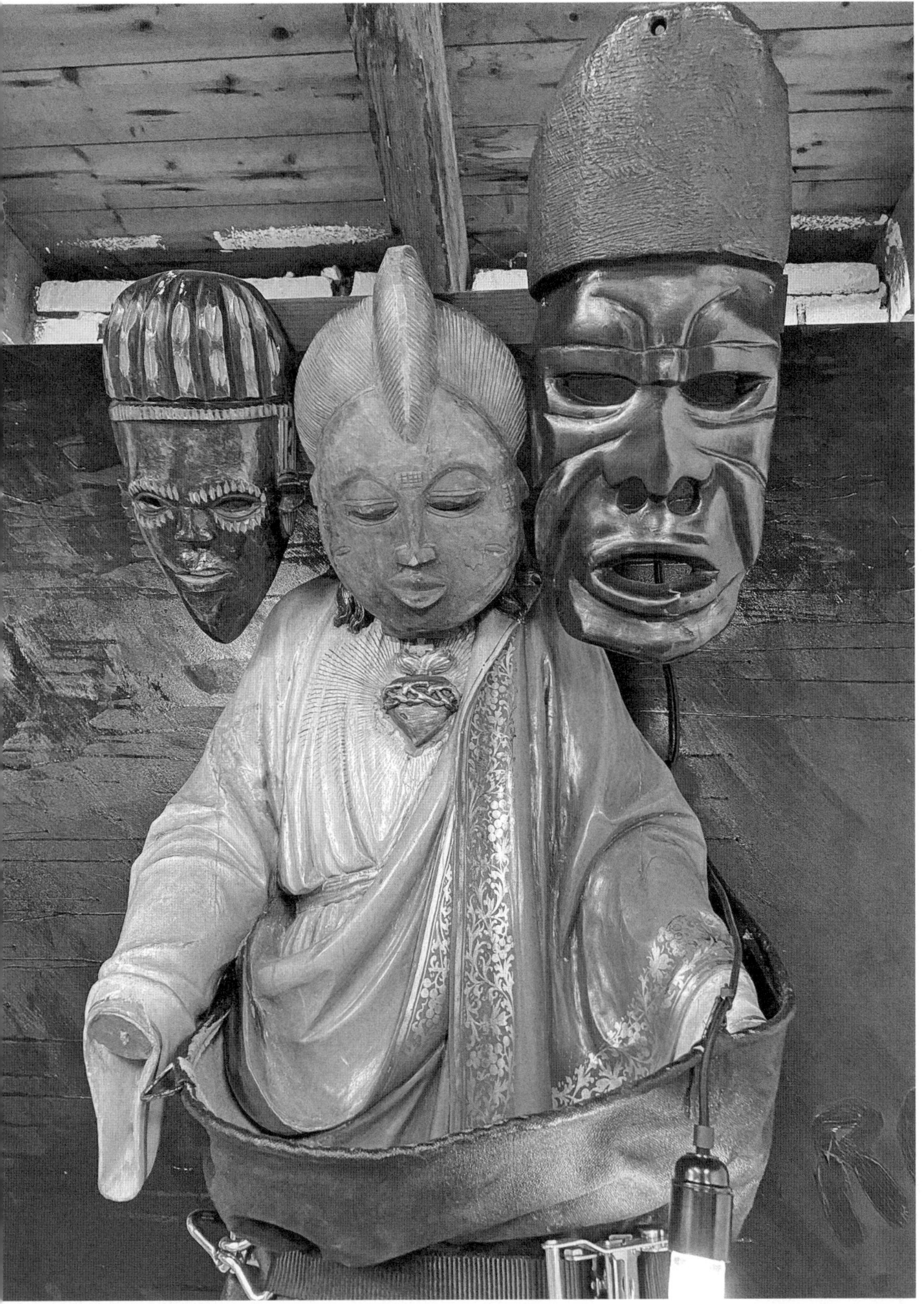

Does this mean I'm ignorant?
Because I don't know the differences?
Am I not aware of it?
....of what's happening in the world?
.....of what's happening in my country?
....my house?
......my car?
....my museum?
...my family?
To be aware
Aware of what?
Colonialism
Slavery
Colour of your skin
Black lives matter
What happened to the other lives?
Is the colour really a reflection of who
I am or who you are?
Or of what you represent?
Is it like your flag?
No, but it sounds SEXY!

resilient
/rɪˈzɪlɪənt/

Leren uitspreken

adjective
1. (of a person or animal) able to withstand or recover quickly from difficult conditions. 'babie are generally far more resilient than new parents realize'
2. (of a substance or object) able to recoil or spring back into shape after bending, stretching, or being compressed.
'a shoe with resilient cushioning'

Is it a way to measure what you're capable of or represent?

Represent.......
Black artist is........
Black art is..............
Barack Obama
First black president.
...o sorry, first Afro American president
First black first lady in White House
O.k. let's start: Buy black made
Buy black owned
Buy black history
Black achievement
B.E.T.
White privilege
Psychological blackmail?

Frighten
Demoralized

....this is placed wrong. I'll come back to this part.....
Moriaantje zo zwart als roet ging eens wandelen zonder hoed.....
Apologize
Who is going to apologize to who?

Is Trump going to apologize? ...oh yeah, he has pardoned a few black rappers

Agree.
Disagree.
Agree to disagree
Victimisation
Science fiction
True story
Based on true events
.........but some of the characters are fictional
Can our past also be fiction?
Or is this only possible with the imaginations of our future?
By the way, my present feels and looks like fiction.
America, America
Hey look can you see...
future, past, present, future or present, past, future?
Social engagement.
Inclusive
Live vest under center armrest
By the way, Sinterklaas.
De zak van Sinterklaas, Sinterklaas, Sinterklaas
De zak van Sinterklaas oh jongens, jongens ....
Here we go again: zwarte Piet
Black face
Veeg Piet
Kleur Piet
Ik mis Piet
Once upon a time,
..a long time ago.
A time that we cannot imagine that it was possible to have existed
Someone invented history
A fist full of Dollars
Avatar
Star Wars, was it invented by George Lucas or Ronald Reagan?
Who inspired who?
Maybe Stanley Kubrick inspired Neil Armstrong or was it the other way around?

Academisch kwartiertje

Inflation calculator
De bedenkers van leugens
Baat het niet dan schaadt het niet
Hunger for reality
Intention of the speaker and reception of the hearer.
Have no power but filled with opinions
Sardonicism
Fuck is part of our protected speech, we have the right to say it.
To have a future in the past
How can I save my past with my future
Kids paradise Rooseveltweg
Kracht van verscheidenheid in de expertise
Management by speech
Chief art officer
Face tune
Systemic racism
Aspirational look
Duurzaam
Creative independence
Random
Real
Coherent
Consistent
Reality
Truth
Wishful thinking
Tradition
Culture
Folklore
Subjective
Waardig bestaan

I'm a perfectionist...

pretending to be a Perfectionist without the knowledge of what perfectionism contains and is Meanwhile, as soon as we make a mistake we seek our refuge in the fact that we are deficient creatures

Plastisch impuls
Self determination
Anthropological damage
Overcoming modern art
Starting over and over again
Tradition
Ideology
Conservatism
Consumerism
Social art

Inclusion sustainability

Social sculpture
Social change?
Change of reality?
Which reality?
..... oh the reality presented by politics, social media or your ego?
In what kind of economy are we living in?
Is it forgiving?
Is it accusing?
Is it causing?
One of power and materialistic greed and nonsense.
Politicization through art
Liberalism
Desire for freedom without activism
Coverup for a poverty of spirit
Institutional art world
Empty Rhetoric
Radical
Joint task in order to answer and resolve
Protocol
Dialogue
Human thought structure
Other persons
Fractioning humanity

Sent from my iPhone

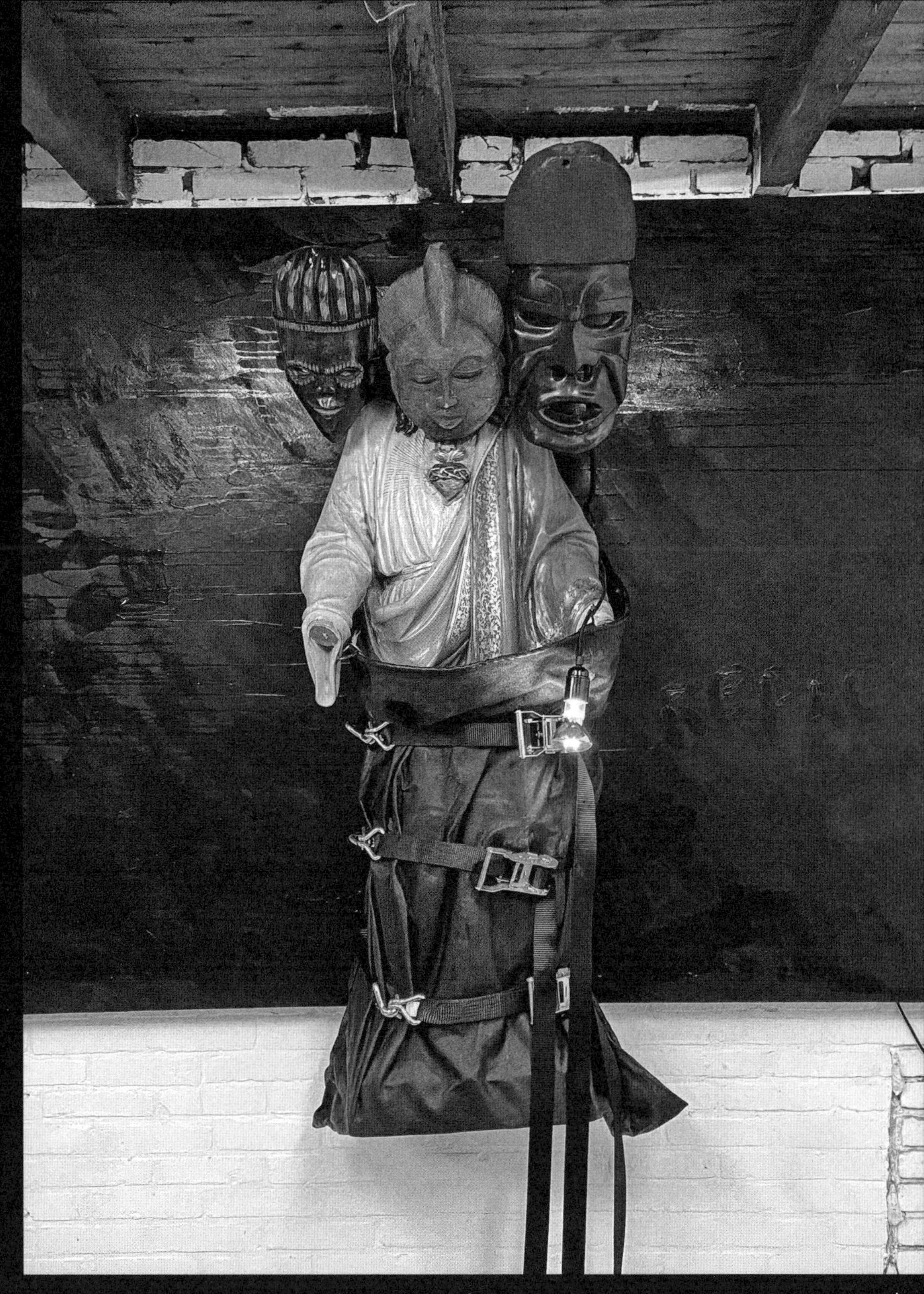

Tirzo Martha, *Represent*, 2020, mixed media.
Photo Tirzo Martha.

ON EXHIBITIONS

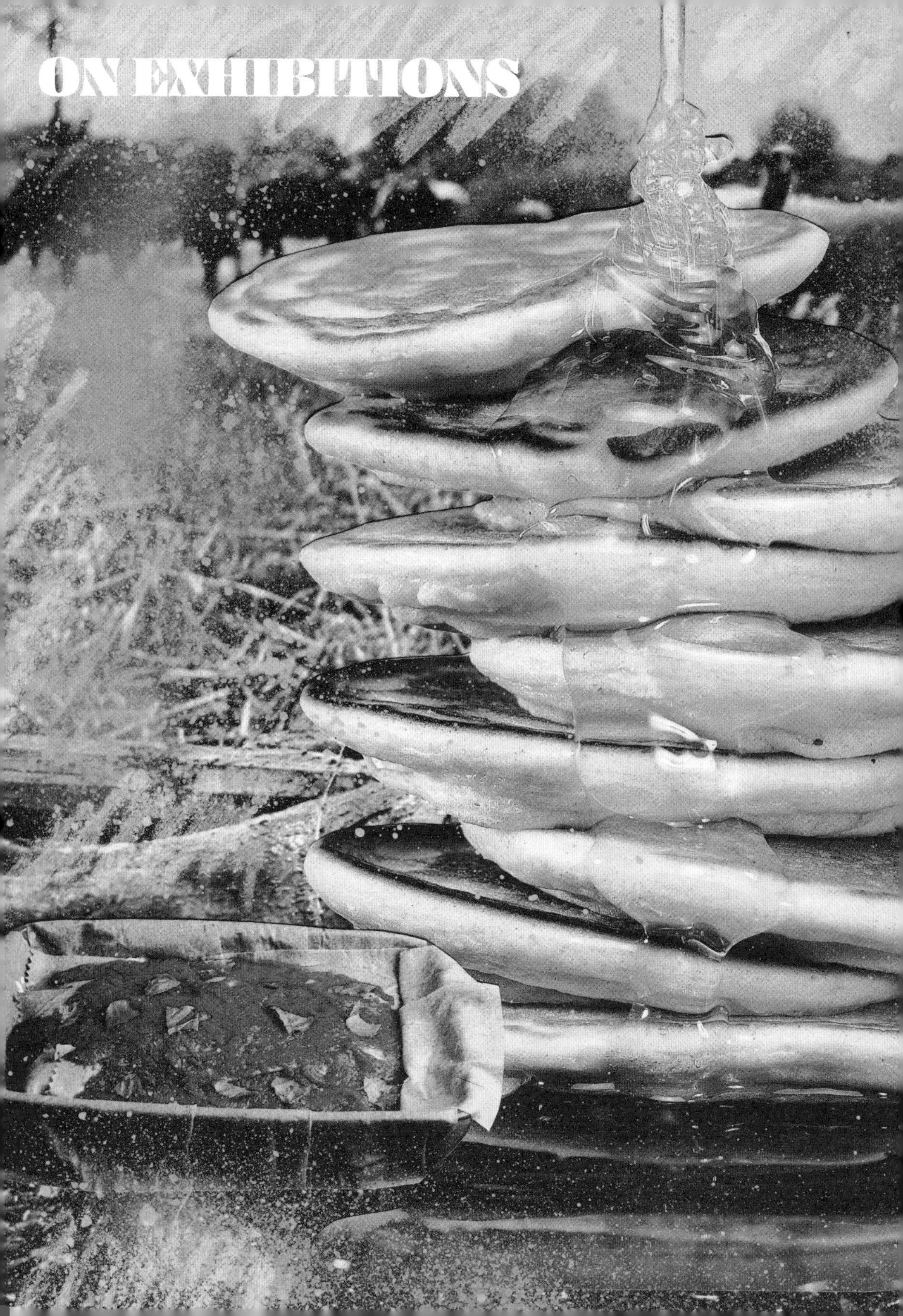

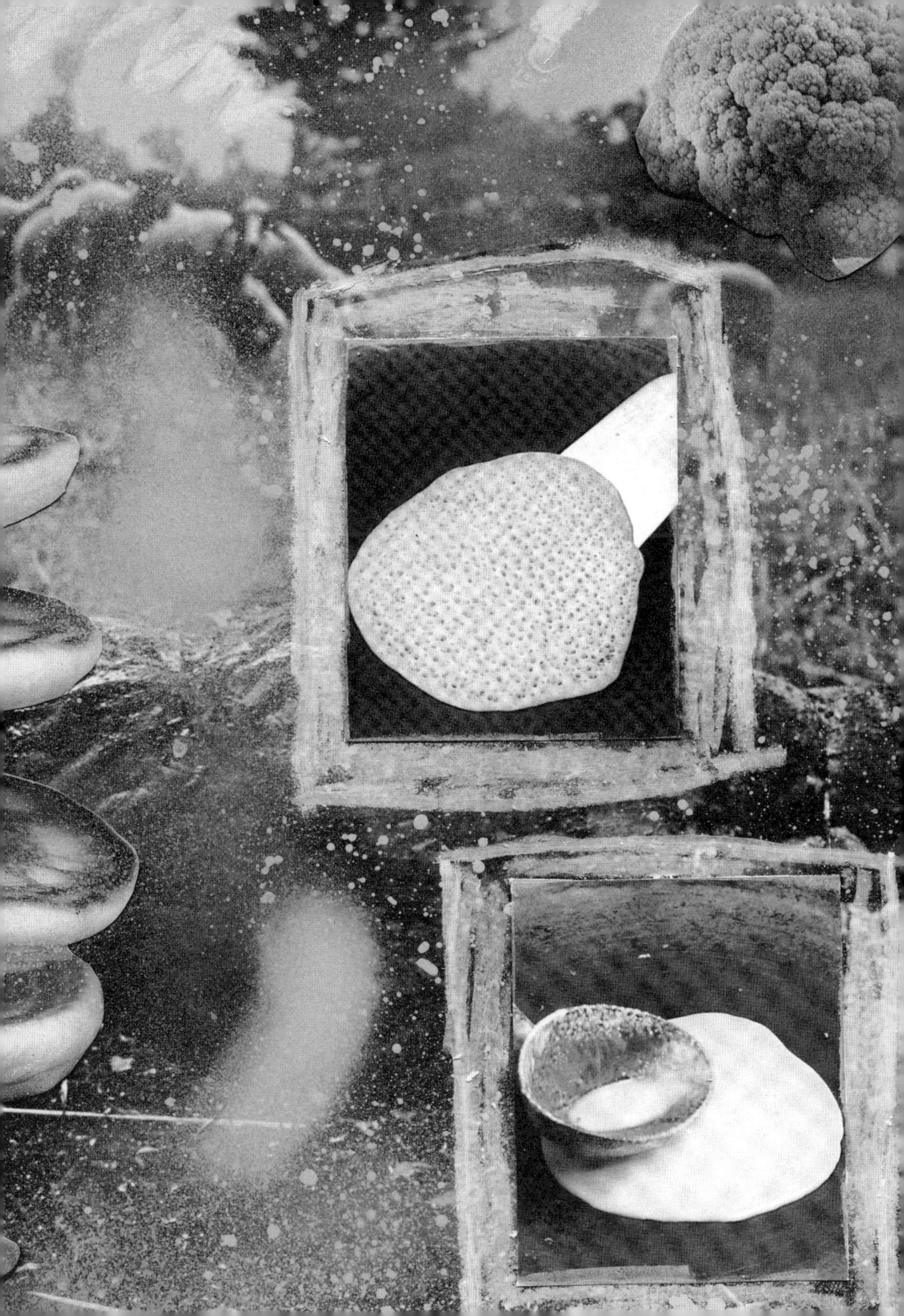

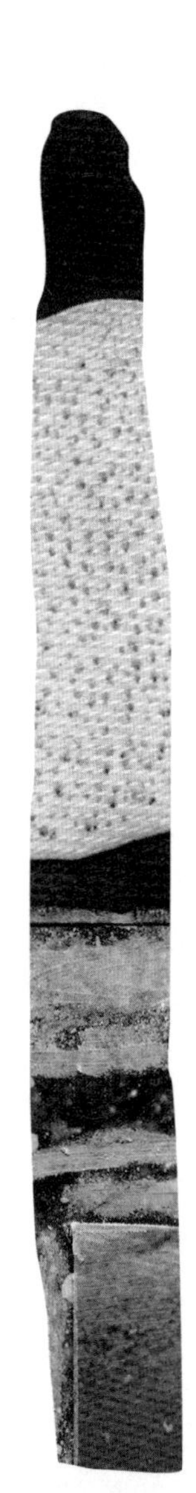

DISHING UP COLONIALISM An Innovative Curatorial Approach to Dutch Colonial History

Anja Novak

INGREDIENTS AND RECOMMENDED KITCHEN PRACTICES[1]:

- 4 maps
- 3 cookbooks and 1 botanical book
- A museum that is open to innovative and experimental curatorial approaches
- A devoted curatorial team with a broad range of expertise and skills
- A strong curatorial concept that helps to let the objects speak
- A collective commitment to transparency regarding the institutional framework and the curatorial team's positionality

Sometimes harsh conditions produce astonishing results. If someone would have told me they were planning to organize an exhibition on the loaden subject of colonialism within a month's time, with a curatorial team consisting of fifteen graduate students, who will only be able to communicate via Zoom and other means of telecommunication, I would have thought they must be joking. But they weren't. This essay is written in celebration of what a team of creative and diligent young scholars and their dedicated supervisors have accomplished under the grim circumstances of the Covid-19 pandemic. It offers a reflection on their innovative curatorial approach to the charged subject of Dutch colonialism.

'From Cartography to Cookbooks. A Web of Dutch Colonialism' is an online exhibition that addresses

1. Cooking is not just a matter of putting ingredients together. To prepare a successful dish we also need a well-equipped kitchen, a devoted chef and kitchen crew, and teamwork. Therefore, this recipe also includes advice on kitchen practices.

life practices of Dutch colonizers in the so-called East-Indies, as well as the views and ideas that these practices epitomize. The exhibition is on view on the website of the Amsterdam-based Allard Pierson Museum—which houses the heritage collections of the University of Amsterdam—from 28 January to 31 December 2021.[2] The exhibition has been conceptualized and constructed by students enrolled in the graduate course Museum Studies at the University of Amsterdam, supervised by Colin Sterling (Assistant Professor Memory and Museums at the University of Amsterdam) and Laurien de Gelder (Curator Ancient Greek World and Near East at Allard Pierson). 'From Cartography to Cookbooks' takes the online visitor on an adventurous, surprising, and often cringeworthy journey to the Indonesian regions that were incrementally colonized by the Dutch from the late sixteenth century onwards. Focusing on a selection of ordinary objects, the exhibition offers astonishing insights into the structural underpinnings of Dutch colonial society.

The exhibition's main curatorial strategy is to address a complex and highly-charged subject through a selection of seemingly plain objects. Maps and cookbooks seem to make an odd pair, given their utilitarian functions in rather different domains of life. Yet their connection to colonialism is evident. Cartography is a profession that was vital to the colonial enterprise as maps were instrumental in gaining access to and control over foreign territories.[3] The cookbooks—aimed at a Dutch public living in the Netherlands and/or in the East-Indies—show how Dutch cuisine was influenced by Indonesian spices, such as pepper, cinnamon, cloves, mace, and nutmeg. The desire to control trade in these exotic spices was the engine that drove Dutch colonial expeditions to these regions. Cookbooks also convey information about domestic life practices in the colonies and the values that they epitomize. In spite of their humble appearance, cookbooks turn out to be rich and revealing historical resources.[4]

The differences between the two types of objects allow the curators to address multiple aspects of what they call 'the web of Dutch colonialism'. Conceptually, this web is addressed through three themes: space, environment, and gender. Each theme, in its turn, is further analyzed by means of a characteristic dichotomy: public versus private

2. To view the exhibition, visit this website: www.fromcartographytocookbooks.com/

3. On mapping as a means of exercising and legitimizing Western hegemony, see Nicholas Mirzoeff, *The Right to Look: A Counterhistory of Visuality* (Durham/London, 2011). On mapping as a globally employed practice of exploration, see Felipe Fernández-Armesto, *Pathfinders: A Global History of Exploration* (New York/London, 2007).

4. On the connection between food and colonialism, see Michael Dietler, 'Culinary Encounters: Food, Identity, and Colonialism', *The Archeology of Food and Identity*, ed. Katheryn Twiss (Carbondale, 2007), pp. 218-242.

5. www.fromcartographytocookbooks.com/menu/exhibition, accessed on 25 March 2021.

space, natural versus cultural environmental features, and male versus female spheres of life. The exhibition shows that these oppositions were inherent in the colonial system and reinforced clear divides within society. It also shows how these dichotomies were interconnected: together they formed a complex web that sustained power relations on which the colonial system was built.

The items on display epitomize these dichotomies in various ways. For instance, maps were usually commissioned by male administrative and military officers and designed by male cartographers, who often accompanied particular expeditions. Not only were maps instrumental in gaining access to foreign territories, they also symbolize the colonizers' endeavour of imposing their own culture upon an environment that they perceived as being in a 'natural' state of primitivity. The private households in which cookbooks were used, were less accessible, and perceived as a predominantly female domain. Yet by literally reflecting the growing Dutch taste for exotic flavours, the cookbooks show how public and private interests were intimately connected and mutually reinforcing. As the curators state in the exhibition: 'Mapping and cookbooks transformed the natural Indonesian environment into a "cultured" space for Dutch colonizers.'[5]

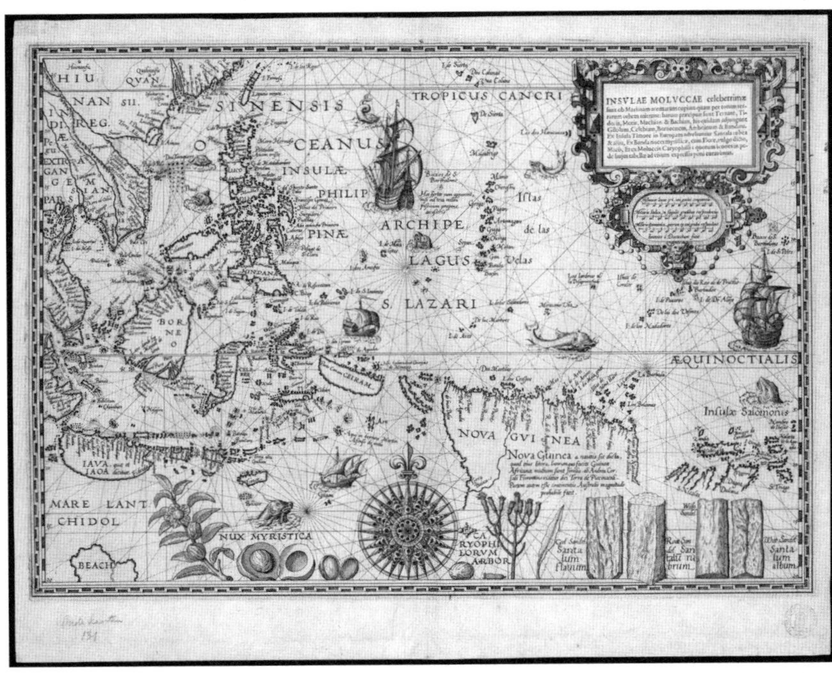

Petrus Plancius, *Insulae Moluccae* [...], 1592–94, copper engraving, 37 × 53.5 cm, scale c. 1:14,000,000. Courtesy Allard Pierson, Amsterdam.

The limited number of objects on display—four maps, three cookbooks and one illustrated book on botany—encourages visitors to explore these objects in detail.[6] The four maps cover a time period from the mid-sixteenth century up to the third decade of the twentieth century. With their elaboration and striking differences, they illustrate profound changes that cartography underwent during the colonial era, as well as the leading position of the Dutch in this profession. *Insulae Moluccae*, designed by Petrus Plancius in 1592–1594, was the most geographically correct representation of the Maluku Islands of its time. It is adorned with fantastic creatures of the sea, Dutch ships, and images of the exotic spices that enticed the Dutch to explore and dominate these regions. The fact that the map was based on Portuguese manuscripts that were stolen by Dutch spies illustrates the severe competitiveness of the colonial enterprise. Made only four years later, Willem Lodewijcksz.'s *Nova tabula insularum lavae*, a map of Borneo, Java, Sumatra, and Malacca from 1598, hits a slightly different tone as it features the Dutch colonizers' perceptions of indigenous populations. As a member and chronicler of the first Dutch voyage of the East-Indies, Willem Lodewijcksz. keenly observed the customs and ways of living of the locals, which are depicted in a number of panels on the top right of the map. The depicted scenes, relating to local customs of jurisdiction, power display, intercultural trade, and shipbuilding, make a striking

6. The texts accompanying the main exhibition section are kept brief. Additional historical information and reading suggestions are provided in the 'Archive' section of the exhibition. All information in this essay is obtained from these two sections, unless otherwise stated.

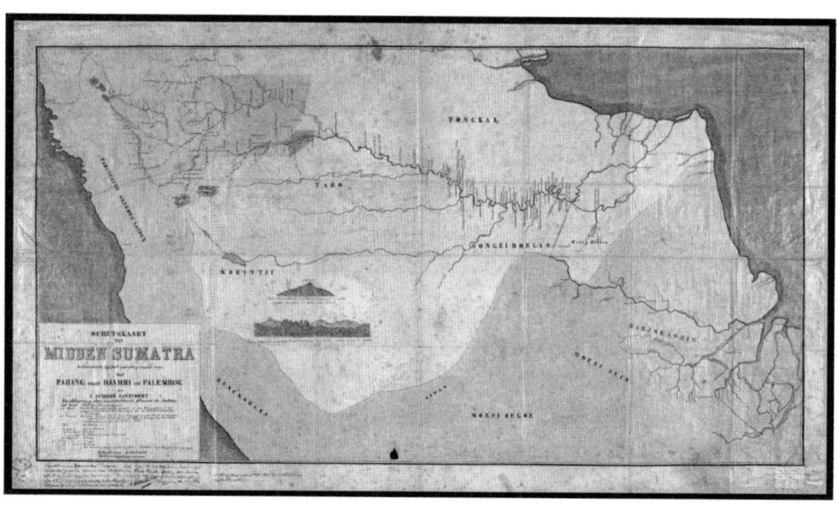

Willem Lodewijcksz., *Nova tabula insularum lavae, Sumatrae, Borneonis et aliarum Malaccam* [...], c. 1598, copper engraving, 36.5 × 52 cm, scale c. 1:5,230,000. Courtesy Allard Pierson, Amsterdam.

contrast with later perceptions of colonized peoples as primitive, lazy, and uncivilized.

Produced almost 280 years later, naval officer Johannes Santvoort's *Sketch Map of Central Sumatra* from 1877 is directly linked to a particular military operation. The map was drawn during the first government-sanctioned expedition to Central Sumatra, a region to which the Dutch did not yet have access. This expedition was explicitly likened at its time to the 'discovery' and 'conquest' of the African continent by European imperialist nations, an enterprise that was about to enter into its most aggressive and reckless phase. In that sense this tranquil map with its abstract and seemingly rational visual language can be read as foreshadowing the unknown atrocities that were committed by avaricious European imperialistic powers in various parts of the world.

The section on maps closes with a *Map of the Dutch East and West Indies* from 1932, designed by S.C. Bruins. With its high degree of detailing, this map exemplifies the astounding progression that cartography made in the course of time. As part of a collection entitled 'Our Colonies' the map brings together the geographically widespread parts of the Dutch national territory of that time. Visually, as well as through the use of pronouns such as 'ours', the maps belonging to this collection express the idea of a geographically dispersed yet fortunately unified nation, suppressing not only profound cultural differences within that nation but its history of violent domination, exploitation and deportation of colonized populations.

The cookbooks cover a smaller period of time than the maps. The earliest cookbook on display was published in 1803 by J.B. Elwe and J.L. Werlingshoff and bears the funny title *Aaltje, de volmaakte en zuinige keukenmeid* [Aaltje, the perfect and frugal kitchen maid]. The woman featured in the title, and directly addressing the reader in the preface, is probably a fictional character that embodies Dutch female virtues such as frugality and diligence. While the cookbook was published in Amsterdam, it contains a remarkable number of recipes that include spices sourced from the Dutch East-Indies. It demonstrates the profound influence of colonialism on Dutch cuisine, which is palpable to this day. An intriguing contemporary addition to the cookbook section in the exhibition is a wrap of a package with a herbal blend for *nasi goreng* (a fried rice dish) by the Dutch brand Conimex. Products of this brand can be found in almost every kitchen cupboard in the Netherlands. One wonders how many consumers will be aware of the fact that Conimex was founded in 1932, at a time when Dutch colonial dominance in Indonesia was particularly prominent.

Next on display is *Oost-Indisch Kookboek* [East-Indian Cookbook]. It had several editions, each of which contains new recipes that reflect the increasing influence of

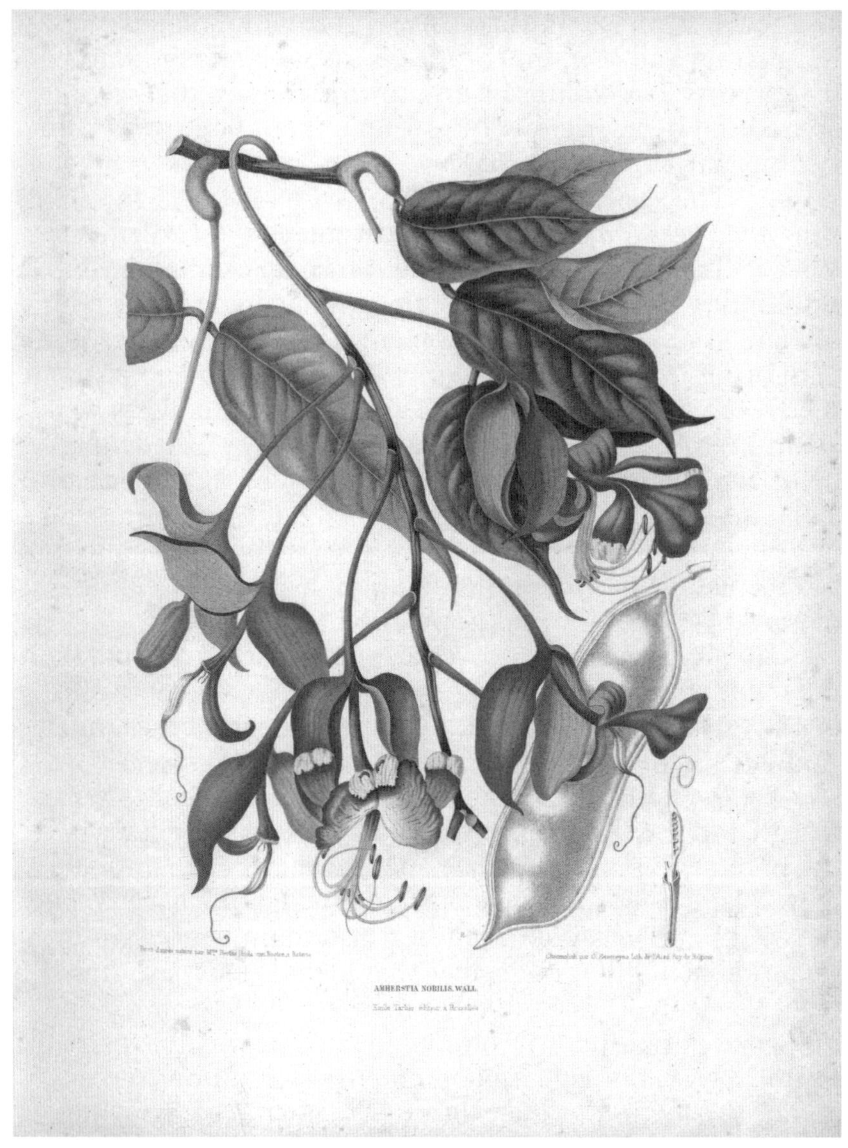

A page from Berthe Hoola van Nooten, *Fleurs, Fruit, et Feuillage Choisis de la Flore et de la Pomone de L'Île de Java*, 1863, chromolithograph by Guillaume Severeyns, 57 cm. Courtesy Allard Pierson, Amsterdam.

7. On the complex connection between food, eating habits, and colonial identities in the Dutch East-Indies, see Susie Protschky, 'The Colonial Table: Food, Culture and Dutch Identity in Colonial Indonesia', *The Australian Journal of Politics and History* 54, no. 3 (2008-2009), pp. 346-357.

8. On women's contribution to botanical illustration, see Heather Pardoe and Maureen Lazarus, 'Celebrating the Contribution of Women to the History of Botanical Illustration', *Collections* 14, no. 4 (2018), pp. 545–566.

the Dutch in the East-Indies. The exhibition features a copy of the second edition, published by G.C.T. van Dorp & Co in Semarang, Java, in 1870. Written in Dutch, it was clearly aimed at a Dutch public living in the East-Indies, as many recipes are based on local ingredients, spices, and cooking commodities. The recipes also show an increasing fusion of traditional Dutch and local tastes and eating habits.[7] Indonesian cuisine also prevails in *Kokki Bitja* [Cook or Kitchen Maid Bitja], the only book in the exhibition written in Bahasa Indonesia, although the spelling of the words adheres to Dutch phonetics. Originally published in 1850, this popular cookbook had its fifth, revised edition in 1859, published by Batavia-based publishing house Land & Co. It contains an editorial note in Dutch to commemorate the death of the author, a woman referred to as Nonna Cornelia [Miss or Misses Cornelia]. According to the obituary Nonna Cornelia had recently passed away under remarkable circumstances: she had suffered a nervous fit followed by a heart attack while failing to produce a perfect *kwee broeder*, a particular type of cake. As the editors suggest with a wink, her unlikely failing may have been caused by a neglected dish that sabotaged the preparation of the *kwee broeder* out of jealousy. This odd obituary, together with a print on the cover that shows Indonesian servants at work in a kitchen, suggests that the cookbook was aimed at Dutch households that employed Indonesian cooks. Even a hands-on collection of recipes such as *Kokki Bitja* reveals a strict social hierarchy, as well as a patronizing attitude of Dutch colonizers toward local people, who were perceived as servants to use and make fun of.

A stranger in the midst of the cookbooks is *Fleurs, Fruit, et Feuillage Choisis de L'Île de Java* [Flowers, Fruits, and Plants, Chosen from the Island of Java], a richly illustrated botanical volume that contains chromolithographs of original drawings of indigenous plants, flowers, and fruits. It was compiled by Berthe Hoola van Nooten, a Dutch schoolmistress, botanist and illustrator, who, after she had been widowed, relocated to Java together with her five children to live with her brother. The book, first published in 1863 with support of Queen Sophie Mathilde of the Netherlands, was Van Nooten's *magnum opus*.[8] It enchants the reader with its beautiful, detailed images and accompanying texts that, apart from minute descriptions of the depicted specimen, offer information on their various uses, particularly also in indigenous culture and cuisine. The eloquent preface is strikingly honest about the authors difficult economic, social, and emotional situation. It is explicitly addressed to female readers, whom the author hopes to inspire to study the riches and beauties of God's creation. Van Nooten plays down her scholarly achievement to avoid accusations of immodesty and of overplaying her hand.[9] The text evokes a struggle with women's position in society that many contemporary women will recognize. Yet *Fleurs, Fruit, et Feuillage…* is also the creation of an educated woman with connections in the highest ranks of colonial society. These privileges allowed her to produce what might be seen as a different kind of map, which provided its European readers access to the beauties and utilities of Indonesian flora.

Whose Narrative?

Looking at the selection of objects highlighted in this exhibition one can marvel and wince at what they reveal about the structural underpinnings of Dutch colonialism. What an object can tell you, clearly depends on the questions you ask, but it also depends on who is doing the questioning. This is pointed out in the closing section of the exhibition, called 'Positionality'. Here, the curators state that a person's experiential history, ethnicity and social position influence the way they perceive the world.[10] They invite visitors to reflect on how their own position and identity shapes their interpretation of the objects.[11] Yet they also critically reflect on their own positionality, as well as on the institutional framework in which the exhibition has taken shape. The Allard Pierson Museum, they state, is a Eurocentric institution with a predominantly white staff, which is reflected by its collections and exhibition history. It is important to keep in mind that the objects in the present exhibition represent the colonizer's perspective on colonial society and the colonized regions, but not that of the indigenous populations. The lack of indigenous views and voices is addressed in a podcast in which three of the curators—Nadine Joinville, Naema Abdi, and Steffi Stouri—discuss the topic of positionality. They regret not having had enough time to

9. On associations of botany and femininity in the nineteenth century, see Sam George, 'Unveiling the Mysteries of Vegetation: Botany and the Feminine', *Botany, Sexuality, and Women's Writing 1760–1830: From Modest Shoot to Forward Plant* (Manchester, 2017), pp. 43–80.

10. Positionality is a concept coined in the field of Human Geography. It addresses the relation between people's geographical, historical, and social position, their views and values, and their understanding of the world. See Luis Sánchez, 'Positionality', *Encyclopedia of Geography*, ed. Barney Warf (Thousand Oaks, 2010). Gillian Rose, 'Situated Knowledges: Positionality, Reflexivities and Other Tactics', *Progress in Human Geography* 21 (June 1997), pp. 305-320.

11. Clearly, my own positionality (European but non-Dutch background, woman, scholar, single parenting mother, keen gardener) has shaped my readings of the objects at display.

engage with Indonesian communities to set up forms of collaboration or look into examples of counter-mapping.[12] They also reflect on how their own backgrounds and origins shape their perception of the selected materials. Visitors are rarely offered such an honest glimpse into the 'kitchen' of heritage institutions.

The strong commitment to transparency articulated in the podcast ties in with the curators' decision to not make generalizing claims about Dutch colonial history but present the chosen materials in a way that triggers visitors to start asking questions themselves; not only about the colonial past but also about how certain ideas, customs, and even tastes inherited from it still shape much of the contemporary world. The exhibition crucially manifests a learning process, for the curating team as much as for the visitors. As Colin Sterling suggested, university collections seem to offer exceptional opportunities for such experimental, learning-centred curatorial approaches.[13]

12. On counter-mapping in Indonesia, see Nancy Lee Peluso, 'Whose Woods are These? Counter-Mapping Forest Territories in Kalimantan, Indonesia', *Antipode* 27, no. 4 (1995), pp. 383–406. Lisa Tilley, '"The impulse is cartographic": Counter-mapping Indonesia's Resource Frontiers in the Context of Coloniality', *Antipode* 52, no. 5 (2020), pp. 1434-1454.

13. Personal conversation with Colin Sterling, 30 March 2021.

The Curatorial Team and their Tasks

Interpretation: Arjun Chandramouli, Kelly Willersen, Marny Garcia Mommertz, Pauline Duijndam.

Project Management: Nadine Joinville, Anna-Rosa van Wees.

Design and Digital: Steffi Stouri, Richard Weaver, Henriette Bloema, Camiel de Kom.

Communications and Engagement: Naema Abdi, Zeynep Özçelik, Tara Khalili, Stien Wouters. Supervision: Colin Sterling, Laurien de Gelder.

I would like to thank the curatorial team for providing this learning experience; Colin Sterling, Steffi Stouri and Anna-Rosa van Wees for sharing with me their thoughts on developing this exhibition; Laurien de Gelder, Charlotte Kleyn and Reinder Storm at Allard Pierson for making available the illustrations; and Marijke Lampaert for proofreading. Most of all I would like to thank my teacher, supervisor, and colleague Kitty Zijlmans for being an inexhaustible source of knowledge, inspiration, guidance, and encouragement.

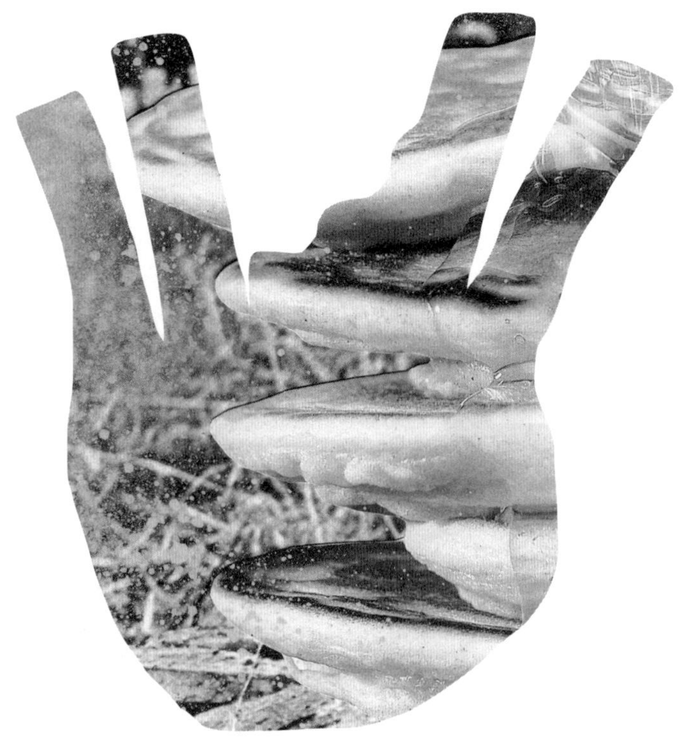

BLACK ART MATTERS
The Successful Branding of Black Lives Matter

Rob Perrée

INGREDIENTS

- Storytelling
- Branding
- Exposure
- Engagement
- Political Awareness
- African American Art

> If you deal with contemporary art, it is self-evident that many of the most interesting artists are African American. And you realize that there were always important African American artists, even if they were not as visible to museums as they should have been. So then you need to address that as well.

This statement was made by Glenn Lowry in an article published on *artnet* on 20 September 2018. Lowry had been the director of New York's Museum of Modern Art (MoMA) ever since 1995 and it had taken him over twenty years to reach this conclusion. Throughout the 1990s, his museum had virtually ignored Black artists, even though a number of them were attracting great interest at precisely that time.

In 1995 I spent time in New York working on a book and exhibition about African American art. The previous year, Harvard professor Henry Louis Gates had published an article in *Time* magazine highlighting the upsurge in Black culture, especially in literature, music and the visual arts.[1] He coined the term 'Black Renaissance', echoing the name 'Harlem Renaissance', used to describe the initial flowering of 'New Negro' culture in the largely Black Harlem neighbourhood of New York in the 1910s and 1920s. His article tickled my curiosity. Whilst I had no reason to doubt what he said, I felt an urge to demonstrate that it was true. I set myself the task of doing so.

1. Henry Louis Gates, 'Black Creativity: on the Cutting Edge', *Time* magazine (10 October 1994).

In the late 1980s, the American art market had suffered a large-scale collapse. Prices and reputations had become over-inflated. The media had conferred a celebrity status on artists that was at odds with reality. When the bubble burst, galleries and artists had to fire staff and assistants. But, as top *New York Times* art critic Holland Cotter says:

> After Black Monday in October 1987 the art was gone too, and with the market in disarray and gate-keepers confused, entrenched barriers came down. Black, Latino and Asian-American artists finally took center stage and fundamentally redefined American art.[2]

Cynical as it may sound, the downfall of some provided an opportunity for others. Galleries suddenly became interested in Black artists: they were not only easy to recruit, but—very importantly—cheap. To disguise this banal motivation, it was often claimed that the welcome given to Black artists was due to a growing interest in politically and socially engaged art.

For whatever reason, galleries opened their doors to artists such as Kara Walker, Glenn Ligon, Carrie Mae Weems, Kerry James Marshall, Gary Simmons, Lorna Simpson, Fred Wilson, Lyle Ashton Harris, and Leonardo Drew—the first generation of Black artists to gain entry to the 'official' art circuit.

Was this positive development a reflection of changes in the social position of Black Americans? Hardly. Gates makes this clear not only in the article mentioned above, but also in the preface he wrote for the Whitney Museum of American Art's 1994 catalogue for the exhibition 'Black Male'.[3] He points out that the existence of a growing Black middle class meant that there were not only more Blacks in decision-making positions on the production side of the cultural industries, but—not insignificantly—more African Americans affluent enough to form a growing Black audience for the arts.

Nevertheless, racism and racial discrimination remained the daily reality; police violence against Blacks was still common; the prisons were full of predominantly

2. Holland Cotter, 'The boom is over, long live the art!', *New York Times* (12 February 2009).

3. Henry Louis Gates, 'Preface', *Black Male: Representations of Masculinity in Contemporary American Art* (New York, 1995), pp. 11–14.

Black youths; murder was the leading cause of death among young Black men; and there was huge Black poverty, while ninety-five percent of those running the country were white and ninety percent of the nation's wealth accrued to white Americans. Gates suggested that this deplorable situation was the driver of the defiant ambition shown by many Blacks. I doubt whether many people shared his optimism.

At the time, there was no widespread awareness of these facts. The choice of Black artists was not bred of any shared consciousness that the time had come to award them equal treatment. That would come later. Had it been the case then, galleries and museums would also have shown works by previous generations. They did so only incidentally. For a long time, Black artists of the past were largely ignored. But having a contemporary Black artist in its stable made a gallery look cool and avant-garde; it was simply a matter of salesmanship.

The 'Black Renaissance' must therefore be seen as no more than a tentative step in the right direction. The number of Black exhibitions remained modest and Black art continued to account for only a small proportion of the works in public and private collections. Whereas twelve percent of the US population was black, museum representation remained for a long time at less than five percent.

The First Exhibition: 'Postcards from Black America: Contemporary African American Art'

To create the overview of contemporary African American art that I had in mind, I was able to take my pick of works by this promising and exceptionally talented generation. I never imagined then that they would, almost without exception, become such stars of the art world.

In the Netherlands, they were still attracting little or no interest, as I would soon learn to my cost.

My exhibition 'Postcards from Black America. Contemporary African American Art' opened in late 1998 at De Beyerd in Breda. It featured work by twenty artists, including Kara Walker, David Hammons, Jean-Michel

Basquiat, and Kerry James Marshall. Early the following year it moved to the Frans Hals Museum in Haarlem.

The opening was thronged but after that 'Postcards…' attracted few visitors. Press coverage was limited to two reviews in national dailies. The book sold few copies. Museum Arnhem was the only other Dutch museum showing an interest in contemporary African American art and, to my amazement, staff at the Mondriaan Foundation

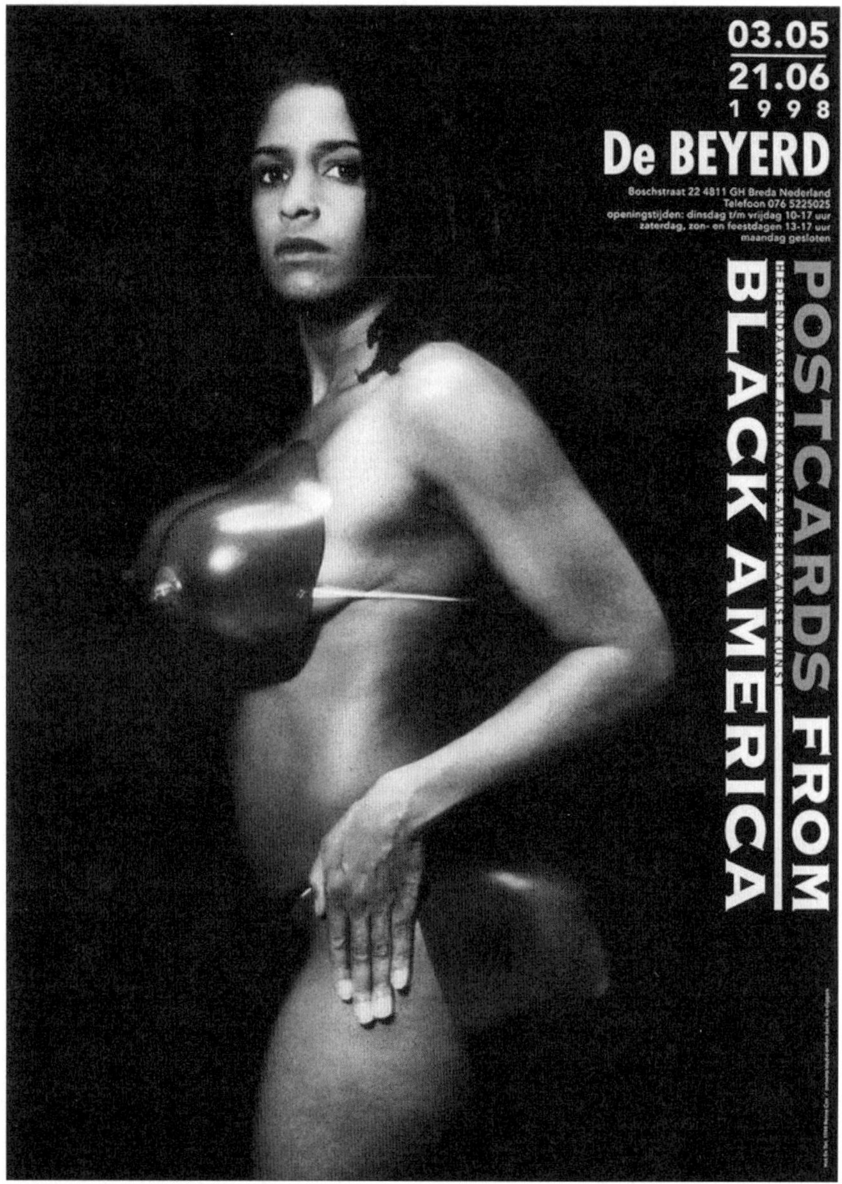

'Postcards from Black America. Contemporary African American Art', 1998, De Beyerd, Breda.

(the Netherland's main public fund for visual art) had advised me not to apply for subsidy for 'Postcards…' because 'who would be interested in Black art from America?' I was dismayed to discover that they were right. My mission to promote Black American art in the Netherlands had failed. The time was not yet ripe.

U-turn?

For a long time, Black artists continued to play only a minor role in the mainstream American art world. It was not until after 2010 that this began to change, at first gradually but after 2015 with increasing speed. Several factors were involved.

Firstly, Nigerian-born curator Okwui Enwezor undermined the overall dominance of the Western canon by focusing public attention on 'art from elsewhere' in 2001 ('Short Century', MoMA PS1, New York) and 2002 (Documenta 11 in Kassel). His universally acclaimed 2015 Venice Biennale would also showcase the work of many Black Americans.

Equally early in the twenty-first century, Thelma Golden, Director of Harlem's The Studio Museum, began a trio of attention-grabbing exhibitions ('freestyle', 2001; 'frequency', 2006; and 'fore', 2012) that gave many (often young) Black artists the chance to display their talents. By introducing the concept of 'Post-Blackness'—'I'm an artist, not a Black artist'—she managed both to influence the Black discourse and to attract the attention of the international press.

Another factor has undoubtedly been the selection of Black artists to represent the US at the Venice Biennale no less than five times: Robert Colescott (1997), Fred Wilson (2003), Mark Bradford (2017), Martin Puryear (2019), and Simone Leigh (selected for 2022).

Meanwhile, the success of the Black Renaissance artists has overcome the prejudices of many traditional art lovers, while the quality of their work has ensured high prices at auction—a point to which America is extremely sensitive.

Other exhibitions have also given a significant boost to the status of Black artists. '30 Americans' has been touring the US ever since 2009. It is based on the African American holdings of the Rubell Family Collection in Miami and new acquisitions are integrated into the presentation at each successive venue. The exhibition attracts a strikingly large young audience—a fact that will prove to be particularly important.

'Soul of a Nation: Art in The Age of Black Power', initially held at London's Tate Modern in 2017, has also been highly influential. It featured work by important artists of the 1960s, 1970s, and early 1980s who were still unknown to many people but who had been involved in the Civil Rights Movement and used their Black identity as a weapon in the struggle for equal rights. The exhibition made the political context clear, so that visitors could link the art of the past to the turbulence of the present. 'Soul…' was originally intended to go on to only two American museums (the Brooklyn Museum and the Crystal Bridges Museum), but its success was such that the exhibition is still touring and—like '30 Americans'—attracting large young and Black audiences.

However, the final breakthrough was due to Black Lives Matter. The organization was launched by three young, Black women in 2013, in response to the acquittal of George Zimmerman for the fatal shooting of Black seventeen-year-old Trayvon Martin the previous year. As their website puts it:

> Black Lives Matter Global Network Foundation, Inc. is a global organization in the US, UK, and Canada, whose mission is to eradicate white supremacy and build local power to intervene in violence inflicted on Black communities by the state and vigilantes. By combating and countering acts of violence, creating space for Black imagination and innovation, and centering Black joy, we are winning immediate improvements in our lives.

And they do not confine themselves to the US:

4. blacklivesmatter.com, accessed on 1 April 2021.

> We are expansive. We are a collective of liberators who believe in an inclusive and spacious movement. We also believe that in order to win and bring as many people with us along the way, we must move beyond the narrow nationalism that is all too prevalent in Black communities. We must ensure we are building a movement that brings all of us to the front.[4]

Apart from its immediate political and social relevance, it is the movement's clever branding—conscious or otherwise—that has ensured its huge impact. The simple three-word slogan reduces a vast problem to its human essence. The phrase encompasses not just the lethal violence that the American police employ against Black men and women, but institutional racism worldwide. It has become an instantly recognizable label for anti-racism demonstrations, debates about racism and measures to combat racial discrimination. Because of its vast international impact—googling Black Lives Matter produces 1,390,000,000 hits—the 'brand' has done a huge amount to raise public awareness of the issue. Moreover, it has proved to have great appeal to young people (whatever their colour). This is important because, by demonstrating on the streets and thus creating further publicity via social media, they have played a major role in propagating the movement. The slogan has been seen and heard at street protests innumerable times, and, as with all effective branding, this constant repetition encourages 'consumption' of the 'product'. Its effect has been reinforced—and this may sound cynical—by the determination of the American police to continue killing African Americans: a situation that reached a new low with the asphyxiation of George Floyd, witnessed on television screens around the world.

The worldwide change in the climate of public opinion has not only created a new interest in young Black artists, but also prompted action by numerous American museums. Realizing the need to catch up with changing attitudes—if only to avoid being confronted with a Black Lives Matter demonstration on their own doorsteps—they have held dozens of exhibitions, not only in the Black southern states but throughout the US.

The Second Exhibition: 'Tell Me Your Story: 100 Years of Storytelling in African American Art'

In 2015 Kunsthal KAdE invited me to curate an exhibition of African American art in Amersfoort. Unwilling simply to repeat 'Postcards…', I chose storytelling as my starting point. The phenomenon is typical of Black culture: 'There is no question that storytelling for Black America is a way of saying I am here and I matter'.[5]

5. Andrea Collier, 'Why Telling Our Own Story Is So Powerful', published on the website of the Greater Good Science Center at UC Berkeley (27 February 2019).

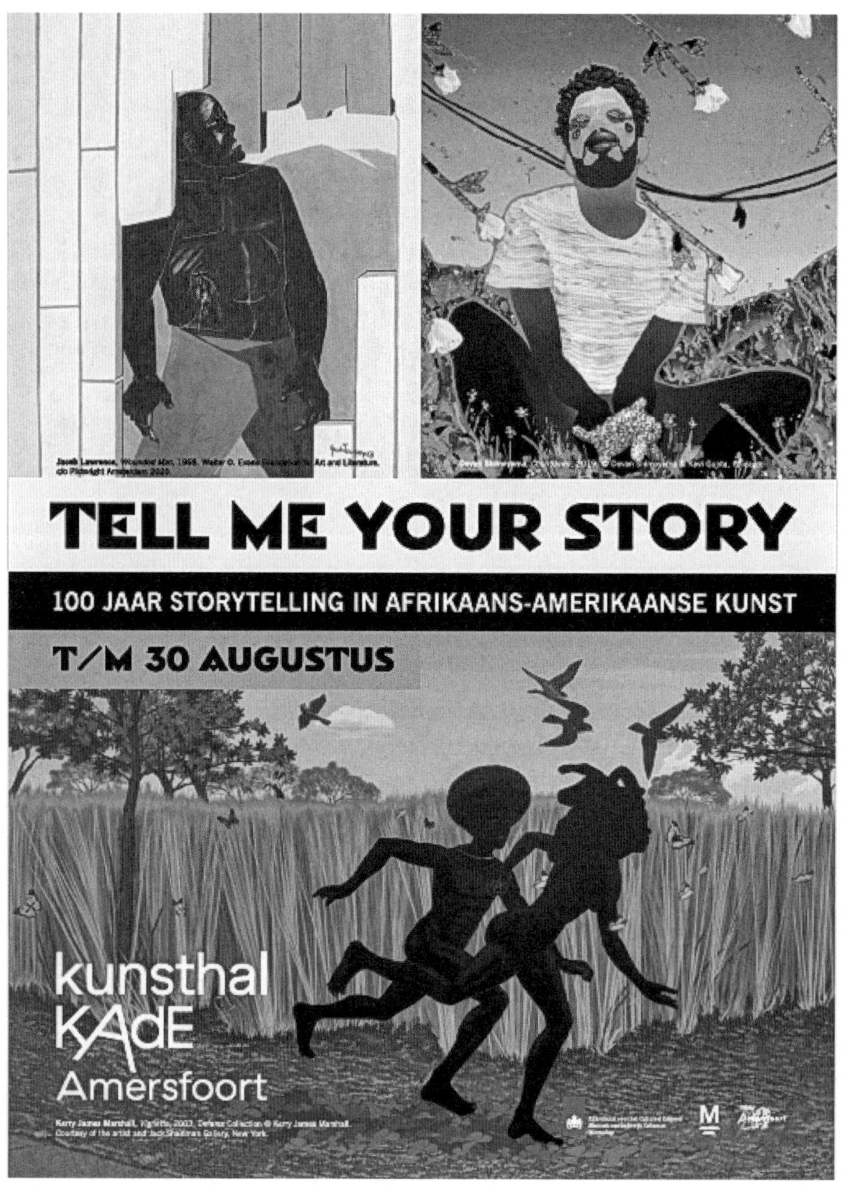

'Tell Me Your Story', 2020, poster KAdE, Amersfoort.

6. www.humanityinaction.org/knowledge_detail/black-pete-analyzing-a-racialized-dutch-tradition-through-the-history-of-western-creations-of-stereotypes-of-black-peoples/?lang=nl, accessed on 1 April 2021.

7. www.theblackarchives.nl/, accessed on 1 April 2021.

I also thought it was important to show how Black art in the US had *evolved* in line with developments in society. That was why the show focused on a whole century of African American art, beginning with the Harlem Renaissance, when Black artists had their first opportunity to show what they could do and to be given credit for it (an unprecedented freedom that was given an ideological basis in philosopher Alain Locke's famous 1925 anthology, *The New Negro*).

Because I invited the artists, as it were, to tell their own (often moving) stories—stories unfamiliar to most people in the Netherlands—the main title of the exhibition had to be 'Tell Me Your Story'. The resulting chronological display of over one hundred twenty works by forty-five artists opened to the public on 8 February 2020.

Unlike 'Postcards…', this second exhibition was a public success. Despite coronavirus restrictions, there were plenty of visitors, including conspicuously large numbers of young and Black people. The latter were estimated to account for between ten and fifteen percent of total footfall. The two versions of the catalogue, in English and Dutch, went into a second edition and even then sold out. And over twenty-five positive reviews appeared in virtually all the Dutch dailies and weeklies, in the Belgian press and online.

Why the success? It is hard to say. Was it the quality of the works? Was it because almost none of them had been shown previously in the Netherlands? Did the public like the exhibition concept? Was it the emotional appeal of the themes? Or just the right thing at the right time? No doubt all these aspects were relevant but, in the end, the decisive factor was the climate of opinion created by BLM. The branding of the movement had also ensured its success in the Netherlands.

In fact, the impact of BLM in the Netherlands was rather different from elsewhere. It was intensified by the existence of a thorny annual debate about the depiction of 'Black Peter' in the nation's traditional *Sinterklaas* festivities, a beloved aspect of children's lives.[6] The BLM movement managed to situate this distinctively Dutch tradition and national debate within the context of the universal issue of racism. The impact was further intensified by the efforts of the Black Archives in Amsterdam, active since 2015 and 'a unique historical archive for inspiring conversations, activities and literature from Black and other perspectives that are often overlooked elsewhere'.[7] I think 'Tell Me Your Story' was seen as an illustration of the BLM movement. The images and stories showed that Black Art Matters.

The worldwide success of Black Lives Matter has created a large audience for the work of Black artists. Not only has there been a major increase in public interest, but museums all over the world are now programming exhibitions featuring work by them.

Kerry James Marshall once said that he aimed to earn a place in the still conspicuously white artistic canon. But should he be doing that? Is not that canon a bastion of a cultural heritage determined to protect itself at all costs within an art world that has long since abandoned all divisions of nationality and race? Should not the canon be demolished? Should not Marshall be glad not to be part of it? After all, the idea that Black Art Matters is well on the way to achieving universal acceptance as unchallenged fact.

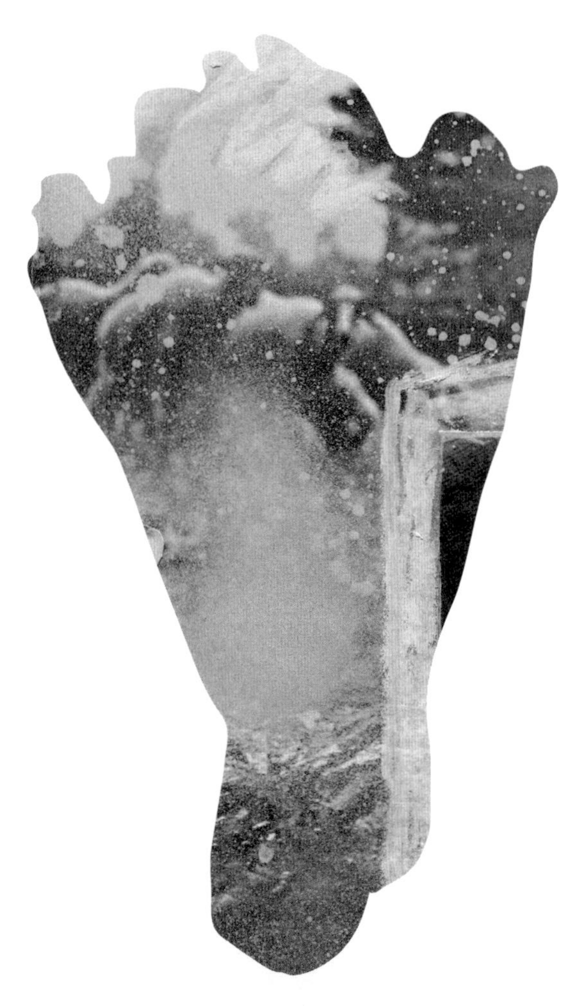

THE PROOF OF THE PUDDING IS IN THE EATING

Stijn Huijts

INGREDIENTS

- Antropófago/ Cannibalism as Postcolonialism
- Global Cultural Interface
- Critical Distance
- Sense of Urgency
- Curiosity
- Intuition

'Variety is the spice of life' is a well-known phrase used in situations where people want to emphasize that a change of perspective can have a positive effect on someone's energy and motivation. The directors of the Mondriaan Foundation and the Prince Claus Fund must have had something similar in mind when they decided in 2003 to collaborate on organizing an annual working visit with the aim of informing Dutch professionals about artistic developments in lesser known, yet nevertheless interesting regions. Both foundations considered it very important for the Dutch art world to become truly international, and to not just focus on the cultural capitals of the West. By organizing these visits, the main aim was to 'contribute to increasing the international knowledge and associated network of Dutch art sectors'.[1]

In May 2005, as the director of Museum Het Domein, in Sittard, I went along on one of these working visits, with China as its destination. In the preceding years, I had gone on a few trips myself to Brazil, first as part of a cultural exchange with the Museu de Arte Moderna Aloisio Magalhães (MAMAM), in Recife, in North-East Brazil, and later also in my capacity as curator of the Dutch contribution to the twenty-sixth São Paulo Biennial. Through my contacts in Brazil, I learned a lot about the context in which modern and contemporary art had developed in the country over the course of the twentieth century. One reference often made was to the *Manifesto Antropófago* of 1928, by Oswald de Andrade, which is

1. In: *Oriëntatiereis China. Evaluatie: Kennismaken met Kunst en cultuur in China. 14-24 May 2005* (Amsterdam, 2006), p. 3.

regarded as an important cornerstone of the modernist movement in Brazil.[2] This 'cannibalistic manifesto', which opens with the words 'Cannibalism alone unites us. Socially. Economically. Philosophically.' is a post-colonial statement based on the metaphor of the consumption and digestion of European cultural traditions, so that they blend with the pre-colonial Brazilian culture and create a new, authentic Brazilian culture.

During the China visit in 2005, the group of Dutch professionals was accompanied by four Chinese artists and two Chinese curators. The visit took us to Beijing, Shanghai, Hangzhou and Guangzhou, in that order. It struck me that the further south we went, not only did the local cuisine keep improving (with the famous Cantonese cuisine as the apotheosis), but gradually the meetings also became more interesting from an artistic point of view. One highlight was the introduction to Hu Fang, one of the founding directors of Vitamin Creative Space, in Guangzhou. At the reception in his presentation space, which was hidden away on a third floor behind a busy market hall, Hu moved me with his impassioned story about the role of Vitamin as a generator of artistic production and reflection in the region. One of the main themes was the confrontation between ancient Chinese philosophical traditions and modern China, as the country was becoming more and more part of a globalized world. It was an approach in which I recognized clear overlaps with the aforementioned cannibalistic manifesto of the Brazilian modernists. For Hu, too, art appeared to revolve around savouring a mix of contemporary and traditional cultural influences, with the goal of arriving at new cultural insights and practices.

After the show of muscle from the initiatives that were promoted as 'creative spaces'—but were actually commercially driven for the most part—which we had seen in the major Chinese metropolises, such as the 798 district in Beijing and 50 Moganshan Road in Shanghai, the combination of engagement and critical reflection revealed by Hu Fang in the 'peripheral' Guangzhou was an inspiring experience. His holistic vision of the role of art and culture in society appealed to me so much that I proposed keeping in touch and looking at the possibility

2. English translation by Leslie Bary, published in: *Latin American Literary Review* 19, no. 38 (July–December 1991), pp. 38-47. Access through this link: jstor.org/stable/20119601.

. *MiMmanual* (Sittard, 007).

of a long-term collaboration. Subsequently, Hu took up the offer of presenting Vitamin Creative Space in Museum Het Domein in 2006. The occasion sowed the seeds for Made in Mirrors (MiM), an intercultural mirroring experiment based on a small-scale exchange of people and ideas with a variety of regional and cultural backgrounds. The starting point for the project was a shared sense of urgency: the conviction that cultural diversity is a question of curiosity and willingness to learn something about yourself by delving into—and reflecting yourself in—the other. The new insights thus gained can help you redefine your own cultural reality in the light of the kaleidoscopic dynamics of advancing globalization and the dominant role played therein by the big cultural centres. Echoes of the cannibalistic manifesto are found here, too, which is maybe why—as an extension of my earlier Brazilian experiences—the director of the MAMAM in Recife, Cristiana Tejo, responded with enthusiasm to my suggestion to link up with MiM. It was a shared enthusiasm, fuelled by the realization that art practices in the periphery are excellently suited—due to their inherent tendency towards critical distance—to making a difference.

An independent foundation (the Made in Mirrors Foundation) was set up, and a joint kick-off meeting in Guangzhou in January 2007 formulated the principles in more detail and outlined the plans for an exchange programme of artistic research, presentations, performances, residencies, and symposia. With support from authorities, funds, sponsors, and donors the plans were then put into practice. In the first year, the emphasis was on the exchange with Guangzhou and the region of Guangdong. After that, a workshop in Recife in December 2007 was the starting signal for a programme in 2008 and 2009, which placed more emphasis on the exchange with Pernambuco. A report of the first project year, 2007, was published in a *MiMmanual*,[3] along with a description of the mission and vision of MiM.

The programme had a multidisciplinary character and involved makers and researchers from diverse backgrounds. Painter Rik Meijers worked in Guangzhou for a period, where he gave a lecture, produced a colouring book for children, and made a wall painting. Other artists-in-residence in Guangzhou were the fashion designers Els Beusen and Hiroaki Kanai, who organized workshops with local fashion students about sustainable design. On the Chinese side, several artists, journalists, and cultural entrepreneurs came to Sittard to conduct research. They included the well-known video artist Cao Fei and the journalists Han Yan and Jiang Jun from the architecture journal *Urban China*, whose research focused specifically on the role and significance of the chemical company DSM in local urban development. Artist Chu Yun researched the influence of Spinoza on Dutch society, and the education department of Museum Het Domein organized a special Made in Mirrors programme for primary schools. In the summer of 2007, the museum presented a special programme of exhibitions and events, entitled 'Chinergy – the China Summer Show'. It included the project 'Forms of Exchange', a special collaboration between Kitty Zijlmans and the Chinese artists Ni Haifeng and Wang Jianwei, comprising the installations *Gift* and *Input/Output*, which reflected on topics such as shared ownership and processes of giving and taking. I still have a porcelain potato, a 'passport' and a plastic squeeze ear as mementos of this project, which formed part of a bigger research project into new possibilities for cultural production in an era of globalization, and thus linked up seamlessly with MiM's programme focusing on the intercultural exchange of people and ideas. The project was accompanied by a publication of the same name.[4]

While various other projects with Chinese artists were still being created, in the course of 2008 the focus shifted gradually to a more intensive exchange with Brazil. For instance, the head of education at Museum Het Domein travelled to Recife for an education project in which primary schools in Sittard and Recife experimented with art-based learning, a methodology that was also reflected on in a special conference for education staff. Various artists were invited to spend periods working in Recife or Sittard. During a residency in Recife, for example, filmmaker Daniel van Hauten made a series of video portraits of people he met on the streets, which revolved around the tension between dream and reality. Under the title Egotrip.tv, he presented these works in SCHUNCK*

4. *Forms of Exchange*, eds. Kitty Zijlmans and Ni Haifeng (Sittard, 2007). In addition, Zijlmans contributed a text about it for the *MiMmanual*.

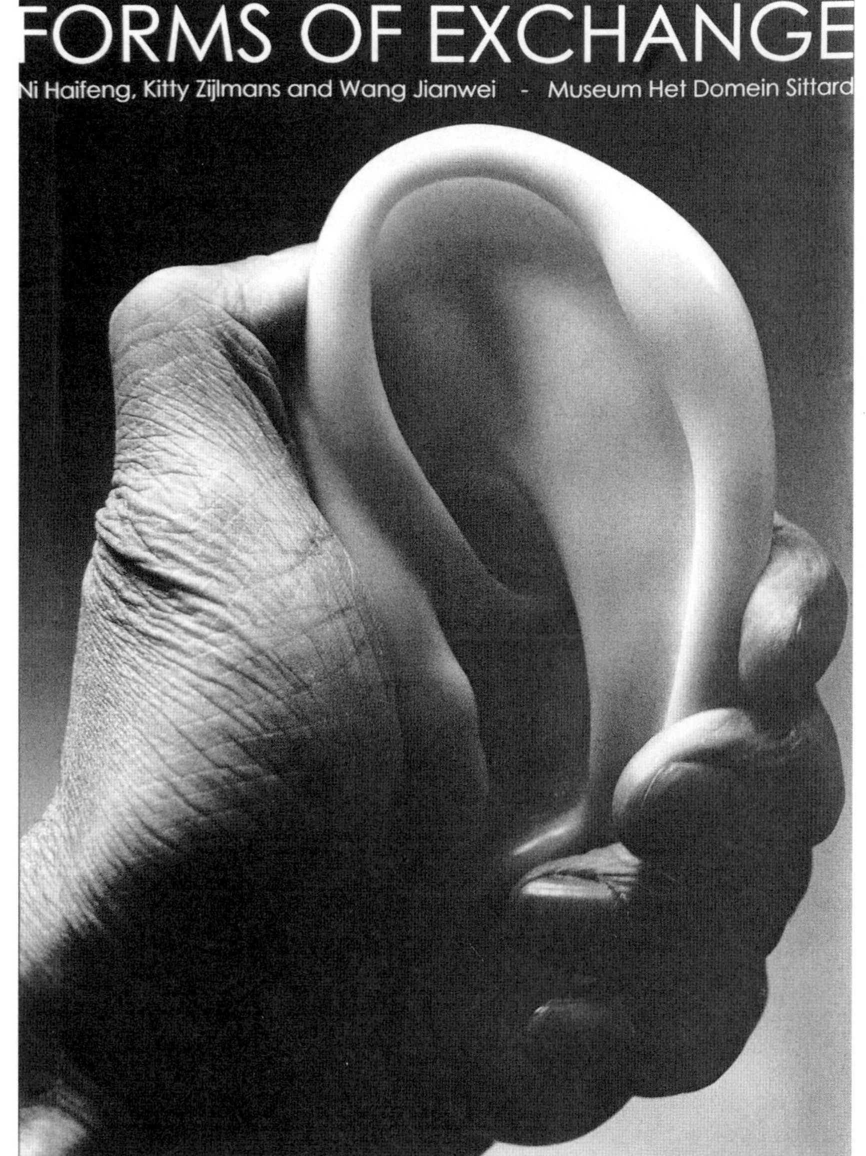

Forms of Exchange, Ni Haifeng, Kitty Zijlmans, Wang Jianwei (Sittard, 2007), book cover: design and photo Ni Haifeng 2007.

in Heerlen, in 2010. In Recife, Maria Barnas did research into the sociocultural implications of the restoration of a small park designed by the famous landscape architect Burle Marx. The Brazilian photographer Barbara Wagner, whose work is concerned with questions of identity and representation, travelled to both Guangzhou and Sittard in 2009. In Guangzhou, she made a photo series about the self-representation of newly-weds, and during her residency in Sittard she pointed her camera at caravan dwellers, who let her portray them in their own environment in the way they themselves wanted. The summer exhibition of 2009 in Museum Het Domein was a group presentation by young Brazilian artists who address socio-political themes in their work. And in the autumn, a 'Week of Cannibalism' was held in Sittard and Heerlen, comprising lectures, discussion meetings, guided tours, and culinary tastings, all focusing on the Brazilian contribution to Made in Mirrors.[5]

To avoid MiM becoming too dependent on the continuity of a limited number of institutional partners (both Cristiana Tejo and myself had changed job in the meantime) and to increase the impact of the project, it was decided to bring the MiM activities under the direction of regional managers, namely Hu Fang, Cristiana Tejo, and myself. As 'MiMmanagers', our ambition was to expand the MiM network to form a global cultural interface. An important step in this development was when in 2009 William Wells, the director of the Townhouse Gallery in Cairo, joined us. I had met him in March of that year, at the Cairo Residency Symposium, a joint initiative by the Townhouse Gallery and the BKVB Fund, which focused on international knowledge-sharing, collaboration, and network forming in the field of artist-in-residency projects in the Middle East, Africa, and Europe. Just like my first encounter with Hu Fang and his Vitamin Creative Space, I was impressed by the visionary way in which William Wells had created a multidisciplinary community-based programme in Cairo, despite the limited resources and the lack of a professional infrastructure. Once again, I realized that in culture everything revolves around a sense of urgency and the sort of engagement that releases the energy necessary for developing cultural and artistic initiatives that help people to better understand themselves and the world they live in.

So, William Wells became the fourth MiMmanager, and in October 2009 a kick-off meeting took place in Cairo, so that Hu Fang, Cristiana Tejo, and myself could further familiarize ourselves with the context in which the

5. These are just a few examples of the many projects realized in the Made in Mirrors pressure cooker in the period 2007–2009. A complete overview of the projects was published in a report by MiM in the spring of 2010: *MiM-report 2010* (Sittard, 2010).

6. *Beyond the Fantastic: Contemporary Art Criticism from Latin America*, ed. Gerardo Mosquera, (London, 1995).

Townhouse Gallery operated and with the local scene of artists and curators in particular. The kick-off resulted in new proposals for residencies, presentations, and a symposium. In the first months of 2010, for instance, the artists' duo Wouter Osterholt and Elke Uitentuis held a presentation entitled 'Model Citizens' in SCHUNCK*. It showed the results of their residency in the Townhouse Gallery: a project in which they had reflected on both the history and the future of the district of Antikhana in Downtown Cairo, in a process of co-creation with the residents. In collaboration with the Fundação Joaquim Nabuco, MiM organized the symposium 'Curating new centralities' in Recife, in April 2010. Inspired by Gerardo Mosquera's anthology 'Beyond the Fantastic: Contemporary Art Criticism from Latin America', curators from various parts of the world, including the renowned Paulo Herkenhoff, discussed the significance of cultural and contextual diversity for curatorship in an age of globalization.[6] 'Curator food' Jeffrey Kuckelkorn, from SCHUNCK*, spent a few weeks in mid-2010 as curator-in-residence in Cairo, where he did research into local eating habits. The results of his research were presented in the form of images, sounds, smells, and tastes, in an exhibition in the Provinciehuis in Maastricht, in October 2010, and in a 'cookery book' with diary excerpts, philosophical reflections, photos and recipes.

Unfortunately, the cookery book still has not appeared in print. At the end of 2010, the funding available to the Made in Mirrors Foundation in previous years dried up, so there was no money to publish the book. To make matters worse, the Egyptian Revolution broke out in January 2011, forcing the Townhouse Gallery to shut its doors for a long time. So, the collaboration with William Wells was ended prematurely. The loss of funds and of an important partner put pressure on the continuity of MiM, and eventually the only course of action was to close down the foundation. However, this did not mean that the goals and principles of MiM disappeared from view, so when I became artistic director of the Bonnefanten museum in Maastricht, in 2012, I was fortunate to be able to use the experience and network I had gained through MiM in developing new, more diverse cultural and artistic perspectives for the museum. For example, the focus of the biennial Bonnefanten Award for Contemporary Art (BACA) became more culturally diverse. Since then, the short list of candidates looks specifically at neglected art practices that transcend the geographical and/or cultural borders of the dominant Western canon, or take place outside it. With a view to this, the jury has since comprised mainly experts who have experience and knowledge of the specific geographical/cultural search area. Partly thanks to the personal contacts I made during the MiM period, this has produced some fantastic award winners in recent years, from Latin America, China, and the Arab world, as well as many interesting collaborative projects with curators and art institutes in these regions. Meanwhile, the changing composition of the BACA jury ensures that the network keeps on growing steadily and that new mirrors are continually being added to the MiM kaleidoscope.

The experiences with Made in Mirrors and the BACA have proved invaluable for my professional work in the cultural sector. Theoretical knowledge alone can never be the catalyst for new and more diverse perspectives for cultural and artistic practices. I have realized that curiosity, intuition, and empathy are far more relevant as the subjective basic skills necessary for doing justice to multivocality. The key concept is cognitive empathy: learning to see the world through the eyes of another; meeting one another; getting to know each other's environment, and exploring local eating habits—in short: sampling the atmosphere. I became convinced that looking one another in the eye and exchanging ideas and experiences over a meal can contribute more to understanding the historical, social, and cultural context in which artistic practices can develop than the study of literature can, and that cultural and artistic development as a driving force for social change benefits from building up and maintaining long-term networks. In other words, where people get to know each other by dining together, during the meal they also consume shared ideas, stories, and experiences, generating new insights in accordance with the best cannibalistic traditions. As far as I am concerned, personal contact and investment in long-term networks form the basis for developing new, culturally diverse perspectives for academic, curatorial, and artistic art practices.

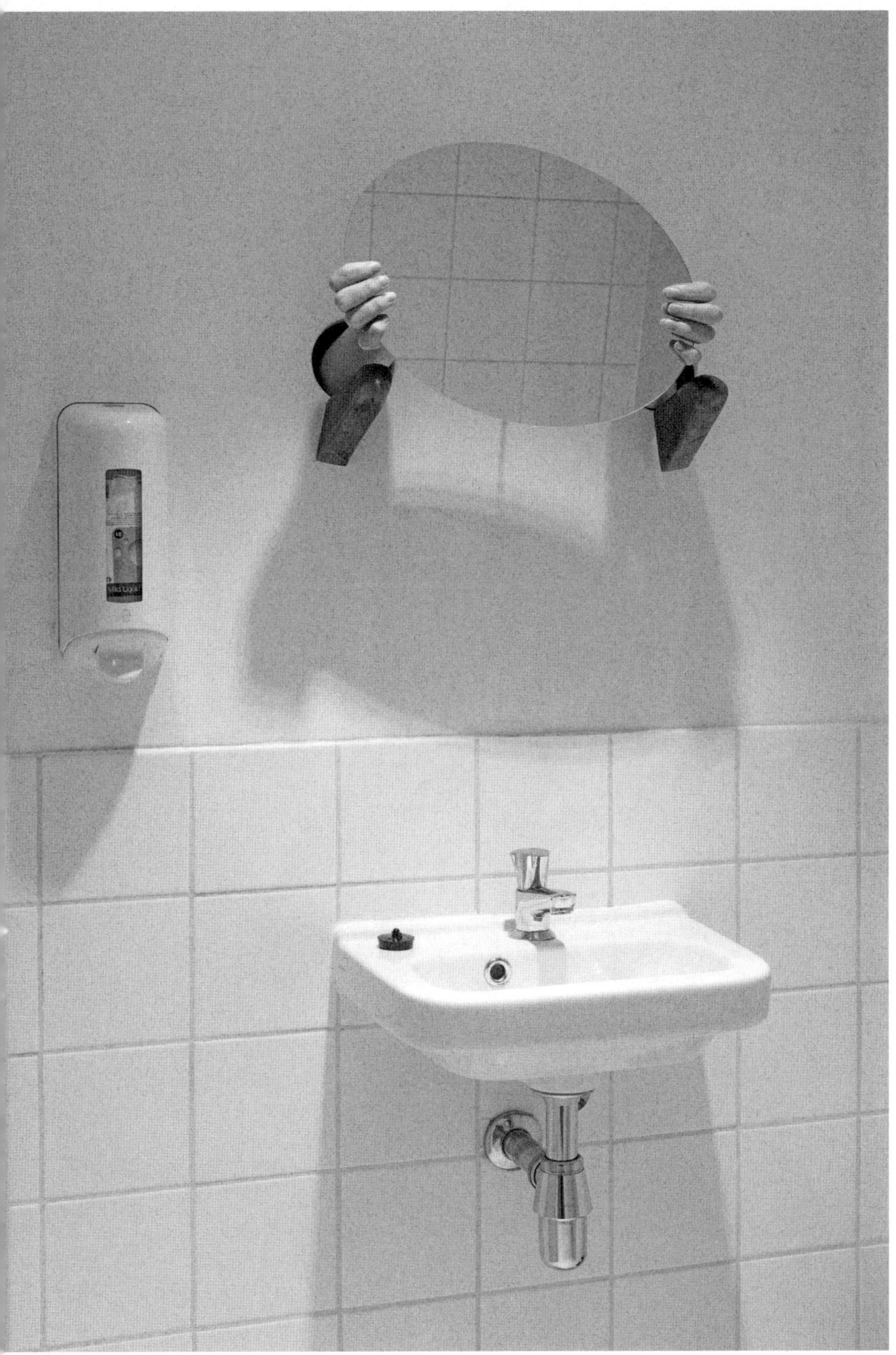

Laura Lima, *Toilet*, 2014, Collection Bonnefanten Museum Maastricht, acquired with the support of the BankGiro Loterij. At the exhibition 'The Fifth Floor' of Brazilian artist and BACA-2014 winner Laura Lima, in one of the washrooms the visitors were surprised by a mirror held by a real person whose hands were coming out of the wall. Photo Peter Cox.

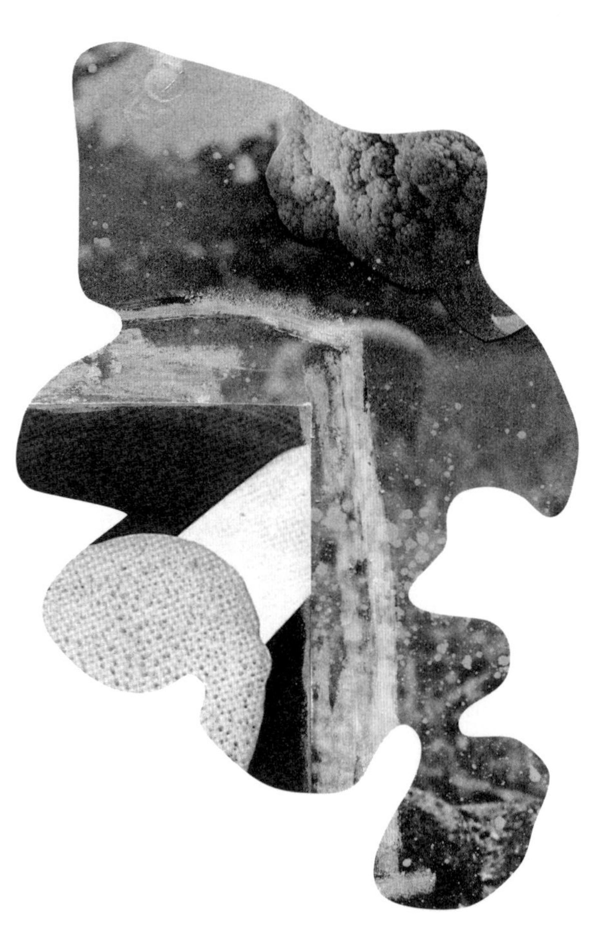

REVISITING OSHOGBO

Paul Faber

INGREDIENTS

- Revisiting Old Projects
- Diachronic Reception
- Inside/Outside View
- Near and Distant Framing

Recently I became aware of the attraction and complexity of revisiting favourite projects of the past, when I got in touch with a granddaughter of Ru van Rossem. Van Rossem (1924–2007) was a well-known Dutch graphic artist who excelled in etching. I had met him in 1980. I studied art history at the University of Amsterdam at the time and did an internship at the Tropenmuseum in Amsterdam. To my delight the museum was about to host a touring exhibition called 'Modern Art from Africa' ['Moderne Kunst aus Afrika'], that was put together in Berlin in 1979. This large exhibition brought together artists and artworks from many different African countries and was the first of its kind anywhere.[1]

At the time I had no idea it was a landmark exhibition, and I didn't realize it would determine my career. It felt like an adventure and I loved to be part of it. I digested art and information, all new to me, and Africa curator Harrie Leyten gave me a free hand. We even wrote a modest book together called *Moderne kunst in Afrika* [Modern Art in Africa].[2]

Several works represented in this exhibition were made by artists from Oshogbo, a town in southwestern Nigeria, with Twins Seven Seven (1944–2011) as the most striking representative. I was quite hooked by these works and by the stories around Oshogbo. These stories became very much alive when Ulli Beier, one of the most important lenders of the exhibition and a kind of godfather to the Oshogbo artists, consented to come over to Amsterdam to open the exhibition.

1. Its importance has often been overlooked, I am afraid, for the simple reason that the catalogue was written in German. See: *Moderne Kunst aus Afrika: Horizonte '79* (1. Festival der Weltkulturen: Ausstellung der Berliner Festspiele), ed. Sabine Hollburg et al., exh. cat. Staatliche Kunsthalle (Berlin, 1979).

2. Harrie Leyten and Paul Faber, *Moderne kunst in Afrika* (Amsterdam/Zutphen, 1980).

It was in this context that I met Ru van Rossem. We had learned that Van Rossem had led workshops in graphic arts in Oshogbo. Leyten and I visited him and talked about his experiences. We looked at his work and he showed some of the African prints he had brought back from Africa. The following year I travelled to Nigeria, visited Oshogbo and met Twins Seven Seven. I saw Twins a few times later on in the Netherlands,[3] I organized a small exhibition of his work in the 1980s, but I never met Van Rossem again and the memory of Oshogbo slowly faded away. From his granddaughter I found out Ru van Rossem passed away in 2007. From her I learned he made many prints inspired by Africa. Soon we reached the same conclusion: we should make an exhibition around Van Rossem's connection to Africa. The research brought me back to Oshogbo forty years after I visited the town.

I soon realized that I was now a much more critical and demanding visitor. Back then I was just fascinated, and intrigued by the stories, impressed and charmed by the striking personalities of Beier and Twins Seven Seven, and I was a fan of Nigerian literature and music.[4] Now I wanted to form a more concrete and reliable idea of the scene Ru van Rossem had entered in the 1960s and what exactly he had been doing there.

My investigations added a few new facts to what I already knew. Van Rossem came in touch with Beier when in 1958 he published a few drawings in the fourth issue of *Black Orpheus*,[5] the famous journal founded the year before by Beier and Jahn. Later Beier invited him to exhibit his work in the Mbari artists and writers club in Ibadan, in October 1961, just a few months after the opening of this experimental cultural centre.[6] Van Rossem's first visit to Africa took place in the summer of 1963, when he led a workshop in graphic arts in Ibadan, for art teachers and students. His second workshop took place in Oshogbo in 1964. In this town, located about a 100 km from Ibadan, a second Mbari-club was founded in March 1962 by Ulli Beier and Duro Ladipo, a Nigerian theatre maker. In 1962 and 1963 short workshops were organized in the visual arts, open to anyone who was interested, mainly young men with little education. In the summer of 1964 Van Rossem gave a more specialized workshop in graphic arts. The participants

3. A Dutch collector, Fopke Fopma, had a large collection of works by Twins, and kept buying work from him.

4. In this period Fela Kuti and King Sunny Ade were performing in Amsterdam.

5. Illustrations of poems by Afro-American poet Paul Vesey.

6. See Isabelle Malz and Nadine Siegert, *The Mbari Artists and Writers Club in Ibadan* (Bayreuth/Johannesburg, 2018), pp. 42–43; Chika Okeke-Agulu, *Postcolonial Modernism: Art and Decolonization in Twentieth-Century Nigeria* (Durham/London, 2015), pp. 131–182.

in his workshop were Bruce Onobrakpeya, Georgina Betts, Samuel Owojo, Rufus Ogundele, and Jacob Afolabi. Georgina Betts was a British artist who came to Oshogbo in 1963, and married Ulli Beier not long afterwards. From 3–8 August 1964, so directly afterwards, she led the now famous third Oshogbo workshop that started the careers of several talented artists: Muraina Oyelami, Adebisi Fabunmi, Jimoh Buraimoh and Twins Seven Seven. After the short workshop these four artists worked under Georgina's guidance for a long time. During this period, she passed on the etching technique she picked up from Van Rossem to Twins. Twins made a series of remarkable etchings, but dropped the technique soon afterwards. The third and final workshop by Van Rossem was given in 1974 in Ile-Ife, together with Bruce Onobrakpeya.

Over the last forty years new sources have become available. In 1980 there were only a few publications on this topic, like Ulli Beier's *Contemporary Art in Africa* and Marshall Mount's *African Art: The Years Since 1920.*[7] From the 1980s onwards, especially after the famous exhibition 'Magiciens de la terre' (Paris 1989), publications appeared that added other sources and perspectives such as *Seven Stories: About Modern Art in Africa*, and 'The Short Century', curated by Okwui Enwezor.[8] New sources were presented, such as testimonies of African artists and essays written by African authors. The Iwalewa Haus in Bayreuth, created by Ulli Beier, also was and is an interesting centre for research and publications. Both Ulli and Georgina Beier passed away, and their substantial archives have been preserved in Oshogbo itself[9] and in the Iwalewa Haus. The Ulli Beier Photographic Estate is a rich source that, for example, enabled a recent detailed compilation of the activities at the Mbari Club in Ibadan.[10] The significance and impact of the Oshogbo art movement has been researched thoroughly, for instance by Peter Probst.[11]

Apart from new facts concerning the workshops and the artists, the most enlightening insight was connected to the reception of the Oshogbo school. In 1980 I was convinced that the Oshogbo artists formed the avant-garde of African modern art, the way forward, a fascinating mix of new and old, modern and ancestral, Western and African. I was influenced by the compelling writings of Ulli

7. Ulli Beier, *Contemporary Art in Africa* (London, 1968); Marshall Ward Mount, *African Art: The Years Since 1920* (Bloomington, 1973).

8. Clementine Deliss, *Seven Stories: About Modern Art in Africa* (London, 1995); *The Short Century: Independence and Liberation Movements in Africa 1945–1994*, ed. Okwui Enwezor (Munich/London/New York, 2001).

9. Centre for Black Culture and International Understanding (CBCIU), Oshogbo.

10. Malz and Siegert 2018 (see note 6).

11. Peter Probst, *Oshogbo and the Art of Heritage: Monuments, Deities and Money* (Bloomington, 2011).

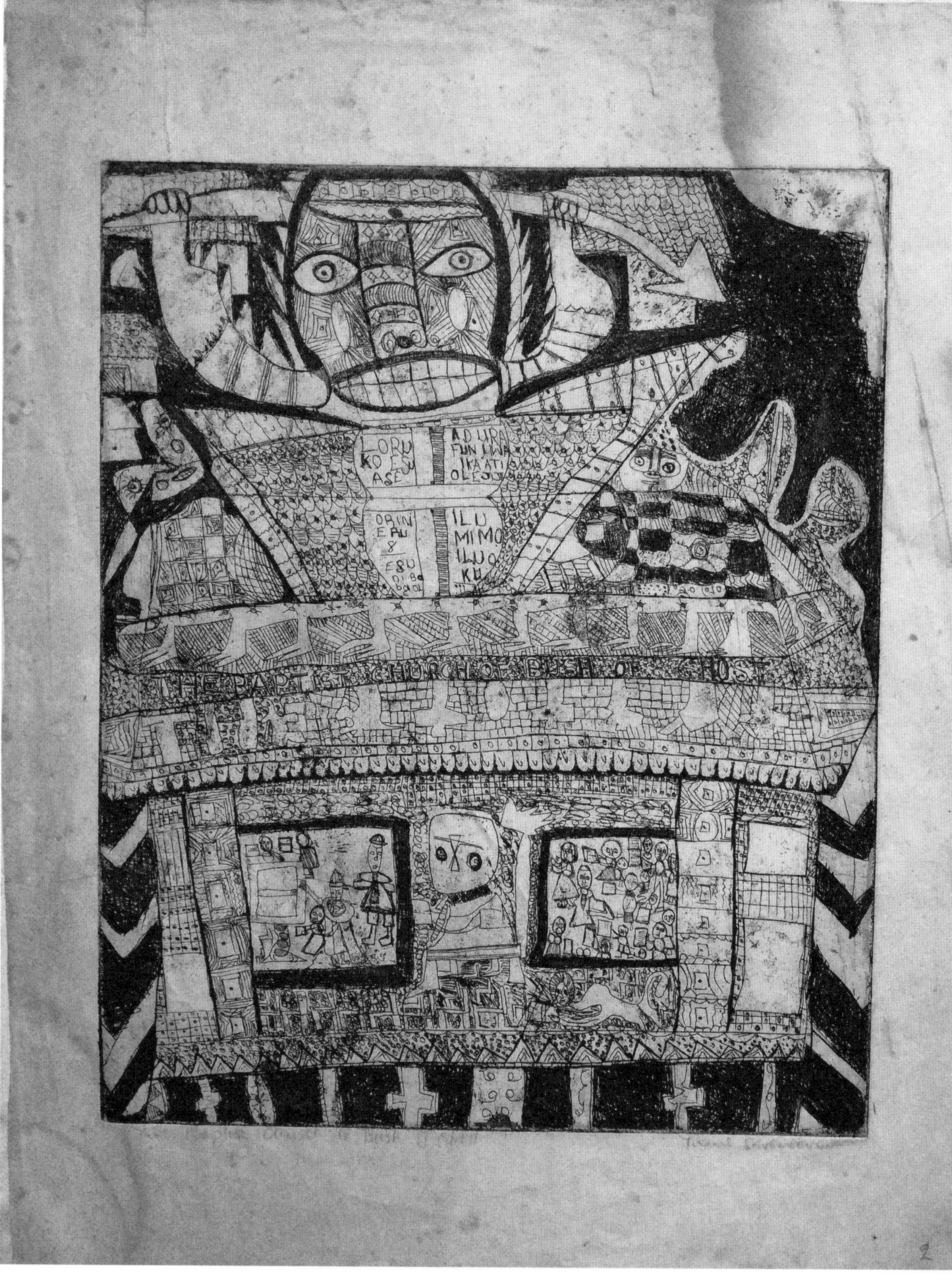

Twins Seven Seven, *The Baptist Church of Bush Of Ghost*, 1964, etching, 38 × 30.5 cm. Private collection.

2. The Swiss collector ean Pigozzi assembled a uge collection of modern African art, inspired by the exhibition 'Magiciens de la erre'.

3. Probst 2011 (see note 11),). 63.

4. Babatunde Lawal, The Search for Identity in Contemporary Nigerian Art', *Studio International* 193, no. 986 (March–April 1977), pp. 145–150.

5. Deliss 1995; Enwezor 2001 (see note 8).

6. Okeke-Agulu 2015 see note 6).

Beier, stressing the revitalization of African traditions that found such an overwhelming outlet in the Oshogbo school. Over the years I had already noticed that the high expectations of the Oshogbo art movement were not fulfilled. In the 1980s not much was heard about the Oshogbo school anymore. For some time, Twins Seven Seven formed an exception. He was represented in the exhibition 'Magiciens de la terre' and several exhibitions based on the Pigozzi collection,[12] but that was it. Now I slowly came to understand this reception process.

First of all, the departure of the Beiers from Nigeria, first in 1966, later definitely in 1974 meant a severe loss of patronage. From the start, Beier, with his international network, managed to realize exhibitions worldwide. But it is also clear now that these were rarely shown in the regular art circles, and the shows were often framed as 'Third World Art' or 'art from developing countries'. In Nigeria itself the reception was even more critical. When Nigeria organized the large Festival of African Art and Culture (FESTAC) that same year, the organization committee more or less banned the Oshogbo artists from participating.[13] The Nigerian critic Babatunde Lawal described Oshogbo art in 1977 as 'a psycho-dramatic outpour of images that invited the comparison with psychotic art…'.[14] So already at the time of the 1980 exhibition, the position of Oshogbo art was rather ambiguous. Over time this valuation changed again. The Oshogbo art school lost its actual significance but became part of Africa's history of modern art.[15] However, when Chika Okeke-Agulu published his thorough *Postcolonial Modernism: Art and Decolonization in Twentieth-Century Nigeria*, he treated Beier's role in the formation of Nigerian modernism and the Mbari club in Ibadan extensively and with great appreciation, but Oshogbo is hardly mentioned at all, and there is not one work of Oshogbo artists among the many reproductions.[16]

What did I learn from this process? Comparing these new insights with my earlier attitude, first of all I realized that I had strongly chosen sides in 1980. I was won over by personalities such as Ulli Beier and Twins Seven Seven, both charismatic storytellers (however different they were), and I got carried away. I was intrigued not only by the imaginative and playful artworks, but also by the many references to Yoruba folklore, religion, and history. Often the imaginative stories written by Amos Tutuola, published in 1952 under the title *The Palm-Wine Drinkard*, are mentioned in the context of Oshogbo.[17] I also read Tutuola, and enjoyed the similarities between the fantastic stories and the artworks and I felt I had a role to play in winning the Dutch audience for these unknown artists. I was not aware of the critical point of view of other contemporary Nigerian artists. From their position they saw uneducated youths who produced folkloric pictures to sell to expats or abroad. In independent Nigeria of the 1970s there was an increasing negative framing of the Beiers as 'saviours of a dying culture'. In the 1960s they were seen as anti-colonial, in the 1970s they were linked to the colonial past.

This shift in reception was connected to the approach chosen in the various workshops. From the start it was clear that they were designed as a free space, without any guidance in content. The workshops made materials and techniques available, but didn't prescribe what to make or how. Beier was inspired by other workshops elsewhere and the concept of *art brut*; the Beiers were aware of the theories of Jean Dubuffet. In Ibadan the workshops were intended to break down conservative academic habits of the participants, who were art teachers and art students. The Oshogbo workshops, however, were primarily targeted at youngsters who had never painted or drawn in their lives. Beier hoped to tap an original and pure sense of creativity, in combination with a deep sense of African culture. The works that were produced here were dynamic and vivid but not very refined, and the artists did not partake in an intellectual discourse on modern art. It was precisely this that made it impossible to connect these works to the emerging modernism in Nigeria.

The case of Bruce Onobrakpeya is interesting in this respect. Onobrakpeya participated in the Oshogbo workshops, and shared the interest in using African folklore and history as themes. But he was then already a graduate from the Zaria art academy, a member of the Zaria Art Society,[18] and had had some training in graphic techniques when he followed the etching workshop with Van Rossem. Three years later he imported an etching press

17. Amos Tutuola, *The Palm-Wine Drinkard* (London, 1952).

18. A group of art students at Zaria who rebelled agains the conservative academic methods.

from Amsterdam to his large studio in Lagos, and built steadily on his career as the most prolific graphic artist from Nigeria, possibly Africa, with Nigerian and international clients.

Thinking back, I realize I felt personally closer to the *art brut* character of the Oshogbo artworks, rather than to the work of artists representing Nigerian modernism at the time, as Demas Nwoko, Uche Okeke and Bruce Onobrakpeya. However, history judged that Oshogbo was a short-lived niche, and it were the Zaria graduates who represented the future of Nigerian art. I realize now I didn't ask myself enough questions in 1980. I was a fan, rather than a distanced scholar.

There were more moments of insight during the research process of the last few months. For instance, I learned the value of psychology, to better understand the personalities that play a role in colonial and postcolonial encounters such as these, and I realize the importance of external and internal power relations in the art discourse. However, the most important lesson I learned is the awareness of one's own opinions, attitudes, likings and dislikings, involvement and commitment, that influence one's vision.

Working as an art historian in the field of international and intercultural art studies requires to take sides, to a certain extent. You have to identify with your subject, to learn, to understand, to be inspired, but you need distance too, and open eyes and ears for other voices, other opinions. This is in my view the ultimate challenge, because it is hard to do. Revisiting old projects represents a unique opportunity to become aware of the traps. So, cherish your old projects. I still believe in the importance of that initial enthusiasm, which makes you a fan. But we also have to be sober and careful, less inclined to judge, and all the more to understand.

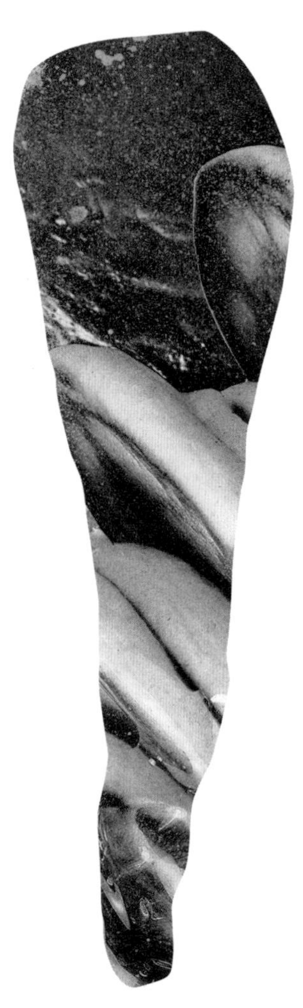

JOHN MAWURNDJUL Towards a Truer Transcultural Exhibition

Georges Petitjean

INGREDIENTS

- Direct and Sustained Involvement of the Artist
- Language of the Artist
- Sense of Place and History
- Dedicated Website
- Indigenization of Catalogue

This essay proposes to distil a number of ingredients for a truer and more equal transcultural or intercultural approach of artworks and practices of curating in future exhibitions. It advances on the pathway taken in the organization of a recent exhibition dedicated to the art of John Mawurndjul (b. 1952) and that includes the viewpoint of the artist as a leading curatorial force. While not new, in this particular case it concerns an Indigenous Australian artist from a remote community whose first language is the local Indigenous Kuninjku.

In September 2018 the retrospective exhibition 'John Mawurndjul: I am the old and the new' opened at the Museum of Contemporary Art (MCA) in Sydney before commencing a regional tour in Australia. The exhibition assembled some 160 artworks by John Mawurndjul spanning the artist's entire career from its beginnings in the late 1970s until now, and covering all mediums of his oeuvre: paintings on bark, sculptures (*lorrkkon* or hollow log coffins, *Mimih*, and other spirit figures), and etchings. Mawurndjul is a leading Kuninjku artist from central Arnhem Land in northern Australia with an impressive international track record of exhibiting, starting in Europe with his participation in the now legendary 'Magiciens de la terre' exhibition (1989) in Paris. This latest Australian retrospective was set up in close association with Mawurndjul and his involvement in this exhibition invested every aspect of this exhibition, ranging from the selection of artworks to the realization of a dedicated website. The structure of the exhibition followed Mawurndjul's directions and the catalogue is bilingual Kuninjku-English. Taking this exhibition as a case study, a number of cutting-edge and profound new curatorial practices can be identified and further developed, in particular for the purpose of an adjunct exhibition in Europe.

Before coming to this, let us first examine the exhibition in question and its precedents in the artist's career. It is in the history of significant exhibitions in Europe and in Australia in which Mawurndjul's oeuvre was honoured, that one can distinguish the seeds that led to this ground-breaking display of artworks. To continue the metaphor of the recipe book, these precedents are test recipes, try-outs before coming to a more final recipe for a dish of excellence.

'I never stop thinking about my *rarrk*'[1]

It was not the first time that a retrospective exhibition was dedicated to the art of John Mawurndjul. His oeuvre was celebrated in a major international exhibition, entitled '<<*rarrk*>>—John Mawurndjul: Journey through Time in Northern Australia' in reference to the cross-hatching so characteristic for the region, which premiered at the Tinguely Museum in Basel in 2005 and subsequently travelled on to the Sprengel Museum in Hannover (Germany). The main section of this exhibition comprised about seventy-five selected works by the artist, several from European private and institutional collections. The ethnographic museum of Basel, the Museum der Kulturen, as a guest institution of the Museum Tinguely, co-jointly presented about thirty-five major works on bark by different Arnhem Land artists that were acquired by Karel Kupka for this Basel museum between 1956 and 1963. Karel Kupka, a collector, artist, and anthropologist, insisted in his writings on the individual creativity in Arnhem Land painting practices. Christian Kaufmann, curator of the Oceania department of the Museum der Kulturen, identified the commissioned barks from Kupka as the foundation stone of the Mawurndjul exhibition.[2]

1. John Mawurndjul in an interview with Apolline Kohen, *<<rarrk>> - John Mawurndjul: Journey Through Time in Northern Australia*, ed. Christian Kaufmann, exh. cat., Museum Tinguely, Basel, 21 September 2005–29 January 2006; Sprengel Museum, Hannover, 19 February 2006–5 June 2006 (Basel, 2005), pp. 25–28; p. 28.

2. Christian Kaufmann, 'Aboriginal art from Arnhem Land: Why in Basel?' Ibid., pp. 222–226; p. 222.

Kupka's emphasis on art, the creative personality and individuality of the artists that he met, and his interaction with European artistic circles reflect the changing perceptions that mark the period in which the works were collected. His assessment of individual creativity went against the dominant assumption that Aboriginal artists were merely repeating unchangeable graphic prototypes. Since then, appreciation of Indigenous Australian art as contemporary art had come a long way. Indeed, it was a logical outcome in 2005, that a retrospective exhibition of this important Arnhem Land artist should take place at a museum of contemporary art, a monographic museum dedicated to one of Switzerland's greatest artists of the twentieth century.

Bernhard Lüthi, a Swiss artist, activist, and curator of '<<*rarrk*>>', who previously had been *chargé de mission* (project manager) for the Indigenous Australian segment of 'Magiciens de la terre', endeavoured throughout his life to give a voice to Indigenous people in the art discourse, actively pursuing direct involvement of the artists. Lüthi insisted on a solo exhibition of Mawurndjul that explicitly presented the artworks in a museum of art and that placed the emphasis on individual artistic development and innovation. Although Mawurndjul, who attended the opening in Switzerland, was highly supportive of this exhibition, it would take more than another decade before an exhibition would open on the artist's own terms.

Born in 1952, John Mawurndjul started painting in the 1970s and became one of the leading figures in the Australian contemporary art scene. Already in 1989, his work was presented in a high-profile international context with the inclusion of a number of bark paintings in 'Magiciens de la terre'. Two paintings on bark that were included in this legendary exhibition were the first works by an Indigenous artist to be registered in the collection of the MCA in 1989. Other important exhibitions in which Mawurndjul's work was included, were 'Dreamings: The Art of Aboriginal Australia' in New York in 1988 and 'Aratjara: Art of the First Australians' in 1993–1994, also curated by Bernhard Lüthi, for which Mawurndjul travelled to Europe. In 2000, his work was amongst that of eight individual Aboriginal artists and collective groups shown at

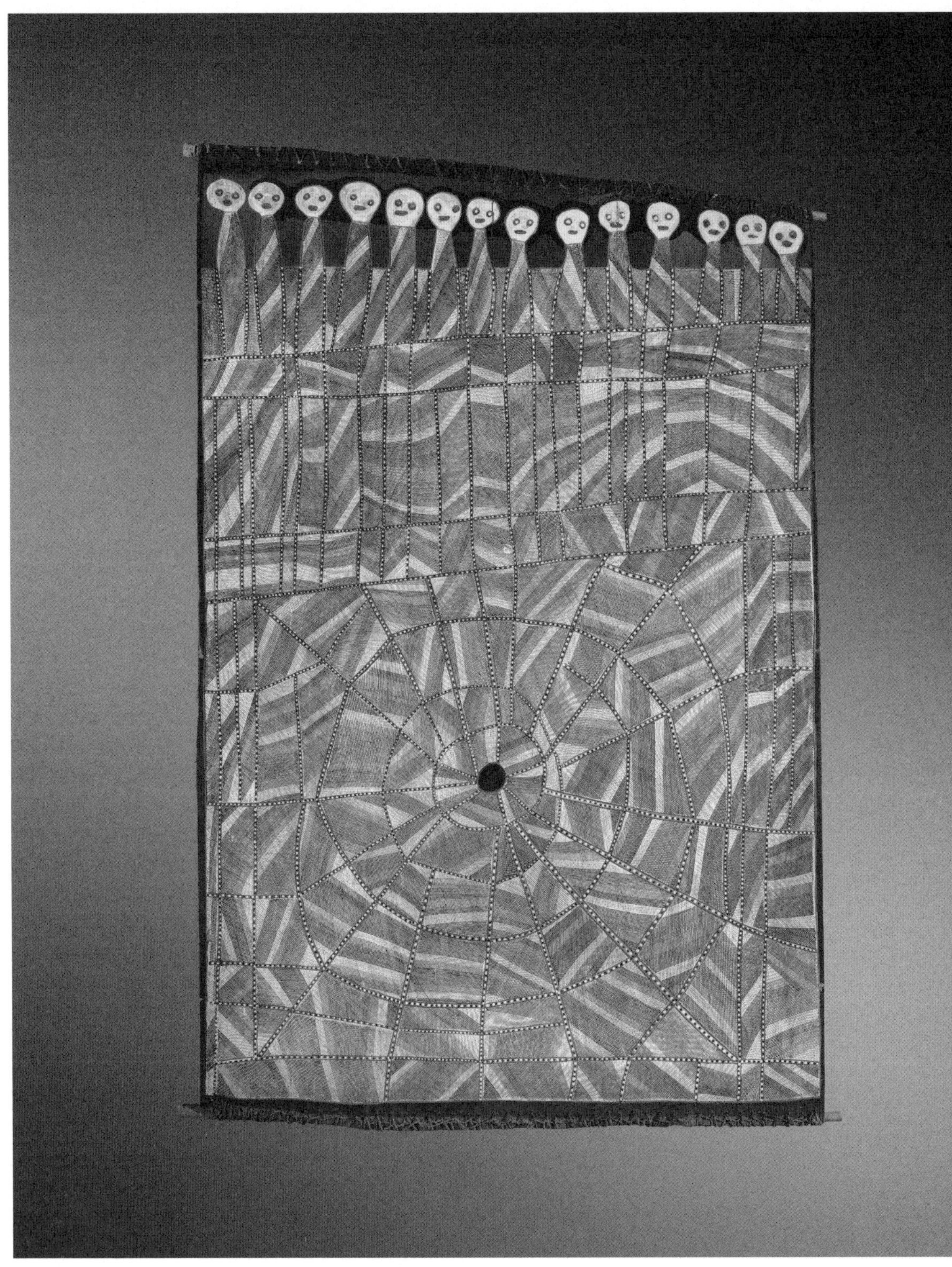

John Mawurndjul, *Ancestors at Milmilingkan*, 1994, ochres and natural pigments on bark, 168 cm x 110 cm. Collection Fondation Opale/Collection Bérengère Primat. Photo Vincent Girier Dufournier.

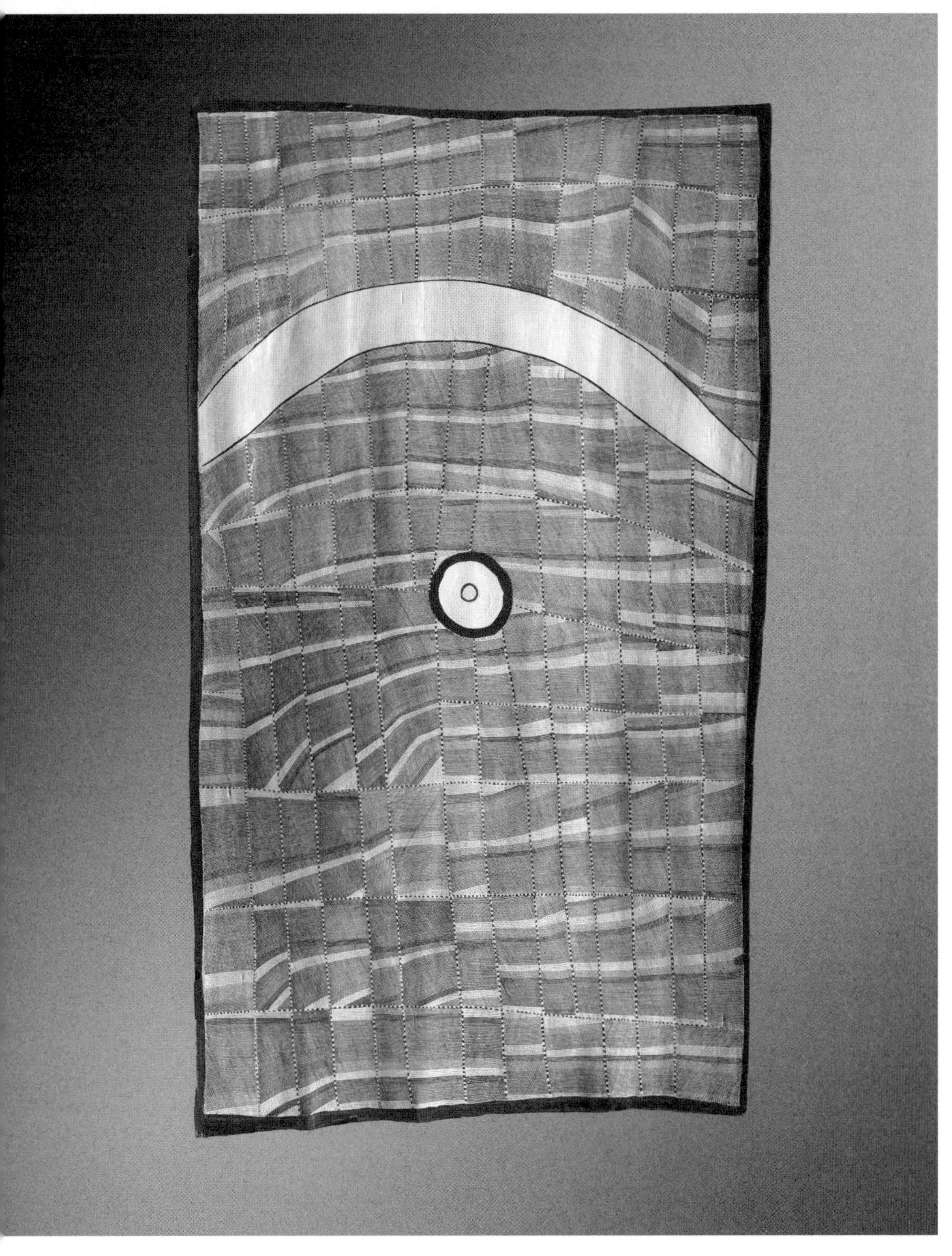

John Mawurndjul, *Dilebang Waterhole*, 2016, ochres and natural pigments on bark, 151 cm x 86 cm. Collection Fondation Opale/Collection Bérengère Primat. Photo Vincent Girier Dufournier.

the State Hermitage Museum in Saint-Petersburg.

His engagement with art from around the world during this imposing artistic trajectory led him to many places. Attending several openings overseas, including in Paris, Tokyo, Cologne, and Venice, provided him with the opportunity to mingle with an international audience. Interactions with *balanda*, non-Aboriginal people, supported his strong belief in the universality of art ('We make art, and it's all powerful. Everybody'). All human beings make images, each with their own particular technique for drawing and all emanating from their own particular culture. This outspoken conviction speaks volumes about Mawurndjul's approach to art on a global, transcultural scale.

Mawurndjul's work questions Western approaches to both seeing and presenting art of Indigenous Australians. The pictorial content in his visually striking artwork is in a continuous process of transformation. Key to this is the use of a cross-hatching technique referred to as *rarrk* in the Kuninjku language. *Rarrk* dominates the entire picture and accords it a particularly shimmering effect. While both a powerful formal aspect, especially in the works consisting solely of *rarrk*, and a narrative element (e.g., skin of the Rainbow Serpent, who represents one of the great and powerful forces of nature and spirit in Aboriginal Australian belief), it heightens the effectiveness of the visual rendition of encrypted meaning that is only accessible to the initiated. This expression of simultaneous luminosity through shimmer is the basis of aesthetics in which the complexity of knowledge forms an integral part of the painting and determines its power, which is reflective of ancestral power.[3]

> I always think of new ways to paint,
> I always look for something different.[4]

The continuous aesthetic innovation in Mawurndjul's oeuvre, and the artist's proactive interaction with tradition and convention, is illustrative of his personal individual approach of art. His work is characterized by a sense of energetic composition and refuses to be categorized.

3. See for a comparative not on the brilliance in Yolngu art of northeast Arnhem Land the seminal article by Howard Morphy, 'From Dull to Brilliant: The Aesthetics of Spiritual Power among th Yolngu', *Anthropology, Art and Aesthetics*, eds. Jeremy Coote and Anthony Shelton (Oxford, 1992), pp. 181–208.

4. John Mawurndjul in an interview with Apolline Kohen, Kaufmann 2007 (see note 1), pp. 25-28; p. 28

In 2020, the year of UNESCO Indigenous Languages, this exhibition and its catalogue were very timely. While bilingualism is not new, the use of bilingualism to this extent—both the exhibition and its catalogue have Kuninjku language—is unprecedented. 'John Mawurndjul: I am the old and the new' is not only a comprehensive survey of one of Australia's most important Indigenous artists. It is also an exhibition that challenges the Eurocentric and Western-centric viewpoints.

As a result of a constraint of budget, there was a lack of works from European collections in the Australian exhibition. This however opened the prospect for a new individual exhibition in Europe, with work sourced primarily from European collections, as adjunct to the landmark Australian retrospective.

A number of elements are key to the success of this exhibition that transcends cultures, of which the culture of the artist is an active part, and should be taken into account for a European adjunct exhibition, indeed for any monographic exhibition of an Indigenous Australian artist in a European gallery setting. Although a European gallery context provides at the very least a geographical distance from an Australian context, a European pendant to this exhibition has to take into account the cultural distance of Aboriginal Australia.

Direct participation and sustained involvement of the artist from the onset, even at an international level, is a crucial ingredient. To make this possible, a strong bond of mutual trust between the artist and the curators should be established, one of exchange and mutual understanding. The artist is a guide to his own exhibition. Curators should travel to the artist's country and visit sites of importance to the subjects of his work under guidance of the artist. It is equally imperative to read transcriptions or hear the artists talk about their work and its sources. Curators should endeavour to empathize with the world of thoughts of the artist and to become intercultural through proactively seeking rapprochement and understanding in order to foster a platform for an understanding for a broad public.

Language is a critical marker of cultural identity. In a world in which diversity, paradoxically, is diminishing rather than increasing, and languages are declining or disappearing rapidly, language more than ever is a critical marker of cultural identity. Some specific concepts that reflect the differences in the approach of art can only exist when using the words for these in the language of the artist. This notably is the case with *rarrk* in the Kuninjku language, which evokes more than just a crosshatching technique, but reflects an entire social, religious, and artistic system behind the image. Another word, *kabimbebme*, for instance, is a Kuninjku term describing the effect of brilliance or a 'painting jumping at you'.[5] The bark painting is judged by the artist in terms of the brilliance and shimmer of its cross-hatchings. Nowhere else is *kabimbebme* more present than in bark paintings and sculptures that relate to specific sites with connected ceremonial knowledge, in which a riveting sense of energy in space is achieved that suggests an evocation of these ancestral places that in turn stimulates an imaginative but overwhelming sense of immersion.

Does this mean that we have to learn an entire language in order to appreciate an artwork? Obviously not, but familiarizing oneself with a particular concept, such as *rarrk*, *kabimbebme* or *kunred* arms us with the necessary openness of mind and broadens our vocabulary towards a better, more accurate and articulate understanding and appreciation of the artwork. This is not entirely unlike the connoisseur of medieval European religious paintings, who needs profound iconographic knowledge to come to a truer understanding of the artwork. One advantage is that this new knowledge and expanded vision of mind also has a beneficial effect of enhancing cross-cultural and transcultural visions in art. This is particularly important when curating exhibitions in which artworks by artists from several cultures and places in the world are juxtaposed. It helps us curators to draw parallels between different works, in finding links and sometimes unthought-of correlations, and ultimately with opening up a new discourse in and about the art world.

A next important aspect concerns the sense of place. Mawurndjul's paintings on bark and sculptures are intrinsically related to *kunred*—the concept of place—through the materials he uses, stringybark (*Eucalyptus tetrodonta*), and ochres and natural pigments mined directly

5. Hetti Perkins, 'Mardayin Maestro', *John Mawurndjul: I am the old and the new*, ed. Clothilde Bullen et al, exh. cat., Museum of Contemporary Art, Sydney, 6 July 2018–23 September 2018; Art Gallery of South Australia, Adelaide, 26 October 2018–28 January 2019 (Sydney, 2018), pp. 20–37; p. 33.

from the earth. Here, country supports culture. While beautiful and powerful abstract patterns to the eyes of the lay visitor, these paintings are powerful representations of notions that are at the basis of Kuninjku culture.

The selection of works for 'I am the old and the new' took place under Mawurndjul's guidance and direction, resulting in a presentation of the most powerful works from his four-decade long career. Mawurndjul outlined the structure of the exhibition during a journey with the curators to places of great significance in his country.[6] He advised that the works should be grouped by moiety—*duwa* and *yirridjdja*—and then consequently follow a path through the *kunred* (places) of his country.[7] Sites and places (equally sites of production) represented in the paintings are a guiding principle in the floor plan of the exhibition. In Mawurndjul's case this is of great importance as an assimilation of the self within the Kuninjku cosmological landscape occurs.[8] Culture and country converge, are inseparable.

All of the above ingredients are closely interrelated, as they are logical consequences of one another. Next to these are two more ingredients, to spice up the dish, that, while still in close association with the artist, offer important transcultural handholds for a general public to acquire an enhanced and more informed appreciation of the artist's oeuvre, culture, and vision.

The first one is a dedicated website and substantial presence on internet, delivered by new digital technology. Especially in recent times with the advent of Covid-19 we have seen an exponential rise of dedicated websites that allow visitors to get an in-depth view into an artwork, exhibition, or art fair. Inclusion on internet and social media platforms should happen in conjunction with the artist and follow cultural protocols. For 'I am the old and the new', a dedicated website was set up by the Head of Digital Media at the MCA, Jean-Pierre Chabrol, who has been following Mawurndjul since 2003.[9] This website, an ongoing project, which will be extended with future projects around Mawurndjul's oeuvre, was conceived in close association with the artist.

Secondly, the catalogue for 'I am the old and the new' is very much the result of an artist-led project, as is

6. Mawurndjul 2015–2016 (see note 1), p. 373.

7. The Kuninjku population is divided into two moieties, Duwa and Yirridjdja. A person that belongs to the moiety of their father marries a person of the opposite moiety. The entire universe is divided on the basis of moiety: ancestral beings, animals, places, plants, even constellations belong to either one moiety or the other. However, the moieties, while separate, are intertwined with one another. The ceremonies are associated with different Mardayin (songs, paintings, sacred objects, and dances) but the themes of the ceremonies overlap and people of both moieties have roles in their performance. The moieties are bound together in a web of kinship. Mawurndjul is *duwa moiety*, but also paints the very small fine cross-hatching associated with the *yirridjdja* moiety.

8. Perkins 2018 (see note 5), p. 33.

9. johnmawurndjul.com. For a possible European sister exhibition, this website will be expanded with new, ongoing biographical data, a new selection of artworks mainly deriving from European collections, and paving the way for an online *catalogue raisonné* of the artist's oeuvre.

the exhibition and the website. Clothilde Bullen, Natasha Bullock, Nici Cumpston, Keith Munro and Lisa Slade, the curators—coming from both the MCA and the Art Gallery of South Australia (AGSA)—of the Australian exhibition, worked in close collaboration with Mawurndjul. Tellingly, their words come at the end of the bilingual Kuninjku and English catalogue in an Afterword, thus leaving the final—or the first—word to this artist. In line with the bilingual approach of the exhibition, the catalogue is bilingual too, and hence renders the artist's thoughts in his own words. This format should be reprised for a European version of this particular exhibition or an individual exhibition with the work by an Indigenous Australian artist from a remote community, although possibly some concepts might require more interpretation for a public with a largely European background. Instead of decolonizing, the catalogue should be an example of Indigenization.

The ingredients listed in this essay propose to combine the old and new ways of curating and should serve as a guideline for European exhibitions of art by Indigenous Australian artists. The right dosage of these ingredients could result in ground-breaking exhibitions that profoundly challenge the Eurocentric and Western-centric viewpoint through a sustained and direct involvement of the Indigenous artists informing each aspect of the exhibition, ranging from the selection and placing of artworks through to the production of a bilingual catalogue and a dedicated website, thus taking into account the artists' vision and intrinsic relationship to the land that is at the core of their art. This should allow for a truer and more equal transcultural approach of the artworks and practice of curating in future exhibitions. Such exhibitions can also provide important precedents, even blueprints, for other exhibitions involving Indigenous artists and to create an openness of mind through providing the necessary tools for better reciprocal understanding.

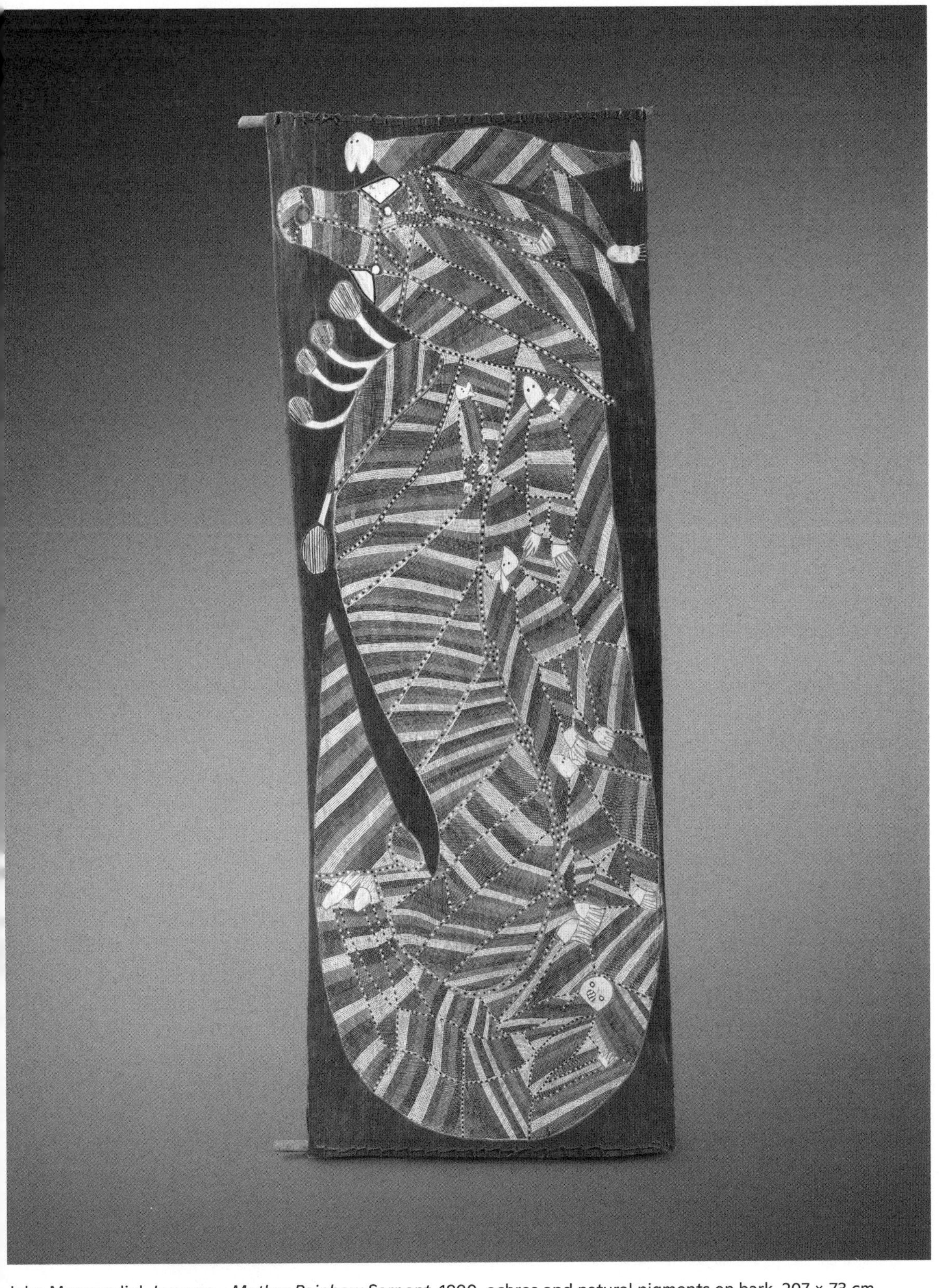

John Mawurndjul, *Ingarna - Mother Rainbow Serpent*, 1990, ochres and natural pigments on bark, 207 × 73 cm. Collection Fondation Opale/Collection Bérengère Primat. Photo Vincent Girier Dufournier.

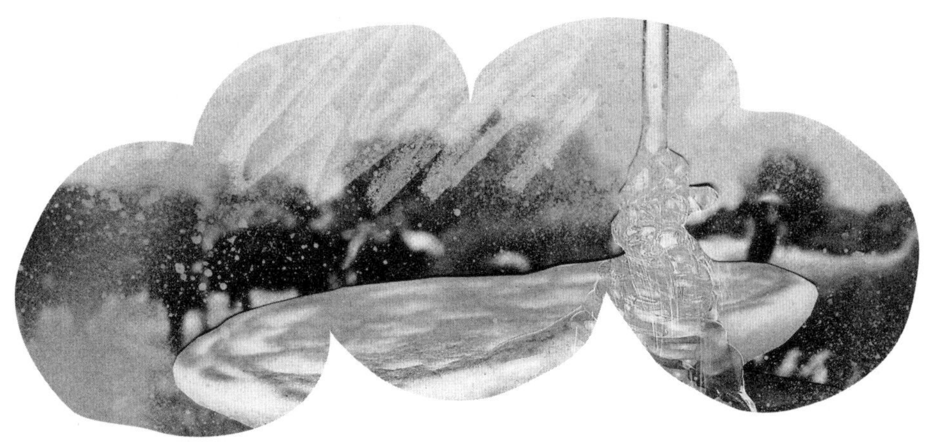

OUR BRAIN IS A MIRROR

Meta Knol

INGREDIENTS

- Magic Wand
- Imagination
- Empathy
- Perspective
- Museum

My mother-in-law recently passed away. While clearing out the house, full of Indonesian bits and pieces, I came across a framed photograph of a work by Gerhard Richter again. It must have been years ago that we had visited the De Pont Museum in Tilburg together. Unexpectedly, I had found my mother-in-law in one of the rooms, in tears. Incredibly upset. Over a cup of coffee in the museum café, she had finally been able to find the words: she had been terribly shocked by a particular detail in that Richter painting. Suddenly, in that abstract green design, she had been confronted with the image of a robbery in Zimbabwe, which she had experienced barely a year earlier, during a trip through Africa, and as a result of which she had suffered a stab wound to her forearm. After she had dried her tears, she went back to the painting, took a photograph of it, framed it, and casually placed it in her bookcase, so that she could begin the process of healing from the corner of her eye. The things that art can do, I thought at the time.

Perhaps it started with that experience: the realization that art and empathy are much more closely intertwined than I had learned from conducting style analyses and memorizing dates during my art history study in the 1990s. We learned a great deal about European painting and sculpture, about movements, oeuvres, materials, and iconography. We were told that the origins of art could be traced back to the caves of Lascaux, and how, gradually, the same Western art rose to great heights. We learned to be in awe, founded on a clear distinction between what was art, and what was not. That whole circus unfolded around the holy grail: the material object. We learned nothing about people, about how individuals look at art, how they interpret and process art. Yet, that is where it all begins: *in the eye of the beholder*. Fortunately, much has changed since I was a student, and mainly in a positive sense.[1] That said, I think there is still a significant area for research between our eyes and art history that lies fallow.

This elusive question continued to haunt me as I stepped out into the world, between all the activities and new jobs: how do people view art? What's going on in that cranium up there? How does meaning arise? Every now and then, I would realize with a jolt that something essential had changed in my own ideas. For example, I once heard a story in the Mondrian House in Amersfoort, of a neurologist in a London hospital who put people through an MRI scanner to measure their brain activity while looking at paintings by Piet Mondrian and Theo van Doesburg. The differences were significant: calm versus agitation.[2] Or, the time I asked a neurologist to write a brief essay about the 'drawing hand'—because the shortest conceivable connection in the triangular relationship between eye, hand, and brain still lies in drawing, the archetype of art.[3] This attention also goes deeper than physical processes, for example to the psychological encounter between the viewer and the work of art. Time and again it became clear that every interaction with art involves an active change of perspective. Artists make us look at the world with different eyes. Every art experience is therefore also an interactive process in which object and subject compete for priority. That makes looking at and experiencing art an interesting type of brain gymnastics. Museum experts often inadvertently get in the way of these more emotional encounters when they appeal to the public on a cognitive level, flooding them with art-historic lessons.

Fortunately, this way of thinking is becoming less and less common, now that the interaction between man and object in a museum context is changing under the influence of advancing social emancipation processes. While I was taught, during my studies, that the visual arts of Western Europe and North America are an exclusive domain that can be entered thanks to the increase in art-historical knowledge, around 2010 the concept of

1. See e.g., Caroline van Eck, *Art, Agency and Living Presence: From Animated Image to the Excessive Object* (Boston/Berlin/Munich/Leiden, 2015); Kitty Zijlmans, *Kunstgeschiedenis* (Amsterdam, 2018 / Elementaire Deeltjes no. 60).

2. Unfortunately, the reader has no choice but to trust my memory, since I can no longer find my notes from that time, and the Mondrian House's website also does not provide a definitive answer.

3. Meta Knol, Jan G.P. van Bergen, Jan van Gijn, *Zinnenprikkelend* (Utrecht, 2000).

4. For more information about the concept of inclusiveness in relation to the Dutch museum world, see e.g.: Nynke Feenstra, 'Putting into Words: The Relation Between Museums, Communities, and the Importance of a Context-Specific Meaning of Inclusiveness' (STUDIO —Stedelijk Museum Amsterdam and Van Abbe Museum, Eindhoven, 2018).

5. Ellen de Bruin, 'Spiegels in de ziel', *NRC Handelsblad*, 14 March 2009, www.nrc.nl/nieuws/2009/03/14/spiegels-in-de-ziel-11697684-a1358973; Marco Iacoboni, *Mirroring People: The Science of Empathy and How We Connect with Others* (London, 2009).

6. Susan Lanzoni, *Empathy, a History* (London, 2018).

7. For an overview of empathy in a museum context, see the collection of essays: *Fostering Empathy through Museums*, ed. Elif Gokcigdem (London, 2016).

inclusiveness made an appearance in culture and society.[4] The postmodern realization that many interpretations are possible, reinforced by the effects of globalization and digitalization, meant that also in museum policy attention gradually turned from the exclusive materiality of the object to more inclusive, human-oriented interpretations of it. In the wake of this development, the focus is slowly shifting from collecting and preserving art to making it accessible and transferring it to diverse people and audiences. Refreshing forms of humanity are entering the museum field.

New scientific discoveries and insights could play an important role in this development, which too often remains underexposed. I vividly remember, for example, reading an interview in a newspaper with the Italian-American scientist Marco Iacoboni, who had written a book about the discovery of the mirror neuron.[5] In the mid-1990s, a team of neurophysiologists from the University of Parma, led by Giacomo Rizzolatti, discovered how nerve cells in the brains of a group of laboratory animals lit up when they observed behaviour by their researchers, such as licking an ice cream. By analyzing movements in the motor cortex of this group of macaques, these scientists had discovered the mirror neuron; a substance that is fired in the brains of humans and animals as soon as they observe the behaviours of others. The magic mirror neuron stimulates unintentional imitation and thus generates unconscious learning processes, such as during interactions between parent and child. In combination with physiological processes that occur in other brain regions and the production of hormones such as oxytocin, this contributes to our capacity for empathy.[6] People who see another person scratching, start to feel itchy themselves. And the same is true when we look at images of reality, because something similar can happen when we look at a photograph.

Our brain thus possesses mirroring properties that contribute to our empathic abilities, even when it comes to depictions of reality. This leads to the interesting question of to what extent this empathic capacity influences the production and experience of art.[7] Recently, a few interesting books have been written about empathic capital by scientists, philosophers, and essayists such as Jeremy

Rifkin, Frans de Waal, Roman Krznaric, and the American historian Susan Lanzoni.[8] At Harvard University, Lanzoni focuses on the history of psychology, psychiatry, and neuroscience. Her book on empathy contains a wealth of information and insights and should be required reading for all art historians. Because anyone who delves into the concept of empathy quickly learns that this stems from the notion of *Einfühlung*: the ability to react empathically to works of art.[9] It was the nineteenth-century German philosopher and aesthetician Theodor Lipps who described *Einfühlung* as 'the projection of one's own unconscious feelings and inner imagined movements into the art object'.[10] At Cornell University, in 1908, the English psychologist Edward Titchener linked the concept with the Greek *Empatheia*, meaning 'physical affection or passion' and, as such, directly derived from the word *pathos*.[11] He explored what he called 'kinaesthetic image': the ability to project our mental faculties onto matter.[12] It is telling that these scientific explorations, circa 1900–1914, of the concept of 'empathy' coincided with the birth of modern art and the invention of abstraction,[13] which saw expressionist artists such as Wassily Kandinsky and Ernst Ludwig Kirchner begin to create penetrating 'emotional images', while at the same time, in related circles, psychoanalysis, invoked by Sigmund Freud and Ernst Gustav Jung, was coined as a new scientific field. The genie was out of the bottle.

Psychology has subsequently made an unprecedented advance from these artistic-scientific circles; a development that led the English philosopher Roman Krznaric to describe the twentieth century as 'The Age of Introspection' in his book *Empathy: Why it Matters, and How to Get It*.[14] Under the influence of the popularization of psychology, the concept of 'empathy' has steadily penetrated our everyday language since the 1950s.[15]

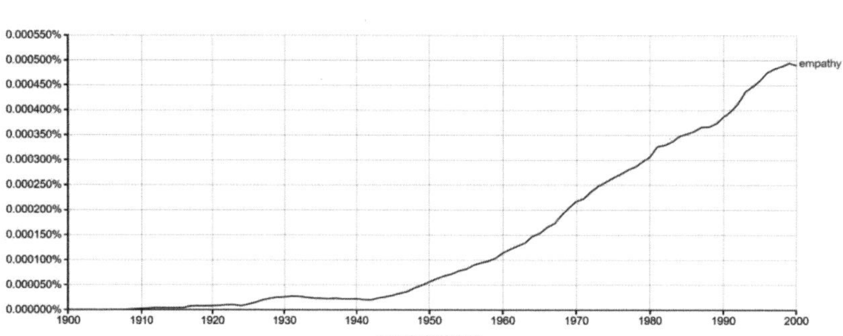

Google n-gram chart showing the frequency of use of 'empathy' in English from c. 1900 to 2000, taken from: Lanzoni 2018 (see note 6), p.198.

8. Jeremy Rifkin, *The Empathic Civilization: The Race to Global Consciousness in a World in Crisis* (New York, 2010); Frans de Waal, *The Age of Empathy: Nature's Lessons for a Kinder Society* (New York, 2009); Roman Krznaric, *Empathy: Why it Matters, and How to Get it* (London, 2014); Lanzoni 2018 (see note 6).

9. Joanna Ganczarek, Thomas Hünefeldt, Martha Olivetti Belardinelli, 'From "Einfühlung" to Empathy: Exploring the Relationship Between Aesthetic and Interpersonal Experience', *Cognitive Processing* 19 (2018), pp. 141-145: 'The notion of "Einfühlung" was theoretically developed in nineteenth- and early twentieth-century German aesthetics, especially by Robert Vischer (1873) and Theodor Lipps (1903, 1906). The term "Einfühlung" literally means "feeling into" and refers to an act of projecting oneself into another body or environment, i.e.—Vischer's terms—to an imaginary bodily "displacement" (*Versetzung*) of oneself into another body or environment, which is aimed at understanding how it feels to be in that other body or environment. In other words, it refers to some kind of imaginary bodily perspective taking, which is aimed at understanding what it would be like to be living another body or another environment'.

10. Lipps quoted in Lanzoni 2018 (see note 6), p. 23.

11. Ibid., pp. 46–51.

12. Ibid., p. 46.

13. Ibid., p. 42.

14. Krznaric 2014 (see note 8), p. XXIII

15. There are different forms of empathy: cognitive, affective, collective empathy, empathy towards others, self-empathy. A distinction is made between sympathy (perceiving), empathy (feeling for), and compassion (offering help). We can talk of 'empathic bias', which means that empathy can lead to identification with like-minded people and the removal of dissenters.

16. Rifkin 2010 (see note 8).

17. On the decline of empathy as an artistic-museum value, see: Lanzoni 2018 (see note 6), p. 93. England 1941): 'Museum curators were advised that empathy was a "now outmoded aesthetic" even if many had been schooled in the empathy tradition.'

18. See e.g. Clement Greenberg, 'Avantgarde and Kitsch', *Partisan Review* (Autumn 1939), pp. 34–49; and Clement Greenberg, 'Modernist Painting', *Arts Yearbook* 4 (1961) (Washington, DC: Voice of America 1960).

It prompted the American social economist Jeremy Rifkin to publish the hefty tome *The Empathic Civilization* (2010), in which he even argues that the development of empathic ability coincides with the evolutionary development of humanity towards ever higher levels of interconnectedness.[16] This triumphant march of the concept of 'empathy' is in sharp contrast to the disappearance of the idea from the art world itself—as Lanzoni also aptly describes it.[17] The whole idea of *Einfühlung* seems to have collapsed under the weight of modernist art theory in the 1950s. The influential, formalistic art critic Clement Greenberg had an eye for the sublime spirituality of artists and their works, but rarely for the complex experiences and individual interpretations of viewers. It led to a devaluation of the audience, which was literally and figuratively forced into a clinical *white cube*. Greenberg also felt that art had to defend itself against the decline of good taste as a consequence of popularization and consumerism.[18] In doing so, he disqualified *en passant* 'other eyes' than those of the artist and the initiated expert. While the neglected bond between viewer and artwork still plagues us, fortunately we are observing a gradual reversal of this.

As far as I am concerned, it is high time that we reconnect the concept of 'empathy' with its roots: the arts. Because when people look at art, they are by no means passive observers; each work of art is subject to change under the influence of individual points of view. In this complex process of viewing, comparing, feeling, distancing, associating, identifying, interpreting, and judging, the artwork takes on a temporary and person-specific shape; what the viewer brings to the table in terms of judgements, prejudices, values and truths, experiences, and feelings, all plays a decisive role in the formation of meaning. Not only visual art, but also film, dance, theatre, and music are invitations to briefly step into the shoes of the other, to look at reality, as it were, through their eyes. Art is pre-eminently a perspective changer: it opens your eyes, offers opportunities to identify, and can lead to different or new insights. An empathic art experience is thus automatically rooted in the emancipation of the viewer, who changes from a passive observer into an active participant.

This insight also fits in with the current trend that spectators increasingly behave as participants. The apparently great need for this is clear from the popularity of 'immersive installations' in contemporary art, of concerts where the audience no longer has to sit neatly on chairs, and in the new forms of co-creation that are gaining ground in the cultural sphere. As Lanzoni recalls: 'The beautiful is not a thing, it is an act.'[19] Or, as Roman Krznaric puts it: 'Art has a long and distinguished history, going back centuries, of kicking our empathic selves into action.'[20] Our reflective, empathic brain continuously translates encounters and collisions with the outside world into our inner world and art, in all its manifestations, could just be a particle accelerator of that process. Incidentally, as scientific research shows, reason and feeling can hardly be distinguished from each other anymore.[21] Yet, we still make a distinction, if only to get a little grip on reality. For example, you could say that, while the modernist view of art is primarily Apollonian in nature, our contemporary art experience is once again shifting in a Dionysian direction.[22] Nowadays, there seems to be more space for the emotional experience of art. The question is, what does this shift mean for art history as an academic discipline?

Lessons in the working of empathy can, in many ways, yield new art historical insights with respect to the relationship between object and subject, and this can directly contribute to opening up this same art history through new perspectives. For example, a global approach to art, in which, in addition to traditional Western art concepts, there is also space for art forms and art experiences from other parts of the world, fits very well with this empathic method. In his book, Krznaric cites the novelist George Eliot (pseudonym of Mary Anne Evans), who already in the nineteenth century wrote: 'Art is the nearest thing to life; it is a mode of amplifying experience and extending our contact with fellow-men beyond the bounds of our personal lot.'[23] He also references the writer and cognitive psychologist Keith Oatly, who showed, through neurological research that: '...the process of entering imagined worlds of fiction builds empathy and improves your ability to take another person's point of view'.[24] Lanzoni, in turn, writes in her wonderful book:

19. Lanzoni 2018 (see note 6), p. 23.

20. Krznaric 2014 (see note 8), pp. 135-136.

21. Lanzoni 2018 (see note 6), p. 273: 'The stark divide often made between emotion and cognition is a historical artifact of outdated moralism'.

22. In philosophy and cultural history, the Apollonian-Dionysian dichotomy is used to indicate certain mental states. The terms derive from Apollo and Dionysus, the two sons of Zeus, from Greek mythology. Apollonian stands for rational thinking, order and logic, mastery and purity. Dionysian stands for irrationality, chaos, emotions, and the instinctive.

23. Krznaric 2014 (see note 8), p. 151.

24. Ibid., p. 152; Keith Oatly,'In the minds of others', *Scientific American Mind* (Nov/Dec 2011), pp. 63–67.

> Empathy depends on the movement between the poles of similarity and difference, of distance and closeness, of immersion and alienation. Empathy marks a relation between the self and the other that draws a border but also builds a bridge.[25]

And the biologist Frans de Waal uses the scientific knowledge that he has acquired about monkey colonies to emphasize the naturalness of encounters between human cultures:

> If we could manage seeing other people on other continents as part of us, drawing them into our circle of reciprocity and empathy, we would be building upon, rather than going against, our natures.[26]

Interesting initiatives are now underway in the international museum world, such as the Center for Empathy and the Visual Arts, which was established a few years ago and is part of the Minneapolis Institute of Art. They focus on conducting research and organizing activities in collaboration with museum staff, social scientists, artists, educators, and others with the aim of promoting 'empathy and global understanding through the power of art'. The results are generously shared with the museum field.[27] The Brooklyn Museum in New York has also started empathy-related programmes, while the Peabody Essex Museum in Salem, Massachusetts, is taking a slightly different approach by appointing a 'neurologist-in-residence'.[28] In the American 'Empathic Museum' initiative, knowledge, expertise, and practical tools are collected and shared with the museum field, after all: 'The qualities of twenty-first-century museums are impossible without an inner core of institutional empathy: the intention of the museum to be, and be perceived as, deeply connected with its community.' They describe the museum of the future as: 'Visitor-centered. Civic-minded. Diverse. Inclusive. Welcoming. Responsive. Participatory'.[29] Interesting initiatives have also emerged in the United Kingdom, such as the Roman Krznaric's sympathetic 'Empathy Museum', which has now embarked on an international tour.[30] His compatriot Matthew Taylor,

25. Lanzoni 2018 (see note 6), p. 17.

26. De Waal quoted in Krznaric 2014 (see note 8), p. 20. See, e.g., also Kader Attia's exhibition 'The Museum of Emotion', Hayward Gallery 2019, www.southbankcentre.co.uk/whats-on/art-exhibitions/kader-attia.

27. Center for Empathy and the Visual Arts, part of the Minneapolis Institute of Art new.artsmia.org/empathy/.

28. See Brooklyn Museum, New York: www.brooklynmuseum.org/about. And: Peabody Essex Museum, Salem, Mass. www.pem.org/press-news/pem-appoints-dr-tedi-asher-as-first-ever-neuroscience-researcher-at-an-art-museum.

29. American initiative 'Empathic Museum': www.empatheticmuseum.weebly.com.

30. 'Empathy Museum' by Roman Krznaric: www.empathymuseum.com/.

until recently president of the Royal Society for the Arts and currently CEO of the confederation of National Health Services, is an advocate of 'empathic universalism'. His website, *cultureofempathy.com*, features lots of information about initiatives, sources, and experts in the area of empathy and culture. Taylor makes no bones about it: 'The emotional foundation of universalism is empathy.'[31]

To date, in the Netherlands, this empathic movement has penetrated slowly.[32] Yet, it is hugely relevant. While the inequality in our society is demonstrably increasing, there is a call from all sides to make the cultural sector more inclusive by opening it up with alternative narratives and new audiences. Museums certainly have a role to play in this. Last week, for example, I read an impressive interview in a Dutch newspaper with the former international footballer Clarence Seedorf, who said: 'It would be good if people reflected more on each other's past, culture, needs, and beliefs. Tolerance can be trained. I think that, in the Netherlands, we are still at the beginning of that process.'[33]

Incidentally, when the same newspaper asked the mirror neuron chronicler, Marco Iacoboni, in 2009, where he hoped this phenomenal discovery would lead, he said:

> If I had a magic wand, I would force countries to use some of their money to allow citizens to travel, so that they can really meet people from other cultures. I think that mirror neurons also help to make people open-minded and to get rid of their prejudices. The most conservative people are those who grow up and continue to live in completely homogeneous cultures. So, if you're genuinely exposed to other people, to how they behave, what they do, instead of just thinking about them in a stereotypical way, that helps. If you really look at people, you will find lots of things that you have in common.[34]

That is nicely put. And I think that if people look closely at art, they will also find a lot of things in common. Because, contrary to what some would have us believe, art never

31. Krznaric 2014 (see note 8), p. 185.

32. A Dutch pioneer in this field is STUDIO i, an initiative of the Stedelijk Museum Amsterdam and the Van Abbe Museum in Eindhoven: www.studio-inclusie.nl/en.

33. Enzo van Steenbergen and Danielle Pinedo, 'Clarence Seedorf: "Ik heb moeten vechten om gehoord te worden"', *NRC* 28 mei 2021, www.nrc.nl/nieuws/2021/05/28/clarence-seedorf-ik-heb-moeten-vechten-om-gehoord-te-worden-a4045263.

34. Iacoboni 2009 (see note 5).

stands alone. It is an essential part of that wide range of commonalities that we call culture. So, if our brain is a mirror, so to speak, and culture is our collective reflection, then art may be that exciting perspective changer that shows, in a challenging manner, that I, we, and they are, ultimately, all sides of the same coin. And the best place to show all those miraculous connections, I now realize, could well be a museum.

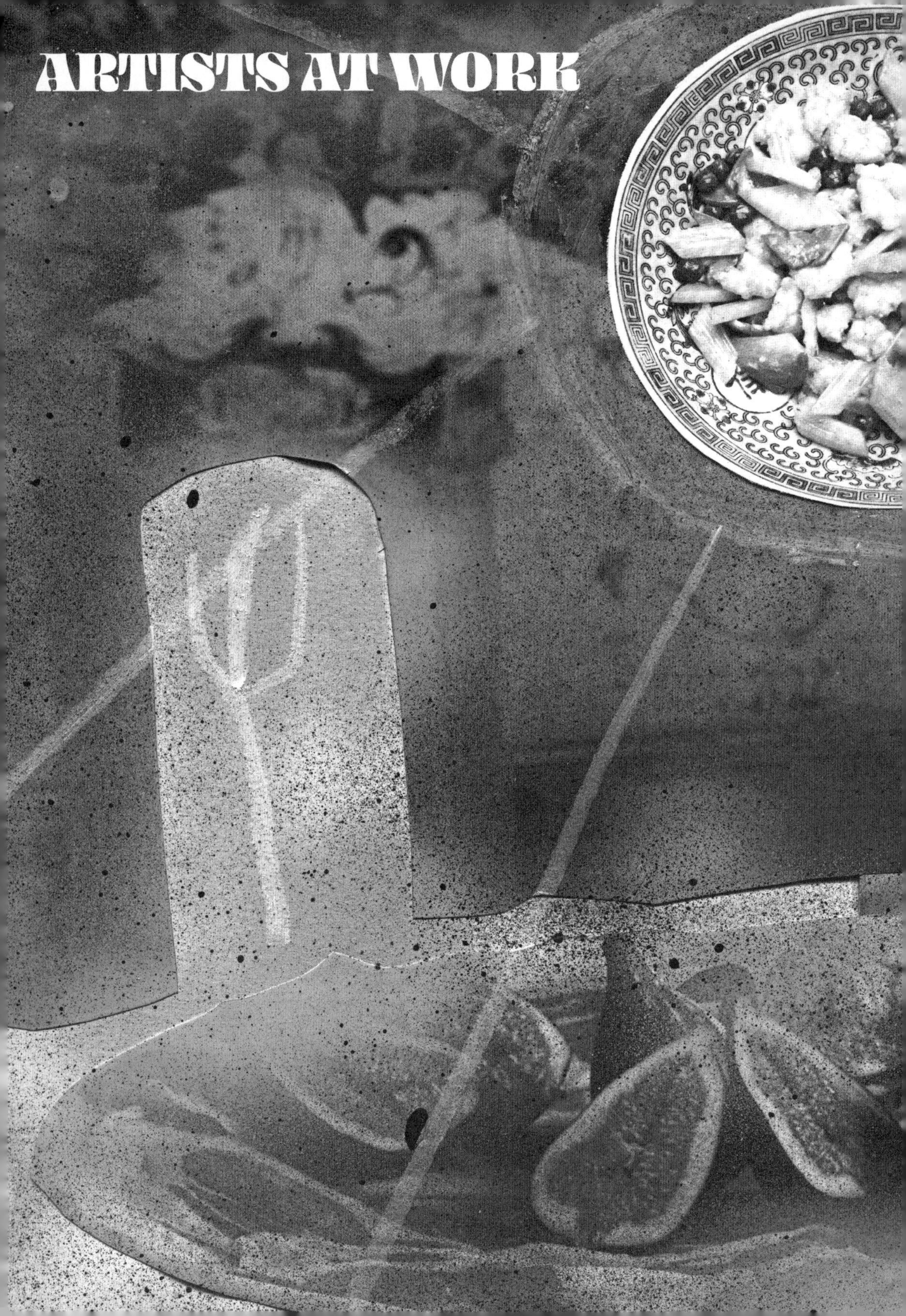
ARTISTS AT WORK

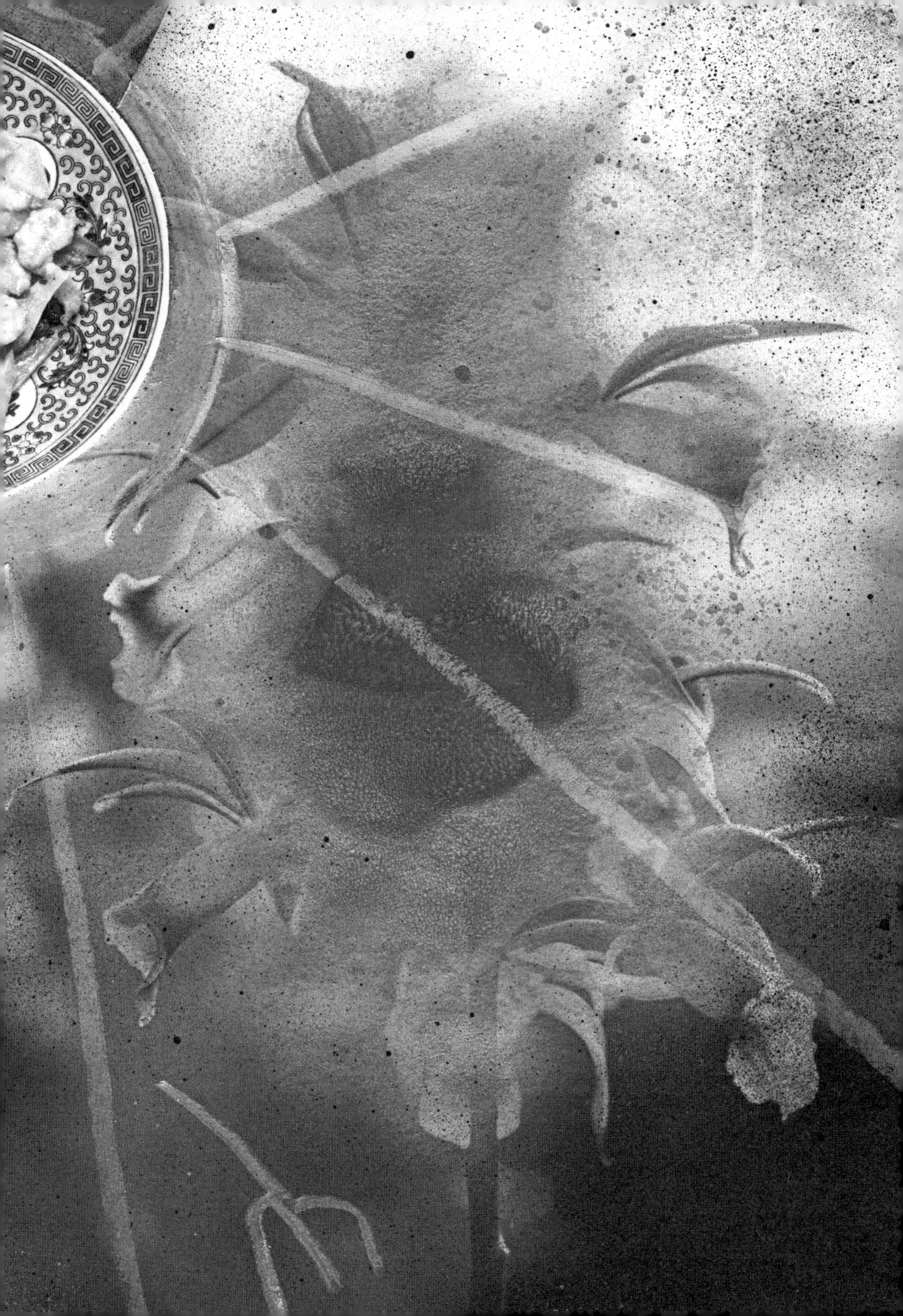

Sonja
van Kerkhoff

MUTABILITY

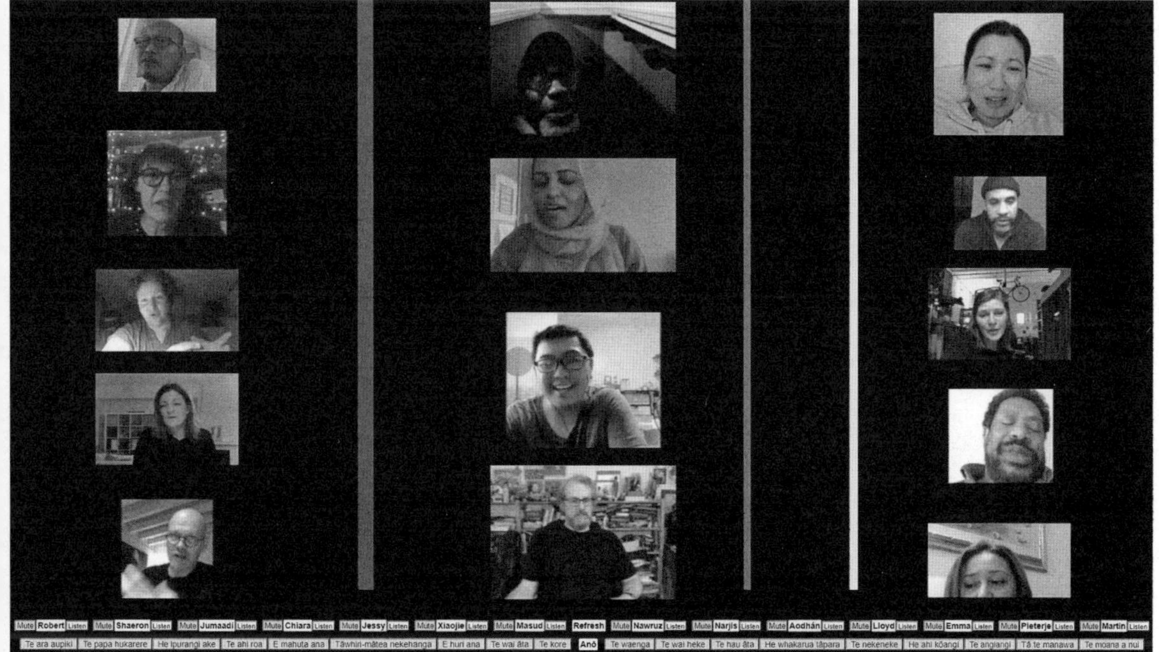

Sonja van Kerkhoff, *He tito nekehanga a waenga / Choreographies of in-between-ess*, 2021, interactive wall projection. Screenshot: When the system begins or if you click the 'refresh' button in the middle, all fourteen voices are speaking at once. Here the animations, 'Te ahi roa' (The long fire) and 'He whakarua tāpara' (double change) are playing.

For the March 2021 exhibition 'E Tiaki – Take Care', shown at artHAUS in Auckland, I selected fourteen artists in countries more stricken by Covid-19 than we are, here in Aotearoa, New Zealand. I partnered them with local artists who would serve as caretakers for the work of the overseas artist. For example, Masud Olufani, based in Atlanta (USA), worked with Ursula Christel. He gave her instructions to buy a copy of Adam Smith's *The Wealth of Nations* and to cut and burn it. Ursula created a wall installation incorporating the charred book and Masud's drawing of an anonymous Black enslaved. Other examples were large digital prints where Cathy Carter merged her own New Zealand sea imagery with Italian Chiara Rubino's landscapes surrounding her home city, Matera, and for the video installation *Nukta* (the meaningful dot) Australian-based Narjis Mirza (originally from Pakistan) provided the materials which Michelle Mayn installed as an interpretation of the ideas Narjis had discussed with her. This exhibition will tour to the Papakura Art Gallery later in 2021. See this page for details: sonjavank.com/takecare

The exhibition process began with zoom sessions where we shared thoughts about the effects of lockdown and how the artists were adapting their practice. A common thread was a sense of being in an in-between space caused by a shift in what used to be the 'day to day'. As Canadian-based Robert Hamilton said, 'It's like living in a space ship'.

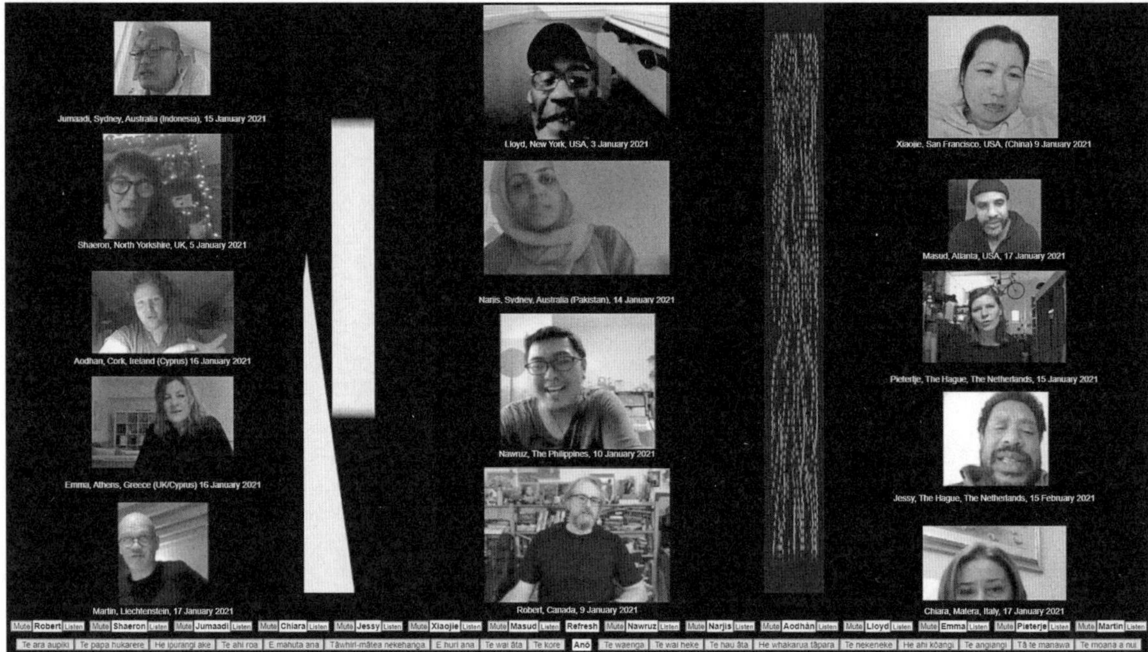

Sonja van Kerkhoff, *He tito nekehanga a waenga | Choreographies of in-between-ess*, 2021, interactive wall projection. Screenshot showing the layout when two animations, 'E mahuta ana' (rising celestial) and 'He wai heke' (gentle water), and each of the artists' names, have been clicked.

He tito nekehanga a waenga | Choreographies of in-between-ess features short video clips of these fourteen artists. When it opens, they all speak at once, so the viewer has to make some choices by clicking on the mute buttons in the row of names. The second row of nineteen buttons bear poetic names in the Māori language, each phrase relating to an animation that runs up or down between columns of videos.

The animations relate conceptually to the vertical tukutuku panels of a Māori Meeting House, which reference the natural world and are set between carved ancestor poles. These animations are abstracted and more organic than the geometrically patterned tukutuku panels, and the phrases also evoke multiple readings. For example, the animation for 'Tā te manawa' (A heart's breath) is the slow descent of a purple column. The choreography of this work shifts conceptually between the natural and the cultural worlds and visually combines minimalist abstraction with documentary.

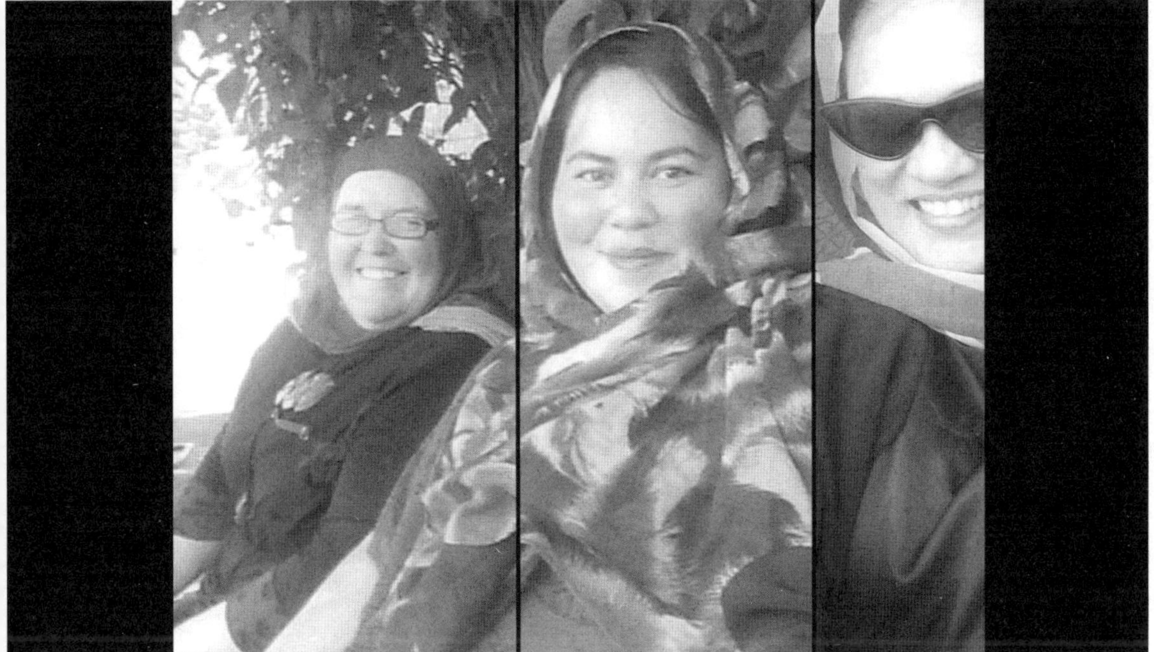

Sonja van Kerkhoff, *Ko rātou, ko tātou* (On other-ness, on us-ness), 2020, 2'48" video.

On 15 March 2019, a man armed with automatic rifles walked into two mosques in Christchurch and killed fifty-one men, women and children. A week later thousands of women from all over New Zealand wore the hijab in an act of solidarity with the Muslim community. I was one of those who wore the hijab for a while. Via the Headscarf for Harmony Facebook group, I met others who took action and discussed the effects of this on themselves, their families, and work environment. The video features thirty-four selfies which I have cropped to make them more like portraiture. The texts in the silent video slide between English and Māori. How much thinking and research did each woman take before deciding to wear the headscarf? Are some of them Muslim? Does this matter? If so, why? I chose to use texts that foreground the empathic rather than taking an analytical approach, to stress that this action of 'othering' was seated in solidarity: not to own, not to claim. The photographs were cropped and framed to bring focus to the face of the woman looking at the lens, which fits with a feminist ethos in much of my work. The headscarf 'others' but it also connects—there is an element of 'us-ness'.

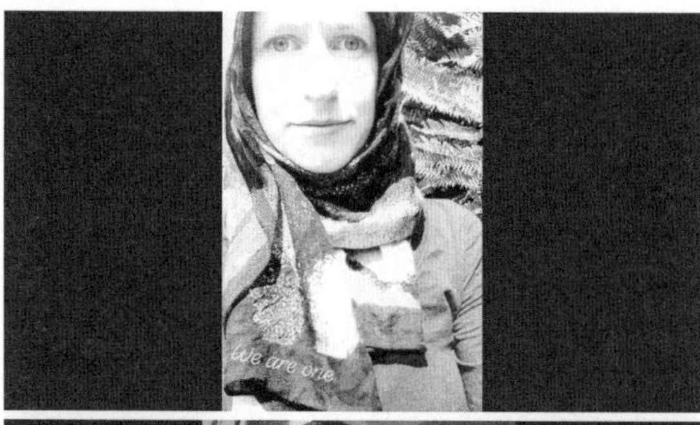

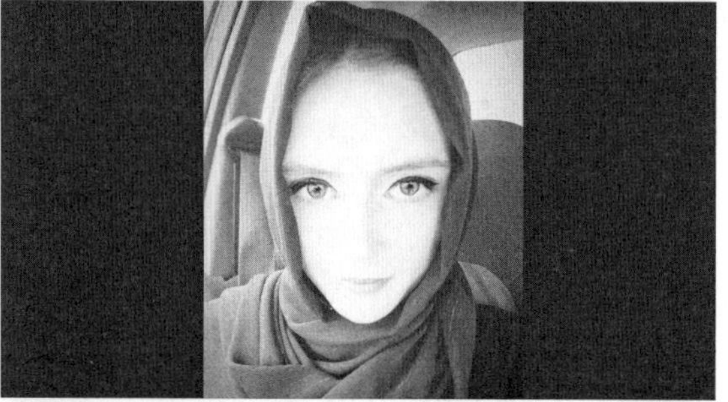

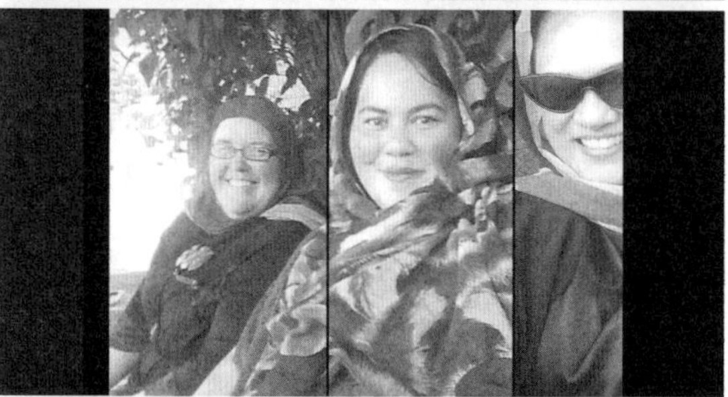

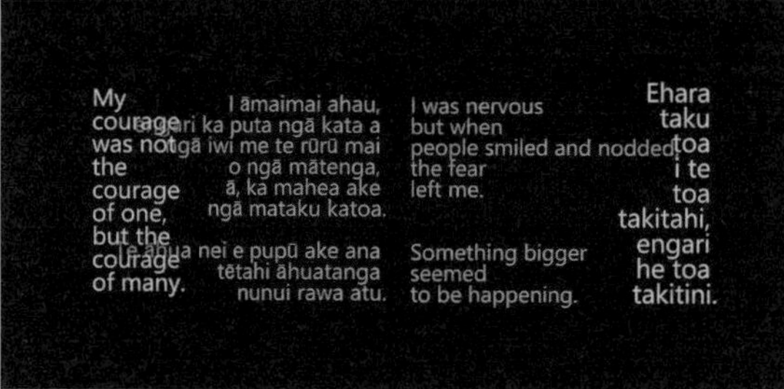

Sonja van Kerkhoff, *Ko rātou, ko tātou* (On other-ness, on us-ness), 2020, 2'48" silent video.

This video was made for an exhibition of the same title that I co-curated in March 2020, where contemporary artists either made new works in response to the Christchurch massacre, to Islam, or allowed me to recontextualize existing works within an Islamitized framework.

I obtained permission to use and re-contexualize these selfies and chose a distilled approach (Black framing) with no soundscape for this video. I wanted the viewer to find their own 'sound' or 'space'—whether as observer (of the images) or participant (remembering their own responses after the massacre). A common phrase used to express solidarity at the time was 'Tātou tātou', (we are one) but to avoid associations of cultural appropriation, in consultation with my co-curator Salama Moata McNamara, we chose the title *Ko rātou, ko tātou* (On other-ness, on us-ness), to stress the other-ness as a marker, in much the way the headscarf changes the look of each woman in this video. This 'othering' has various ramifications in relation to the themes of 'other/us', including the question of appropriation in the context of these women's empathetic responses to the tragedy.

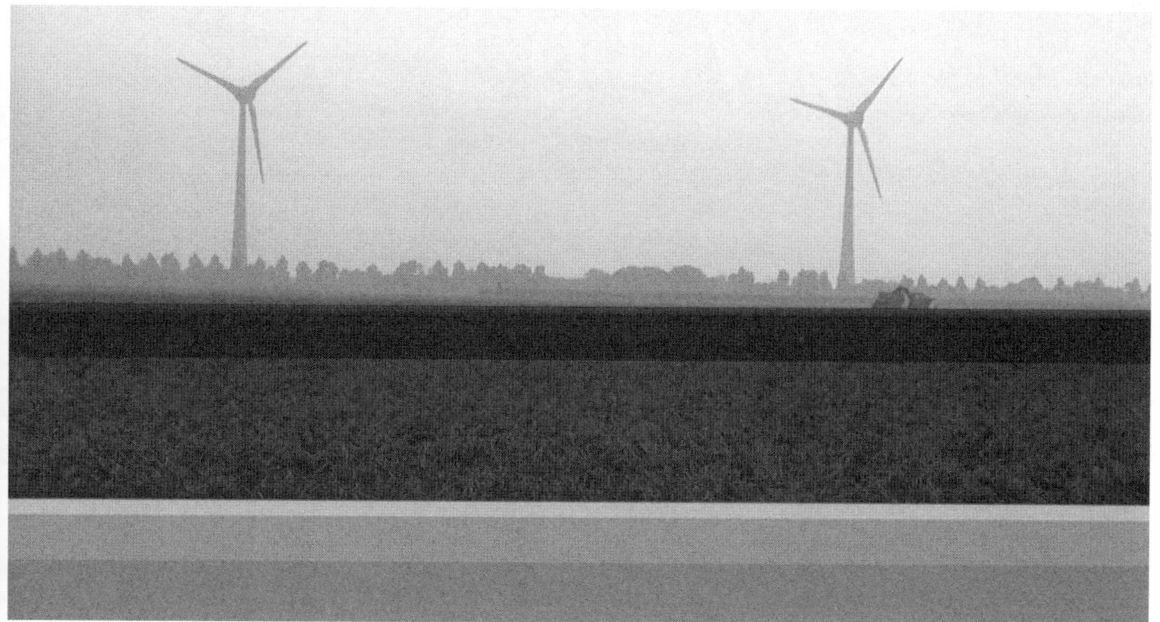

Sonja van Kerkhoff, *An unfinished symphony*, 3'50" video, 2019.

Music arranged, performed, and produced by Semay Wu (UK). It is a mutation of Schubert's *Unfinished Symphony*. The European road movie features animated colours of the LGBTQ rainbow over sea and landscapes in motion. Being European (part-European in my case: my father was Dutch), is a never-ending symphony of mutability.

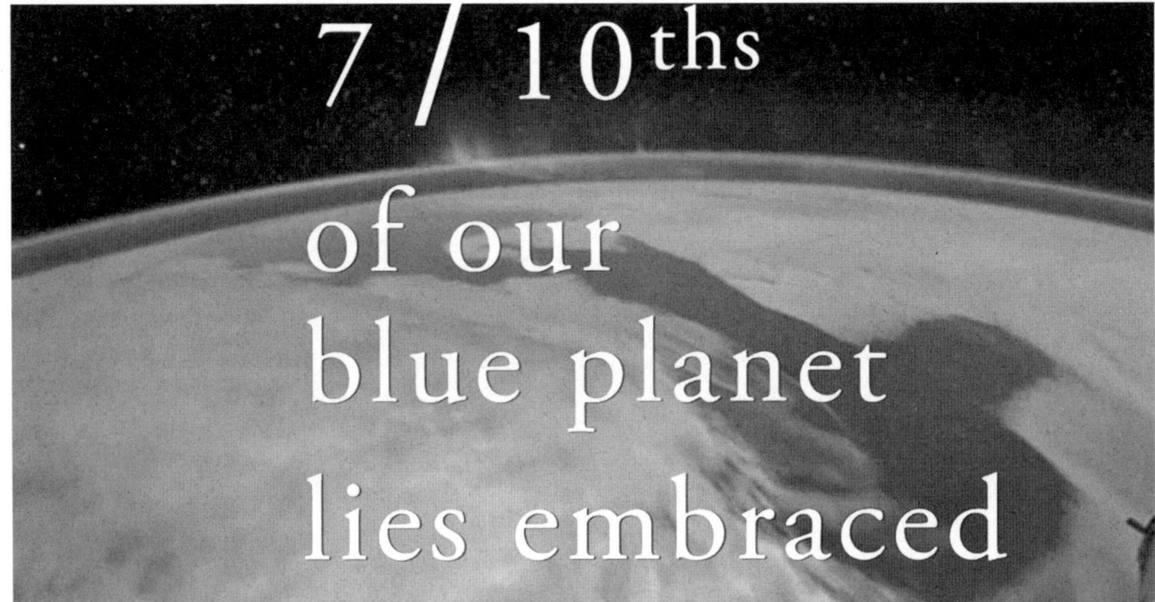

Sonja van Kerkhoff, *Once our world had edges*, 3'22" video, 2017.

Music: 'a distant backdrop' by sink \ sink, on the album 'a lone cloudburst' (2013). Written and performed by Gareth Schott. The footage is found objects from the archives of the NASA International Space Station.

Text and music are used to transform the imagery from the analytically objective into a story of the inner and subjective. The punchline is that the earth is analogous to the flow and movement of our own body.

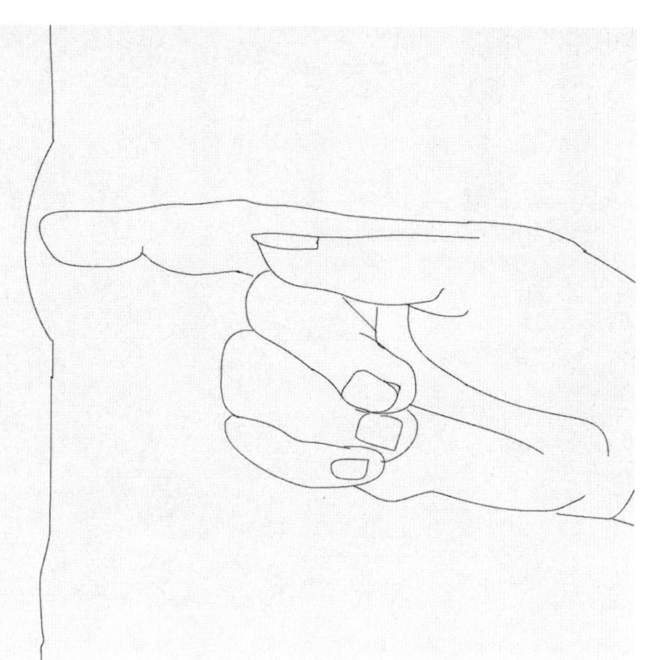

Sonja van Kerkhoff, *Deus ex machina*, 1' animation, 2021
Music: 6 July 2020 improvisation by Craig Denham.

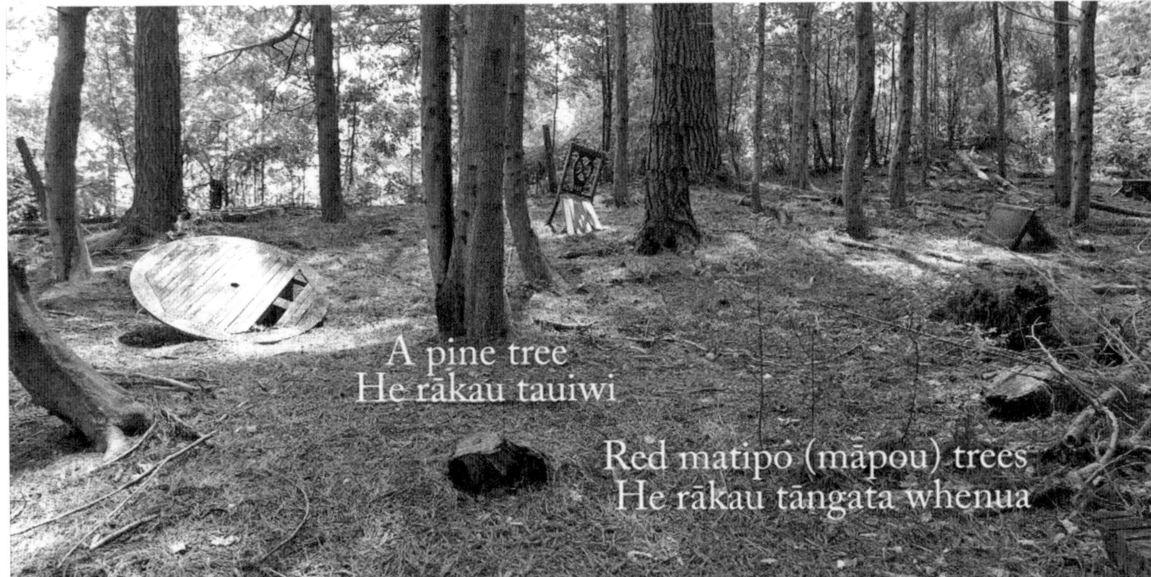

Sonja van Kerkhoff, *Somewhere, in the forest | I te wa, i te ngahere*, 2020, 7'22" video. Music by Craig Denham, *Excerpt from an improvisation on 15th April 2020*. It features, *It is not a tale invented... (two chairs, a table, and a bench)*, a suite of absurdist furniture in a forest by Sonja van Kerkhoff and Sen McGlinn at Kaipara Coast Sculpture Gardens, 1 Dec 2019–4 November 2020. The text in Māori refers to imported/immigrant trees (the pine) and to native trees (trees indigenous to Aotearoa / New Zealand).

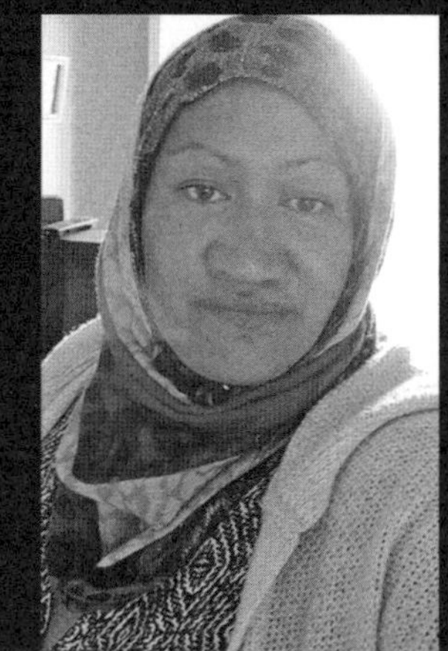
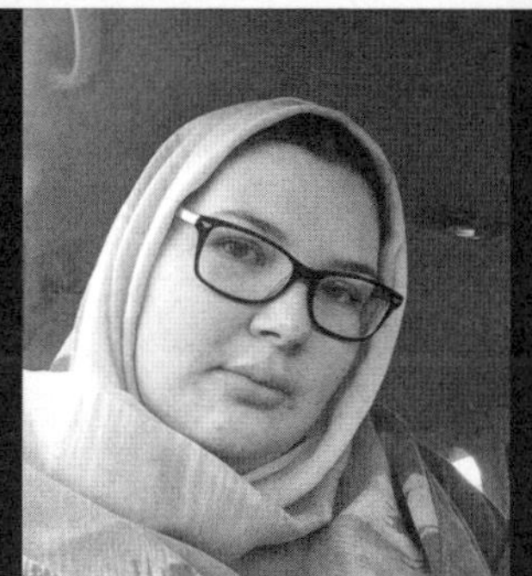
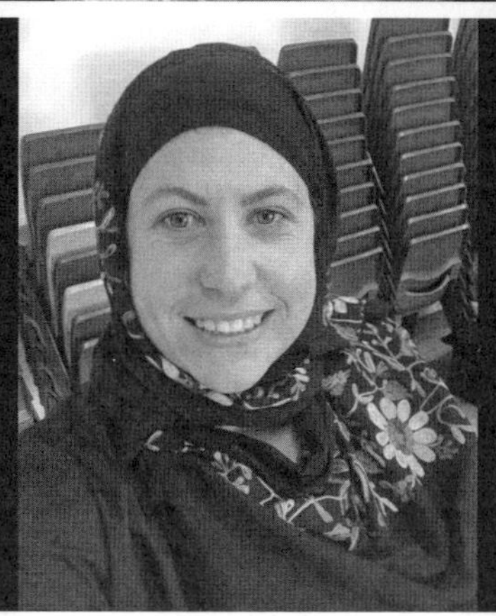
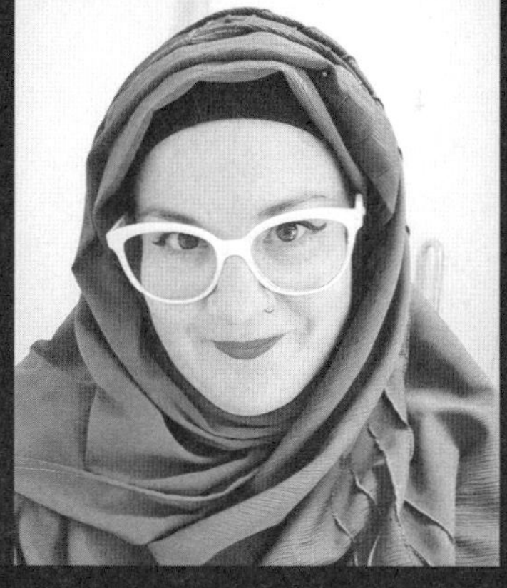

Sonja van Kerkhoff

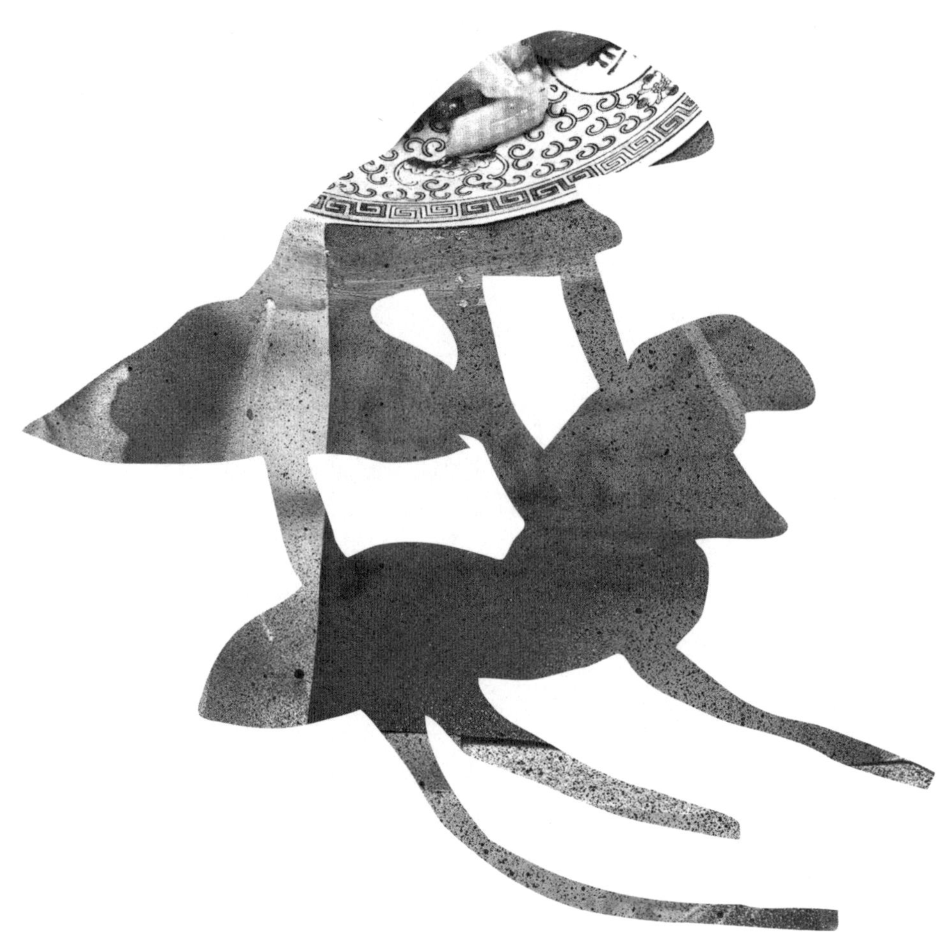

THE ART OF GERARD CARIS AND THE WORLD
A Neural Approach

John Onians

INGREDIENTS

- Neuroarthistory
- Neuroscience
- Mind and Matter

Neuroarthistory was developed, on the back of the rapid expansion of neuroscience, as a response to World Art Studies' challenging agenda of engaging with all art, however defined, wherever and whenever it was made.[1] Its goal is thus to explore the extent to which new knowledge of the brain may provide fresh access to the minds of the makers and viewers of art from any place or time, access that is not dependent on the medium of language.[2]

One of the discoveries of neuroscience is that all our experiences, actions, and feelings require the use of particular neural networks, and that, because of neural plasticity, these are strengthened the more that use is repeated and/or intense.[3] They thus become an integral part of an individual's neural make-up, potentially influencing their later actions and feelings. This means that the more we know of an individual's experiences, actions, and feelings the better we will be able to reconstruct their personal neural resources and the more we will understand the actions and feelings to which these predispose them. Such a neural approach can be productively applied to the study of any maker or viewer of art from any place or period, but is especially applicable to contemporary artists and viewers. Since, in their case, we can know more about the nature, the intensity, and the frequency of the experiences that shape their neural make-up than we can with earlier generations, we are necessarily in a better position to understand the

1. For the expansion of neuroscience see Semir Zeki, *Inner Vision* (Oxford, 1999).

2. John Onians, 'World Art Studies and the Need for a New Natural History of Art', *Art Bulletin* (June 1996), pp. 206-209. This is not to underestimate what can be achieved by a sophisticated study of texts, such as Post-Minimalist Horizons and Relational Aesthetics: Rereading Gerard Caris' in Grant Pooke, *Projecting Pentagonism: The Aesthetic of Gerard Caris* (Canterbury, 2018), pp. 25–54.

3. John Onians, *European Art: A Neuroarthistory* (New Haven/London, 2016), pp. 9–10.

role of that make-up in shaping their (artistic) life.

This is especially so when the aspect of that life that we are studying is as complex as a major artist's relationship with the whole world, in our case that of Gerard Caris. In that context the value of a neural approach appears unsurpassed because it potentially includes all dimensions to that relationship. All we have to do is reconstruct the salient elements in Caris' neural formation from his birth in Maastricht (the Netherlands) in 1925 through his experiences in many different environments.[4]

Our first insight into Caris' neural formation is provided by a photograph of him, as a student, standing at a metalworking lathe. A glance at his eyes already reveals his exceptional passion for engineering and the intensity of his sensory alertness. That intensity is also confirmed by his memories of the first irruption of the wider world into his life during World War II. He vividly recalls how the German invasion in 1940 was announced by the rasping of their steel-shod boots on Maastricht's cobble-stone streets, and how the relief of their departure four years later was sealed by the arrival of American soldiers, their footfall softened by rubber soles.[5] He was evidently already building up the neural resources for the discrimination of the sounds and textures associated with different materials, and these will have been enriched by the even more evocative contrast between hardness and softness that he experienced soon afterwards, when he volunteered to help the United States military liberate Pacific islands from the Japanese and

4. What follows is an expansion of the chapter on Caris, ibid., pp. 341–349.

5. This observation, like others in this paper, draws on many conversations with Caris from our first meeting in a café on Rotterdam station in 2010, through visits to his studio, until a phone call early 2021.

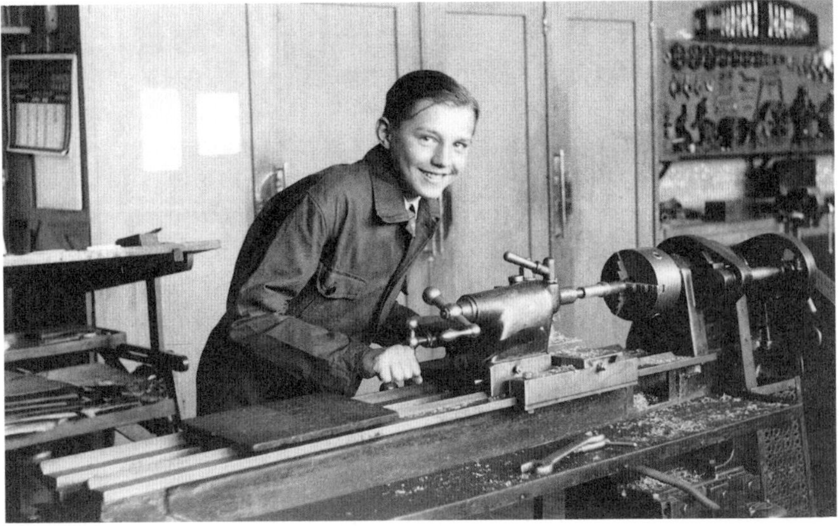

Gerard Caris at Technical School, Maastricht 1942.

found himself practising the disembowelling of the enemy by repeatedly bayonetting bags of straw, an activity only brought to an end by Japanese surrender.

By this time he had a good realization of the raw power of steel on the foot or in the hands of humans. But he also had an appreciation of the much more subtle power of steel when guided by a machine, especially one under his control. This he first acquired at technical school in Maastricht and then developed professionally as a petroleum engineer. He honed his skills working on oil-drilling rigs in Indonesia, New Guinea, Nigeria, Turkey, and Saudi Arabia between 1948 and 1961, and refined them when, in 1957, he was employed calibrating Leitz microscopes in New York City, where he also began to study art and philosophy. His varied technical activities all contributed to the laying down of rare neural resources, whose quality, in 1961, earned him an appointment at the cutting edge of the emerging space industry, as site manager for the construction of the Horn Antenna at Andover Maine, its function being to receive microwave signals from the first satellite to transmit television images, Telstar 1.

The neural resources he built up during this demanding assignment were to become vitally important for his deeper involvement with art, following his enrolment at UC Berkeley 1964-67. One of the reasons for this was the similarity between the antenna and the Jean Tinguely sculpture, *Homage to New York*, whose auto-destruction Caris had witnessed in 1960. The chance resemblance between the two complex assemblages of moving metal components will have ensured that he viewed the antenna using the neural resources recently laid down by looking at the Tinguely. This meant he would necessarily have seen the antenna also as a work of art, which became significant as he began to train as an artist. We can sense the surprising impact of this unique neural relationship in his first major works. In the acrylic painting *Birth of Form* (1968) the innovative band of light that descends from top left and then bends to leave bottom right is evidently inspired by his neural empathy with the way the antenna captured the signal from the satellite high in the sky in its horn receiver before transmitting it onwards to ground level, but the power of that neural empathy comes out more forcefully in the monumental painting *Feeding Force of Creation* (2 x 3 metres) from 1968. There it blends with Caris' intense neural memory of the visual forms of the Abstract Expressionist works which had amazed him in New York, to generate a work of ambitious scale and dynamism. It was also to a similar combination of sources that we owe the acrylic *Creation of the Pentagon* (1969). The structure of its composition suggests that the origin of the five-sided figure that would be the key to most of his later art, launching a new 'ism', Pentagonism, lies in a neural empathy with the beam of microwaves fused with a neural memory of the trapezoidal forms of the model of the protype of the Andover antenna, which confronted Caris every day on his desk while working on the project. From this point onwards it becomes clear that Caris' unique achievement will depend on his exceptional neural sensitivity both to visible forms and invisible forces.

The visible 'forms' that absorbed him are easily identified, as are their far-flung and highly diverse sources. The combinations of regular solids and metal wires in the sculptural series of *Polyhedral Net Structures* from 1971 onwards, for example, are manifestly the product of neural networks shaped by intense and frequent exposure to the configuration of rods and geometrical volumes of his beloved Maine antenna installation.[6] By contrast, the repetitive arrays of regular solids in his subsequent series of *Relief Structures* have so much in common with the rows of basins and bidets, the sanitary ceramics, which were Maastricht's principal product, that they must testify to the impact of early visits to the Sphinx factory in the company of his potter grandfather who worked there. Much more exotic were the personal experiences behind the two-dimensional designs of the later *Eutactic Star* series, built around pentagons and triangles. Their combination of geometry and colour was shaped by his memories of the tile patterns that had impressed him on his frequent visits to mosques when working in the Middle East in the 1950s. Caris' awareness of this dependency then influenced him in his search for patronage from the same area. After he learned of the potential power of unconscious neural response from a knowledge of my writings, he used these designs to generate both an invitation to participate in the Third Fadjr International Festival of Visual Arts at the Tehran Museum

6. For illustrations of these and other works see *Gerard Caris: Pentagonismus/ Pentagonism*, eds. Gregor Jansen and Peter Weibel (Karlsruhe, 2007).

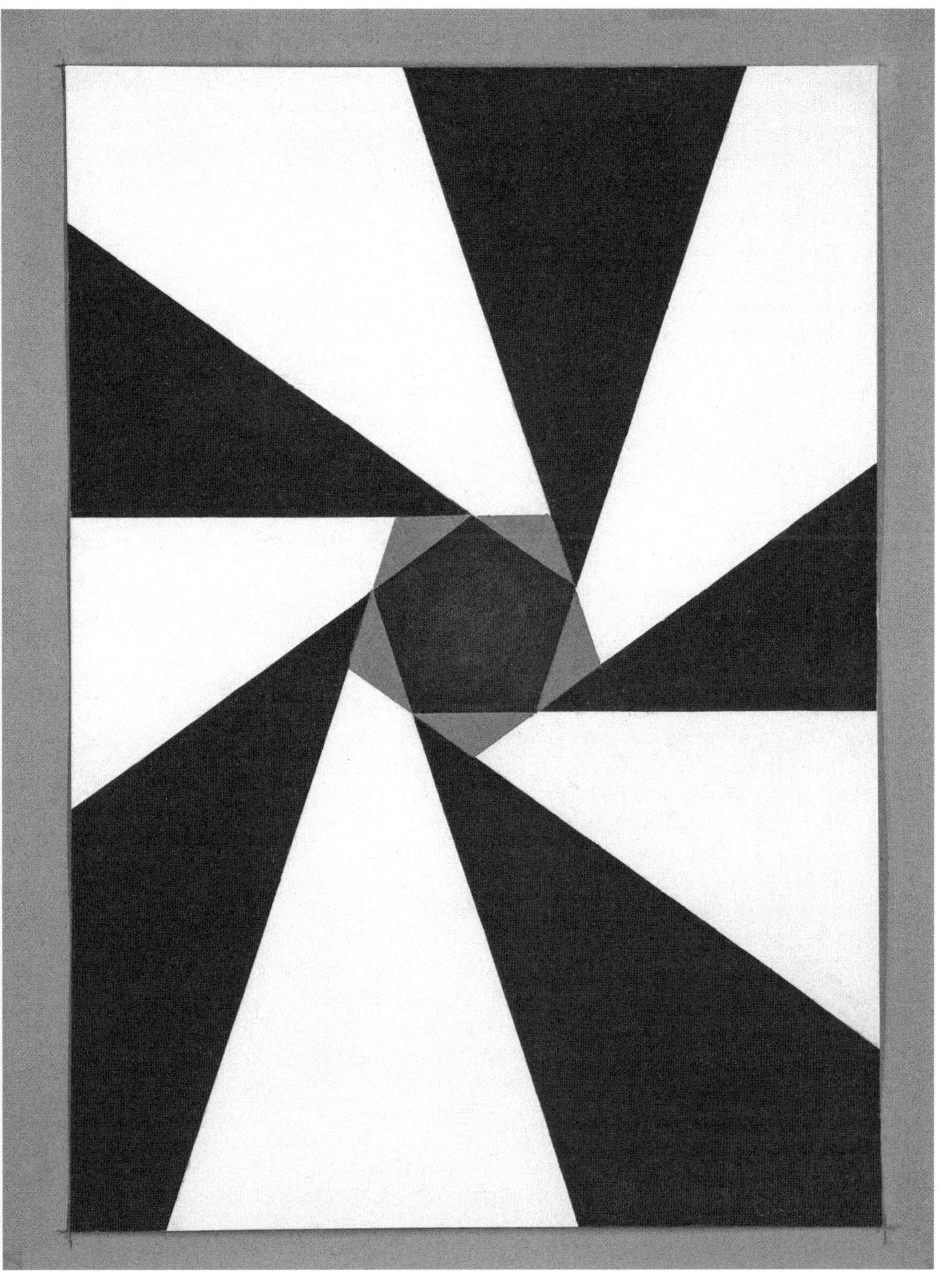

Gerard Caris, *Pentagon Radiation # 1*, 2017, pencil, oil pastel, paper, 73 × 51 cm.

of Contemporary Art TMOCA in 2011 and the commission of a major exhibition, 'Pentagonism', with associated catalogue at the Kuad Gallery Istanbul in 2012.[7]

7. Beral Madra et al. *Gerard Caris – Pentagonism / Besgencilik* (Istanbul 2012).

The roles of the different 'forces' that engaged Caris are more obscure. They begin with the miraculous intervention of atomic energy in his life, through the detonation of the bombs at Hiroshima and Nagasaki. That event brought about Japanese surrender and released him from bayonet practice. It also initiated his life-long interest in nuclear fission, which was given substance twenty years later when Caris was studying art at UC Berkeley and found himself regularly taken to the Berkeley Radiation Lab. There he had conversations with people working on both the military and civil uses of nuclear power and he became fascinated by its scientific context in particle physics and its role in the formation of the universe. Out of this emerged the *Universe* series from 1969 and 1970, the *Cosmos* series of acrylics on canvas 1969–72 and the *Nucleation* series of 1970 and 1971. All expand on the pentagon, which had arrived mysteriously from space in *Creation of the Pentagon* (1969), suggesting how it could be the key to a pattern extending through space in any direction. All also share formal properties with the 'radiation hazard' sign, which had been created at the Berkeley Radiation Lab in 1941 and which will have regularly confronted Caris on his visits. The depth of the sign's embedding in his neural make-up is evident from the way it surfaced again more explicitly fifty years later in the *Radiation* paintings of 2017 and 2018, where the use of variations on the hazard sign's yellow colour viscerally enhances its message of warning.

NEURAL RESPONSES

Just how important the concepts of radiation and of invisible forces were to Caris is evident from one of his most important pronouncements in a lecture at the Parsons School of Design in New York in 1981. Developing a critique of the heavy rectangular architectural forms characteristic of the city he advocated the construction of polygonal buildings in light experimental materials. These would respond much better to the human body:

> Space is not only perceived with the eyes, but with our whole being. There exists bodily radiation which is felt to interact with physical objects and

8. Gerard Caris, 'Conjectures and Observations', Guest Lecture delivered to the Parsons School of Design, 16 March 1981, gerardcaris.com.

> creates tensions. These tensions are subject to change in direction and force, dependent on the size, shape and direction of the walls of our rooms.[8]

Caris' sensibility to forces acting on the body had many dimensions. One was sexual desire. At Berkeley in the 1960s there was a culture of free love and the female models in Caris' 'life' classes were part of it, as we sense from the passion of his drawings concentrating on the genital area. Another was heat, as we learn from a watercolour executed just after Caris' admission to the university, *Bodies feeling the heat of the desert sun* (1965). This work shows two bodies reduced by the force of a hot sun above to bowed heads, eroded torsos, and frail legs. It is highly original as a representation, not of a traditional subject such as a body's external physical appearance or internal psychic state, but of the internal physical experience of extreme heat, when, as he told me in a recent phone call, the individual feels only their muscle and bone. It needed Caris' especially intense and frequent experience of heat to equip him with the neural resources that predisposed him to such an unusual expression of a hidden inner sensation.

Most important was his unique personal history as a petroleum engineer, working for years in temperatures of over 40°C, a credential he supported in the last painting by adding at the bottom an aerial view of an Egyptian pyramid. The impact of his experience of high temperatures can also be sensed in three early acrylics, all produced at Berkeley in 1967, each of which bears the name of an exceptionally hot place where he had worked ten years earlier, one, *Enugu*, a city in Nigeria, and two in Oman, *Mugshin* an airstrip in Arabia's desert 'empty quarter' and *Salala* a major ancient port. It was only the strength of the neural resources built up by his intense experiences of these places that allowed him to generate such powerful works of art. Whatever the importance of their shared heat, the difference in their forms seems to reflect the impact on him of other aspects of their environments. The colourful curved shapes framed by black in *Enugu* may reflect the bold forms of local Egpo masks and the bright hues of African costumes. The more cuboid and rounded forms of the *Salala* diptych may suggest an urban setting. The black rectangles of *Mugshin 2* may recall above all shadows in the heat.

The only other works by Caris that are attached by their titles to a particular place are the series of *Salzuflen* pencil drawings of 2007 and 2008 and four *Salzuflen* acrylics of 2010. All refer to the resort, Bad Salzuflen, in the German Teutoburgerwald, where Caris went for rehabilitation after a hip operation. All also feature an upper half filled with a pattern of small pentagons similar to that of the liquid with which Caris filled his *Polyvynil Alcohol Foam Machine* (1976), while the lower half is dominated by a row of large triangular shapes. As one of the first, more representational, pencil drawings *Salzuflen 3* shows, these triangles were initially inspired by the silhouettes of fir trees. These are still evoked in the flat green shapes of *Salzuflen One*, but become progressively more threatening as the triangles first become three-dimensional, and then lose all reference to the organic, until in *Salzuflen 4* their white and grey colours turn them to points of steel.

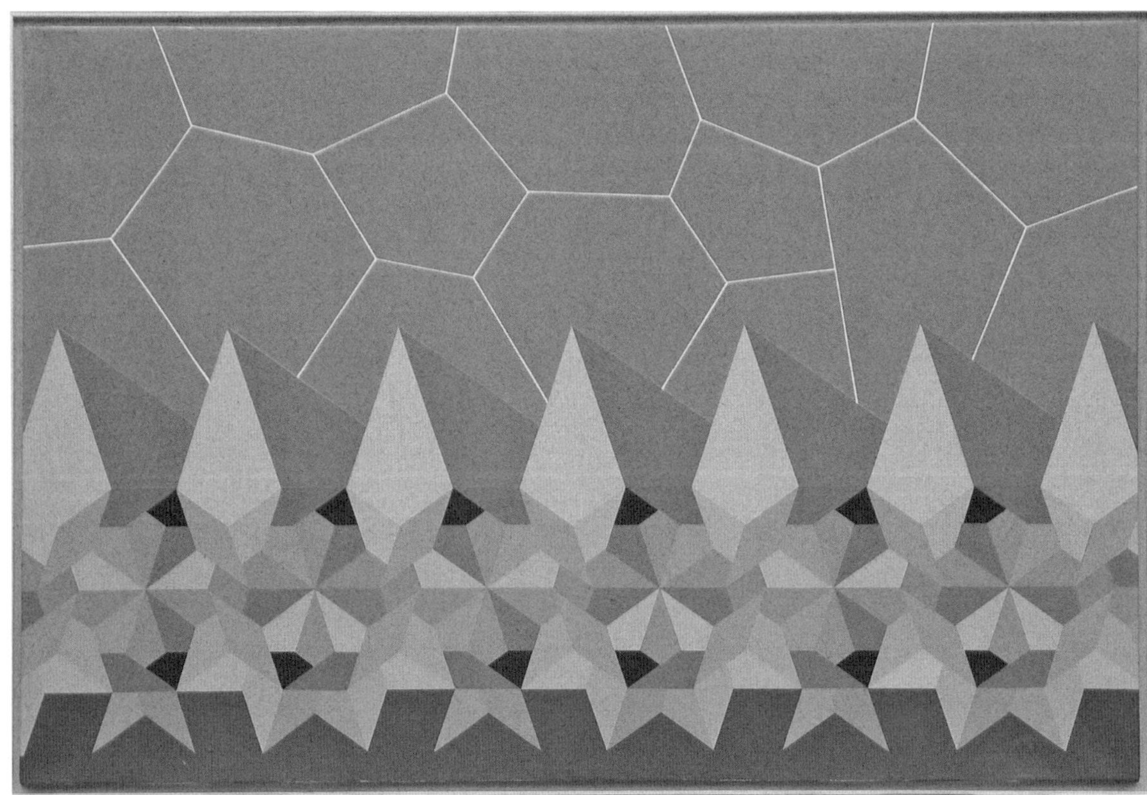

Gerard Caris, *Salzuflen # 4*, 2010, acrylic on linen, 102 × 150 cm.

When I first saw these images a few years ago I felt that the neural resources guiding Caris' hand were those formed by his deadly exercises with the bayonet, and this apercu was confirmed recently when Caris explained that his time at Bad Salzuflen was spent in conversation with German soldiers who had participated in the horrific hand-to-hand carnage of the Battle of Stalingrad. Their memories were, he said, too terrible to share with me. It was against the background of their stories of suffering that repeated exposure to Salzuflen's pointed pine trees reactivated the neural resources formed fifty years earlier in his own brain when he, as a young and passionate engineer, had been repeatedly exposed to the power of the steel bayonet.

This last passage documents the way Caris' recent work is crucially inflected by resonances between his own post-war experiences and those of German soldiers in Stalingrad. As with the other examples adduced, it vividly illustrates how a knowledge of neuroscience can contribute to our understanding of art. In each case we use an understanding of a well-established neurological principle, the way an individual's experiences are liable to affect the formation of their neural resources and so influence their later behaviour, to shed new light on their art-making. This approach offers new access to the mental life of any artist. In Caris' case it reveals how experiences of many different kinds in many places around the globe so affected his neural make-up that their traces are visible in art produced in other places often decades later. The range and power of Caris' work depends on the many dimensions of his response to the world. Without a knowledge of neurological principles, it would be much more difficult to appreciate why this is so.

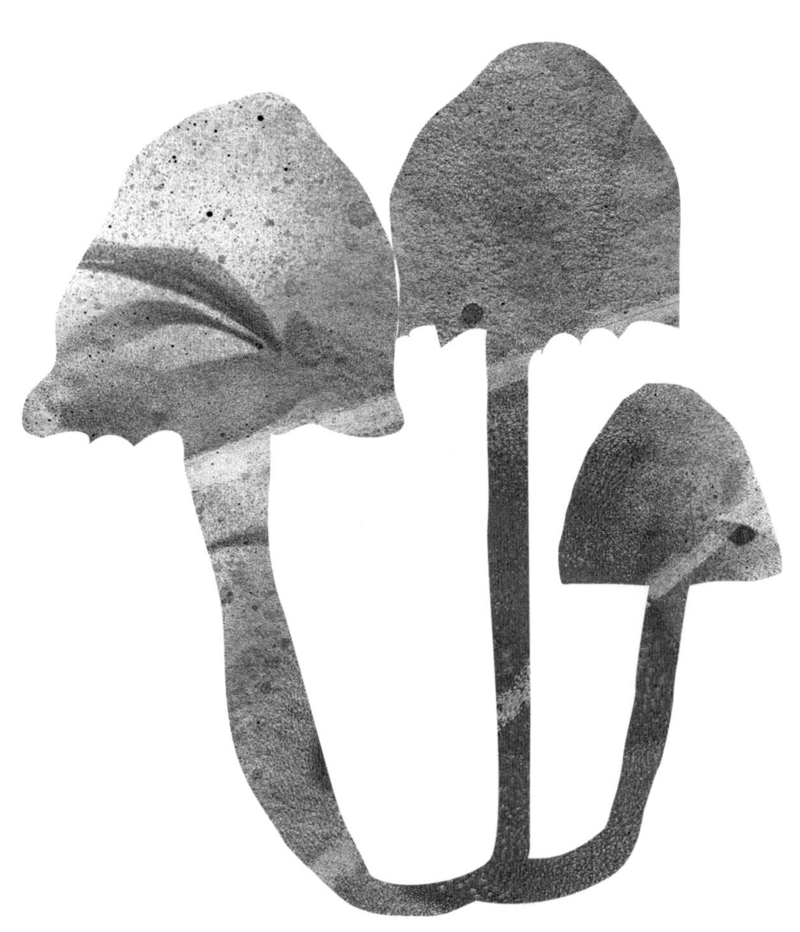

MENTAL FUSIONS

Henk Slager

INGREDIENTS

- Artistic Research
- Connectivity
- Materiality
- Pensive Images
- Transcultural
- Transnational

Preliminary

At the end of the last century, a new generation of emerging Asian artists received their graduate education at leading academies in Europe and the United States. For them, however, this did not mean to indiscriminately follow the Western canon and its related discourse, but above all to establish cross-connections and generate layered practices to be interpreted from multiple contexts and concepts. These practices could be described as panhuman, postconceptual, transcultural, and transnational.

In this contribution, I will situate the work of the Korean artist Kyungah Ham (b. 1966)—who was trained at the School of Visual Arts in New York—from that perspective. In so doing, the text will focus on her artistic thinking processes and visual strategies characterized by materiality and connectivity. Such a way of working that can be described in terms of a mental agility is, in my opinion, characteristic of world art.

Subject

Being a student in New York in the 1990s would turn out to be crucial for artist Kyungah Ham's artistic thinking and her related visual strategies. At that point in time, a clear and critical discourse emerged in this city—in particular in art and theory magazine *October*—produced by authors such as Hal Foster, Rosalind Krauss, and Benjamin Buchloh and artists such as Mark Dion and Renee Green. Also, extra-institutional activities such as the Whitney Independent Program came into view whereas the introduction of Critical Studies within existing institutions effected a new, and above all engaged form of thinking and researching.

The archaeological method of French philosopher Michel Foucault was particularly decisive for this critical form of reflection. His ideosyncratic approach to writing history demonstrated that the way power and knowledge are organized should be rethought radically. In his groundbreaking publication *The Order of Things* Foucault introduced, therefore, the concept 'episteme' linked to the often discontinuous way historical systems and orders are able—through binary bifurcations such as reason and non-reason or true and false—to exclude and disqualify some parts of experience, speaking, and knowing.[1]

1. Michel Foucault, *The Order of Things: An Archeology of Human Sciences* (New York, 1970).

(DE-)CONSTRUCTING HISTORIES

Diagnostics

Initially, these new insights signified a deconstructionist activity where Critical Studies served as a toolbox to reveal and unmask disciplining, narrative structures: structures resulting from a way of speaking organized with the aim to construct 'history'. Over time though, this new form of cultural diagnostics shifted its attention from discipline to stylization; criticism became mostly an authentic way of life characterized by the 'glorious task' of inciting different modes of thinking and topical forms of speaking 'truth'.

A more or less similar development can be seen in the artistic thinking of Kyungah Ham. In her work Ham focuses both on the construction of history/ies and on how an individual relates to that phenomenon. In her early days as an artist, Ham also seemed to see no possibility whatsoever for the existence of a (historical) reality outside discursive regulatory systems and organized forms of speaking. In her work *Chasing Yellow* (2001) a clear link is made between dialogic speaking and mapping subjective histories. In this video work—characterized by 'an explicit research attitude' says Tatehata Akira (curator 1st Yokohama Triennale, 2001)—Kyungah Ham has random encounters with people wearing yellow in public space in various locations in Asia; for example, a fortune teller in Singapore, a water seller in China, a theater manager in Japan, a zoo employee in Singapore, and a student in Korea wearing a required

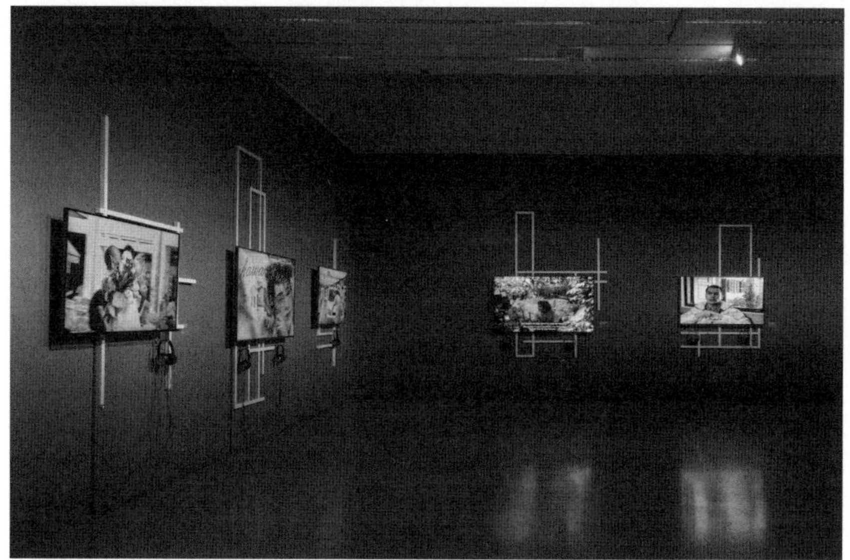

Kyungah Ham, *Chasing Yellow*, 2001, 8-channel video installation, colour, sound, 55″ LED TV, headphones, powder coat on steel. Exhibition view at National Museum of Modern and Contemporary Art, Seoul, 2019–2020.

yellow uniform. At a time when video was just being discovered by the art world, *Chasing Yellow* deconstructs the western view of Asia—often colored by an overly yellow perspective, as the artist noted—and emphasizes that, contrary to what is proclaimed by the rhetoric of linear history, it is possible for different historical subjectivities and forms of awareness to coexist. Furthermore, it demonstrates that the private and the public, myth and reality, can subtly mingle.

Schizophrenia

In the second half of the 2000s the artist continued to produce a number of works dealing explicitly with historical representation and the question of how art can develop an adequate criticism of ideology. Initially, Ham focused her research on the museum as the pre-eminent institution for historical legitimization and rhetorical communication of an ideological perspective as proposed by prevalent powers. Schizophrenic as the museum deep down is, it tolerates or simply obscures the fact that many prestigious temples of culture are filled with treasures stolen in colonial times. To bring this to public notice, Ham developed the project *Museum Display* that was shown at various venues and in various guises up to 2010. The work follows the classic logic of the display system: transparent showcases, linear arrays, and a dominantly present labeling system. Not surprisingly, at first glance the work looks like a museum presentation of antiquities, but in reality it is something completely different. What is shown are objects the artist has misappropriated from museum shops and museum cafes all over the world. This way she emphasizes the irrefutable truth about the criminal core of art-historical reality.

Amnesia

The work *Odessa Stairs* (2008) also critically deploys the disciplining perspective of the museological display system. On a freestanding, staircase-like presentation platform Ham displays garbage remnants found near the home of former Korean president Roh Tae-woo—golf shoes, carpet, pipes, tiles, construction material, English learning materials—in such a way that a picture is evoked of a military allegory, due to a visual similarity to weapons and radar systems.

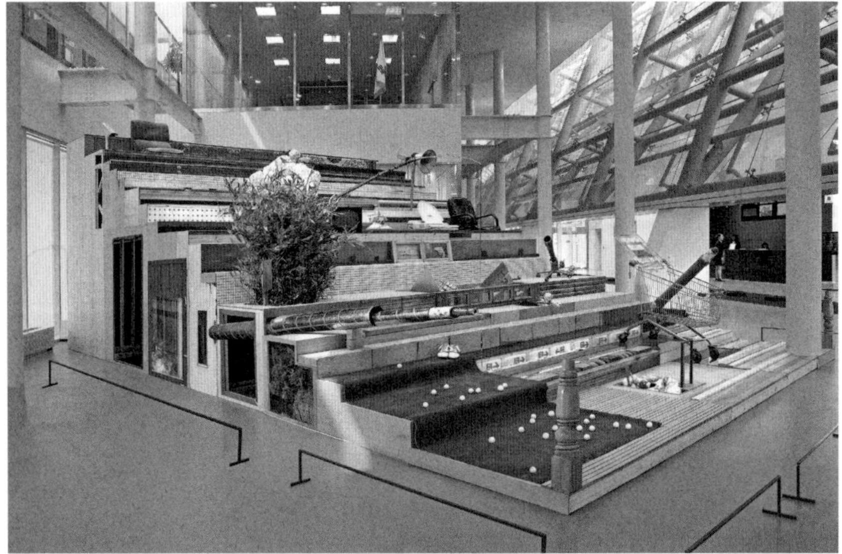

Kyungah Ham, *Odessa Stairs*, 2008, constructive material, furniture, bidet, carpet, TV, golf shoes and ball, videotape, bamboo tree, sofa, supermarket cart, fishing rod, 6 × 9 × 3.3 m, Permanent Collection Exhibition view, Gyonggi Museum of Modern Art, 2009.

2. Gilles Deleuze and Félix Guattari, *Anti-Oedipus: Capitalism and Schizophrenia* (London/New York, 2004).

By referring in the title to a scene in Eisenstein's film classic *Battleship Potemkin* (1925) an extra layer of signification is added. This film shows how at the time of the Russian Revolution the ordinary populace is butchered by Tsarist troops on the stairs of Odessa. This makes *Odessa Stairs* a precarious and possibly paradoxical monument for remembering and re-thinking the Gwangju Massacre (1980). After all, despite the obvious involvement of dictator Roh in this besmirching of the nation's history, he was allowed to live a luxurious and by and large undisturbed life after the end of the period of dictatorship. *Odessa Stairs*, therefore, seems to emphasize that as long as modern Korea suffers from historical forgetfulness it will be impossible to establish a form of justice in this society.

Bipolar

A similar reflection on the bipolarity of a culture shaped by power and desire is given in the work *Blue and White Porcelain* (2008): a museum presentation of porcelain vases decorated with reproductions of romantic landscapes by Hitler as well as an ultramodern weapons arsenal entirely manufactured from porcelain. What we in fact see here is the schizophrenia of capitalism as described by Gilles Deleuze and Félix Guattari in *Anti-Oedipus*: a form of preservative thinking that on the one hand attaches great value to fragile historical artifacts, but on the other hand is based on a military industry focused on destruction.[2]

With these two latter works Ham's attention shifts to the historical situation of the—divided—Korean peninsula. Something she became even more aware of in 2008, when she picked up a propaganda leaflet that had been dropped outside her home by the North Korean regime. She then realized it was time to talk back and open communication with the unattainable half of the country. A communication about a historical situation that cannot as yet take the shape of a dialogue, or be spoken out loud, but perhaps could start with a whisper. As artistic strategy for such a whispering communication, the artist developed an entirely new process of production: she sent her digital images to a contact in China who served as an intermediary and next

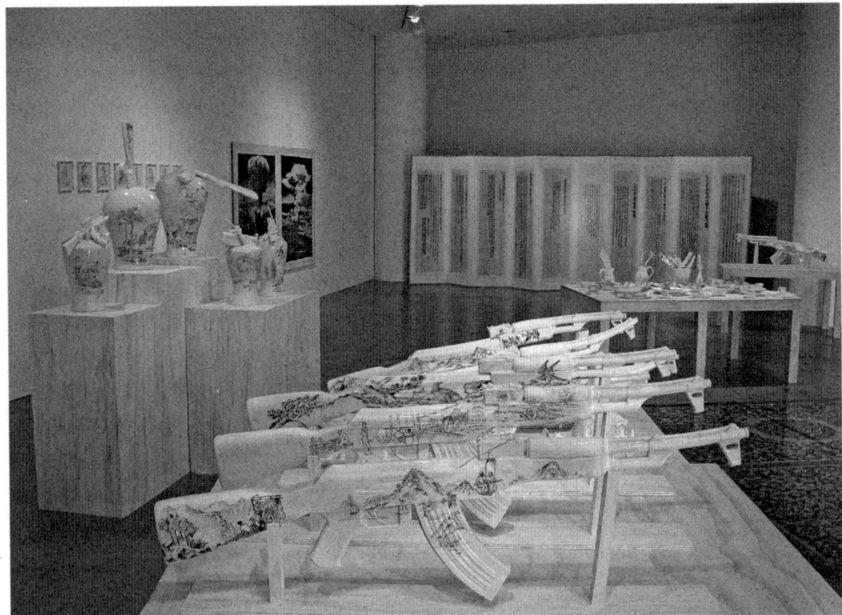

Kyungah Ham, *Blue and White Porcelain*, 2008, drawing of traditional landscape, reproduction of Adolf Hitler's painting and traditional painting, porcelain, wood. Exhibition view at Art Sonje Center, Seoul, 2009.

forwarded the images to North Korean artisans who then translated them into the traditional analogue medium of embroidery—a medium that the regime also uses for propaganda purposes. After approximately a year, a number of the translated images returned to Seoul—political officials confiscated quite a few others. In this roundabout way, says Ham in her contribution to the catalogue of the fifth Guangzhou Triennial (2016), there is communication: 'The mute responses from North Korea can pass through the eye of the needle as a thread that offers to weave wishes.'[3]

3. Kyungah Ham, *Mona Lisa and the Others from the North*, catalogue *Asia Time*, 5th 'Guangzhou Triennial', eds. Zhang Qing and Henk Slager (Guangzhou, 2016).

Division

One of the first images translated into embroidery was *Hiroshima Mushroom* (2009): iconic pictures of the first atomic bombings of Hiroshima and Nagasaki were the starting point. The monochrome presentation somewhat abstracted by the artisans shows a subtle multi-layeredness.

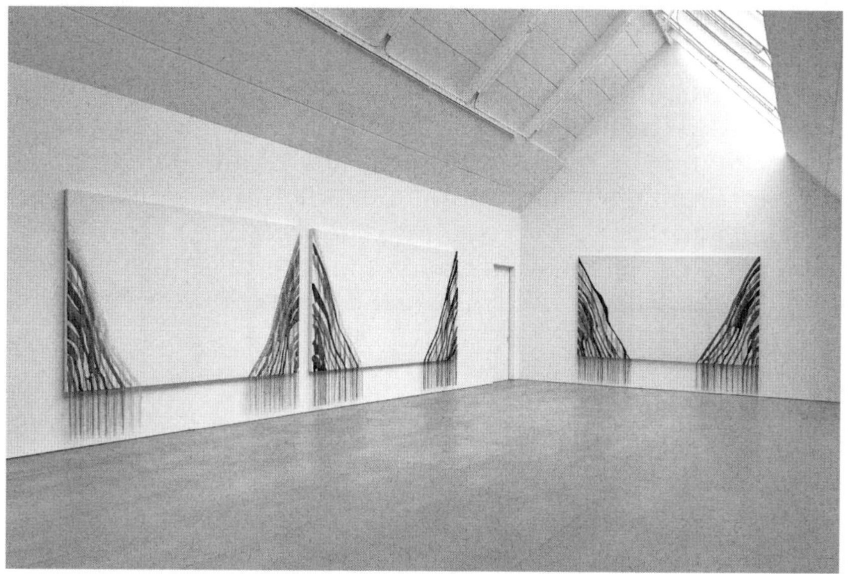

Kyungah Ham, *Abstract Weave/ Morris Louis AlphaLambda1961*, 2012, embroidery, 250 × 320 cm (frame 180 × 320 cm); *Abstract Weave/ Morris Louis BetaKappa1961*, 2012, embroidery, 250 × 334 cm (frame 185 × 334 cm); *Abstract Weave/ Morris Louis AlphaLambda 1961*, 2012, embroidery, 250 × 320 cm (frame 180 × 320 cm); Installation view, solo exhibition at Carlier Gebauer, Berlin, 2017.

A cloud-like image symbolizes the historical defeat of Japan and the end of colonial occupation. At the same time, a new power game started that would ultimately lead to the division of the country. *Hiroshima Mushroom* also represents the threat that emanates from North Korea's current nuclear ambitions. However, it also invites us to dwell on an episode in history almost forgotten in the euphoria of liberation: the many Koreans who were killed in both bombed cities because of being interned there.

A subsequent, multi-year series, *Abstract Weave/ Morris Louis*, concentrates entirely on the iconography of Abstract Expressionism: a form of art focusing on a pure idiom and an aesthetic quality. But also a form of art promoted by the CIA during the Cold War in the 1950s as an expression of a free and open society and as an alternative to the realism associated with Stalinism. It is this kind of Cold War thinking that is still raging in the Korean peninsula. Therefore, the question is what Ham's circulation of images means and accomplishes in this context.

But also, how do the embroidery workers—who have no idea of abstract art whatsoever—actually understand these images? Would they also be able to understand the abstract images with their twin-like colours and empty centre as a representation of the Korean peninsula? And could the way they apparently made the colour stripes run on deliberately be interpreted as an expression of an open-ended conversation and of the hope that potential meetings outside the frame can break down ideological barriers?

Memory

The political game played by the super powers and the significance thereof for the Korean division is also presented in the *Chandelier Series*. Again the artist deploys art-historical memory: a pointillist iconography reminding us of heroic, allegorical painting with strong references to the dwellings of power. But what does the chandelier in mid-fall symbolize? Does it make us think about a possible historic collapse? And what to think of the glowing light? Does it refer to an in-between, the lingering gap between

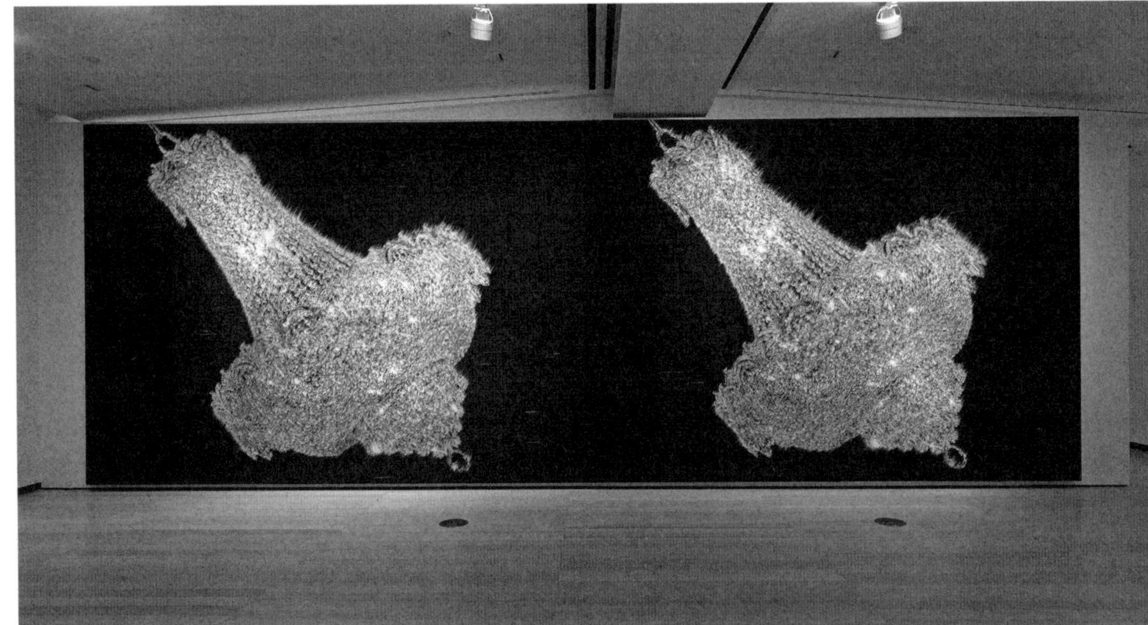

Kyungah Ham, *What you see is the unseen / Chandeliers for Five Cities BR 02-06, BK 02-07*, 2016–2017, 2018, North-Korean hand embroidery, silk threads on cotton, middleman, smuggling, bribe, tension, anxiety, censorship, ideology, wooden frame, approx. 1900hrs/4persons, 265 × 365 cm, 265 × 355 cm. Exhibition view at Asia Society Museum, New York, 2020. Courtesy of the Artist and Kukje Gallery.

4. Roland Barthes, *Camera Lucida* (New York, 1981).

5. Jacques Rancière, *The Emancipated Spectator* (London/New York, 2009).

the real world and our ideological phantoms? Or is it, because of its dark background, particularly about seeing the unseen: the existence of people who live in an unreachable darkness?

In the years that followed Ham would continue her strategy of having appropriated texts and images translated and re-contextualized. Over time, this communication process would allow space for more personal messages. In the SMS series, for example, short messages from internet and lines from popular songs are incorporated, such as 'Are you Lonely Too', or 'Money never Sleeps'. What stands out is that needle marks are left now during the processing of the digital material. Do these material traces mark the moments the artisans stopped sewing to take a look? What does this material presence say about the lived reality and existential tensions that lie behind the production processes? And what were the artisans thinking at those points?

Pensiveness

The image of the needle inevitably brings Roland Barthes' concept of 'punctum' (*Camera Lucida*) to mind.[4] And specifically the way philosopher Jacques Rancière recently reframed the notion of being affected by an image in *The Emancipated Spectator* seems very significant for the works Kyungah Ham realized in collaboration with North Korean artisans. In this context Rancière speaks of 'pensive images': images that do not immediately tell a story or signify a connotation, but represent a train of thought through their form and material. Like the punctum this pensiveness breaks through the narrative layer of the image and acts as punctuation that interrupts interpretation. The pensive image, says Rancière, shows us something that, even though it is contained in the image, is as such ultimately not a part of the composition: it is a direction, or a process of thought.[5]

This is an artistic approach that is not necessarily semiotic in nature—as was still the case in Ham's earlier artistic research into historical representation. No longer do the art works produced require to be decoded, instead they try to articulate what goes on outside of the code or the conscious signification. Precisely this pensiveness allows Ham's embroidery projects to escape coding or categorizing in a tight framework of analysis.

Through the attention for the artistic thought process—and more particularly through an idiosyncratic articulation of the 'pensive image'—the artist has contributed significantly to the further development of the discourse. Already twenty years ago, in her work *Chasing Yellow*, she anticipated the paradigm that would completely dominate the first decades of this century, that is to say: artistic research. During more than ten years she would realize a number of meaningful projects along these lines, where she would deploy and develop that form of research in a strategic and deconstructive way. Again she was among the first to recognize the eventual shortcomings of the artistic knowledge-based practice. Especially in an era characterized by cognitive capitalism, it is up to art to think beyond the boundaries of static knowledge frameworks and to explore new vistas, the artist maintains. So far, we can only speculate about the eventual significance of these investigations for artistic image production and about a possible revision of the research discourse. Particularly in an inspiring combination of material working methods, artistic thinking processes, and the dissemination of imaginaries focused on different futures, the artist seems to detect new possibilities for a more urgent form of research. In any case it is clear at this moment that this connective way of working allows Kyungah Ham to put something unthought-of and authentic in motion—at the same time stilling the culturally coded thoughts of the spectator.

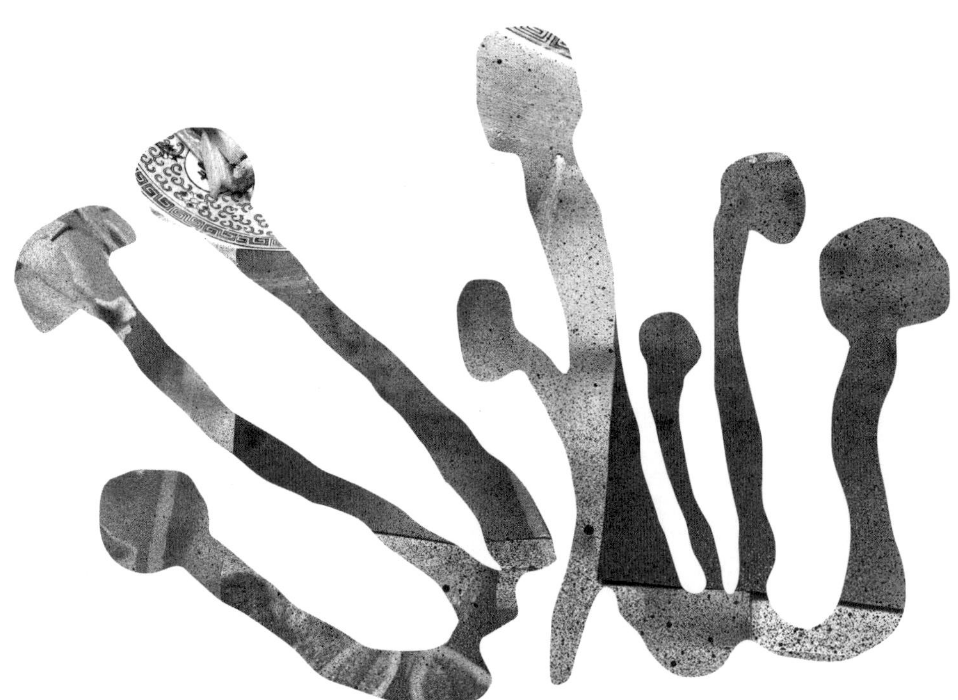

ARTLESS AESTHETICS

Elisabeth de Bièvre

INGREDIENTS

- Aesthetics
- Artlessness
- Well-being
- Senses
- Perception
- World Art Studies

It is a challenge and a pleasure to contribute to this festive dinner. Our main dish will offer a tender piece of aesthetics, which, although about two-and-a-half thousand years old, as served by me will taste fresh and up-to-date. These properties will emerge fully once we have defined what we mean by 'aesthetics' and 'artless' and applied these concepts to the analysis of three contemporary artworks made by different individuals in different places around the world.

Our aesthetics is different from the one we are used to for the last two or three hundred years, which treats art and beauty in terms of qualitative appraisal rooted in social and economic imperatives. *Our* definition is based on imperatives that are instinctive and physical, the importance of which are brought out by Herodotus, the fifth-century BCE Greek historian.

At a crucial moment of his story about the selection of a new king, he tells how everything depends on a stallion *aisthomenon*, 'perceiving by his senses' the smell of a mare.[1] This process, the perception by the senses, is as common and important in the human as in the animal domain. It is an experience, which is familiar to all people at all times and in that way helpful to an understanding of art worldwide, and a constructive basis for World Art Studies. Our concern is not the appreciation of beauty or of art as such, but the sense of well-being derived from a particular perceptual experience and from the positive associations it evokes in individuals and communities, analogous with the pleasure that Herodotus' stallion derived from the perception of the scent of a mare to whom he had been introduced the night before.[2]

1. Herodotus, *Histories*, III, ca. 425 BCE, transl. G. Rawlinson (London, 1897), p.87. First use of *aisthomenon*, translated into English as 'perceiving by the senses'.

2. Ibid.

This aesthetics is 'artless', not because art is excluded, but because art is denied its central position. This aesthetics is not founded in art, but in many domains of which art is only one. Its manifold sources are in personal inclinations, ways of life, belief systems and patterns of social organization. It also owes much to people's relations to the natural and made environment, which frame those behaviours and mental and physical activities. It is these spheres that collectively provide the foundation of an individual's and a community's well-being.

One of the benefits of understanding aesthetics as stemming from such everyday experiences is that it makes it much easier to treat all art equally, whoever made it, in whatever medium, wherever in the world. It also helps us to understand how and why an artefact made in one place at one time looks different from one made elsewhere at another time. Different experiences give rise to different art. This makes it essential to recognize the irreducible importance of the role of difference of natural setting and cultural context in creating a sense of well-being specific to the place. These are too often downgraded or ignored in celebrations of 'superior' values imported by immigrants, invading armies, colonists, or travellers. In our approach, each place can be treated as the centre of the world and the independence of its contribution acknowledged.

Our World Art Studies will not ignore the universality of certain phenomena and the similarities in cultural habits globally, but we will prioritize the effort to understand their differences. This is the context of our study of how three different art works may shed light on the experience of death in three different communities around the world, each unique in its local priorities, special interests, and traditions. With each of these three artefacts I have a personal relationship. Although two of them and one similar to the third, now sit comfortably in my home, I first came upon them in very different settings: a market stall in Sub-Saharan Africa, a shop in Himalayan Nepal and a gallery in Norfolk, England.

The work that caught my eye on a market stall in Foumban, capital of the Bamun kingdom in Cameroon, is a drawing executed in ballpoint using three colours. The contrast between the subject, the death of a king, and the Total Oil calendar on the back of which it is made, is striking. The artist was later identified by our host, Germain Loumpet, an archaeologist and member of the Foumban court, as Issah Mouliom, a known 'maître de Coran'.[3] He died in his early sixties in September 2002, not long after Germain found him, just long enough to support him through his infirmities by supplying him with red, black, and blue ballpoints. The price of each work was based on the number of pens used up, a finished drawing being calculated at ten. In this medium Mouliom expressed passionate feelings in agitated, but precise movements covering every available surface of the drawing.

As I learned, Mouliom's work would have pleased locals because it corresponds to the norms of the tradition of 'Bamun Drawings', developed since around 1920, after the arrival of the French colonial administration. His art is, however, radically different from the drawings created by the famous, slightly earlier artist, Ibrahim Njoya, a member

3. My warm thanks go to both Germain Loumpet and Alexandra Galitzine-Loumpet for informing me about many aspects of Bamun culture. Any errors are my responsibility. Alexandra Galitzine-Loumpet,'Reconsidering Patrimonialization in the Bamun Kingdom: Heritage, Image, and Politics from 1906 to the Present', *African Arts* 49, No. 2 (Summer 2016), pp. 68–81.

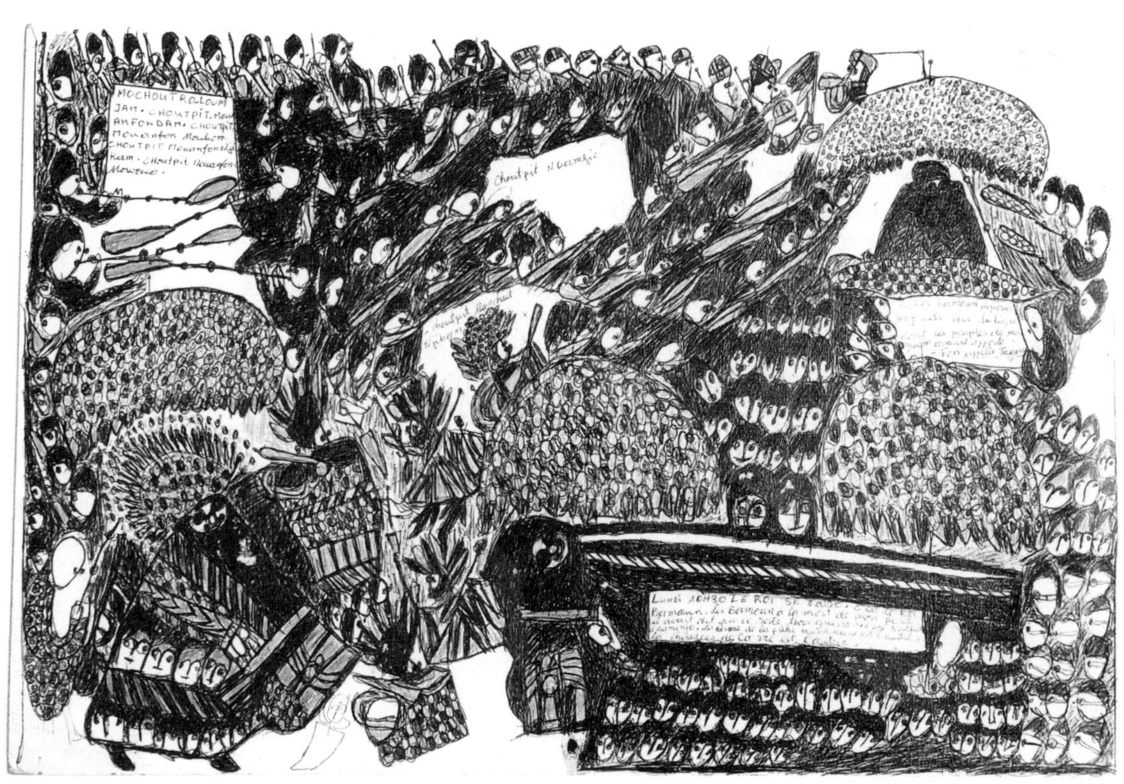

Issah Mouliom, *Untitled (The Funeral of Fon Njimoluh Seidou)*, 2002, ballpoint on cardboard, 40 × 60 cm, private owner. Photo Charles Onians.

of Foumban's royal family. Mouliom concentrated on documenting his private, personal relationships with local history and institutions. With his ballpoints he captured Islamic religious themes, such as the pilgrimage to Mecca, together with some of the most important events in the life of his community, especially the sacred rituals surrounding the coronation and funeral of the *fon*, the king.

In our case the funeral shown is that of Fon Njimoluh Seidou (reigned 1933-1992), son of the celebrated Fon Njoya, the last independent ruler of Foumban and creator of a new modernizing culture. At first sight the complete surface seems covered with rivers of hundreds of heads. These crystallize into densely packed groups, roughly identifiable as soldiers, musicians, and spectators, articulated around four colourful canopies. We seem to hear the steps of the soldiers and the music from the trumpets. The flow of the composition suggests movement and reminds me of the way the subject of most local music is the singing, and sometimes the dancing, of history.

The king dominates the event, being represented at least four times. Larger than any of the other figures, he appears in different poses and outfits. The two representations in the foreground are elaborate, one in full ceremonial dress, headdress and dark glasses, and one, also with sunglasses, lying down on a long and narrow bier. In one of the four inscriptions, which mix the Bamun language with French, and which are both historic and prophetic, looking backward and forward, the name of the maker, Mouliom, appears, suggesting self-confidence on the part of the artist.

The contrast with European funeral imagery associated with a head of state is telling. Instead of stability and organization, we are carried away by the intensity and dynamism of the event. The qualities that Mouliom has distilled, because they gave him a sense of long-established well-being, are communal participation and institutional continuity, both emanating from the person of the *fon*. These are the properties already manifest in early photographs of around 1900 showing elaborate patterns printed on the 'wings' of the 'dancing' costume of the king and in the generous displays of patterned textile hangings and voluminous robes associated with court ceremonies.[4] Having been present in person at several large events in

4. Bernhard Ankermann, *Tanzkleid des Königs. Rechte Hälfte*, 1908, black-and-white positive, VIII A 5331, Staatliche Museen zu Berlin-Ethnologisches Museum. Reproduced in Jonathan Fine, 'Selling Authenticity in the Bamun Kingdom in 1929-30', *African Arts* 49, no. 2 (Summer 2016), p. 65.

the wide open space in front of the palace, I can recognize that, although the reality of large crowds in different festive and formal outfits can be disturbing for outsiders, for the Bamun it is reassuring, a much loved image in everybody's mind.

Our next work of art, which was waiting for me in a gallery shop in Kathmandu in Nepal, is a painting of a rather menacing blue head, which fills, like a perfect circle, the nearly square painting surface. When I saw the figures crawling over the large face I was reminded of the pilgrims I had earlier that day seen clambering over the enormous memorial *stupa* of Boudha a few yards away, before I joined them in the *kora*, the circumambulation of this, one of the most holy sites of Asia, containing a relic of a Buddha. The

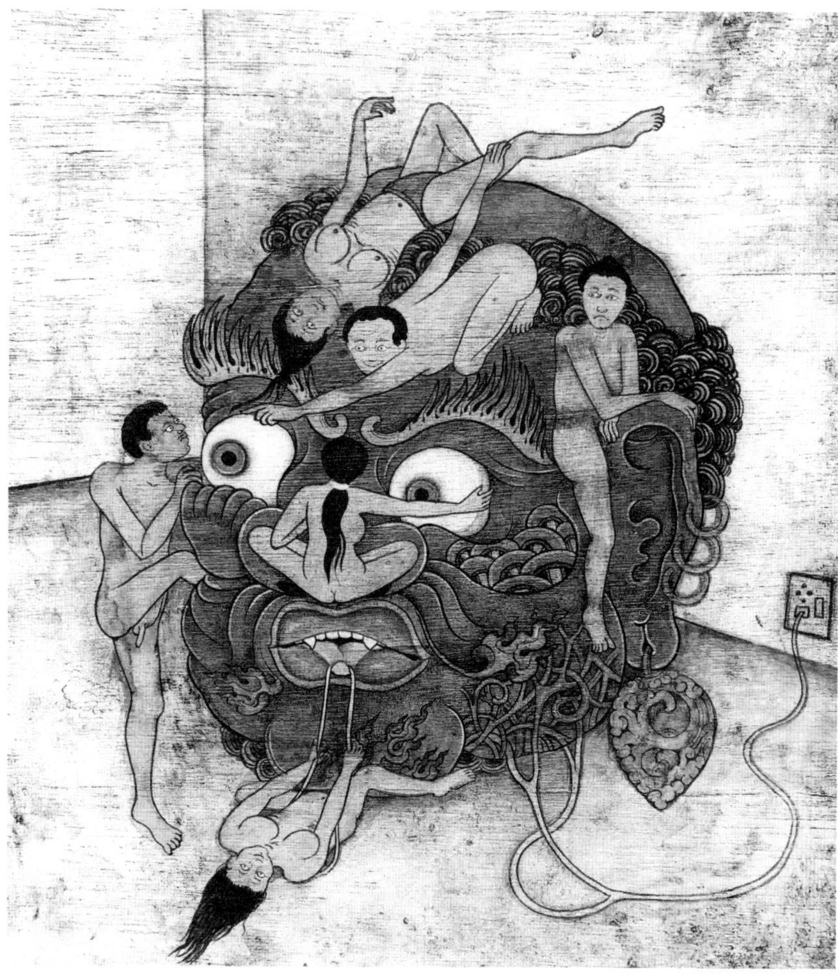

Dorjee Karmarong, *Untitled*, 2017(?), oil on wood, 31 × 35.5 cm, private owner. Photo Charles Onians.

painting connected me to an ancient ritual, but its modernity was puzzling. I wanted to take it home in order to get to know it better. What could this particular work of art by this individual maker tell me about the artless aesthetics of Kathmandu? What was it that provided the artist or viewer with a feeling of well-being?

The beginning of an answer to these questions was the realization that the geometry of the composition resembles that of a generic *thangka* painting, a traditional sacred object of Buddhist meditation, but that it breaks with the customary layout on silk or cotton by using a small rigid piece of wood and by promoting only one subject out of the usual crowd of spiritual examples. In doing so the artist liberates his imagination to depart from the severe iconographic rules of the past by introducing new partners to the dance around religious proprieties. His blue circle is still recognizable as the head of Yama, the divine judge of the dead and assessor of worldly lifestyles, emphasizing skull-like features. With his shaven tonsure and wreath of curls on top, the leaf-shaped eyebrows, the white eyes with dark pupils and the open mouth showing tongue and top front teeth, he is reassuringly the Yama whose image we usually meet on a religious feast-day in Tibet or Nepal, temporarily unrolled and displayed in a shrine, temple, or monastery. However, this image is different. Although our painter, Dorjee Karmarong (b. 1980), while living in remote mountain areas between the ages of seven and twenty, had been schooled as a monk focused on ritualistic performance, his subsequent involvement with the senior artist Tenzin Norbu Lama in Kathmandu encouraged him to display his own more profane longing for modernity.[5] He has moved the deity from its sacred, public setting into a sober whitewashed domestic space, where the intrusion of profane time and mechanical energy is expressed by an artless, electric cable, which, like a vein, connects a power point to the divine brain. The electricity seems to energize the six nudes, three men and three women, who are reduced to the size of nose, eyes, mouth, and ears, draped over Yama's head. Possibly representing the senses of sight, smell, taste, hearing, touch and perhaps even more, they are engaged in awkward relationships, expressing emotions of doubt and fear on their faces and through the dramatic

5. Dominik von Bohlen, 'The Lama Artist', *ECSNEPAL*, no. 13 (June 2013).

postures of their naked, eroticized bodies. At the centre of the composition we find the back view of a woman, whose cross-legged pose refers to ancient rituals, but whose physical handling of the divine eye suggests the modern activity of driving a motor vehicle, both references potential sources of well-being for Karmarong and the local viewer. Although Karmarong's apprenticeship to a *thangka*-making *guru* (teacher) had made him an expert religious painter, he considers himself a lay artist, who perceives his environment, both cultural and natural, with all his senses.

With these strong, but ambivalent feelings about how to make the right decisions about living and dying according to what we perceive with our senses in our surrounding, we move to the Netherlands to find Jan Eric Visser, whose work I got to know in Norfolk. Like that of Dorjee Karmarong, his youth was characterized by extreme tensions. When only twelve years old, he experienced the death of his father, soon followed by that of his much-loved older brother. These inexplicable 'wastes of life' led him to seek to resolve his traumatic relationship with both death and waste.[6] He realized, that 'making art' was 'the closest' he could get to 'usefulness and meaningfulness, to life and death…'. This resulted in his first sculptures at the Kampen Art Academy being made out of discarded pieces of wood picked up from the studio floor and then shaped into skull-like assemblages (1986). His most direct expression of the relationship between death, waste, and art is *Untitled 1988-89*, a coffin shaped cardboard box with lid.[7] Once opened, an undefined mass begs to be touched and fondled, possibly moulded and shaped. The juxtaposition of the mysterious, rounded shape and rectangular box recalls Karmarong's composition and reminds us that some themes—such as the contrast between the round and the rectangular, and death and decay—are not only local, but also universal.

The salience of 'the local' in Visser's case comes out in the contrast between the controlled shapes and linear abstractions he created when dominated by the daily experience of the urban and industrial life of Rotterdam, where he moved about fifteen years ago, and his more recent work, produced after an increased exposure to the countryside that he discovered on day-trips out of the busy harbour city.

6. What I write about Jan Eric Visser and his work is indebted to conversations with the artist himself and to the catalogue of his work, entitled *Veritas*, which combines photographs of a majority of his work of the preceding thirty years, interlaced with Visser's own splendid aphorisms and with an introduction by Elisabeth de Bièvre, 'Vorm Veranderend Afval. De Beeldhouwkunst van Jan Eric Visser / Shape Shifting Waste. The Sculpture of Jan Eric Visser', *Jan Eric Visser. Veritas* (Kemzeke, 2017), n.p. All quotes in this part of the text come from this publication.

7. See image p. 301.

The significance of this contrast was intensified in early 2021, when he spent a period as 'artist in residence' in Viervaart in Zeeland, where he was required to use 'local material'.[8] This made him aware of the resonance between problematic local artefacts and local natural resources. While his senses may have been pleasantly touched by the artless—here in the sense of 'having no connection with art'—bulging forms of the grass silage-bales in the freshly mown fields, he was alarmed by the thought of where all the plastic used to make these bales would find its final resting place, until he decided to transform it into art. 'Bad' plastic became the carrier of a dramatic new interpretation of the environment. Visser compressed reused silage-bales, cardboard, inorganic household waste, clay, and votive candle residue into 'sculptural objects' and made them look like the rolling masses of stormy waves and furrowed fields.[9] By mixing some city-bound shapes with the deep blue of Zeeland's *zee* and the black of the heavy clay of her *land*, Visser reconciles the urban and the rural, the artificial and the natural, the mind and the body.

The three samples of artless aesthetics here discussed illustrate the important connection between an art object and the context of its emergence. In each case we find that critical aspects of the work derive from characteristic features of its environment to which we have access through our senses. These are the sources of the maker's well-being and if we get to know that environment by concentrating on and studying the unfamiliar art object in all its dimensions, they can also become the source of ours.

8. 'Artist in Residence' in Viervaart, Groede, Zeeland from 1-2-2021 to 30-4-2021

9. 'Sculptural objects', such as *Without Title, Plastikos II*, 2021, 139 × 100 × 70 cm.

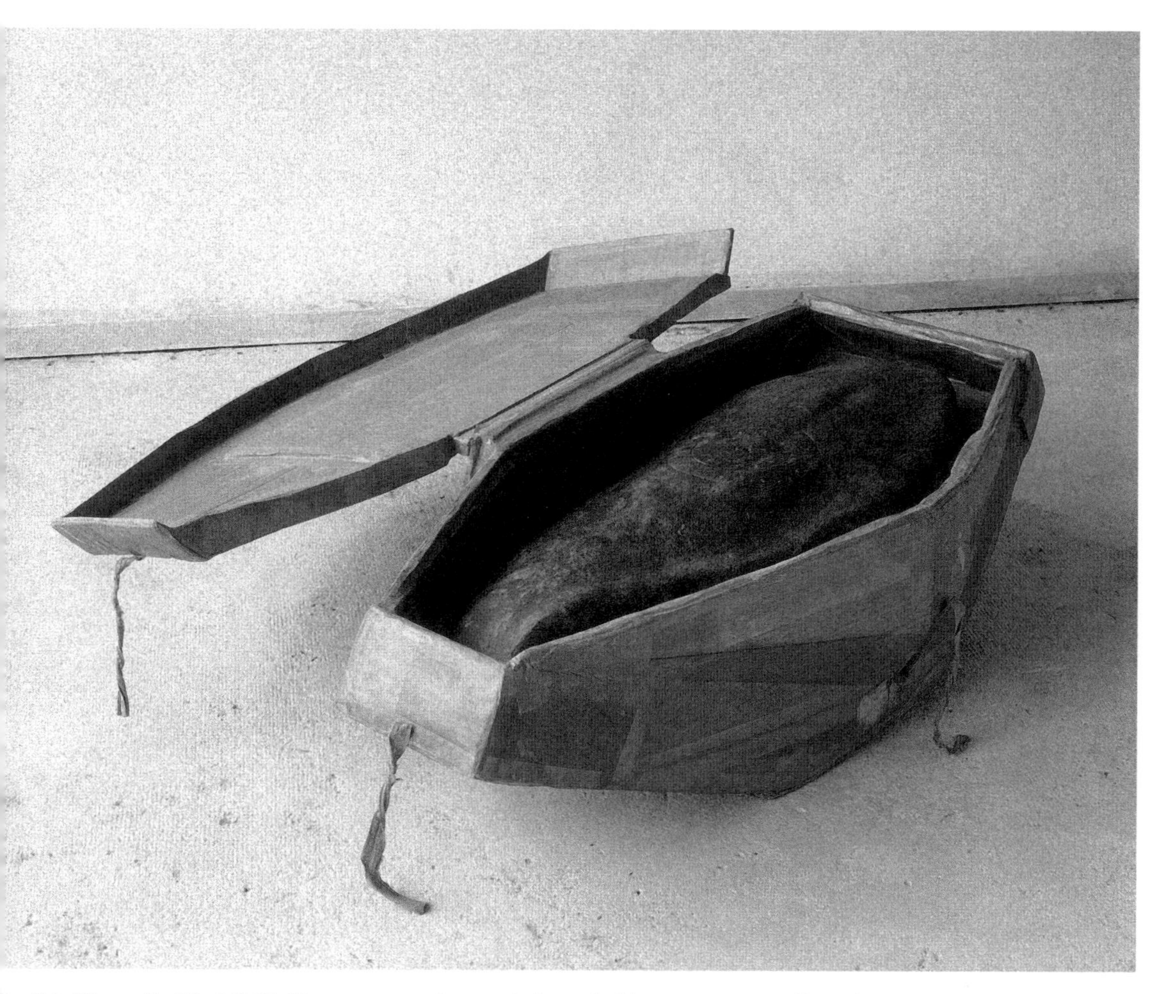

an Eric Visser, *Untitled 1988-89*, newspaper, inorganic household waste, wax, cardboard, cotton, bone glue,
2 × 100 × 103 cm. Artist Collection. Photo D. Mackaay.

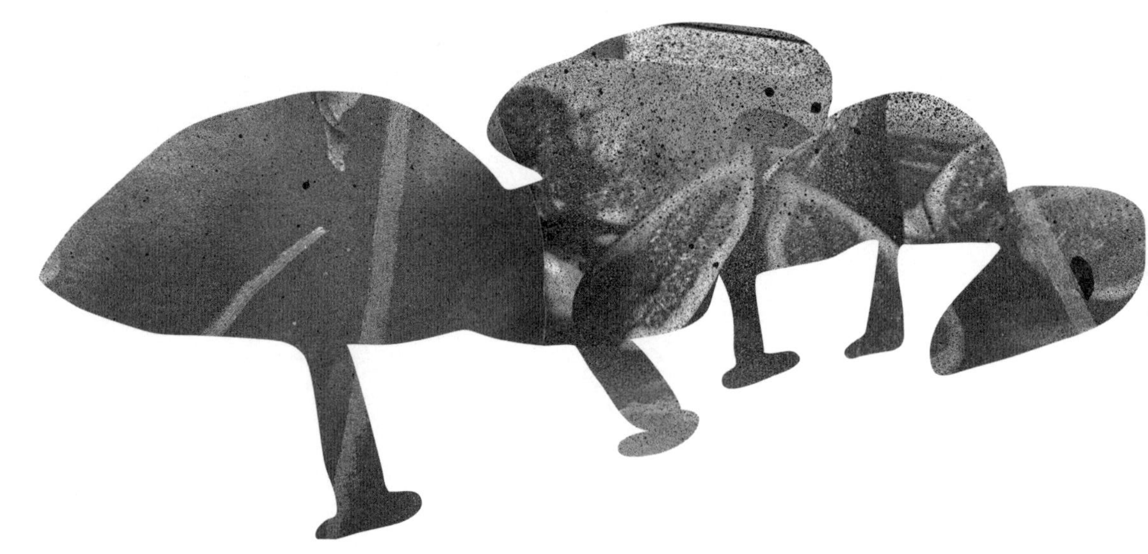

Spiral Retelling
Kitty Zijlmans in Conversation with Charl Landvreugd

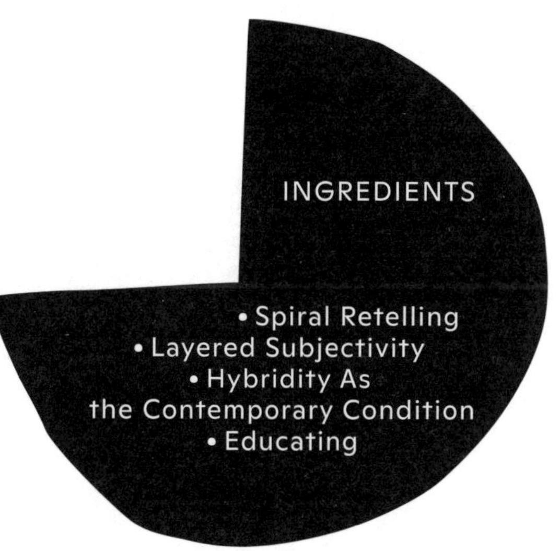

Charl Landvreugd, artist-researcher-educator, has been the new head of research at the Stedelijk Museum Amsterdam since October 2020. His remit in the museum is an extension of his position as artist-researcher-educator and hence (part of) his *work*. We discussed his interpretation of the notion 'work' in the context of the current debate about inclusiveness and diversity and the role and place of the museum with respect to modern and contemporary art in this regard.

CL The perspective of educator for the museum is very important to me; teaching runs in the family and it is something that comes naturally to me. In this case, the educator is not a top-down manager, but someone who strives to engage people in an acquired understanding of the processes of social change. The change in the museum's character, from within, so that it is more tailored to today's requirements, demands a theoretical conceptualization in which we all recognize the essential problem. What I can do, based on experience and study, is offer tools for approaching that fundamental issue. Effectively, the circumstances change, the question never does. The question in this case is, how do you design the museum in such a way that it will still be relevant as a structure in society in fifty or a hundred years' time?

KZ According to Landvreugd, we have reached a tipping point of changing consciousness; he explains:

CL I believe that this moment is our '1968' or '1989', with the fall of the Berlin Wall, Tiananmen Square, and 'Magiciens de la terre', or even a '9/11'. We have reached another juncture and whether it was 2016 with the election of Trump or 2020 when he left office, there is no doubt that there was or is now such a moment. There have been, at least in the Western world, a number of those shock events and each shock basically propels the change further forwards. You could almost say that this moment is a kind of postmodernism gone wild.

KZ What do you mean by 'postmodernism gone wild'?

CL At a certain point, a thinking arose in art that there is more, that you can mix things. That you can mix styles, genres, and backgrounds. Society as a whole now has this awareness and that causes turmoil, commotion. And that's exactly when art matters. Ideas evolve in art and philosophy and then it takes about twenty years before they work their way into the rest of society. I wonder whether that postmodernist idea is actually having repercussions in wider society, or whether society as a whole is now starting to behave like the arts did then.

KZ I think you have a point when you say that these processes are currently underway in society, but there is also a lot of resistance. White monoculture, and that also means modernism, is no longer accepted, because, of course, it was never reconciled with the complex reality.

CL That is no longer accepted, no, and you can see that those changes have accelerated. Art policy lags behind social change. In fact, it has always been the case, but now it is becoming very obvious. What you see is that many art institutions are currently trying to catch up. They are trying to 'get with the programme'—they have to keep up with the changes in society.

KZ So, are we really talking about inclusiveness here?

CL Yes, and then you get a kind of overcompensation, where absolute inclusiveness can never be guaranteed. By this, I don't just mean that you cannot achieve some intersections, but also that white people and specifically white men are explicitly left out. I find that problematic, because I don't think that inclusiveness means a different hegemonic pattern now becoming dominant. What I see as a problem is that, for some, the call for more diversity and inclusiveness is about a changing of the guard and that it is less about coming up with a new power

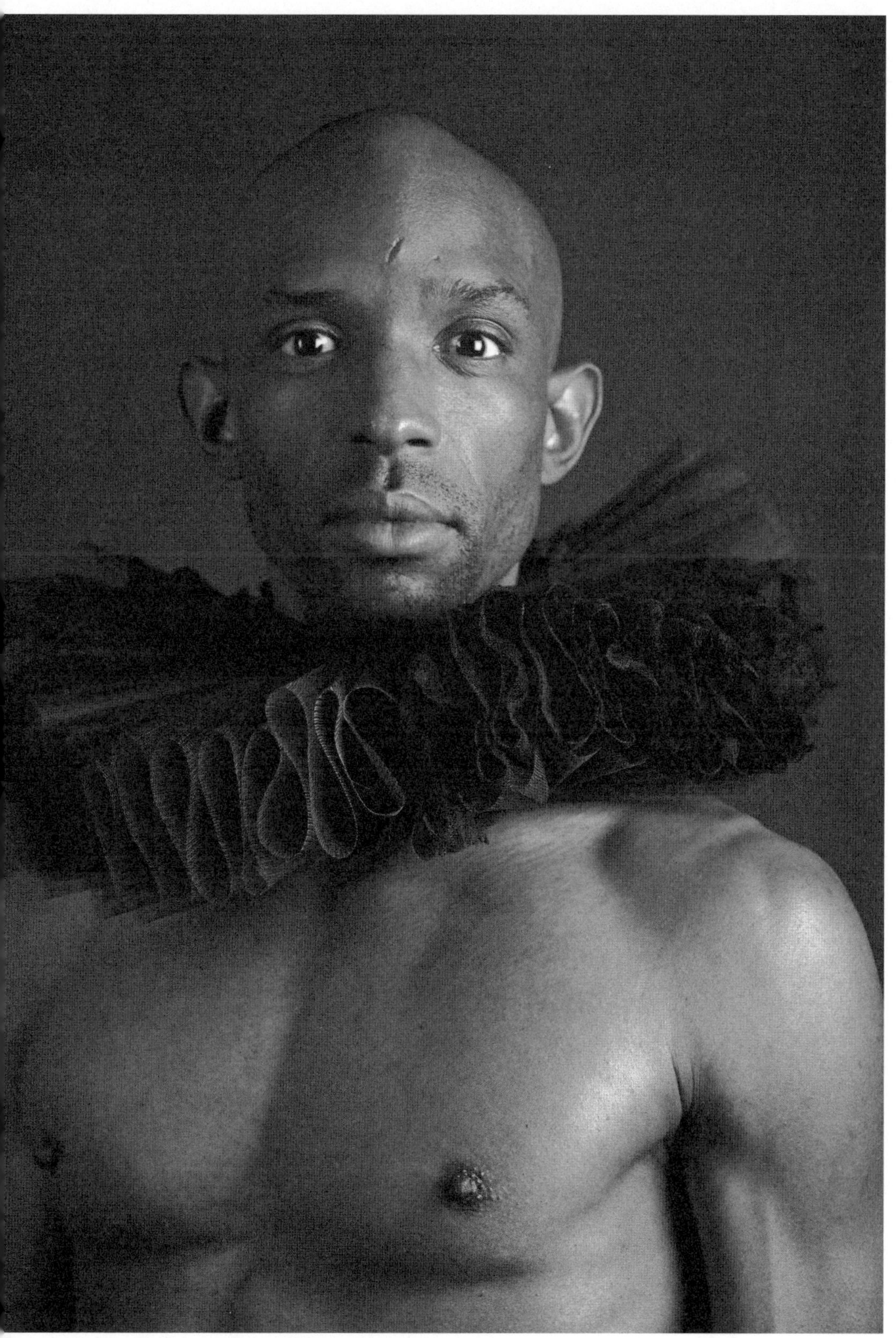

Charl Landvreugd, *Millstone Ruff*, 2010, photograph.

structure. If you replace whiteness with blackness, the world remains equally miserable because nothing changes. Personally, I am very interested in people who are thinking about how we can come up with a different structure, where those old and colonial hierarchical models can no longer apply.

KZ The crux is in that *can*.

CL It is an exercise in thinking; we have to think about this *now* and teach our results, so that it can become reality in twenty, thirty years' time.

KZ Is this way of thinking the reason why art and artists are so important? After all, thinking from the point of view of art involves taking other paths than those involving purely rational processes.

CL I always say, you have to imagine it first, otherwise it can never become reality. Reality only comes into existence in and through the imagination. Sometimes, you can think something and it is only at the moment that you have made something that you see that the work is further ahead than you are. That sounds very abstract, or perhaps very weird if you are not an artist, but you can make a work from a thought, and then, when the work starts talking back, that's when you see that it is actually doing something different, that it is further ahead in its 'thinking' than you are. So, there's a discrepancy there, or at least a difference, in what you know intuitively and what you know intellectually. It is at this point where the work of art, co-informed by intuition and not only by intellect, can provide answers to problems, to issues that cannot yet be resolved.

KZ When a work, an image, starts to speak, does it also transcend you as an artist?

CL Yes, and then you just have to be quiet and listen, as an artist. As far as I'm concerned, that is the whole process, that when you are quiet again, you listen and look at what the work is telling you. I made a work, the one with that black millstone collar. I made it in 2010, at the start of the Black Pete debate. I had tried lots of things and in the end, this work materialized. The nice thing about the work is that I still don't know what it means, while it just stands there being itself. What is it saying now? It is so self-evident that it has taught me that being naturally present, just being yourself, without having to prove or explain yourself to the other, is perhaps one of the greatest qualities.

KZ I think that the strength of the work, and fortunately that applies to many works, is that it can evoke all kinds of references.

CL Yes, yes, but it is mainly just itself and that, I think, is inherently beautiful. Essentially, what I mean is this: I think in structures, and that goes back to my Bachelor's degree when I had a Japanese tutor in my first semester who said to me: the artwork is only a polaroid of that one moment in your process. The process, that is the work. So, I see the entire process, from the moment that I started with my BA until later, when I am dead. That, in its entirety, is THE work. Not these things that are emerging now. In that sense, working at the museum is part of the work, the process. The thing that I am trying to make.

KZ It's about the process, rather than the output and, by extension, that also means your work at the Stedelijk?

CL For me that is part of the work, because now I have the opportunity to apply everything that I have tried and conceived, all the input from professors, fellow students, and my current students with whom I have spoken, all the information that has fed into it. It's a chance to ask, is everything that I have researched and produced until now useful? What have I learnt so far?

KZ So, the Stedelijk is actually a testing ground?

CL The Stedelijk is one big studio. Just one big studio with people.

KZ Like working with students?

CL Yes, it's like that too. I enjoy working with students most when I see their eyes light up. Suddenly, the light goes on and then, that is what I am waiting for. Then I'm done, then I've done what I had to do. And that light never goes out. That educating, that is perhaps my contribution. I'm not saying that the museum is a student, absolutely not, because that's not what I mean. But once the light goes on, it never goes out again. With students, I hope that one of them turns out to be more brilliant than all of us who are currently working.

KZ That way you also transcend your own ego?

CL If that happens, if I got to teach that person, well, then I can be happy, that would be a huge honour. With all of your work you hope to inspire people, you hope to inspire people somewhere to get to certain places. When I was appointed at the Stedelijk, I received all kinds of messages, one of which was from a Black student from London who had just started a Master's, and they wrote: 'It's great to see you appointed to this role, because I have been wrestling with myself about why I am studying art, but now I see you there, I remember why I have to do this.'

KZ To return to the question of what you mean by *work*. That *work* has a process-oriented character and education is an aspect of this, because, ultimately, it is about those deeper structures?

CL Structures that we, as educators, can provide. You see, that is the change that is taking place in the world right now. It is because of the educators who came before us, and what we are doing now will have repercussions in twenty years' time.

KZ So, people that you have educated or guided are now in the same position that you have achieved?

CL Exactly, and they are making great strides.

KZ And in terms of a New Outlook? A new outlook also has a long history, of course, but if I were to ask you to formulate what is essential for you now, for the study of contemporary art or art today, in the wide context of a globalized world, what do you consider the markers to be?

CL One marker is that everything has already happened before. I believe very much in history. It is spiral retelling, we are just doing the same circuit every time, albeit slightly differently. If you look back and see what has happened, then you see that we are now making the same loop again. With that in mind I don't necessarily go for the word intersectionality; I would rather talk about layered subjectivity, or at least recognize a super layered subjectivity. There is a child somewhere, now, whose father was born in Japan and its mother in Brazil. The child was born and raised in Switzerland, but goes to study in Abuja (Nigeria), and there they will meet a nice Australian. That is the world.

KZ And there should be greater recognition of that?

CL Exactly, you have to embrace hybridity as the—new—starting point, and we just have to let go of the idea that there is a pure form, culturally, artistically.

KZ Postmodernism gone wild resonates here. How does this relate to what, in your dissertation, you call cultural nativeness?

CL In my dissertation, I spoke first about Afropea, but I have let that go, because it could create the impression that I am only talking about people of African origin in a European setting, and that is not my point. What I'm talking about is the contemporary condition in which someone like me is physically African, ethnically South American, and culturally European. This is something that has actually been true for migrants for many decades: you had an uncle in Mexico, an aunt in Morocco, you had family everywhere, you were always travelling. Now, it turns out, at least for us in the West, that there is a generation that also travels and has people everywhere. This is only now becoming a reality for the majority group, but for migrant groups this has always been their reality. Previously, it used to be cool to have an aunt on another continent. Now, it's your love who lives there. Good luck with that! So, layered subjectivity as the starting point, that is the contemporary condition. Reality only really comes into existence in that imagination.

PRESENT IN THE MOMENT

Kitty Zijlmans &
Charl Landvreugd

POSTCOLONIAL PERSPECTIVES

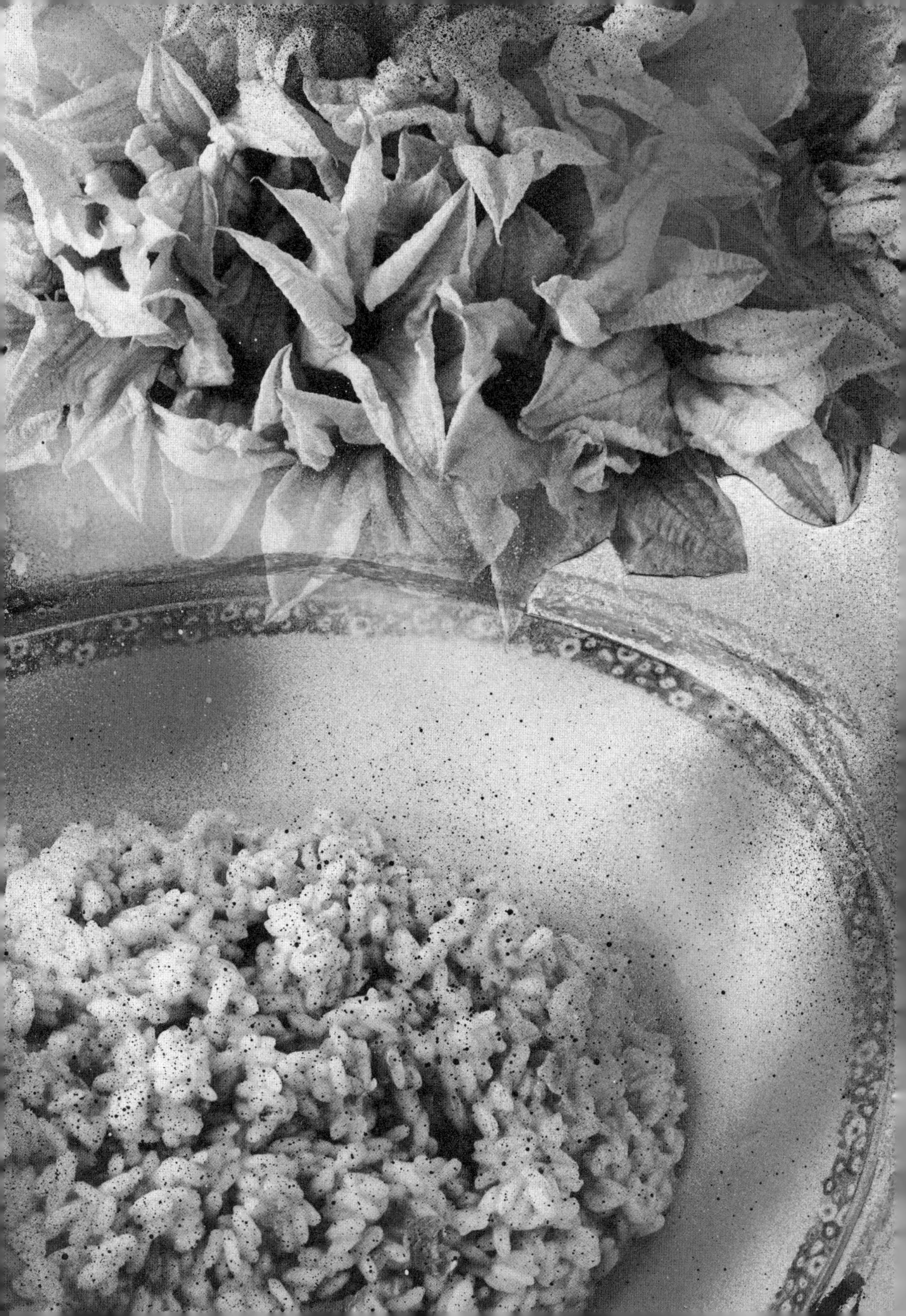

Sophie Ernst

THE SILENT EMPRESS What Should She Have Said?

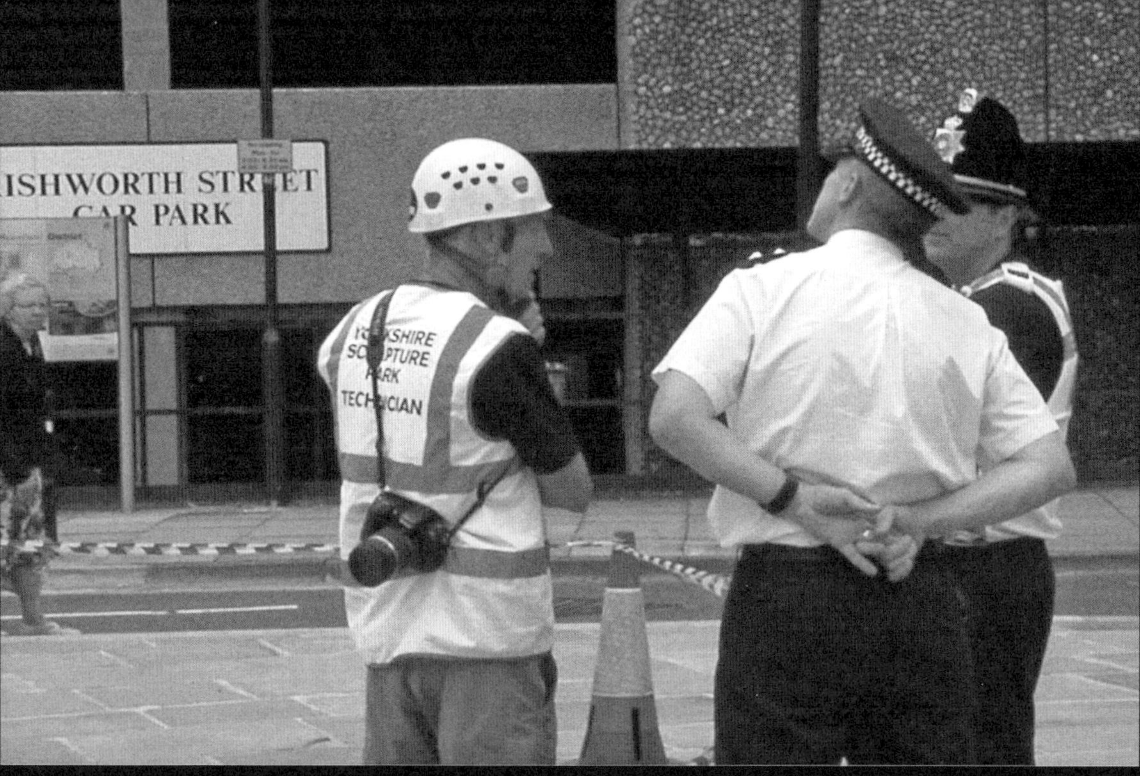

Sophie Ernst, *Silent Empress*, 2012, video still, Wakefield, Yorkshire Sculpture Park.

1. Hannah Arendt, *Responsibility and Judgment* (New York, 2003), p. 265.

2. Sophie Ernst, *Silent Empress*, sound-tag, 2012, Wakefield, vimeo.com/289354487, accessed 16 June 2021.

'I must be held responsible for something I have not done, and the reason for my responsibility must be my membership in a group (a collective) which no voluntary act of mine can dissolve.'[1]

Hannah Arendt

It was the first time I met a Rastafari. Masimba Musodza is a Rasta, he is also a declared Yorkshire man, as you may tell from the picture here. I met Masimba during a residency at the Yorkshire Sculpture Park. He was one of many Yorkshire-based refugees I interviewed for a project that accompanied my exhibition at the Park. He had fled Zimbabwe, where his work as a playwright had put him in difficult circumstances. Our encounter made a deep impression on me. He did not tell me a story of the deprivations and hardships of a refugee, although he probably experienced all that. It was more like he extended a hand and helped me recognize my role in the colonial legacy. Shortly after meeting Masimba, I made a public intervention called *The Silent Empress* (2012).[2] The artwork was a brief disruption on a statue of Queen Victoria.

The Silent Empress embodies our silence as a society. Europe is still reluctant to apologize for its colonial wrongs. Looking at the dark sides of Europe's past is

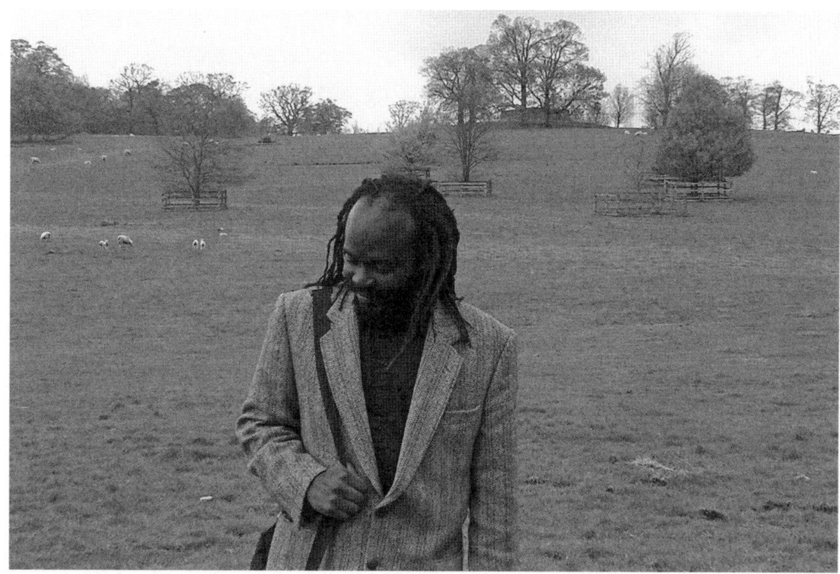

Masimba Musodza at the Yorkshire Sculpture Park, 2012. Photo Sophie Ernst.

politically risky because European states do not know where it might lead to (or what it will cost). 'We have', says Hammad Nasar, 'developed a collective amnesia that blinds us to Empire's complex role in the construction of Britain'[3]—and the whole of Europe, we may add. Why do I believe that Europeans should apologize for the wrong committed by former colonial powers? The principal reason is: by apologizing, we bring ourselves not only at eye-level with the victims of colonialism, but a sincere acknowledgement of a wrong also removes old hierarchies. As a result, it has the potential to diffuse misguided notions of entitlement to resources. Several recent events illustrate how failing to recognize past injuries upholds an attitude of misplaced imperial nostalgia.[4]

Remember the 2010 poppy skirmish when David Cameron insisted on his right to 'free speech', and wore a Remembrance Day poppy in China?[5] The poppy is a sacrosanct symbol of military heroism in the UK with its origins in World War I. Was Cameron unaware of the utmost distress the poppy had brought to the Chinese during the Opium Wars when he insisted on wearing the flower on a state visit to China? Also, you may have followed the 'Rhodes must fall' campaign in Oxford. Cecil Rhodes, the British imperialist who founded Rhodesia (part of which is now Zimbabwe), has been honoured with a memorial in Oxford. Students and faculty have called for the removal and a reckoning with the University's involvement in colonialism. The college has been torn between ethical considerations of better representation of non-white culture and the financial pressure by money-heavy conservative donors.[6] Public statues like that of Rhodes and Queen Victoria, as well as the remembrance poppy, are forms of remembering that claim permanence.

Critical awareness of one's own difficult history is indispensable to change thinking and acting. However, we tend to 'petrify historical discourse, lather it in cement, hoist it high, and insist on it as a permanent statement of fact, culture, truth and tradition that can never be questioned, touched, removed, or recast', as Gary Younge observed.[7] *The Silent Empress* exposes this heroic form of remembering; it shakes and pushes at the regal silence of

3. Hammad NASAR, 'In order to be British we must acknowledge our "Indianness"', *TATE ETC*, no. 41 (2017), www.tate.org.uk/tate-etc/issue-41-autumn-2017/opinion-hammad-nasar-british-indiannes, accessed 16 June 2021.

4. According to a poll by data analytics firm YouGov almost sixty percent of the British public feel proud of the British Empire. Will Dahlgreen, 'The British Empire is "something to be proud of"', *YouGov*, 26 July 2014, yougov.co.uk/topics/lifestyle/articles-reports/2014/07/26/britain-proud-its-empire, accessed 16 June 2021.

5. Michael White, 'David Cameron should not have worn that poppy in China', *The Guardian*, 10 November 2010, theguardian.com/politics/blog/2010/nov/10/david-cameron-poppy-china-michael-white, accessed 16 June 2021.

6. Michael Race, 'Cecil Rhodes statue will not be removed by Oxford College', *BBC News*, 20 May 2021, bbc.com/news/uk-england-oxfordshire-57175057, accessed 16 June 2021.

7. Gary Younge, 'Why every single statue should come down', *The Guardian*, 1 June 2021, theguardian.com/artanddesign/2021/jun/01/gary-younge-why-every-single-statue-should-come-down-rhodes-colston, accessed 16 June 2021.

8. Ibid.

9. Nick Smith, *I Was Wrong: The Meanings of Apologies*, University of New Hampshire/ Cambridge University Press, 2008.

the Queen. As a community, we remember the past in its present-day meaning and will permanently re-examine history in view of present actions. (Needless to say, colonialism is not only wrong from the present-day point of view. It has always been wrong.) 'Heroic' forms of remembering try to make history a-historical and, consequentially, feed the narrative of the political right all over Europe. They will 'detach the past from the present, the present from morality, and morality from responsibility'.[8] So, if I do not acknowledge the colonial wrongs and, as an artist, fail to make this explicit, I am complicit in the rise of conservative nationalism in present-day Europe. Silence is not an option.

The intervention on the statue of Queen Victoria in Yorkshire revealed several instances of silence. For one, power is silent, the Empress has her regalia to evoke authority and needs no words. Furthermore, the singular view on history the statue represents silences other voices, i.e., those of the formerly colonized. Then, the intervention was stopped by the city officials, which amounted to censorship. But the silence most pertinent is the silence of Europe that does not apologize. The monologue of *The Silent Empress*, very consciously, is a *fauxpology*, an incomplete apology. Some have pointed out that apologies often are insincere, commodified, or otherwise flawed. Apologies may act as a licence to 'move on', and bad apologies are like 'hiccups of etiquette'.[9] But what is a valid apology? A valid apology admits a wrong. It tells the history of that wrong and points at its consequences. Furthermore it will correct the wrong. Acknowledging a wrong consolidates a dark part of our history as part of our identity. Masimba told me how, in Zimbabwe, he grew up with the belief that if we commit a wrong, the ghosts of the victims will haunt us for generations to come unless we acknowledge the wrong and apologize. It is only then that both can look eye to eye again and continue in friendship.

1. David Cameron, 2009, www.conservativehome.com/platform/2009/07/david-cameron-proud-to-be-british.html, accessed 28 May 2021.

‘We must never forget that Britain is a great country with a history we can be truly proud of.’[1]

Sophie Ernst, *Silent Empress*, 2012, video still, Wakefield, Yorkshire Sculpture Park

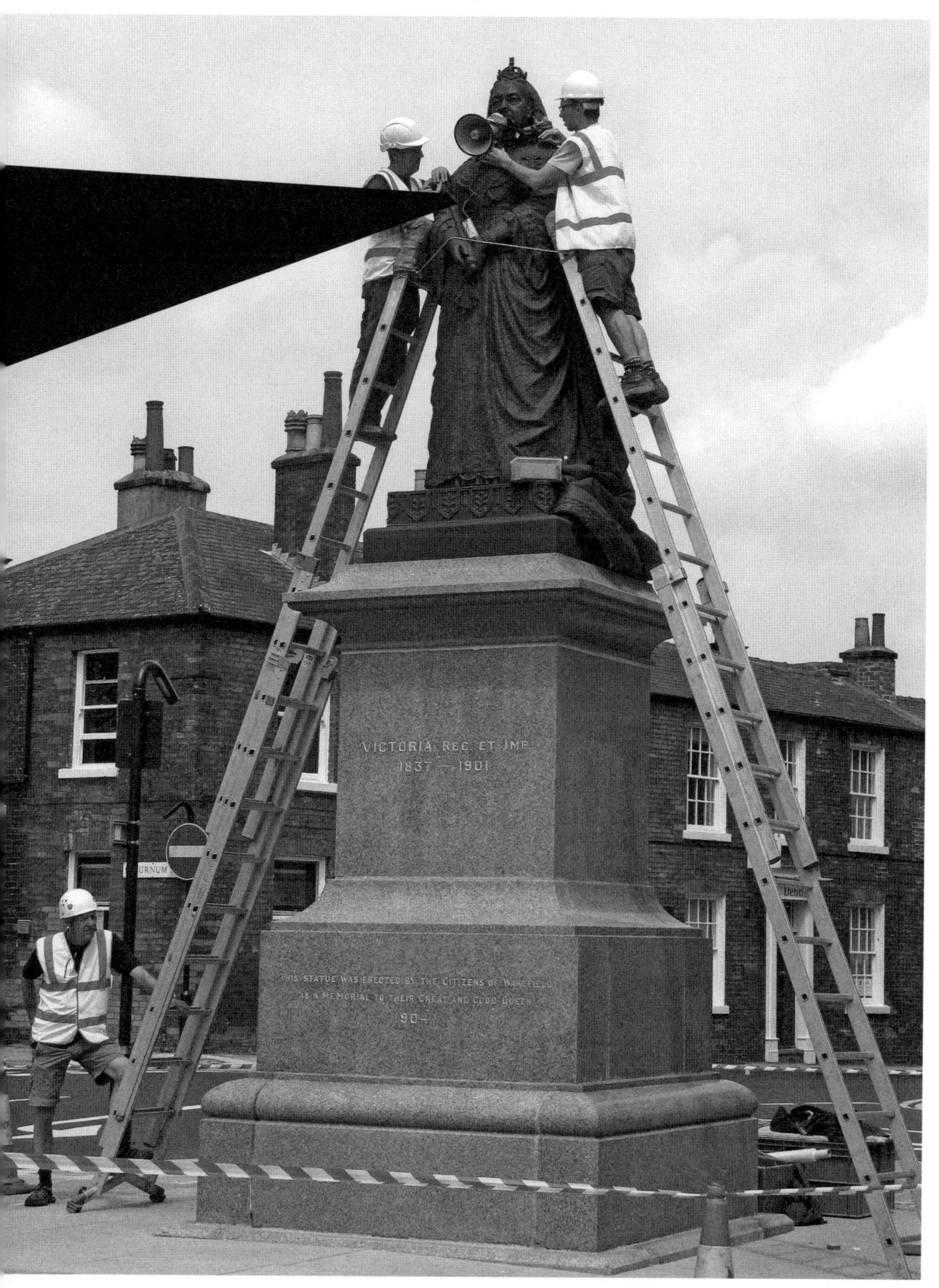
VICTORIA REG ET IMP
1837 — 1901
THIS STATUE WAS ERECTED BY THE CITIZENS OF WAKEFIELD
AS A MEMORIAL TO THEIR GREAT AND GOOD QUEEN
1904

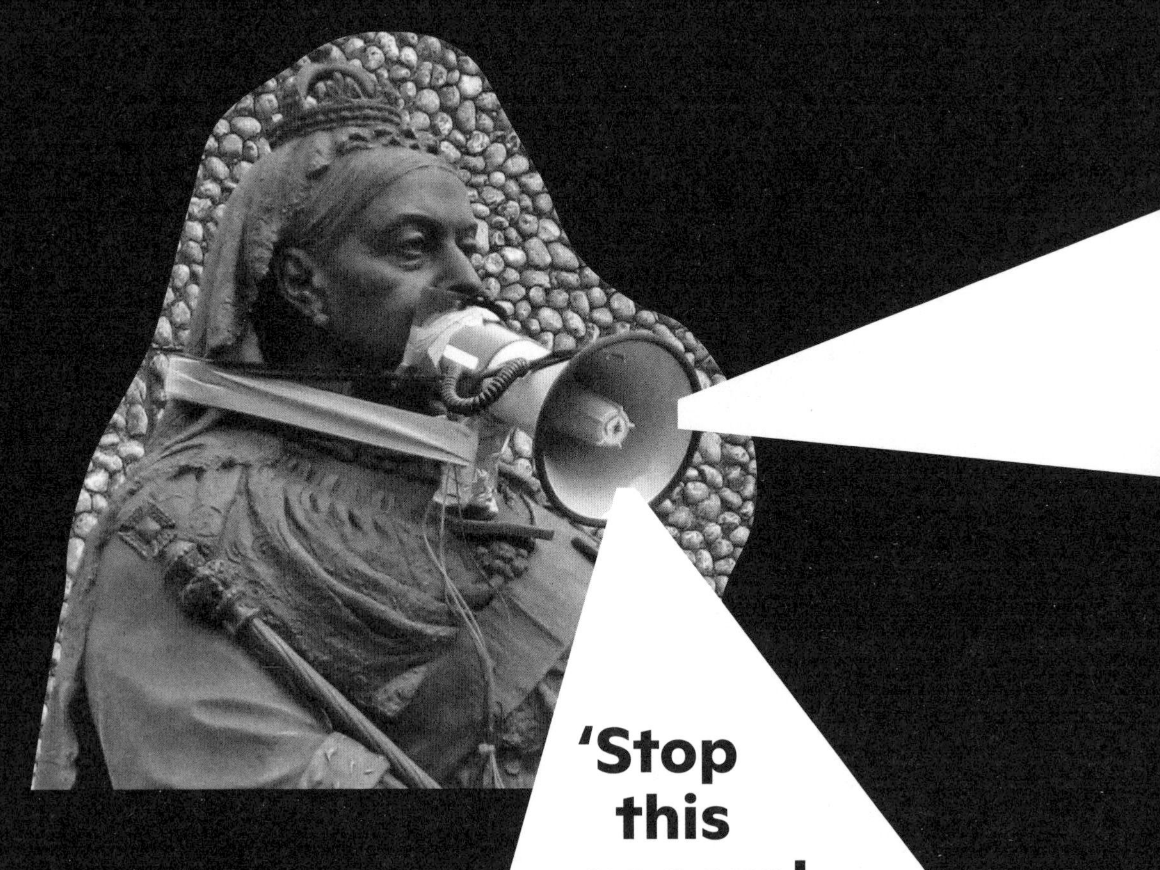

Sophie Ernst, *Silent Empress*, 2012, video still, Wakefield, Yorkshire Sculpture Park.

2. Gordon Brown, 2005, www.dailymail.co.uk/news/article-334208/Its-time-celebrate-Empire-says-Brown.html, accessed 28 May 2021.

3. Boris Johnson, 2020, www.twitter.com/ITVNewsPoliticsstatus/1298235883364265986?s=20, accessed 28 May 2021.

‘We should celebrate much of our past rather than apologise for it.’[2]

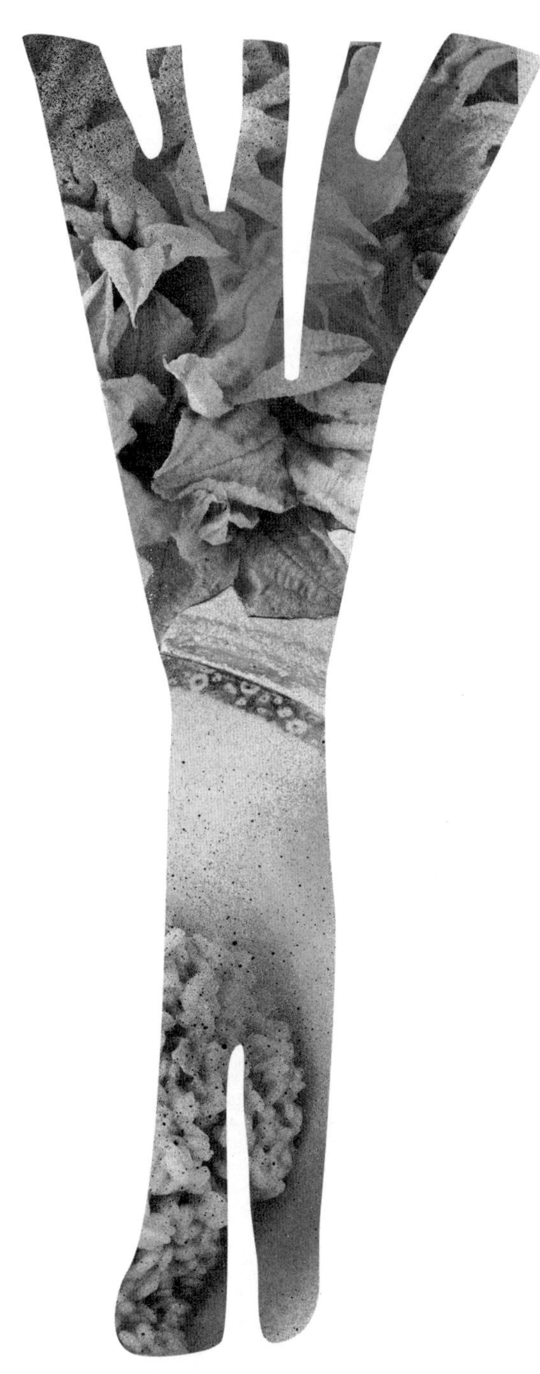

REHUMANIZING ACTS
An Outlook on (the Meaning of) Dutch Slavery Research

Nancy Jouwe

INGREDIENTS

- Reading the City as Archive
- Making the Unseen Seen
- Mapping
- Critical Fabulation
- White Innocence
- Positionality

'The greatest insult is to be ignored. To be in the room but treated as if you simply do not exist. And this is part of what struck me in my research of Dutch art history in finding so many Black figures that were not just not named but apparently unseen and not commented upon.'

(Historian Alison Blakely in documentary *Painted Black*, 2008)

In this essay I would like to discuss some of the implications following the growing attention for the history of Dutch slavery by Dutch researchers, artists, curators, and scholars in the last one or two decades. What has this knowledge brought us as a community interested in art, heritage, and the colonial past? What has changed because of this knowledge production? Has it shaped our thinking differently, and if so, how? And who is 'we'?

As someone who is interested and engaged in the history of slavery, having curated public programmes and published several books that centralize the history of slavery in Dutch cities and landscapes, I learned a couple of things. One: Dutch people in general know very little about this history. Two: there are several emotional reactions attached to this history: fear, resistance, anger, guilt, or shame. And there is also surprise, curiosity and shock. Three: there seems to be a general lack of context. Especially white people have trouble finding something to compare it with: the white Dutch mind finds it hard to imagine what it was like and how it relates to them. A recent British survey showed that at least half of the Dutch population were proud of their imperial past, the highest percentage of countries surveyed, including Britain, Spain and France.[1]

This is not surprising. First, there were simply no plantations on Dutch European soil. These were to be found in Dutch colonies in Asia, Africa, and the Americas. Furthermore, as Alex van Stipriaan noted, twentieth-century Netherlands was coated in silence with regard to the Dutch history of slavery, both in public discourse and in the education system.[2] Actual visual references of the Dutch colonial past, as displayed in internationally renowned museums such as the Rijksmuseum or the Mauritshuis—up to very recently—either showed a lack of reference or a particular lens used to refer to Dutch colonialism. The Dutch audience was shown the riches, beauty, and cultural and economic power it brought, captured in the phrase: the Golden Age.[3] The set-up of the Gallery of Honour at the Rijksmuseum, which leads to Rembrandt's *The Night Watch*, is a case in point. And as Dutch, 'we don't do race', as Gloria Wekker argued in her book *White Innocence*.[4]

In the following segments I will offer some ingredients that have helped me and others to better understand what it is we do when we try to critically unpack this hidden part of Dutch history. As we try to unlearn, to purposely consider our idiom and unearth or reinterpret sources, I have come to realize that we engage in rehumanizing acts.[5]

Before I became actively involved in researching the history of slavery and while working within the philanthropic community, I visited places such as Elmina in Ghana, the infamous slave fortress and the city of Salvador in Brazil, cradle of Black Brazilian culture. Somewhat earlier, as a student, I travelled to Jakarta, vaguely familiar with the fact that it was the main port city of the Dutch East India Company but unaware that it was the second city of the Dutch republic by the year 1700 (Batavia including its surrounding area had 17,500 inhabitants) with over sixty

1. See theguardian.com/world/2020/mar/11/uk-more-nostalgic-for-empire-than-other-ex-colonial-powers.

2. Alex van Stipriaan, 'Hunne vrijmaking zou zoo veel geld kosten', *Trouw*, 31 March 2001, pp. 49–50; Alex van Stipriaan, 'Stilte! Niet storen De slavernij is afgeschaft', *De Negentiende Eeuw* 29, no. 1 (2005): 'Verdwenen in de negentiende eeuw', pp. 45–61.

3. See nytimes.com/2019/10/25/arts/design dutch-golden-age-and-colonialism.html.

4. Gloria Wekker, *White Innocence: Paradoxes of Colonialism and Race* (Durham/London, 2016).

5. *Words Matter: An Unfinished Guide to Word Choices in the Cultural Sector* eds. Wayne Modest and Robin Lelijveld (National Museum of World Cultures, Works in Progress 1) (Amsterdam, 2018).

percent of enslaved people in the eighteenth century. These travels to three different continents unconsciously set the tone for me and as I became a curator working locally in the cultural sector in Utrecht, I seemed to be asking different questions than my peers. A 2010 op-ed by the late Anil Ramdas that spoke of a heartless slavery debate, triggered me.[6] I wondered if a city such as Utrecht, with its rich cultural history of almost two thousand years, had a colonial history, a city traditionally un-associated with slavery and colonialism.

During this quest, looking at my own city anew, an understanding slowly grew that the official archive could stay silent whereas the city can speak. It involved learning how to look, to use a different lens and to learn and see what remained unseen to a general public's eye. It also involved learning to understand what it is that we see. Who actually lies below the tombstones in churches, who lived in the lavish houses along the canals, who is remembered in street names and what do gable stones and ornaments tell us? The building of the Amsterdam Archive at the Vijzelstraat used to seat the Nationale Handels Maatschappij [National Trading Company] and has three statues of colonial empire builders attached to the top of the building: Jan Pieterszoon Coen, Herman Willem Daendels, and Joannes Benedictus van Heutsz. Often their statues go unnoticed for passers-by. It is just one example that made me realize, together with peers such as Esther Captain and Jennifer Tosch, that we could read the city as an archive.

Over the past two decades, more knowledge production on slavery coincided with activists critically engaging in the Dutch colonial past (e.g., the installation of a national slavery monument, the Royal Golden Coach, Dutch military executions during the war of independence in Indonesia, decolonizing the museum, Black Pete, looted colonial objects). As a result, museums were engaging (or were compelled to engage) differently with their own collections.[7] When our project 'Traces of Slavery Utrecht' started in 2010, the city curator of the Centraal Museum stated that they did not have objects in their collection that referred to slavery. Several museums would have given a similar answer at the time. But it is a

6. nrc.nl/nieuws/2010/07/06/debat-over-slavernij-is-harteloos-en-rancuneus-11916470-a128313.

7. See Jos van Beurden, *Ongemakkelijk erfgoed* (Zutphen, 2021).

matter of interpretation. A decade later, the Rijksmuseum Amsterdam exhibit, simply called 'Slavery' (June–August 2021), included a reinterpretation of Rembrandt's full-length portraits from 1634 of an elite couple: Marten Soolmans and Oopjen Coppit. Obtained by the museum in 2016 in a nail-biting high-profile purchase, the young pair embodied the Golden Age. In 2021, Marten and Oopjen were reframed within the exhibit as having profited heavily from sugar production, made possible by the labour of the enslaved during colonial times.

Reinterpreting high-profile art pieces can happen in more ways than one. Black visitors would notice a Black boy in a large painting next to Rembrandt's *The Night Watch*. Curator of History of the Rijksmuseum Eveline Sint-Nicolaas, who is white, acknowledged that throughout her professional life she had looked at that same painting, *Schutters van wijk VIII* by Bartholomeus van der Helst, was familiar with all the names of the dignitaries portrayed, but had never noticed the Black boy in the middle of the painting. Now, she cannot unsee him anymore. It is an example of how the presence of a white gaze, despite, or rather enhanced by a Western art-historical training, creates and upholds an inability to notice a Black person in historical paintings from the Golden Age. It implies that Black people remain unseen and are only understood, especially in paintings produced in the early modern age, as props that enhance a white, gendered presence. The Black presence enhances the beautiful white skin tone of women and the economic prowess of white men (and women) who can afford a Black servant.[8] Thanks to both external and internal pressure and processes, the historicity of museums, established during the heyday of European and Dutch imperialism, has increasingly become the focus of attention. Museums have become implicated institutions that (re)produce a white Eurocentric art/cultural canon that excludes and/or marginalizes everything outside that realm.

While resorting to a formal archive for research on slavery, the realization can hit that the archive is a violent place. People who have been treated like cattle, or objects, similar to furniture, are listed as numbers and amounts in rows of bookkeeping records. How does one begin to unpack this? Important work by women historians in the

8. See Nancy Jouwe, 'Notions of In/visibility', *What Is Left Unseen*, ed. Rosemarie Buikema et al. (Utrecht, 2019), pp. 31–37.

9. Marisa J. Fuentes, *Dispossessed Lives: Enslaved Women, Violence, and the Archive* (Early American Studies) (Philadelphia, 2016).

10. See parool.nl/nieuws/in-de-gouden-eeuw-was-amsterdam-het-epicentrum-van-de-cartografie~b9077a9e/?referrer=https%3A%2F%2Fwww.google.com%2F.

11. Elizabeth Sutton, *Capitalism and Cartography in the Dutch Golden Age* (London/Chicago, 2015), p. 39.

12. See Nancy Jouwe, 'Introduction', *Gendered Empire* (Hilversum, 2020), pp. 25–40.

United States and the United Kingdom, two nations heavily implicated in colonial slavery, provide innovative ways of knowledge production, stemming from the realization that the archive is, indeed, violent. Award-winning historian Marisa Fuentes interrogates the archive and its historical production to expose the effects of white colonial power. In her publication *Dispossessed Lives* she used the mere fragments that she could find about enslaved women (enslaved and free Black women were the majority in eighteenth-century Bridgetown in Barbados but were mostly absent in the archive) and used interdisciplinary scholarship to weave an innovative historical account.[9] Her work is indebted to the scholar Saidiya Hartman, who coined the term 'critical fabulation', a writing methodology that combines historical and archival research with critical theory and fictional narrative. Thus, the marginalized or untold stories of enslaved (and free) Black women are finally heard, told, and seen.

To see and map the unknown, was the business of mapmakers. They were sought after in the seventeenth century. Dutch men such as Joan Blaeu and Jodocus Hondius were mapmakers who lived around the Dam in Amsterdam and made the city the epicentre of mapmaking in Europe for a large part of the seventeenth century.[10] As art historian Elizabeth Sutton argued, the maps these mapmakers produced created a 'pictorial rhetoric' that could forge a discourse within the metropole: 'Maps codified and made coherent what was only a cacophony of voices in meeting rooms and on the street.'[11]

With the public history project 'Mapping Slavery' we wanted to map the temporality of colonial history in the Dutch metropole itself. By gathering empirical data and mapping them into visual and narrated stories, 'Mapping Slavery' debunks the notion of Dutch colonialism, including slavery having taken place somewhere else, out of sight and therefore out of mind, hardly a part of Dutch history. This was very much the dominant mindset of Dutch people in 2013, the year we started. Within the Mapping project, the Dutch colonial empire—stretching from parts of Southeast Asia to West-Africa and the Americas—is considered as one analytical entity.[12] Furthermore, the Dutch colonial project and its afterlives were understood as a continuum, through understanding colonial history and current race relations (an under-researched topic in the Netherlands) as deeply interconnected. Similarly, the well-received publication *De Slavernij in Oost en West: Het Amsterdam onderzoek* [Slavery in East and West: The Amsterdam Investigation],[13] commissioned by the municipality of Amsterdam, showed how the cities' involvement in the colonial slavery system was worldwide, not just trans-Atlantic and argued that the afterlives of slavery is a reality we should not ignore. On the basis of this research (which involved around forty researchers), on 1 July 2021 Amsterdam mayor Femke Halsema officially apologized for the cities' involvement in the worldwide slavery trade and system. It was the first time that a Dutch City Council officially took this public stance. In earlier years, Dutch politicians had uttered only regret and remorse.[14]

Inspired by a feminist anti-racist tradition, I end with some notes on positionality. Considering that the Dutch art realm has been dominated by a white and colonial gaze for so long, a gaze that is still active, it has become increasingly important to become aware of our own individual positions within the art community. The Dutch art world thoroughly lacks a self-critical stance on its whiteness and the implications it involves, especially in the workplace. How do we engage, what are our politics, how do we position ourselves? The conservatism of the arts sector combined with individual complacency hinders us in our capacity as a community to step into the future. Wekker's *White Innocence* provides us with necessary intellectual starting points, which can be helpful in our practices.[15] White Innocence translated into the realm of the arts means that we remain comfortable in reproducing a Western art canon materialized in its institutions and ignore its colonial roots.

Unlearning white innocence can be practiced, for instance, through a heightened awareness of the history of slavery. New questions, not posed before, surface: can we imagine how the lives of the enslaved looked like?

Can we move beyond the Black person as a prop or an object? Can we grasp the magnitude of the dehumanization process that took place and do we realize that this process was reproduced within the arts? Do we find these

13. *De Slavernij in Oost en West. Het Amsterdam onderzoek*, ed. Pepijn Brandon et al. (Amsterdam, 2020).

14. In 2013, vice prime minister Asscher expressed regret and remorse during the 2013 commemoration of the abolishment of slavery and in 2001 during the Durban conference state secretary Van Boxtel similarly uttered regret, see parool.nl/amsterdam/historische-keti-koti-amsterdam-maakt-excuses-voor-slavernijverleden~b62ac7a8/.

15. Wekker 2016 (see note 4).

16. 'Musea Bekennen Kleur' ('Museums show their colours') is a recent platform of Dutch museums focusing on diversity and inclusion, museabekennenkleur.nl.

questions important enough to discuss? Can we fathom the radical notion that the enslaved were subjects, actual people? Seeing, naming, and giving (new) words are acts that rehumanize.

Similarly, the history of slavery makes us aware that race is a defining concept. This knowledge can make people very uncomfortable. It becomes an intersectional endeavour that relates to ourselves. It implicates all of us because every person has a particular intersectional position. If that position has a multitude of dominant aspects (white, male, able-bodied, affluent, cis), you are often not aware of it or simply take it for granted as opposed to a person who predominantly occupies marginalized positions. The bottom line is that this positioning impacts our lives in different ways, which means that we have to do different work. This is why positioning oneself purposely is so important. To understand that you have an ethnic position as a white person and that this positionality always brings privilege and often fragility is something to really sit with. Practices of white innocence and white fragility produce clashes, especially in multi-ethnic working environments.

For art institutions (museums, art academies) and their communities there is work to be done, as they well know.[16] Simple yet difficult questions include: what do students want to be trained in and with which curriculum? What stories do these institutions want to tell, how are they narrated and for whom? What is the history of their institution, when was it founded and under what circumstances? Does the staff represent today's world we live in, including its glocal trends and are they trained well enough to answer and tackle the dynamics of the twenty-first century? These are questions that need answering.

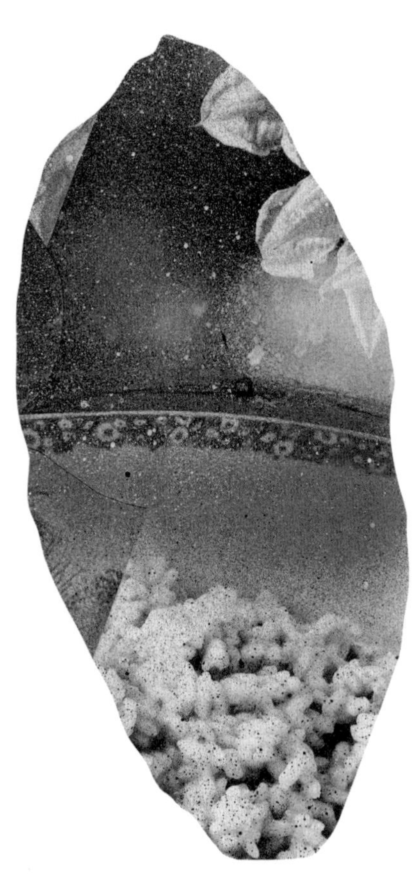

ART HISTORY ROOMS, DECOLONIALITY, AND LIBERATURE

Practicing Art History in the Heerenlogement at the Turfdraagsterpad

Christa-Maria Lerm Hayes

INGREDIENTS

- (Im)possibilities of Dutch Art History
- Sites of Art History Education
- Decoloniality
- James Joyce as Liberature
- Art Research
- Modernism

The Chair in Modern and Contemporary Art History at the University of Amsterdam (UvA) was established for Hans Jaffé in 1963 and is the world's first in this field (*Moderne en hedendaagse kunstgeschiedenis*). I was appointed to it in 2014.[1] The UvA Department is located on the Turfdraagsterpad of the *Binnengasthuisterrein*, formerly a women's hospital, where my office overlooks the so-called three-canal-corner. Where first impoverished and criminalized women had to 'drag' turf up the canals and, afterwards, often pathologized women were ordered to rest by male doctors, the Heerenlogement occupied this prime location in Amsterdam's architectural city centre ensemble (now a UNESCO World Heritage site). In this Heerenlogement,[2] auctions took place: plantations throughout the Dutch colonies were bought and sold, including the dehumanized, enslaved human beings working on them. With the same money, art was also auctioned there. For decolonial thinkers

1. In the committee served, among others, Kitty Zijlmans. I thank her. I also thank Sarat Maharaj for generous comments on my essay, and Jessica Lentz and Maya Dong for their work as student assistants. See: Christa-Maria Lerm Hayes, *Writing Art and Creating Back: What Can We Do With Art (History)?*, Inaugural lecture 537 (Amsterdam, 2015), www.oratiereeks.nl/upload/pdf/PDF-6174DEF_Oratie_Lerm_WEB.pdf.

2. See: nl.wikipedia.org/wiki/Oudezijds_Heerenlogement.

it is clear: Modernism (Jaffé's domain) and contemporary art (some of it now 'appreciated' in freeports) are still intimately connected with the colonial matrix of power; as is the university itself, still based on the 'enlightened' thinking that enabled dehumanization. Art history here (and elsewhere) is thoroughly implicated in abusive power structures: an impossibility.

I had come to Amsterdam from Northern Ireland, where Iconology or Visual Culture were preferred terms for a partially reconstituted, valuable field: it is a healing, societally vital thing (an 'ecumenical' one) to 'find words pertaining to images' (Aby Warburg). Politicians and university functionaries were not particularly interested in listening. On the island, Joseph Beuys had made a sandwich with warmth-giving matter: two turf briquets and a pound of butter in between. He called the work *Irish Energies* (1974). What then can positive, healing artistic and art-historical energies be—and can they be dragged to (or out of?) the Turfdraagsterpad?

Decolonial scholars and makers are not suggesting that we never look at a European site, artwork, or author again, but it is important from where one begins.[3] There is some commonality between Ireland (which partially gained independence in 1921) and my origin in East Germany (socialized in dissident circles): practices in an expanded field of art suggest themselves for creative (I curate) and scholarly attention, even canonization, when they are social, relational, and holistic in their analysis. They highlight connectedness: *vincularidad*. In decolonial scholarship, largely conceptualized in South America, 'Vincularidad is the awareness of the integral relation and interdependence amongst all living organisms',[4] global historical, political, and economic interdependences, an invitation to comparative empathy.

In considering the affordances of locations for practicing art history against all the odds, I choose to begin with the room in which Sarat Maharaj studied the subject: the Art History room at the Apartheid era 'University for Blacks of Indian Origin' on Salisbury Island, Durban, Natal. In twisted Apartheid logic, some subjects were deemed more suitable for some races. Indians were vaguely

3. Walter D. Mignolo, Catherine E. Walsh, *On Decoloniality: Concepts, Analytics, Praxis* (Durham, 2018).

4. Ibid., p. 1.

seen as 'ethnically artistic'. Years later, in the UK, the South African artist Clifford Charles gave Maharaj a photograph of this room. On that basis, when he was Visiting Fellow at the UvA in 2018, Maharaj asked my students probing questions about whether scholarship was colour blind and what sort of art history would bolster or uphold the kind of knowledge that Apartheid touted. The photograph shows an array of global art in reproductions, grouped in some sort of hierarchical order around Breughel and the Greco-Roman, Euro-Art tradition—with the inference that anything, certainly anything 'beautiful', can be reeled into a world view of one-dimensional and violent, dehumanizing certainties. But was this propagandistic, hierarchical, evolutionary reading of the room the only one possible? Could not the same constellation of art objects be seen as interacting with and rubbing up against one another to produce a new, different sensibility and aesthetic?

There were, for the purposes of this far too brief and undoubtedly deficient summary (taken from my notes), four elements that showed or introduced cracks in the system that formed Maharaj's path as a curator, art historian (with a focus on Marcel Duchamp and Richard Hamilton) and leading theoretician of Art Research (what is strangely called Artistic Research now). Mahatma Gandhi had spent twenty-one years in South Africa. It was in his tradition of non-violent resistance, that Maharaj had grown up. Nevertheless, for all those—Christian, Muslim, Hindus, Jewish and others—struggling to forge a common ethical stance of resistance, families would come to be divided when it came to the issue of 'armed struggle' against an unjust system. Before this background, how does one think for oneself (about art and education) and interrogate this Art History room? The elements introducing 'cracks' in the system of disconnectedness (Apartheid) are:

1) Through the window of the Art History room, one can see a train carriage, a waggon like those used for animals. With it, prisoners, all of them black, were regularly transported to the campus to work in the University's gardens.
2) The prehistorical cave paintings of the Drakensberg mountain range, marking the border

between the more English/Zulu/Indian Natal province from the rest of the more 'Dutch' parts of the country, provided evidence of what was not acknowledged in the Apartheid era: that the arrival of the Indigenous population (San and Buntu) had not occurred simultaneously with the Dutch and others, but thousands of years earlier: there was something artistic, holistic that preceded the thinking that reigned.

3) In this room, Sarat Maharaj read a then 'disapproved' author: James Joyce. He found new ways of thinking about the world, diversity, art, and life: Joyce was liberating 'liberature'.[5]

5. Katarzyna Bazarnik derives her beautiful term differently: from the Latin word for book. Katarzyna Bazarnik, 'Sociological Contexts of Liberature', *Teksty Drugie*, no. 2 (2016), pp. 223–241.

6. James Joyce, *Finnegans Wake* (London, 1939), 019, 08.

Joyce's two major works (*Ulysses*, 1922, and *Finnegans Wake*, 1939) both begin with or in (quasi-)prehistorical edifices: a colonial, anti-Napoleonic / anti-indigenous Martello Tower and a 'museyroom' under the Wellington Memorial's obelisk that doubles as a prehistoric passage tomb with objects from all eras (and regions) to form an alternative world history: 'A middenhide hoard of objects!'[6] *Finnegans Wake* is the work of a migrant, doubly exiled from his native tongue that was never 'his' (the Irish language was prohibited under British colonial rule). The book uses around forty languages for neologisms and portmanteau words, thus demands (assumes) relationality: groups of readers, as differently educated and acculturated as possible. Maharaj was telling my students (and the audience at his Stedelijk Museum lecture) that both Joyce's and Duchamp's terms, shifting and coined playfully, are important. To narrate contemporary space and (art) history in a linear way is impossible: it excludes, is partial and restricted. Timelines in exhibitions are pathetic and tangled together. No history will rise to this challenge, except for Joyce's *Finnegans Wake*. It brings together non-sequential elements. Joyce's future of the past is a 'paleo-present'. My students learned from Maharaj that art alone is able to raise questions without putting communities (always unevenly developing insights) in the defensive. Raising matters obliquely might provide a way ahead.

. Mignolo and Walsh 018 (see note 3), p. 7: 'By isobeying the long-held elief that you first theorise nd then apply, or that ou can engage in blind raxis without theoretical nalysis and vision, we ocate our thinking/doing a different terrain.' See: arat Maharaj, 'Know-How nd No-How: Stopgap Notes n "Method" in Visual Art as nowledge Production', *Art nd Research: A Journal of deas, Contexts and Methods*, no. 2 (Spring 2009), www. rtandresearch.org.uk/v2n2/ aharaj.html.

. Sarat Maharaj, 'erfidious Fidelity: The ntranslatability of the ther', *Art of the Twentieth entury: A Reader*, eds. Jason aiger, Paul Wood (New aven/London, 2003), pp. 97–303. See: Christa-Maria erm Hayes, '"The Joyce ffect": Joyce in the Visual rts', *A Companion to James oyce*, ed. Richard Brown Malden/Oxford, 2007), pp. 18–340. Christa-Maria Lerm ayes, *Joyce in Art* (Dublin, 004).

. Darby English, *1971: A Year the Life of Color* (Chicago, 016).

). Hilde Van Gelder's orthcoming book *Ground ea: Photography and the ight to Be Reborn*, lup.be/ roducts/126210.

4) Maharaj suggested that, during the Fellowship seminar, we would 're-create' the Art History room from Durban, in order to approach this tricky constellation. We rose to the challenge of assembling objects—personal ones, historical ones, those that show traces, reveal uncertainties and our not-knowing–so as to assemble something other than the certainties of value and canonicity that echoed through the Durban room. As academics, we were multiply enriched and had to bear 'no-how'.[7]

With the investigation of the Art History room Maharaj evidenced that we should and can learn to live with the differences that we produce. Rather than treating difference as something that has to be managed away (with statistics etc), the contact—what he calls 'rub-up'—between human beings produces further difference. How can being in multiplicity and difference become creative and appreciated, rather than antagonistic? The 're-creation' methodology produced a kind of 'rub-up', and studying it means taking seriously the promises of inquisitiveness and open-ended enquiry that both art and the academy (say they) offer.

I have long been attempting to conceptualize an indirect or negative efficacy in and of art, an effect that Maharaj's lovely formulation of 'perfidious fidelity' still captures best.[8] Examples for this I found in how artists had approached James Joyce (since his work had let them sense such a method). In current art history, I would see as related Darby English's focus on the exhibitions of abstract art that African American curators put together in 1971, having been given the opportunity following the then recent Civil Rights demonstrations.[9] Another example for me is Hilde Van Gelder's response to the 'refugee crisis' and the impossibility of (empathically) photographing refugees for fear of identifying them and damaging their chances as asylum seekers.[10] In East Germany (and totalitarian regimes generally), the ability to say something not regime-conform directly, in art or beyond, was (and is) severely curtailed. This leads narratives of solidarity, care, or *vincularidad*, to be formulated poetically. It may be necessary for art history to attune to such differences in register and embrace necessary indirectness.

To express something similar in the vocabulary of decoloniality:

> For us, the pluriversal opens rather than closes the geographies and spheres of decolonial thinking and doing. … While not accepting [the assumptions of coloniality] could be termed resistance, our interest and proposition here [are] with re-existence, understood as 'the redefining and re-signifying of life in conditions of dignity'. It is this resurgence and insurgence of decolonial conviviality, venues and paths that take us beyond, while at the same time undoing, the singularity and linearity of the West.[11]

It is immediately clear that these two perspectives at once beautifully align, especially also in relation to Art Research (thinking/doing), and, at the same time, seem fundamentally to contradict each other: Maharaj (in Apartheid-era Durban) took James Joyce, the dead, white male and—even worse—foremost modernist in the European literary canon to provide precisely such a path beyond, a crack in the system, as well as a basis for his thinking and doing in the art context. How can this be? Any answer must have profound effects on whether I can teach Joyce and artists responding to his literature (such as Beuys) at the UvA, or Joyce's contemporaries in visual art on the site of the Heerenlogement.

Again in Mignolo and Walsh's words:

> If socialism in the Soviet Union and decolonization during the Cold War failed, one of the reasons is that both projects confronted the content, not the terms of the conversation … [the] assumptions, principles, regulations … of the type of knowledge.[12]

What is at stake, therefore, is not to avoid reading European (or male, or canonical, or academic) sources, but to find and focus on (learn from and comparatively, intersectionally utilize) forms of language, art and scholarship that eschew (colonial) domination. Whether a dictatorship calls itself socialist, or a university calls itself diverse: the

11. Mignolo and Walsh 2018 (see note 3), p. 3.

12. Ibid., pp. 231, 222.

13. Christa-Maria Lerm Hayes, 'Art and Research: A Portrait of a Humanities Faculty as an Inclusive Workspace', *Krisis*, no. 1 (December 2020), pp. 180–202, krisis.eu/issue/view/4732.

14. Mignolo and Walsh 2018 (see note 3), p. 229: 'The other [starting point] is the critique of modernity from its receiving end, the darker side of modernity, the decolonial praxis of living'.

organizational principles (and people at the receiving end) will reveal whether that is the case or not.[13]

Terms and symbols tend to ossify, but they can also (I hope) be re-considered, enlivened. Maharaj appreciated how Joyce's background let the writer grapple with the rise of totalitarianisms in specific ways: Irish independence was nothing to cheer about if it meant substituting one source of domination for another: that of Catholic orthodoxy. Like his near-contemporary, the art historian Aby Warburg, who fought his Jewish background's orthodoxy and whose research institute had to flee the Nazis: these are Europeans, who took a clear but often (necessarily) indirect stance against rising Fascism and dehumanization. They developed methods and vocabularies to steer clear, if possible, from being reinscribed into that which they were fighting.

The methods of Joyce (and the many artists who have responded to the politics implied in his works), Warburg and Maharaj and many more inspiring figures are gentle and necessarily tentative, eschewing final truths and disciplines. And they become allies of larger decolonial endeavours, minus the stereotypical sequestering of the West and the 'non-West': when attempting to follow such notions, an art history conveyed to students in Amsterdam would gain, of course, if (rather than me) there was a colleague teaching decolonial thinking and doing from the perspective of the Andes. If that was framed in the curriculum as one possible, 'true' art history alongside European hegemonic practices, the result would still be rather impoverished.

This appears to point towards several fruitful intersectional lines of solidarity: turning to those who experienced the 'darker side'[14] of colonial modernity includes much that is already there: *turfdraagsters* and other women, thinkers-doers such as Joyce or Aby Warburg, who turned their experiences of marginality into still-valid cultural forms and methods. There is also Hans Jaffé, who, as a German-Jewish emigrant, scholar, and curator, turned to the twentieth-century's constructivist movements not because they were already canonical and could spell domination (what they undoubtedly became at the MoMa in New York). It was a practice that eschewed the touch of the normative genius, aligned itself with workers—and had first been received as 'degenerate' art, a Fascist marker of dehumanization and impending murder. Jaffé and others rendered a practice valuable, i.e., canonical, which they experienced as liberating. To re-consider such work for its social constructionist, epistemological allegiance, for the vision that the practice conveys of systemic interventions and change through art: that appears to me to be of value.

Mignolo and Walsh identify the dangers inherent in liberating practices becoming canonized, including decoloniality. The preceding remarks already express, I believe, a thinking in two directions in this regard: I suggested the possibility to return to various marginal practices to re-read and re-enliven the 'canon' in order to attempt to unearth its liberating import. I would encourage my students, for example, to make a special effort to re-read *Max Havelaar* (or the Bible) as 'liberature', rather than to cut Multatuli from curricula, because of the boredom and indifference felt (as students tell me) when reading in school.[15] The second suggestion is to view decoloniality as in solidarity with (not in competition to) world art studies, global art histories, and general critiques of dehumanization—and to invent new terms, when the old ones become canonized and stale.

There has been renewed interest in comparative research, and 'clusters' of interest are emerging: Connor Habib is a blogger who recommends books on Beuys, is now leading a *Ulysses* reading group 'for the rest of us', and has interviewed Dan Gretton on his book *I You We Them*: a historically comparative study of desk murderers, beginning with those responsible for the Irish Famine.[16] Isabel Wilkerson's *Caste* is inspiring in highlighting corresponding societal mechanisms of exclusion and dehumanization in the Southern US States, India, and Nazi Germany (the last actively sought to learn from the first).[17] She may view German efforts to overcome dehumanization with slightly rose-tinted glasses, but any evidence of humans' ability to break the cycle or long shadow of coloniality's all-round destruction I find welcome.

It is arguably with a focus on dignity and its enabling epistemic possibilities that liberating avant-gardes (critical of modernity) can be taught. Not knowing about them and how they became bureaucratized and (ab)used

15. Concerning re-reading the Bible: 'Notes on Activist Practices Behind the Iron Curtain: Liberation Theologies, Experimental Institutionalism, Expanded Art and Minor Literature', *Conceptualism—Intersectional Readings, International Framings: Situating 'Black Artists & Modernism' in Europe*, ed. Nick Aikens et al., exh. cat. Van Abbemuseum, l' Internationale (Eindhoven, 2019), pp. 332–351, vanabbemuseum.nl/en/research/resources/articles/conceptualism-intersectional-readings-international-framings/.

16. See: bookshop.org/lists/aewch-128-dan-gretton.

17. Isabel Wilkerson, *Caste: The Origins of Our Discontents* (New York, 2020).

18. Mignolo and Walsh 2018 (see note 3), pp. 11, 57, 58–59.

19. Christa-Maria Lerm Hayes, 'Beuys's Legacy in Artist-led University Projects', *Tate Papers*, no. 31 (Spring 2019), www.tate.org.uk/research/publications/tate-papers/31/beuys-legacy-artist-led-university-projects.

20. Mignolo and Walsh 2018 (see note 3) p. 81.

21. See: www.mediamatic.net/en/page/236688/rederij-lampedusa.

will not help. No work, term or movement's legacy will ever have stable characteristics. If there is a liberating element, art history can help through detailed scrutiny, analyze assumptions, institutions, and terms (not just content) and hold those using traditions to account. All this is a communal and intercultural task.[18] I consider it valuable for interdisciplinary scholars, curators, and artists to join forces in both artists' educational projects and public universities,[19] and help to combat dehumanization in all its forms. And it is encouraging to know that there is a community of artists, students, and colleagues with whom to tackle this work. But it does remain a perpetual question, an inherently unending struggle, which Walsh puts like this: 'Decoloniality ... does not imply the absence of coloniality but rather the ongoing serpentine movement toward possibilities of other modes of being, thinking, knowing, sensing, and living; that is, an otherwise in the plural.'[20]

The Amsterdam Art History room on the three-canal-corner does not have a spatial connection to prehistory as the one about which Maharaj lectured. Its 'ground' is water. A Dutch scientist, I hear, coined the term Anthropocene, which draws larger historical lines conceptually, instead of materially. Water in *Ulysses* connected Joyce's characters in Dublin with Odysseus on the Mediterranean. The energies conducted by the water beyond the recently-crumbled Amsterdam canal wall outside the department extend to the women working a few hundred meters further, who have come from all over the world, willingly or not, often as a lasting shadow of colonial matrices of power. Still a little further North are two boats, moored near the Central Station. They were overloaded with refugees when they reached Greece from North Africa. Rederij Lampedusa is a social art project that links their stories with those of pleasure boaters on the canals: bringing the EU's policed borders into the world heritage site.[21] And from Central Station, train tracks are the conductors of energy, goods, and people. They feature in Beuys' work as veins across the European continent that echo humans' early migrations westwards across the Eurasian landmass—and the later ones: during Beuys' time, the tracks transported human beings to extermination camps further East: three quarters of Jews in the

Netherlands did not survive. A student, a Muslima, has made the emergency staircase beside my office her 'prayer room'. The Heerenlogement's tympanum will be restored and a process is underway to see how best to reveal and address through it the dark histories of the site: both artistically and communally. 'riverrun, past Eve and Adam's, from swerve of shore to bend of [canals ...]'.[22]

22. Joyce 1939 (see note 6), 003, 1-2.

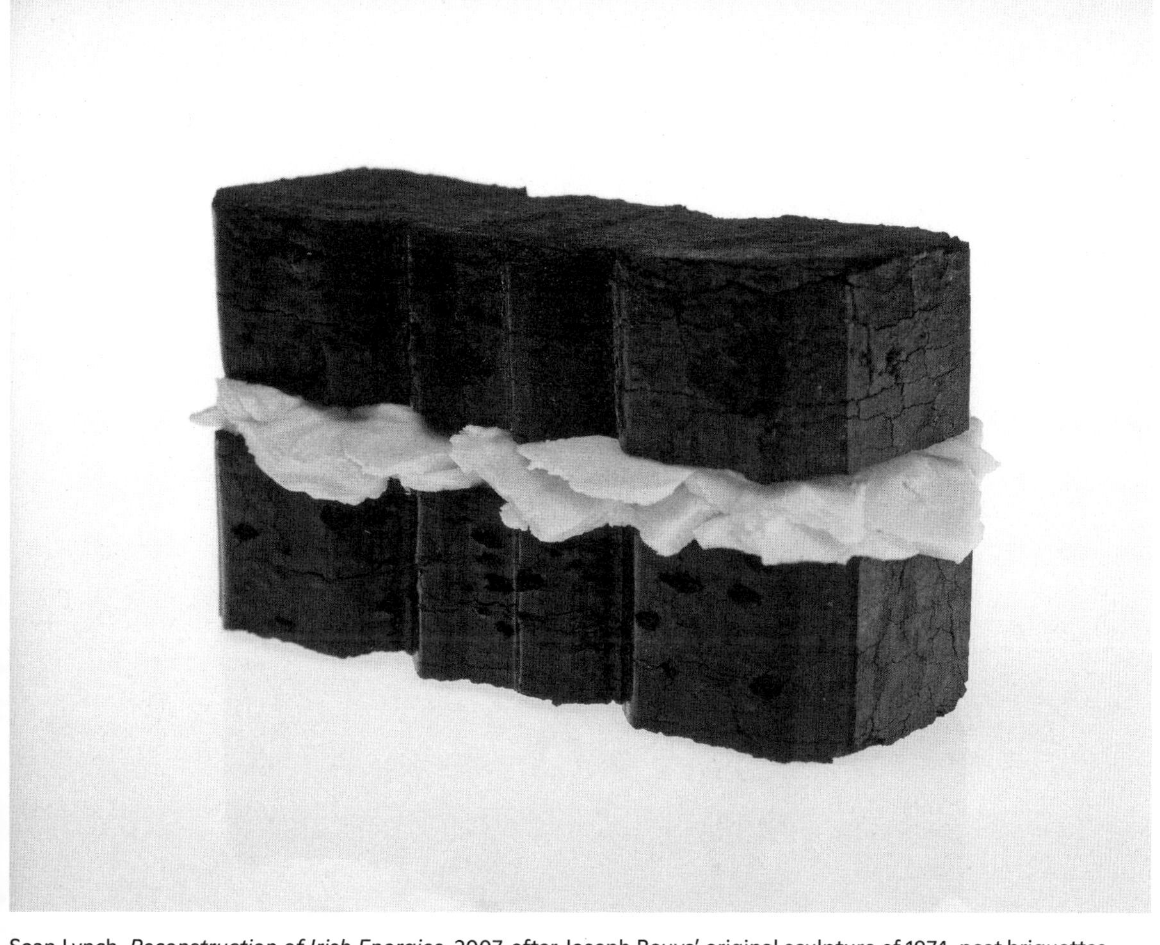

Sean Lynch, *Reconstruction of Irish Energies*, 2007, after Joseph Beuys' original sculpture of 1974, peat briquettes, butter, 12 × 19 × 7 cm. Courtesy of the artist.

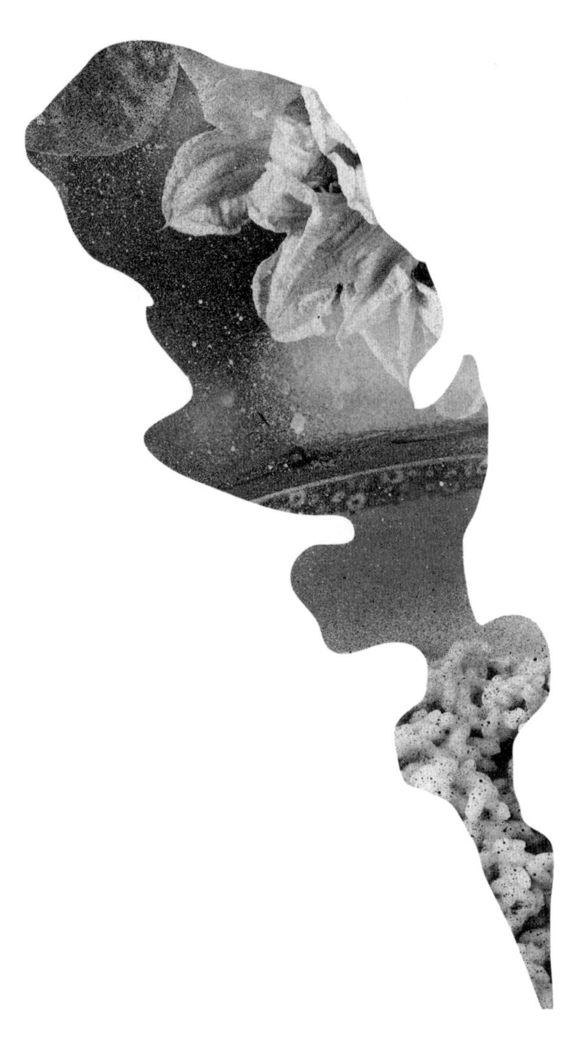

THE ART FOODIE'S LAMENT
Vegan Soundings of the Omnivorous Contemporary Art Circuit

Sarat Maharaj

INGREDIENTS

- Vegan Codex Alimentarius
- Anecdoted Art History
- Aconceptual Epistemics
- Sapid Knowledge

A globalizing contemporary art circuit is on the ascendant: it has few qualms about taking on board any kind of art and thinking as long as it is on its terms. It is a ravenous 'anything goes' force (Feyerabend).[1] Oddly, it has a disarming, liberating air. It places disparate art forms and modes of thinking on equal footing in freewheeling circulation *sans frontières*. But its gargantuan appetite is legend—not least for sundry 'against-the-grain' art forms and modes of thinking such as the 'marginal, tribal, Aboriginal, Dalit, Trans, Indigenous' and the like. They are little more than grist to its mill in the name of 'diversity, high visibility, and inclusivity'.

What looks like an enlightened dispensation still feeds off a Eurocentric diet. Its 'circuits of acceptance' may not look like 'colonial assimilation processes', but they are no less about filtering out unpalatable strands of 'other systems of art and thinking' to render them 'comprehensible and digestible'. Post-Holocaust versions of 'xenocidal' drives (Adorno[2])—the erasure and elimination of multiplicity and variability—hang on Post-Apartheid and Euroliberal avatars of 'multicultural managerialism'—locking out the doggedly untranslatable, gagging, troubling opacity,

1. Paul Feyerabend, *Against Method: Outline of an Anarchistic Theory of Knowledge* (London, 1975).

2. Theodor W. Adorno, *Negative Dialectics*, transl. E.B. Ashton. (London, 1973/1990).

critical difference, and otherness—flourish in favour of easy 'diversity'.

How to offset this algorithmic, all-consuming drive? The contemporary figures of the art punter and the foodie—world art gamers and world food enthusiasts—cheer on the circuit. They see it as 'tasting and celebrating diversity'. At odds with this, the Art Lover and the Apprentice Sous Chef look like quaint, left-behind connoisseurs. They look on askance at this all-devouring force. Against this omnivorous circuit, what chance for a vegan mode of thinking—'knowing the other and other ways of knowing'? My contribution is a prelim sounding of some of its possible components.

It will take overall shape as *A Vegan Codex Alimentarius of Art in the Global System*. Why fight shy of a 'How to do' instructional recipe manual? Because a Codex is more guidelines, less hard and fast rules. It delves into the underlying structures of thought—the deep sediment of 'Eurocentric *mentalité*'—that time and time again throws up new versions of Eurocentric attitude and expression. Two core queries are up for grabs here:

(1) Beyond 'Grand Narrative Art History' how to write an Anecdoted, 'Paleo- Present, Pastless Now' Art History?
(2) Beyond the 'Slaughterhouse of Conceptual Thinking' how to write in an *aconceptual* mode?

(1) The grand models of historical thought and writing—models of dialectical advance, liberal unilinear progress, cyclical repetition, and their variants—were tied up with the rise of Europe and its colonizing scope. They tended to deny both 'history' and the capacity for historical consciousness and refection to non-European, 'other' cultures.

These claimants to hardnosed history with 'scientific' rigour come to grief in the global age. If we see them decline and fall into disuse, the Eurocentric stomach for the timeline of 'past-present-future'—lingers on. How to develop a roomier notion of history based on the episodic and epiphanic? That is, a history composed of anecdote

3. Norman Malcolm, *Ludwig Wittgenstein. A Memoir* (Oxford, 2001), p. 28.

4. Daniel Spoerri et al., *An Anecdoted Topography of Chance* (New York, 1966).

5. See David Newbury, 'Contradictions at the Heart of the Canon: Jan Vansina and the Debate over Oral Historiography in Africa, 1960–1985', *History in Africa*, vol. 34 (2007), pp. 213–254.

annotations upon anecdotes—a 'history' that mobilizes a temporality of scrambled time zones that we might call a 'paleo-present, pastless now'.

(1.a) A trigger for the above is Wittgenstein's reputed quip that a philosophical treatise might be made up entirely of jokes and jests.[3] Further suggestions:

• *An Anecdoted Topography of Chance*, Daniel Spoerri et al.[4]

• Jan Vansina et al. rethink of African 'oral' traditions as different types of historical Thought.[5]

• Rethink of India's 'Puranic Ithihas' (archives of oral/textual histories and myths on the material causes—the cycles of emergence and dissolution of the cosmos, realms of the gods, humans and creatural life) as a different species of fabulated historical thinking.

(1.b) An Anecdoted Annotation: Star Activist Writer versus Star Chef Eurocentric thinking today pops up anywhere: it is not simply associated with its original source in the West. The 'global art-foodie circuits' take in all cardinal points and geographic quarters—North, South, East, West—even if some zones are more favoured than others.

A few years ago, the art foodie circuits were abuzz with rumours of a strange novelty dish in India—the weaver ant egg chutney. It is an *outré* insectile item normally on the menu of certain jungle tribes. It sounded like something beyond the norms of Indian cooking but not taboo to all. YouTube and social media billed it as a 'new' taste sensation and experience. Gordon Ramsay—of Glasgow working-class background, from the top international culinary scene—sets off to his tribal jungle contacts. The quest is on for the incredibly tart, pungent ant egg chutney. Suresh and grandmother are his hosts. Gordon downs several rounds of fierce palm wine with her. Sloshed, he seems utterly at one with them: lifelong mates, surely. The next morning, with Suresh he climbs up a tree to plunder the ant's nest. Suresh grinds and mashes up a chutney. Gordon licks his fingers. In the thick of the mix, the chutney's 'hotness' comes to equal the intense circuit between hosts and guest.
Arundhati Roy, evangelist of Leftie Causes is more than

a match for the zeal that she berates in her opponents. She too is onto that outlandish ant egg grub. She recounts the anecdote in the midst of her 'ethnographic' of living and trekking with a band of Maoist insurgents. A dutiful note solemnly records that it is a formic acid that gives the sauce its sharp kick. The novelist eye catches the detail of the fading, chipped nail varnish on a gun toting boy guerrilla's pinkie. Throughout her stay in the jungle, she seems plugged into the typical observer-informant circuit 'objectively' jotting down encounters with them. Alongside, we sense her keenness to express comradeship and solidarity with individuals she gets to know in the band. With whom do we get a passing taste of Eurocentric thinking—the star chef and foodie hero of the global circuits or the champion of the downtrodden, star activist of the global art-literary circuits?

(2) An abiding strand in Eurocentric *mentalité* is the notion that sharp, clear-cut, precision thinking is overwhelmingly conceptual in character. It chops up arguments, analyzes muddled logic, cuts through blubber and neatly parcels out the meat of meaning. This is likened to the artful butcher's prowess in not mangling the animal's carcass or breaking its bones. They deftly 'unfasten' its tendons and sinews till the flesh flops out onto the cutting slab. An impressive skill. But the brute point is that the animal is dead. A switch to a vegan mode of thinking is not about taking up an anti-conceptual stance. More likely, it opens up the search for aconceptual ways of knowing and thinking—for inventing an *aconceptual* epistemics. What would a language look like where the 'concept is in neutral gear' that is made up of free-flowing, syntaxless sequences—an agrammatical lingo.

Henri Bergson refers to Plato to expound on the strengths and pitfalls of the conceptual abattoir: Jean Baudrillard does much the same with reference to Zhuang-Zi. In mapping a Vegan Codex Alimentarius, the Art Foodie—hanging out either at the Tate or on TikTok—is not able to get moving without a nod towards Jacques Maritain. The latter had an inkling of the creep up of industrial concepts and desiccated critical jargon that we are so prone to in writing about Art today. It is telling that both evoke the gustatory: the former with their omnivorous eye and tongue, the latter by touching on a sort of art thinking that is not scentless, that has a distinct taste, that is flavoursome—a 'sapid' knowledge.

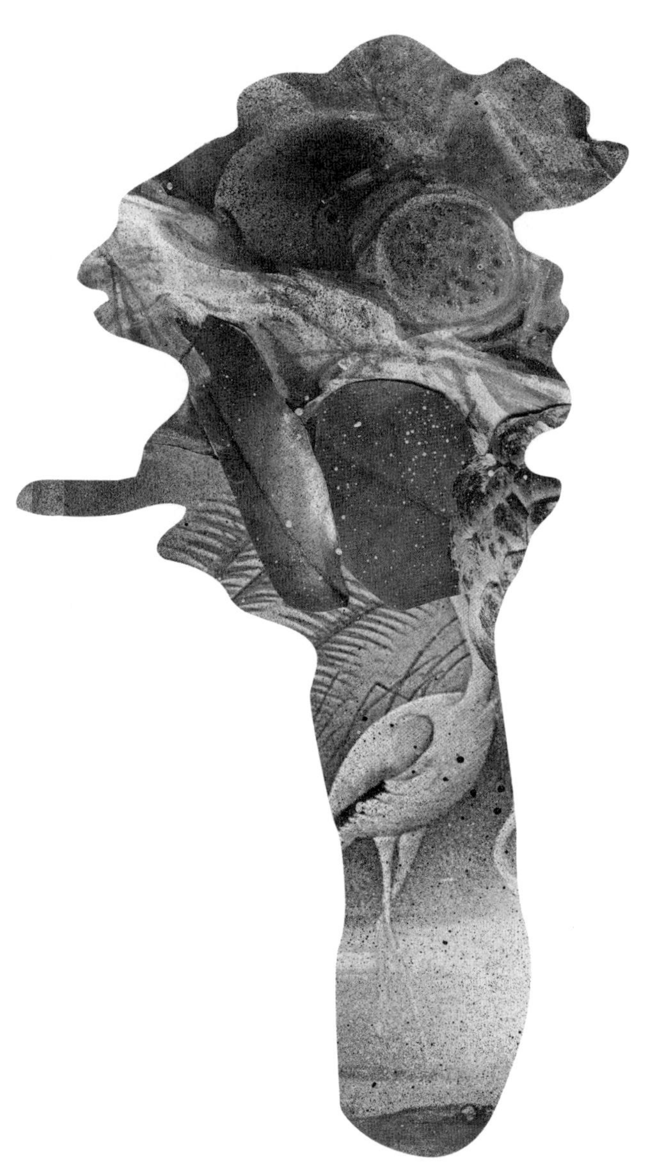

THE PARALLAX EFFECT

Leon Wainwright

INGREDIENTS

• Collaboration
• Strategic Phenomenology
• Theory of Practice
• Cultural Economy

Some scholars, among whom—to be placed with prominence is Kitty Zijlmans, have been an abiding presence and guide for me during the last three decades. Even when scholars live in different countries or continents—we reside in the United Kingdom and in the Netherlands, respectively—they can enjoy the impression of proximity regardless of that distance. This creates something like a parallax effect, which bridges a geographical divide and has lent character to our ever-evolving academic discipline. Thanks to an invitation from Donald Preziosi and Claire Farago, back in 2006 we took part with others[1] in a conference panel in Leeds (UK) entitled 'Taking Back Art History'. The organizers had in mind a panel that would reckon with the pressure to make the discipline of art history 'useful' to the wider society, such as in its adjacent organizations and structures like the museum and the heritage sector. Kitty and I would speak about feeling the first tremors caused by a shift to instrumentalize the teaching and research of the histories of art, to show what 'impact' we were having beyond the confines of intellectual space.

At that stage in my career, I had returned fairly recently from fifteen months in Trinidad and Guyana, where a fellowship funded by the Leverhulme Trust had supported me in looking at 'art and agency in the Caribbean'. My use of that phrase was telling of someone reaching out to social anthropology as an art historian, restating the need for interdisciplinarity. The project had yielded some insights and a published work by which I tried to issue a sort of *j'accuse* to the academy at large (my first book *Timed Out: Art and the Transnational Caribbean*)[2] and

[1]. Marquard Smith, Amelia Jones, Anna Brzyski, Matthew Rampley, Jae Emerling and Marius Kwint.

[2]. Leon Wainwright, *Timed Out: Art and the Transnational Caribbean* (Manchester, 2011).

art history was put in the dock. The charge? I suppose, the 'wilful forgetting' of the Caribbean and its 'subtraction' from the canons of artistic modernism, followed closely perhaps by a concomitant way of commoditizing the very vocabulary of globalizing change and 'differencing' that the Caribbean had bequeathed to scholars, such as in so much curatorial riffing about 'global contemporary art'.

Timed Out suggests to its readers that the dominant centres for the production of knowledge have wanted to ignore the deep and continuing history of relationships between the Caribbean and the wider Atlantic world. While people have moved in flows and waves, travelled, sojourned, and migrated across this wide and transnational geography, so have artworks been on the move, as well as ideas about them and the artists who created and carried them. It is far too commonly assumed that art of the Caribbean lags behind the lead and the cutting edge of art, that the Caribbean field is backward or belated and anachronistic. It is positioned as thus marginal or provincial in histories of creativity chiefly by being denied its place in the 'here and now'. So distinctively geographical and temporal are such outlooks—being implicitly about space and time—that the basis of such thinking has to be undermined from certain angles. That is what I set out to achieve in this line of work, quite trenchantly, without apology. But *Timed Out* pushes farther than that, I like to believe. It demonstrates why we deliver a form of social justice through working in art history once we refuse to accept any of the conventional 'common sense' about the art of 'distant' places being synonymous with a condition of backwardness. To put it in a way that is both more abstract and yet can be generalized outwards to the wider discipline of art history, this is all about refusing the equation of 'over there' with 'back then'—an absolute spatial as well as temporal division between the art's putative centres and peripheries. The Caribbean region formed the very crucible for early modernity—the plantation system, capitalism at its first flush—and its diaspora has reached and transformed every shore of the Atlantic. But the art-historical record of the Caribbean has simply not responded accordingly. Instead, the Caribbean has suffered (with great dignity, I should

3. Leon Wainwright, *Phenomenal Difference: A Philosophy of Black British Art* (Liverpool, 2017).

emphasize) a *chronic disregard*, to use the phrase advisedly, a fate suffered by its art above all else.

What does this mean for the university curriculum as taught in the 'metropolitan North' in view of this deepening epistemic violence, these myths perpetuated about the Caribbean by art history with the effect of furnishing the latter's vaunted self-image? It is a question that could be asked of attitudes to diaspora communities more broadly, for which the particular condensation of circumstances in Britain that brought together artists of African, Asian, and Caribbean backgrounds seems to provide a suitable answer. Indeed, this was the territory of my second book *Phenomenal Difference: A Philosophy of Black British Art*,[3] a detailed philosophical account of artworks by individuals of Black and Asian backgrounds working in contemporary Britain (I cast these under the porous heading of 'Black British' but they include an entire spectrum of ethnicities, the artists Hew Locke, Henna Nadeem, Juginder Lamba, Perminder Kaur, Manjeet Lamba, Mona Hatoum, Sonia Boyce, Keith Piper, Yeu-Lai Mo, Johannes Phokela, Zarina Bhimji, Chila Burman, and Sonia Khurana). In that book I have explored a vivid range of intimate, bodily relationships with works of art, in a manner that speaks to interest among scholars in the arts and humanities as they have come to focus, in particular, on the senses and perception, the emotions, affectivity, and what has come to be captured under the rubric of the 'new materialism'. At the same time, the book problematizes the basis on which the significance of Black British art has been staked in cultural criticism and curatorial practices, namely the weight of attention to identity politics and theories of representation and cultural diversity. Yet there is no intention here to set aesthetics on one side, politics on the other—far from it. Rather, the book represents a detailed case for recognizing the role of Black British art and artists in shaping a more layered and philosophically open account. Focusing on the materiality and immediacy of artworks, *Phenomenal Difference* isolates and demonstrates how the 'phenomenal' qualities of artworks are what allow audiences to enjoy distinctive and complex perceptual encounters that are enriched by cultural differences.

In short, what this line of work does is to emphasize the fundamental aesthetic character and objecthood of artworks themselves. It seeks to heal this field after so much tokenism and what may be called the 'semiotic reductionism' of attitudes and public discourse on Black and Asian British art and artists. Hardly surprising then that the book results from a long period of personal contact with artists, arts organizers, and curators of diverse backgrounds in Britain and here it brings a significant focus on the art of women and those of South Asian backgrounds. Drawing on picture research and supported by a sort of 'strategic phenomenology', I show why theoretical reflection may be used to try to counter the misunderstanding that these artists continue to face, which includes the overreliance on discussion of issues of cultural identity and ethnicity which have tended to preoccupy commentators of this art. Through a wide range of detailed aesthetic analyses of specific artworks, the book shows why it should now be necessary to see Black British art for the 'phenomenal difference' it brings.

These are two strands of work, focused on the politics of art historiography in the first case, and on philosophy as a critical intervention in contemporary art discourse in the second. It was through a collaboration with Kitty Zijlmans (as Co-Investigator) that I was able to bring them together and push and develop them further, what became in that sense a third strand of research. The opportunity came with the project *Sustainable Art Communities: Creativity and Policy in the Transnational Caribbean*, which took a direct look at the complex realities attendant upon the conditions of art production, circulation, and reception for artists of Dutch- and English-speaking Caribbean backgrounds. The project team held conferences in Amsterdam (at the Tropenmuseum) and London (at Iniva, the Institute of International Visual Arts), each of them filmed (this material is archived in an open access repository at the Open University), and consolidated our progress in a special issue of the *Open Arts Journal*, an open access peer-reviewed publication, which was subsequently developed into a major book anthology.[4] Through the project, artists from Aruba, Curaçao, Germany, Japan, Canada, Trinidad, Jamaica, Barbados, Surinam, the Netherlands,

4. Funded jointly by the Arts and Humanities Research Council (AHRC) and the Netherlands Organization for Scientific Research (NWO). See: www.open.ac.uk/Arts/sac/ (accessed 1 June 2021); and Issue 5 of the *Open Arts Journal*: www.openartsjournal.org.

and the United Kingdom (around fifteen in all) shared a platform in order to speak for themselves. They did so with eloquence and patience, and often with force, directing their views to the funding agencies, arts bureaucracies, curators, art historians, and cultural policymakers that operate within as well as outside the Caribbean.

The project traced the similarities and distinctions between Dutch- and English-speaking contexts of the Caribbean and its global diaspora. It sought to find strategic ways to support this community's rich cultural heritage by assessing how the Caribbean region has stood as a locus for global cultural communities. In particular we wished to exchange perspectives on how activities of networking can help to transform both creativity and a sense of Caribbean location. The book that resulted bears witness to how the Caribbean sits in dialogue with current (neoliberal) arts discourse, comprising of various public programming and arts funding policy frameworks, as well as art-historical interests. Through this and the surrounding project, we uncovered the significant pressures and difficulties felt by Caribbean artists at the local, regional, and international scales.[5] Among them is the frustration that artists have felt, especially towards the way that common buzzwords such as *sustainability*, *community*, or *transnationalism*, have come to be traduced, subverted, and misused. That was a surprising finding, given that the same terms are virtually everywhere in the funding policies and curatorial celebration of Caribbean artists, venues and mechanisms that are usually held to be a source of support and means of 'visibility' for Caribbean creativity. Hearing about the experience of Caribbean artists and finding that there are cross purposes and conflicts here with their objectives, as an art community centred in the 'global South', is salutary. The artists that we worked with, helped to identify the need to foster a sustainable arts community that may nurture the broader Caribbean culture and society. We pinpointed a key aim, articulated in numerous ways by artists in the course of the project, which was about placing responsibility on the visual arts to serve as a site of living heritage that in turn could inform the academy.

5. See also: Leon Wainwright, 'Transatlantic Movement and the Taste for Ethnicity: Art and "Exchange" between Suriname and the Netherlands', *Etnofoor* 24, no. 2 (2013), pp. 13–40; 'Global Change and Contemporary Art of the Caribbean: Notes on the Futurology of a Sustainable Art Community', *Who More Sci-Fi than Us? Contemporary Art from the Caribbean*, ed. Nancy Hoffmann (Amsterdam, 2012), pp. 80–84; Kitty Zijlmans, 'Art and agency in contemporary Curaçao: Tirzo Martha's "Blijf maar plakken"', *Sustainable Art Communities: Contemporary Creativity and Policy in the Transnational Caribbean*, eds. Leon Wainwright and Kitty Zijlmans (Manchester, 2017), pp. 91–101; and Kitty Zijlmans, 'Globalisation and Localization: Two Sides of the Same Coin', *Changing Perspectives. Dealing with Globalisation in the Presentation and Collection of Contemporary*, ed. Mariska ter Horst (Amsterdam, 2012), pp. 214–228.

I was fascinated to work together in tracing such diverse experiences in this shifting and contemporary cultural geography. Artists of the Caribbean, when they spoke of their various groupings, migratory lines, and archipelagic routes of travel and settlement, spoke also of a history of creativity that makes new demands on art history. Flipping the script on this, as we tried to do, was to suggest that art history can be a window onto these worlds; without it we would not be able to grasp, for example, how artists operate in national contexts where the sense of community is being drastically changed through those artists' mobilities and networks. Thereby, the *Sustainable Art Communities* collaboration has been a recursive and iterative way of accounting for the original roles that the Caribbean can hold in theorizing and historicizing art in the present situation. It suggests at least one very effective means by which art-historical researchers can embrace the Caribbean's visual, embodied, performative, and immaterial approaches to creativity.

The outcome of that analysis—crossing linguistic boundaries—brings our entire field onto fresh and original ground. As a project that has an impact upon current scholarly attitudes as well as on the social and political climate in which artists live and work, it also brings my short discussion here round full circle, back to our first meeting in Leeds ('Taking Back Art History'). The parallax effect as I have felt it is ultimately the effect and the yield of a lasting dialogue. I have sketchily set out a recipe for its longevity and success here. What needs emphasizing a bit more though, in closing, is the lasting concern that that can be identified with finding or positing a 'theory of practice', a way to ensure that artworks are to be analyzed always as a mode of agency and a materializing of 'affect'. Where and when needed to be critical, scholars should embolden one another to raise and develop objections about the failure of endeavours (such as scholarship or exhibition curating) to recognize that art and artists have value beyond the lexicon that has come to be used on them. That means unfolding them from the cultural economy in which social identities are drawn within globalized, metropolitan settings. Can our discipline transcend histories of marginalization and exclusion? It not only can, it must.

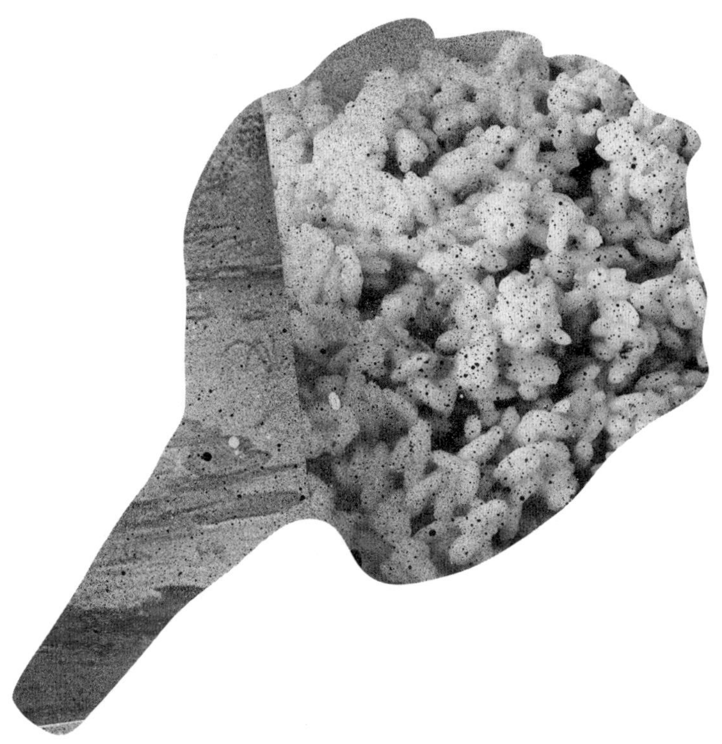

COOKING A TRANSCULTURAL PEDAGOGICAL EXPERIMENT
A Recipe to Turn a Global Art Course into a Vehicle for Change

Isabel Hoving

INGREDIENTS
(PER PERSON)

- Some Uneasy Questions
- Generous Amounts of Openness and Self-reflection
- A Sense of Urgency (Rasheed Araeen would do well)
- 750 gr of Fieldwork
- The Wish to Avoid Naive, Simple Solutions (for example 250 grammes of Jacques Rancière, Slavoj Žižek, and/or Yogita Goyal)

In a lively part of a sprawling, dirty, noisy city, a group of people sit on the ground, engaged in creating objects out of plastic, reed, wood, photographs, jewellery, and paint. Statues? Masks? The people smile when asked. Come and see, next week, during the ceremony in that open space over there. You're welcome. On a field in front of a community building far from there, three people are working on a complicated, colourful sand pattern. In another place, a young woman frowns while she considers the disturbing tapestry she has just created. Are the references to slavery too implicit, or are they too blunt? How will her grandmother react? *Her* grandmother had lived through the last days of slavery; she still remembers her stories.

She turns around and asks her sister, the art student, for advice. The art student puts down her smartphone. A fellow student just sent pictures of an artist community she met during her travels. She is very eager to buy these masks, or statues, she says—just look, they're *insane*!—they would look *absolutely* fabulous in the gallery she works for. And it would be kind of humanitarian work, too, wouldn't it, to give these poor people money for their creative work? The art student ignores the remark, but before she can answer her sister, another picture pops up. Contemporary aboriginal sand art... it's immediately appealing, even if it speaks a language she hasn't mastered. 'I feel like I'm on an alien planet, or in another universe'—adds the art student who just sent the picture—'I feel utterly irrelevant, with my privileged background.'

How to travel through the landscape of world art studies? These three students all picked their own trajectories. They carve out their journeys according to the patterns we, their teachers, have been feeding them. My contribution to this book will focus on the dishes we serve our students during their Arts and Culture Studies, and on the meal we might wish to prepare instead, as a test recipe for future courses.

Some Uneasy Questions: Reflections on the Diet, the Kitchen and Kitchen Utensils Needed

How to come to terms with the mind-boggling diversity of the visual and verbal arts of globalization? This is the question that inspired Kitty Zijlmans and me to develop Master courses for students who were interested in interculturality, in literature and art from around the world. We have been busy in the same kitchen, to create our pedagogical meals together, have worked with writers and artists from all over the world, and through these personal contacts have become deeply aware of the inequalities and injustices that still shape the art world. The cookery books that have been used throughout the art world have led to obesity in some privileged art circles, and malnourishment in many artists in

1. Rasheed Araeen, 'A New Beginning', *Third Text*, no. 50 (2000), pp. 3–20.

2. I learnt this wonderful term from prof. em. Barbara Love, social justice educator, coach and consultant in trauma recovery and (anti-) racism.

the less privileged regions of the world. There is an urgent need for change. But if we listen to curator and writer Rasheed Araeen, founder of the journal *Third Text*, who spoke up in 2000, we must acknowledge that decades have passed, without any fundamental change, in spite of the efforts of many.[1] We can ask ourselves to what extent the situation in 2021 has improved when compared to 2000.

So, how can our students come to terms with the diversity of global art when the field itself is still struggling to change into a truly diverse, intercultural, and transcultural art practice? Many of the existing kitchens, the cookery books, recipes, and ingredients have been aiming at metropolitan tastes for a long time, and change is slower than we wish. Should we not rather aim at teaching our students to understand the powers that are still hampering the development of a truly inclusive art world? In one of our course descriptions, we invited students 'to participate—on a professional level—in the passionate but complex academic discourses that address these intriguing arts', and asked them 'to develop their own response to these discussions'. But should we not also ask them to develop their own tactics to *intervene* in these academic and art policy *practices*? We need our students to become curators and art critics that will help speed up the transition of the global art world to one that is (also) defined by the global majority.[2] If the generation of our students will not succeed in doing this, who will? How can we design a course that inspires them to do just that?

One of the main obstacles is that the kitchen we work in imposes its own serious restrictions. The preparatory study programmes students have followed, and are still following, are both enabling and disabling. The first obstacle is well-known to all teachers in our international Master programmes: some students are well versed in critical theory and post-critique, whereas others have barely received any education at all in critical reflection about the relation between art and society. Secondly, their prior education may already have established an unproductive idea of the relation between art (as merely the raw material for the first world art market, or art scholarship) and the metropolitan academy (as the site of the sophisticated labour that would produce value). The second student mentioned earlier, who is passionate about the commercially promising masks, is a case in point. Thirdly, they may have internalized a sense of white privilege, or, in contrast, may be disillusioned by the insight in their own systemic marginalization and exclusion. They may have cultivated an individualist, (neo)liberal, universalizing approach to all social and cultural issues, or they may be politicizing everything, within a narrow framework. They may feel irrelevant, or overwhelmed by the insight that they have not even started to scratch the surface of art in its global complexity.

So, we cannot just start making our own meals, in every which way we want. The kitchen we have to work in is already there. Let us remember Gayatri Spivak's statement, though: the academy is an institution you cannot *not* want to inhabit. It is still one of the main institutions that produce formal knowledge and that intervene in the dominant ways of producing knowledge.[3] World Art Studies is one of the productive interventions. So, the question is: How to tweak our meal, within the context of this kitchen? How to tweak it in such a way that it will energize our students to contribute to changes in the art world? Let us enter the kitchen, then. Let us taste the ingredients, and the dishes that are already cooking. What is in them that dampens our students' ability to act? The first thing that jumps out is this: this soup is very, very complex. We, as teachers, appreciate the subtlety and richness of the combination of ingredients: Giorgio Agamben,[4] Judith Butler,[5] Yogita Goyal,[6] Achille Mbembe, Jacques Rancière,[7] Yoko Tawada,[8] and so on, but some students just do not recognize any of the ingredients. They do not suit them and do not nourish them, so that they can reflect and act.

Theory comes from practice. It comes from the practice of critically engaging with social and artistic work, in a local and intercultural and international community. Can we make our students take a step back, and ask them to immerse themselves in these practices first? My contribution to this book will focus on the dishes we serve our students during their Arts and Culture Studies, and on the meal we might wish to prepare instead, as test recipe for future courses.

3. Sara Danius, Stefan Jonsson and Gayatri Chakravorty Spivak, 'An Interview with Gayatri Chakravorty Spivak', *boundary 2* 20, no. 2 (1993), p. 42.

4. Giorgio Agamben, 'The Paradox of Sovereignty' and 'The Camp as the "Nomos" of the Modern', *Homo Sacer: Sovereign Power and Bare Life* (Stanford, 2005).

5. Judith Butler, 'Survivability, Vulnerability, Affect', *Frames of War: When is Life Grievable?* (London, 2009) pp. 33–62.

6. Yogita Goyal, 'African Atrocity, American Humanity: Slavery and Its Transnational Afterlives', *Research in African Literatures* 45, no.3 (2014), pp. 48–71.

7. Jacques Rancière, 'The Paradoxes of Political Art', *Dissensus: On Politics and Aesthetics* (London, 2010).

8. Yoko Tawada, 'From Mother Tongue to Linguistic Mother', *Manoa* 18, no.1 (2006), pp. 139–143.

9. Aminata Caïro is a cultural anthropologist and consultant, who uses art and academic research to empower communities.

Openness, Self-reflection, Awareness

Practical experience gives one an awareness of how art relates to social problems. It often leads to an openness to other social, spiritual, and sensual functions of art, and helps in developing the active will to *learn* about these aspects. But one can only benefit from this practice if one already has a certain openness.

Fortunately, the students who follow our electives do so because they already have a certain degree of openness. The first preparatory two classes of our transformed course profit from this and from the fact that the student group is very international, and very diverse, not just in terms of prior education, but also in terms of their social position (shaped by gender, age, socio-economic background, ethnicity, religion, health, sexual orientation, and so on). The programme for the first class is simple: talk to each other. After a general intro, we embark on that very task. The inspiration for this exercise is Aminata Caïro's Let's Talk-sessions.[9] In small groups, the students share their life stories, and the reason why art (visual art, literature, film, dance, video games…) is important for them. The assignment for the others is to listen carefully, and actively. As a preparation for the second class, students study the art works their fellow students have mentioned as powerful (as a consolation, eye-opener, life-changer…). They also share what they learnt during the first class. They may realize that they never thought much about the experiences their fellow-students spoke about.

In my own teaching career, a student once shared that without art, they simply would not have been able to survive. Another student found in art—in this case music—a sudden revelation about how their family history related to other colonial family histories, which suddenly gave them the words to make sense of their own history. Another student created art to give visible form to inexpressible psychological pain.

The teachers act as mediators throughout the two classes, in the first place by creating a safe space. An important task is to make students respect each other's boundaries; nobody will push anyone in sharing more than they feels safe to do. The teachers contact the students before the first class, explain the plan, and ask them to consider whether they would like to contribute. This may mean that it may not be possible to do the talking exercise described above, or to restrict it to those who are willing to share their stories. The teachers may decide that the insights and questions that emerge from these sessions need to be complemented. They can offer videos in which artists talk about their own efforts at creating significant art—art that helps one to survive, to reflect, to reach out, to criticize, to make the invisible visible. At the end of the second class, all students are asked to articulate one or more issues they would like to learn more about.

Fieldwork

The next ingredient is fieldwork. This means: the students and teachers leave the kitchen, and take as much distance from the academic kitchen rules and cookery books as they can. The teachers propose a particular form of fieldwork to each student, based on the aims they have articulated themselves. Preferably, they work in pairs, and, most desirably, spend four weeks in an artist community of people of colour (in Europe or elsewhere), or in a multicultural group of activists (antiracism, climate change, for example) or in a community centre or gallery where art is used to address social issues, or in a local gallery or art centre that seeks access to the more well-known museums, art fairs, and exhibition centres. They interview artists, activists, gallery owners, community workers, and curators, and do participatory fieldwork to find answers to their questions, such as: what is the role of art in this community? What are the obstacles to making art as effective and meaningful as possible? How can art bridge differences between the communities? What are the obstacles to ethnic, cultural, socio-economic, and other forms of diversity in the mainstream art institutions?

Practice-based Theory: Avoiding Easy Solutions

We understand this fieldwork as the gathering of a wealth of ingredients for these students' own 'global' dinner. When they are back in class, in the kitchen, they share their experiences and insights, and present their own reflections on the tensions and contradictions they discovered.

The next four weeks are dedicated to further study. During the fieldwork and this next stage of the course, the teachers keep stimulating students to think critically about their experiences. The motto for the next month is: avoid easy solutions. Depending on the particular problematics explored by the students, we ask them to study for example Jacques Rancière,[10] Slavoj Žižek,[11] Yogita Goyal,[12] or others. This allows them to explain why critical art will usually not have any direct political effect (Rancière); why a simple critique of ideology will not lead to institutional change (Žižek); and why a humanitarian (human-rights) approach may not at all be helpful to excluded people (but may increase white privilege) (Goyal). The students explore the pitfalls of a facile, unspecified ethical approach, based on an unproblematized understanding of empathy and sympathy (Arendt[13] and Bloom[14]). They study European diversity policies and learn to differentiate between neoliberal approaches to diversity, and critical approaches.[15]

In this way students can begin to understand the use of theory as the deliberate adoption of *other perspectives*, as a means to see a vexed problem in another light, and to recognize its complexities. Theory is nothing but a way to avoid reductive analyses and ineffective solutions. Theory can give one the words to talk about new, productive views and approaches (Bal and Boer[16]). One of the discussions to have in this class therefore is: what is the relevance of theory? And: what is the relevance of art?

At the same time, the class is invited to problematize the practice of doing theory. What theoretical approaches are helpful? Which approaches developed by non-metropolitan thinkers are helpful, and which ones are helpful in spite of being developed in a metropolitan context? Are the critical approaches of a decade ago still useful, now that Michel Foucault's analysis of biopower

10. Rancière 2010 (see note 7).

11. Slavoj Žižek, 'Tolerance as an ideological category', *Violence* (London, 2008), pp. 140-177.

12. Goyal 2014 (see note 6).

13. Hannah Arendt, *On Revolution* (New York, 1963).

14. Paul Bloom, *Against Empathy: The Case for Rational Compassion* (New York, 2016).

15. For a thorough study of diversity in academia see www.leru.org/publications/equality-diversity-and-inclusion-at-universities.

16. *The Point of Theory: Practices of Cultural Analysis*, eds. Mieke Bal and Inge E. Boer (New York, 1994).

in the disciplinary society is complicated by the fact that we are now living in a society of informatics control? The critique of ideology, and discourse analysis are still very useful to analyze in what ways race, religion, nationality, gender, sexual orientation, and so on, are mobilized in the service of power (the extreme right and the governments that are exploiting extreme-right views are a telling example of the necessity of such a critique). However, this analysis neglects affective dimensions—and therefore the decisive reasons why art moves people, and why art can unite or divide. This is why we bring in postcritical approaches too, to help our students to make sense of the tensions they observed during field work. Sara Ahmed[17] and Judith Butler are some of the useful voices here.

17. Sara Ahmed, 'Affective Economies', *Social Text* 22, no.2 (2004), pp. 117–139.

Practice: Cooking a Nourishing Meal for Significant Others

This is the menu we hope to serve our students. They cooked part of it themselves; now it is their turn to prepare a whole meal. In the final three weeks the students write a plan of action for, for example, a gallery or museum in Leiden, The Hague, or elsewhere, to help them succeed in increasing the ethnic and cultural diversity of the artists whose work they are exhibiting, or to help realize a collaboration with other (more ethnically and culturally diverse, or more influential) communities and organizations. They write the plan of action in collaboration with the artists and activists they have met during their fieldwork. Their final assignment is evaluated and graded by the last group, the gallery people, and the teachers. The proof of the pudding is not just in the eating, but also in what happens next; the course is only successful when all those involved feel that they are now part of a new inclusive network, a small but promising part of the broad global network that is dedicated to speeding up the transformation of the world of global art.

INTERSTITIAL SPACES: DRC NO.12

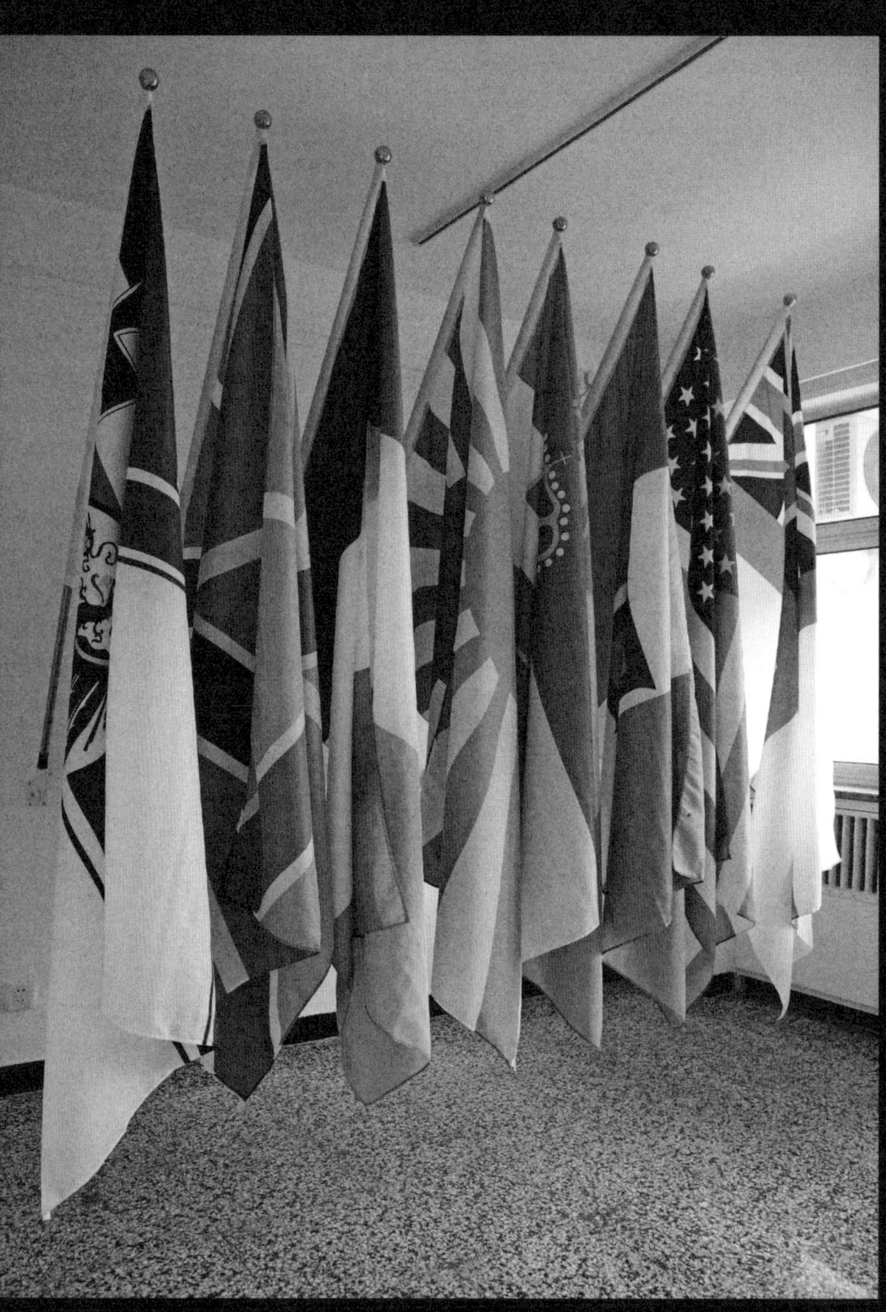

Ni Haifeng, *55 Days at Peking*, 2017, site-specific installation, work in progress, flags, flag poles, vinyl letters, newspaper, books, printed matters, TV screen, video, 79,200 min., installation view.

What kind of world are we living in at this precise moment? The disrupted supply chains, closed national borders, travel restrictions, trade wars, the shifting world order, international terrorism, regular financial crises, refugee crisis, climate change, inequality, the rise of popularism and nationalism, all seem to suggest that the once euphoric globalization has lost momentum. As the global pandemic lingers on, on the one hand we find ourselves increasingly marooned in the suspended global world, while on the other hand we are provided with an exceptional time to contemplate globalization. While the world is irreversibly interconnected, globalization in its current iteration becomes increasingly untenable. What about art and its global circulation? Is that also an unsustainable model? The answer may lie in our approach to the globalized art world.

The art world in the age of globalization is not a singular, continuous international space for the production, circulation, and consumption of art, but consists of plural, parallel, superimposed multiple global networks, and the 'panhuman' experience of art is not a smooth continuum of a global phenomenon, but rather the aggregation of disparate localities, ethnographies, temporalities, and spaces, simultaneously separating and connecting us from each other. In such a topography of art worlds, the flow and mobility of art, artists, and global cultural agents form multidirectional trajectories, differing from those in the age of nomadism, hybridity, and diaspora, which emphasize the unidirectional transmigration of 'Third World' artists to the metropole.

We must also realize that the kaleidoscopic worlds of art imagined above are superimposed on the current condition of globalization and are still somewhat Western-centric or perhaps also capitalism-centric. Deconstructing cultural dominance and hierarchy will always remain an unfinished project, the success of which, I think, will rely on the multiplicity of other geographical and cultural locations, and spaces, for the production and consumption of art outside the global circuit and the usual routes of capital flow, such as biennales, art fairs, and global speculative and blue-chip art market. Globalism is not a solution but part of the problem of perpetuating cultural dominance and hierarchy. I see globalization as a homogenizing force, setting up a new form of inclusion and exclusion—between those artworks that can be circulated alongside global symbolic capital and those that are not. We need to 'reterritorialize' cultural space and propagate a new form of 'localism', creating other loci to defy the totalizing force of the globalization of art. This 'localism', however, should not be understood as the antonym of the global, nor in the sense of an oxymoron that they used to call 'glocal', it is, rather, the concrete constituents, the disjointed, overlapping, and juxtaposed multifarious realities of the global world, or the loci where the production of different cultures takes place. In short, outside the traditional centres, there is a necessity to establish more localities, ex-centric sites, more constant and persistent presence than those biennial and triennial gatherings in 'elsewhere' that leave a vacuum in their aftermath. Not only in the geographical peripheries but also within a locality and a system, we need to create interstitial spaces, where different strains of contemporary art can take root in their immediate socio-political and cultural realities that would otherwise be lost in the global mobility of art.

In order to illustrate the ex-centric localities discussed above I propose both an experimental art space, DRC No. 12 in Beijing, and my project *55 Days at Peking* (2017)—tailored for this space—for this special volume as 'ingredients' and a part of the material culture of contemporary art for world art studies, or as both a case and an event.

Located in the Chaoyang District in Beijing, the Jianguomenwai Diplomatic Residence Compound (the DRC) was built in 1971 to provide offices and living spaces for foreign diplomatic missions, international news outlets, and international organizations. It was the only international community in China that enjoyed diplomatic privileges. In the 1980s, the living rooms of the diplomats and foreign residents in the Diplomatic Residence Compound became the first venues for contemporary art exhibitions and other underground cultural activities, because of the lack of institutional support for contemporary culture. Around the same time, the Diplomatic Residence Compound also functioned as an information hub that contributed to the early discoveries and internationalization of Chinese contemporary art. Established five years ago as a non-profit art organization, DRC No. 12 is one of the few art spaces that are embedded in the real social fabric of China, amidst the otherwise booming spectacle of contemporary art that rides the free wave of capital. DRC No. 12 is an apartment space located in the Diplomatic Residence Compound and has since been functioning as an ex-centric site in this 'trans-national', 'extraterritorial', and peripheral space right in the heart of the city. The borderline character of the art space reflects its orientation in the interstices of institutional systems, global art circuits, capital and politics, bringing together art and a complex historical, political, and cultural context, in an effort to redefine the contemporary. *55 Days at Peking* is a project attempting to redefine the present, renew 'the past', refigure it as "in-between" space that innovates and interrupts the performance of the present. 'The past-present' becomes part of the necessity, not nostalgia, of living'.[1]

1. Homi K. Bhabha, *The Location of Culture*, (London 1994).

20 June–14 August 1900

In present-day China, the Diplomatic Residence Compound (DRC), like an embassy, is extra-territorial; it is within Chinese territory but separated from it. Ever since its establishment in the 1970s, it has been tightly guarded by the People's Armed Police, and Chinese citizens are denied free movement in and out of the compound. The guarded gate can be equated to a frontier, separating two very different worlds inside and outside the DRC. The DRC is a rather unique Chinese phenomenon. The rationale behind it is to segregate foreigners from the local population and to manage foreign influence effectively. It is also a legacy from the earlier Communist era—an arrangement to provide foreign nationals a better living condition while the overall living standard in China was considerably lower. Today, the role of DRC is changing; it is no longer exclusively occupied by foreign diplomats, embassy personnel, journalists, and foreign company executives, as was the case two or three decades ago. It is now available to all foreign nationals. The aura of DRC is fast fading, and perhaps DRC itself will soon become history.

That brings me to the disused legation quarter—Dongjiaominxiang, the earliest legation area in Beijing where foreign diplomatic missions concentrated during the Qing dynasty (1636-1912). It is the predecessor of

2. 'Boxers' was the name of a Chinese secret society known as the Yihetuan (Righteous and Harmonious Militia), which practiced certain boxing and calisthenic rituals in the belief that this made them invulnerable. In the late nineteenth century, because of growing economic impoverishment and a series of unfortunate natural calamities, the Boxers began to increase their strength in the provinces of North China. Initially, as part of the wider anti-Qing rebellions, the Qing Court persuaded the Boxers to drop their opposition to the Qing Dynasty and unite with it in destroying the foreigners. By November 1899, the boxers started openly attacking Western missionaries, Chinese Christians, and anyone who sided with foreigners. The Boxer Rebellion was eventually suppressed by an international force, known as the Eight-Nation Alliance (see note 3), in September 1901.

3. Empire of Japan, Russian Empire, British Empire, France, United States, German Empire, Kingdom of Italy, Austria-Hungary.

today's diplomatic districts and the abovementioned DRC in Beijing. In 1900, during the Boxer Rebellion,[2] the Boxer and Qing Army soldiers surrounded the area in an attempt to kill foreigners and Chinese Christians living there, and the incident ended with the Eight-Nations Alliance attacking Beijing. The historical episode is known as the 55-day siege in the Legation Quarter, which lasted from 20 June to 14 August 1900.

Despite the arrogance of the Imperial court and Chinese literati towards anything non-Chinese, China has a long history of encountering foreign cultures. Nestorian Christianity was found in the Tang Dynasty China (618-907). The Jesuit missionaries reached China as early as the sixteenth century, and in the following centuries they were allowed to establish churches all over China. The missionaries played an important role in the cultural transfer between China and the West. The recent history of China is, however, fractured by major cultural, political, and military conflicts with hegemonic foreign powers. With the two Opium Wars (1839-1842 and 1856-1860), the First Sino-Japanese War (1894-1895), the Boxer Rebellion (1899-1901) and the ensuing retaliation from the Eight-Nation Alliance,[3] the course of the nineteenth century left a deep scar in China's modern history. To this day, the wounded pride and sense of humiliation are a constitutive part of the collective psychology of contemporary China, which often ignites nationalistic sentiments whenever national pride is in question. The century also marked the beginning of China's long and reluctant process of opening up to the world.

The official historical narratives (Chinese and Western) focus on the western colonial aggression against China but rarely on Chinese xenophobia. The Boxer Rebellion was at least partly spurred by a xenophobic sentiment, which is still alive in China today. The Boxer Rebellion is an acutely controversial and ideologically charged historical incident, the true nature of which has always been obscured by the official narrative throughout the era of the People's Republic.

The different views and attitudes concerning the Boxer Rebellion reflect the divide among Chinese social classes.

I. The Boxer Rebellion is a very complex story, not only because of so many opposing views, but also the difficulty to locate its moral coordinates. The incident is embedded in the broader context of Western colonialism and China's century of humiliation that left many so-called unequal treaties. Nevertheless, with its mob character and violence, the movement was spurred by a tremendous amount of rumours, disinformation and superstition. Its narrative has been carefully shaped and instrumentalized by official history of the People's Republic of China. After 1949, communist historians rushed to re-interview the last surviving boxers, attempting to affect the historical materials and re-edit the history of the Boxer Rebellion from the ground up. The diverse and critical views toward Boxers from the previous republican years disappeared in official discourses, and the incident was reframed as a proletarian uprising in a Marxist-Leninist framework. In today's China, where nobody thinks about Marxist-Leninist, Boxers are now synonymous with patriotism.

The Boxer spirit is ghostly latent in today's ostensibly modern China, ready to morph into whatever form of mass hysteria against whoever challenges China's pride.

20 June–14 August 2017

55 Days at Peking is a 1963 American historical epic film produced by Samuel Bronston and directed by Nicholas Ray. The film is a dramatization of the siege of the foreign legation compound in Beijing during the Boxer Rebellion, which occurred in China between 1898 and 1900.

II. *55 Days at Peking* was produced in 1963, around the time I was born. The film can be considered a special case in Western film history, echoing the history of the West's understanding of the Oriental. As most scenes were shot in Spain, the images of China appear fake and all the protagonists, such as Ci Xi and Rong Lu were performed by Western actors. As the film needed thousands of walk-ons and extras, the film crew asked almost every Chinese living in Spain to participate in the shooting. Consequently, during the filming process nearly all the Chinese restaurants were shut down.

What attracts me the most in the film is the idea of casting Westerners as Asians in the film, which betrays a tint of Orientalism. They imagined what the Chinese ought to look like and selected Westerners whose features conformed with the 'imagined Chinese' for the leading roles in the film while relegating the real Chinese (the walk-ons and extras) to backgrounds.

The exhibition is named after the film. It is structured to coincide with the timeline of the real historical events in 1900. As if to call forth the historical event as a rehearsal, the exhibition started on 14 June when the Boxers surrounded the foreign legations and ended on 14 August when the Eight-Nation Alliance ended the siege 117 years ago. By the coincidence of time and the juxtaposition of the past and the present, history here appears as a horizontal stretch of every day, while the historical event, in turn, frames the exhibition duration as a (present) historical course.

In the main room, a tripod-mounted monitor shows the epic historical film *55 Days at Peking* (1963) in extreme slow motion. It is stretched to a duration of 1,320 hours to coincide with the 55 days of the real historical event and the exhibition period. That is to say that the film began to play as the exhibition opened and ended as the exhibition closed.

III. As the movie is in such extreme slow-motion, an execution scene at the beginning of the movie appeared on the third day of the exhibition, in which it took a falling sword more than 8 hours to reach the condemned. The duration of the sword frozen in the mid-air causes a rupture in the temporal continuum, disrupting the naturally established relations between life and death.

The diplomatic compound apartment (DRC No. 12 Space) was spatially arranged in a temporal structure. The south side room housed black and white navy ensigns or national flags of the then Eight-Nation Alliance when they attacked Beijing in 1900. The lack of colour neutralizes the highly symbolic impact of ensigns and flags, and they, in turn, create a temporal distance. From the ceiling of the north side room seventeen contemporary national flags are hung, in full colour, of the original Eight-Nation Alliance, which has now disintegrated into seventeen nations.[4] The corridor functions, symbolically, as a temporal passage linking the past to the present.

IV. History could be imagined as a palimpsest that is constantly erased, rewritten, coded, and deciphered.

A double row of dates of 55 days—the real historical event in 1900 and the entire exhibition duration—in the form of numbers, such as 20-06-1990/20-06-2017, in vinyl letters, are printed on the walls, starting at the corridor, continuing into adjacent rooms and spreading throughout the entire space. It can be seen as a numerical form of time, unfolding in a fragmented fashion. The numbers are like the names of the days, and they call forth the 55-day historical duration into presence and arrest the 55 present days from the current flow of time. This timeline also serves as a grid for both the historical storytelling and contemporary everyday narratives to unfold. Within the 55 days of the exhibition duration, progressively, things, images, video clips, and texts

4. As the Austrian-Hungarian Empire dissolved into Austria, Hungary, Czechoslovakia and Yugoslavia, and the latter two further divided, respectively, into the Czech Republic and Slovakia, and into Bosnia-Herzegovina, Montenegro, Macedonia, Croatia, Slovenia, and Serbia.

were added to the space around the timeline to interpret and reinterpret the days from both the year 1900 and 2017. Within the double durations, each double day is regarded as an archaeological site for both the artist and audience to excavate what has been in the immediate past on the one hand, and reinvent the historical readymade on the other. The project aimed to create a double narrative, a parallel temporality that is simultaneously historical and present, both truthful and fictional.

The project is about time, about the visibility and the perceptibility of time. It is as if various temporalities, from the fictional cinematic time to the unfolding of the present, are inserted into the rigid frame of 55 days, the real historical duration. The project posits that history is a form of time and that it resides in the distorted cinematic time, in the deconstructed historical continuity, and in the fragmented everyday life. History becomes real when it is freed of its monumentality. History should be ordinary and full of anecdotes. It is the total sum of ceaseless fluxes of time.

V. The history we know is always full of key moments, turning points, watersheds, monumental events, heroes and villains, rarely about ordinary life or mundane moments. History is a high abstraction of the past, leaving a huge blank space in the representation of the lives lived, and the time passed. Anecdotes are minor narratives, amusing or sometimes unreliable, and they are here to perform as dynamic and subversive quotidian 'histories'. I see anecdotes as the marginal space of history. To borrow a Postcolonial jargon, it is the 'subaltern' history.

It is only a little more than a century that sets apart the 55-day siege in Dongjiaomingxiang and the 55-day exhibition in DRC No. 12. A century is at the same time long and short in our increasingly relative perception of time and history. Over the century, China has marched from feudal-colonial times to the age of global capitalism; a lot has changed, but some subterranean blind forces, which often triggered regressive momentum in history, have remained constant. Depending on one's perspective, sometimes the past appears nearer than it actually is, at other times one finds a cyclic motion in historical processes. With the 55 days at DRC No. 12, can we not imagine that we are under siege again, this time by the invisible forces from within?

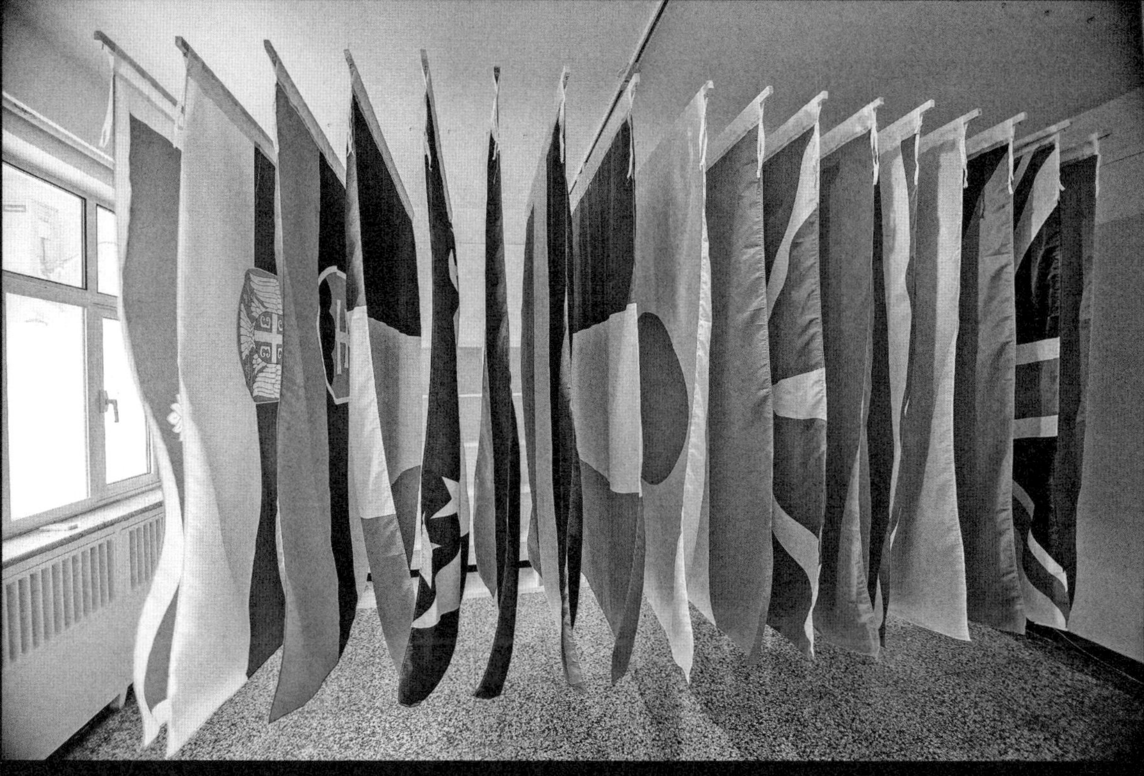

Ni Haifeng, *55 Days at Peking*, 2017, site-specific installation, work in progress, flags, flag poles, vinyl letters, newspaper, books, printed matters, TV screen, video, 79,200 min., installation view.

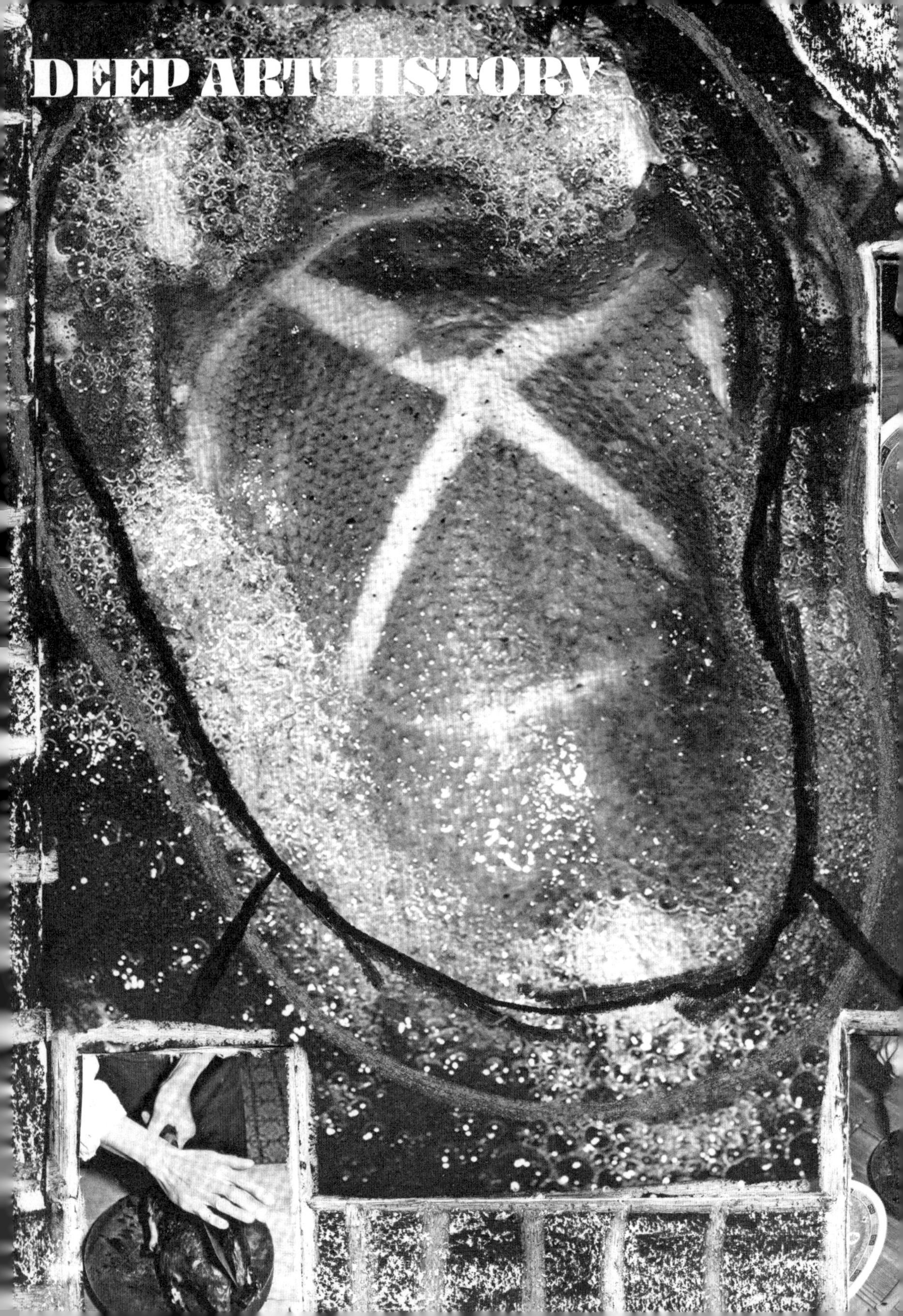
DEEP ART HISTORY

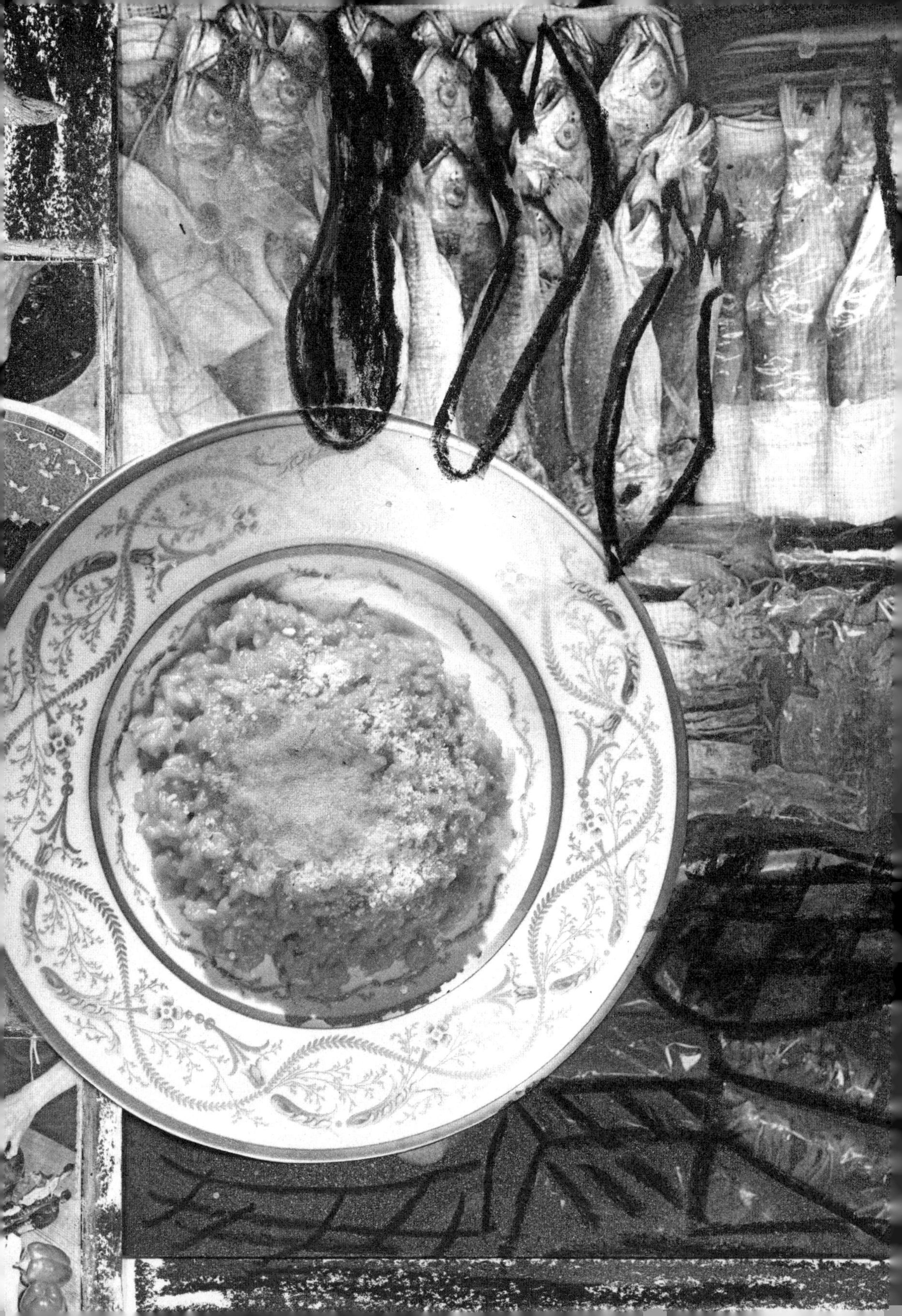

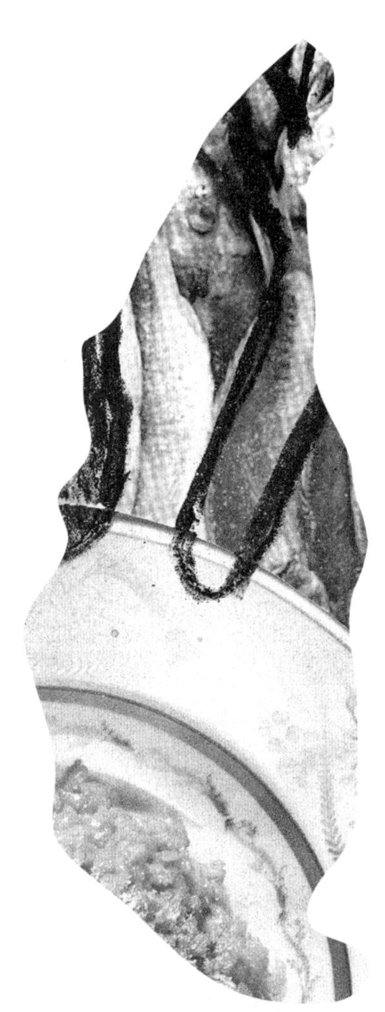

EVOLUTIONARY APPROACHES TO ART
A Fusion Dish

Larissa Mendoza Straffon

Prepare the Ingredients

INGREDIENTS

- Evolutionary Theory
- Anthropology of Art
- Ethology
- Archaeology
- World Art Studies

Ideas on the biological roots of the arts have been around since Charles Darwin, who in *The Descent of Man*[1] embedded human aesthetic preferences in the framework of the natural sciences. From then on, various scholars have followed up on his efforts to explain the role of biology in the arts and, conversely, the role of art in human evolution.[2] No group of scientists made better advances in this regard than the ethologists.

In the mid-twentieth century ethology arose as a discipline dedicated to the biological study of behaviour. Before then, animal and human behaviour had been the exclusive subject of psychology, which at the time focused primarily on the influence of external stimuli and emphasized the study of so-called stimulus-response mechanisms, in the manner of I. Pavlov and B.F. Skinner. In contrast, ethology proposed to study behaviour as any other physiological organ, i.e., as an intrinsic, functional, adaptive part of the organism, with its own evolutionary history and purpose.[3] Ethology, then, aimed at explaining the causes, functions, development, and evolution of the behaviours that are characteristic of a species.[4]

Art practices have been recorded in every known human culture around the globe and can be undertaken by any person, from childhood to old age, irrespective of quality. So, the arts were soon identified as characteristic human behaviour and adopted as a topic in ethology.[5] Once classified as a (partly) biological phenomenon, prominent

1. Charles Darwin, *The Descent of Man, and Selection in Relation to Sex*, 2nd edition published in 1879, with an Introduction by James Moore and Adrian Desmond (Harmondsworth, 2004).

2. Yrjö Hirn, *The Origins of Art: A Psychological and Sociological Inquiry* (New York, 1900).

3. Niko Tinbergen, 'On Aims and Methods of Ethology', *Zeitschrift für Tierpsychologie*, 20 (1963), pp. 410–433.

4. Konrad Lorenz, 'Evolution of Ritualization in the Biological and Cultural Spheres', *Philosophical Transactions of the Royal Society of London. Series B, Biological Sciences* 251, no. 772 (1966), pp. 273–284.

5. Julian Huxley, *A Discussion on Ritualization of Behaviour in Animals and Man* (London, 1966).

ethologists such as Desmond Morris,[6] Irenäus Eibl-Eibesfeldt[7] and, particularly, Ellen Dissanayake[8] set out to answer the question of what art evolved for.

Since then, ethological and evolutionary approaches to art and culture have become commonplace, and nowadays constitute a thriving multidisciplinary field of research.[9] However, some commentators from the humanities still argue that studying the arts as behaviour means reducing them to mere biological mechanisms. In this essay, I argue that such objections stem from a misunderstanding of the aims and methods of evolutionary research, and show that it is not only possible but also crucial to reconcile art history with human evolution studies if we want to understand art as a panhuman phenomenon.[10]

I will focus primarily on three frequent criticisms directed at evolutionary studies of the arts. The first being that evolutionary scenarios of the arts are purely speculative. The second criticism addressed here is that the study of the evolution of art, particularly of art's origins and its ancestral function, is irrelevant to art history. Finally, I examine the complaint that modern and contemporary art escape evolutionary explanations and thus, evolution-based methods are not useful for examining art as a current practice.

Mix and Stir: Art and Evolution, How Do We Know?

Questions about origins are never easy to answer. Especially when these regard aspects of the human mind or of human traits that have left no direct material traces in the fossil or archaeological records, such as language and symbolic cognition. To study the emergence of such traits, researchers must either rely purely on theory[11] or have to turn to indirect evidence, for instance by inferring that the creation of certain artefacts involved the said capacities. One example is transposing what we know about cultural display and identity in living societies to argue that the presence of personal ornaments in populations of modern humans over 70,000 years ago indicates that they possessed

6. Desmond Morris, *The Biology of Art: A Study of the Picture-making Behaviour of the Great Apes and Its Relationship to Human Art* (London, 1962).

7. Irenäus Eibl-Eibesfeldt, 'The Biological Foundation of Aesthetics', *Beauty and the Brain. Biological Aspects of Aesthetics*, eds. I. Rentschler, B. Herzberger, and D. Epstein (Basel, 1988), pp. 29–68.

8. Ellen Dissanayake, *What is Art For?* (Seattle/London, 1990).

9. Joseph Carroll, 'Why We Need a Journal with the Title Evolutionary Studies in Imaginative Culture', *Evolutionary Studies in Imaginative Culture* 1, no. 1 (2017), pp. vii–xii.

10. Wilfried van Damme and Kitty Zijlmans, 'Art History in a Global Frame: World Art Studies', *Art History and Visual Studies in Europe*, ed. Matthew Rampley et al (Leiden, 2012), pp. 217–229.

11. Geoffrey Miller, *The Mating Mind: How Sexual Choice Shaped the Evolution of Human Nature* (Portsmouth NH, 2000).

language and symbolic thought.[12]

Due to the problems inherent to these methods, research that looks into the origins of language, music, art, and human cognition in general has often been said to be too speculative to be taken seriously.[13] Whereas these speculation claims may be true in some cases, for example those that disregard any material evidence, generalizing them to the whole field seems unfair. Despite the 'epistemic disadvantage' that historical sciences have compared to the 'hard' sciences,[14] researchers of human evolution are able to and frequently do put forward hypotheses based on evidence of past activity, observations of current patterns of behaviour (from anthropology or psychology), techniques for simulating, modelling, and comparing data (from AI, linguistics, or evolutionary biology), and the general existing corpus of scientific knowledge (evolutionary theory). In this sense, the evolutionary research of human behaviour is no different from disciplines such as geology, palaeontology, or cosmology,[15] and like these, it is constantly improving its methods to propose sounder hypotheses and better testable models.

Furthermore, if incorporated into evolutionary hypotheses, the archaeological record offers a way to test different scenarios for the origins and evolution of art[16] and much like other scientific models, evolutionary explanations of art are continuously reassessed according to new data, the refinement of scientific techniques, and the input from different disciplines. Until recently, palaeontologists were convinced that we would never know the colour of dinosaurs.[17] Advances in molecular palaeobiology have now made it possible to learn about dinosaur coloration,[18] and studying the colours of dinosaur skin, eggs, and plumage has quickly become a booming area of research. This illustrates that what seems impossible at some point, may not remain that way. Likewise, over the past decade, the problem of the origins of language has undertaken a complete revision as new information about the genetics and cognitive abilities of extinct humans (e.g. the Neanderthals) have come to light.[19] Thanks to developments in research and technology, such as genomic analysis, our knowledge of the human fossil and archaeological records have also taken great leaps, and like those studying dinosaur colour, we can now make better-informed

2. Francesco d'Errico, hris Henshilwood, Marian anhaeren, and Karen an Niekerk, 'Nassarius raussianus Shell Beads rom Blombos Cave: vidence for Symbolic ehaviour in the Middle tone Age', *Journal of Human volution* 48, no. 1 (2005), p. 3–24.

3. Whitney Davis, Beginning the History of rt', *The Journal of Aesthetics nd Art Criticism* 51, no. 3 1993), pp. 327–350; onald de Sousa, 'Is Art an daptation? Prospects for n Evolutionary Perspective f Beauty', *The Journal of esthetics and Art Criticism* 2, no. 2 (2004), pp. 109–118; ichard Lewontin, 'The volution of Cognition: uestions We Will Never nswer', *An Invitation to ognitive Science* (Vol. 4), ds. Daniel N. Osherson, aul Sternberg, Don carborough (Cambridge, A, 1998), pp. 107–132; atthew Rampley, *The eductions of Darwin: Art, volution, Neuroscience* State College, 2017).

4. Derek Turner, *Making rehistory: Historical Science nd the Scientific Realism ebate* (Cambridge, 2007).

5. W. Tecumseh Fitch, Preface to the Special Issue n the Biology and Evolution f Language', *Psychonomic ulletin & Review* 24, no. 1 2017), pp. 1–2.

6. Larissa Mendoza traffon, 'Evolution and the rigins of Visual Art: An rchaeological Perspective', *andbook of Evolutionary esearch in Archaeology*, ed. . Prentiss (Missoula, 2019), p. 407–435.

7. Turner 2007 (see note 14).

8. Fucheng Zhang, Stuart . Kearns, Patrick J. Orr, ichael Benton, Zhonghe hou, Diane Johnson, Xing u, and Xiaolin Wang, Fossilized Melanosomes and he Colour of Cretaceous inosaurs and Birds', *Nature* 63, no. 7284 (2010), pp. 075–1078.

9. Lawrence Barham and aniel Everett, 'Semiotics nd the Origin of Language n the Lower Palaeolithic', *ournal of Archaeological ethod and Theory*, no. 28 2021), pp. 1–45.

inferences about the evolution of hominin cognition and behaviour.

Admittedly, evolutionary explanations of (the origins of) art have often ignored the material evidence for the earliest art, or have been based upon information that is now outdated.[20] That does not mean, however, that learning about why and how art became a usual component of the human behavioural repertoire is not a valuable endeavour or that it will linger in speculation looking ahead.

Bring to a Boil: Does Evolution Matter to Art History?

Another frequent complaint raised by art historians against evolutionary hypotheses of art and its role in human life is that, for all their interesting propositions, they do not directly address the key questions of art history and art scholarship.[21]

It may be useful to note that there is no single unified evolutionary model for art's origin and development. On the contrary, there are several models and hypotheses that offer many different explanations that suggest very different scenarios and often oppose each other, even if they all have evolutionary theory as a common starting point.[22] In spite of such variety, most of these hypotheses are mainly concerned with one of two themes, one being the origin of art, i.e., since when and under what circumstances humans started producing art. This question requires a rather empirical approach and is usually the subject of archaeology, bioanthropology, cognitive science, and genetics. The second theme examines what art evolved for, i.e., the evolutionary function(s) of art and the potential selective pressures that gave rise to it, some of which may be inferred from art's current uses. This is more akin to the fields of human ethology, evolutionary psychology, and evolutionary aesthetics, and often aims at determining the role of art and aesthetics in human existence since ancestral times.

Both themes are interested in the deep roots of art in human biology. Therefore, they generally adopt a broad concept of art that includes prehistoric, traditional, and

20. Straffon 2019 (see note 16).

21. Davis 1993 (see note 13); De Sousa 2004 (see note 13) ; Dennis Dutton, 'Aesthetics and Evolutionary Psychology', *The Oxford Handbook for Aesthetics*, ed. J. Levinson (Oxford, 2003), pp. 693–705; Jonathan Jones, 'God, Sex or Evolution—Why Did Humans Start Making Art?' ,2016, www.theguardian.com/artanddesign/jonathanjonesblog/2016/nov/03/on-the-origins-of-art-exhibition-tasmania-why-did-humans-start-making-art-comment; Rampley 2017 (see note 13).

22. Ellen Dissanayake, 'What Art Is and What Art Does: An Overview of Contemporary Evolutionary Hypotheses', *Evolutionary and Neurocognitive Approaches to Aesthetics, Creativity, and the Arts*, eds. C. Martindale, P. Locher and V. M. Petrov (New York, 2007), pp. 1–14.

'non-Western' practices,[23] many of which formal art history would perhaps consider 'crafts' but certainly not art 'with a capital A'.[24]

Art historians, for their part, have a more restrictive concept of art and very different study questions from the ones mentioned above. For example, they may want to trace the history of a motif as a subject in artworks, establish the relationships between particular artists and their artistic production, reveal the connections between specific styles or practices of art-making, find out how individual preferences for certain forms or styles arose, and most importantly, determine what separates art from non-art.[25]

Given the different conceptualizations of art and diverging interests of art scholars and evolutionary studies of art, some commentators have doubted the validity of the latter because they do not attend to key issues in art scholarship and the questions they do address 'are of little use to most researchers in art history in particular and the humanities in general'.[26]

I argue that such concerns stem from confounding the different units and levels of explanation of each field. Evolutionary studies of behaviour are usually guided by research questions formulated according to four levels of explanation, nowadays known as Tinbergen's four questions, after the Dutch Nobel laureate who first described them.[27] These are **1)** causation: the immediate mechanisms that trigger and control a behaviour, **2)** ontogeny: how a behaviour pattern emerges and changes through the life-course, **3)** function: the role of the behaviour in the organism's life, i.e. how the trait contributes to survival and reproductive success, and **4)** evolution or phylogeny: the history of the behaviour, i.e., the origin and plausible selective pressures that shaped the behaviour. The first two levels are referred to as 'proximate' explanations as they correspond to the immediate mechanisms that underlie a behaviour, whereas function and phylogeny are called 'ultimate' explanations because they attend to the evolutionary history of the behaviour.

Evolutionary approaches to the arts are mainly concerned with ultimate explanations (function and phylogeny) and aim at finding out their influence in a population (often the species) over long periods of time,

3. Wilfried van Damme, ntroducing World Art tudies', *World Art Studies: xploring Concepts and pproaches*, eds. Kitty ijlmans and Wilfried van amme (Amsterdam, 2008), p. 23–61.

4. Stephen Davies, 'Ellen issanayake's evolutionary esthetic', *Biology & hilosophy* 20, no. 2–3 2005), pp. 291–304.

5. Dennis Dutton, 'But They on't Have our Concept of rt', *Theories of Art Today*, d. Noel Carroll (Madison, 000), pp. 217–225.

6. Rampley 2017 (see note 3), p. 72.

7. Tinbergen 1963 (see ote 3).

whereas art scholars generally address proximate questions (causation and ontogeny), and frequently target particular individuals or small groups of artists in specific eras. We would not ask of someone who studies the evolution of the human diet to explain the recent rise in popularity of the Slow Food movement. These topics are related to the extent that they both concern human feeding behaviour, but to explain the first, one would need to know about nutrition science, biology, and (palaeo)anthropology,[28] whereas for the second, one would need to be familiar with contemporary history, sociology, and economy.[29] Likewise, it seems unjust to condemn scholars interested in the evolution of art for not answering art historical questions, when they have a different aim and focus on different units and levels of explanation. This does not mean that ultimate questions are of more or less value than proximate ones. In the end, it is only by putting together all four levels of explanation that we get a complete understanding of a behaviour.

Simmer and Reduce: A Link to the Present

The final concern dealt with here is that evolutionary approaches cannot account for modern and contemporary art and therefore cannot be applied to study art as a current global phenomenon. As discussed before, evolutionary approaches have a broad working concept of art, one that encompasses all those practices and objects that are purposefully made and displayed aesthetically and skilfully, i.e., things and activities that are 'made special'.[30] These 'special' practices and objects take a wide array of forms, varieties and qualities, are found in every society from prehistory to today, and in principle can be enjoyed and undertaken by every person whatever their background. Here 'art' includes the crafts as well as, for instance, tribal art, folk art, domestic art, and religious art, alongside so-called fine art, all having the common denominator of being aesthetic and 'special'.[31]

This democratized view of art is at odds with traditional Western art scholarship, in which art denotes a constrained set of items, made by a small group of people

28. Richard Wrangham, 'The Evolution of Human Nutrition', *Current Biology* 23, no. 9 (2013), pp. R354–R355.

29. Sophie Bossy, 'Slow Food Movement', *The Wiley-Blackwell Encyclopedia of Social and Political Movements*, eds. D.A. Snow, D. della Porta, B. Klandermans, and D. McAdam.

30. Dissanayake 1990 (see note 8).

31. Ellen Dissanayake, 'The Arts After Darwin: Does Art Have an Origin and Adaptive Function?', *World Art Studies* (see note 23), pp. 241–263.

(talented or trained 'artists'), is contemplated and displayed in specialized curated spaces, and assessed by educated critics and patrons.[32] Some critics have said that the whole-encompassing evolutionary view of art is misguided and we should not 'confuse decorative instincts, or even the sense of beauty, which hand axes suggest evolved very early in the human story, with the higher, more complex activity that is art as we know it'.[33]

Just like traditional art history had trouble accommodating modern and contemporary disruptive art, such as the Dada movement, sceptics argue that if the term art refers to 'special' objects made with skill, then the evolutionary definition cannot account for anti-art either.[34] Ready-mades and Pop Art pieces are often meant not to be aesthetic or 'special'. These are a far cry from the painted caves of the European Palaeolithic or the sacred items of many small-scale societies, and a sound theory should be able to account for both.[35]

The fact is that art 'as we know it' originated from those ancestral decorative instincts and sense of beauty, even if nowadays it does not look like it. Biologists classify penguins as Aves even if they have lost most of the traits that we normally associate with birds, like having wings, feathers, and being able to fly. They are birds because their lineage can be traced back in the bird phylogenetic tree[36] and because they still share many typical bird characteristics even if less obvious than the ones mentioned before. In the same way, all art can be traced back to a common origin, even if over time some of it has specialized and changed so much that at first glance we can barely observe the similarities between old and new forms. So, an evolutionary perspective could in fact explain contemporary anti-art, for instance by applying a phylogenetic approach.

Serve and Enjoy

World Art Studies and the anthropology of art have often embraced evolutionary explanations of art. Art history and art criticism have often been hostile to these approaches and have put forward the objections I have reviewed here, among others. I have attempted to answer to claims

32. Dutton 2000 (see note 25); Tim Ingold, 'Beyond Art and Technology: The Anthropology of Skill', *Anthropological Perspectives on Technology*, ed. Michael Brian Schiffer (Albuquerque, 2001), pp. 17–31.

33. Jones 2016 (see note 21), para. 8.

34. Rampley 2017 (see note 3).

35. Jones 2016 (see note 21).

36. Kerryn E Slack, Craig M. Jones, Tatsuro Ando, Abby Harrison, R. Ewan Fordyce, Ulfur Arnason, and David Penny, 'Early Penguin Fossils, plus Mitochondrial Genomes, Calibrate Avian Evolution', *Molecular Biology and Evolution* 23, no. 6 (2006), pp. 1144–1155.

that evolutionary hypotheses are speculative, irrelevant to art history, and disconnected to art in the present, by suggesting that these criticisms are in fact misplaced and likely stem from misunderstanding the different research aims and questions pursued by art historians and evolutionary scholars, respectively. Calls from biological approaches to abandon the views and methods of the humanities[37] and, vice versa, from the humanities to disregard evolution[38] are unnecessary and harmful to a complete understanding of art. There is no reason why art should not be studied from every perspective and with a plurality of methods, as each will reveal a different aspect of this multi-layered and most intriguing of human behaviours.

37. Alex Mesoudi, Andrew Whiten and Kevin N. Laland, 'Towards a Unified Science of Cultural Evolution', *Behavioral and Brain Sciences* 29, no. 4 (2006), p 329.

38. Rampley 2017 (see note 13).

EVOLUTIONARY VIEW

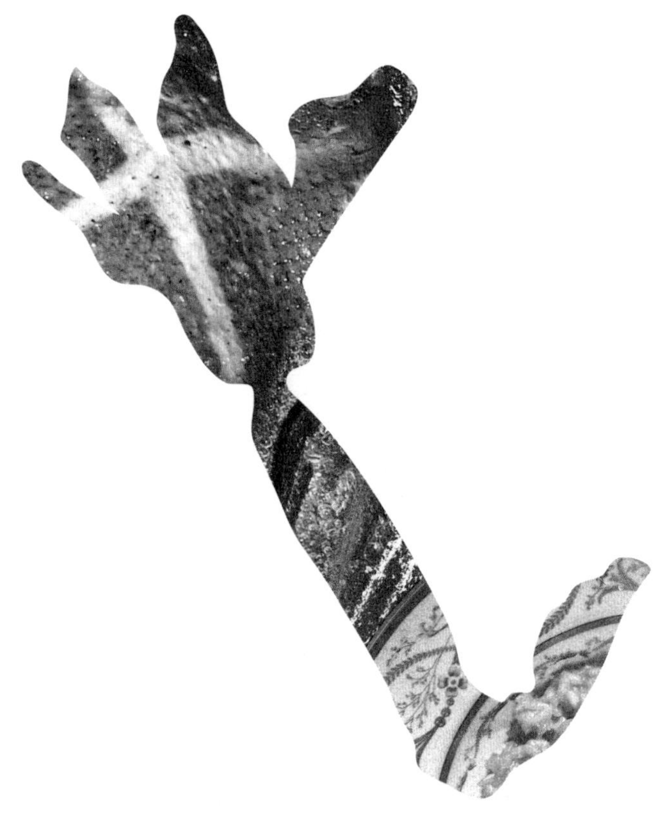

WORLD ART HISTORY
The Dialogue between the Prehistoric and the Contemporary

Thomas DaCosta Kaufmann

INGREDIENTS

- Deep Art History
- Tool Making and Art
- Primate (Orangutan) Studies
- Neuroarthistory
- Chauvet and Sulawesi Cave Paintings
- Blombos Cave Discoveries

At first glance, the vastly incomplete record of creations by early humans presents an extreme contrast with the abundance of works by artists produced in recent times. However, the apparent incommensurability of these phenomena may be as misleading as it is in other cases where this notion has been invoked to limit the possibility of writing global history (and art history).[1] What has been called 'prehistoric' may participate in a dialogue with the contemporary. Since the late-nineteenth century, when scholars began to realize that human beings have been on the planet for a vastly long time, and especially since circa 1900, when cave paintings were confirmed as human-made, very early works have stimulated artists such as Picasso as well as contemporary critics and theorists. The astounding discoveries of 'prehistoric' art that will continue to be made parallel the continuous outpouring of contemporary artworks. This brief essay suggests how these apparent opposites may inform each other in illuminating approaches to world art history.

1. Sanjay Subrahmanyam has repeatedly argued against this objection to doing global history: see e.g., *Courtly Encounters: Translating Courtliness and Violence in Early Modern Eurasia* (Cambridge, Mass., 2012). For art history see Thomas DaCosta Kaufmann, 'Reflections on World Art History', *Circulations in the Global History of Art*, eds. Thomas DaCosta Kaufmann, Catherine Dossin, and Béatrice Joyeux-Prunel (Aldershot/Burlington Vt., 2015) pp. 23–45.

In recent decades, the discipline of history has expanded in both space and time in ways comparable to art history. Historians now study all parts of the world, while proponents of 'big history'[2] and especially 'deep history'[3] have bucked tendencies in the Humanities to concentrate on the 'modern' and increasingly on the past half century. 'Deep historians' have incorporated the remote past into longer stories, challenging the division formulated in the nineteenth century between history and 'prehistory' that followed from defining history as a study based on written sources. Many historians utilize a wide variety of evidence from DNA to objects to materials, including traces of the past uncovered by archaeologists.[4] Art history has of course been associated with archaeology since its beginnings, and in as much as art historians have studied objects ('material culture') they already anticipated what some 'strict' historians do. Art history has also expanded its purview: art historians work on all geographical areas, while many advertisements for jobs specifically call for a global approach to chronological subdivisions. But while art historians also resemble historians in increasingly concentrating on recent art, no contrary movement towards 'deep art history' yet exists. It is fair to say that aside from a few specialists, art historians have in general displayed little inclination to engage seriously with prehistoric art in more than textbooks and similar surveys, other than through the lens of modern art and theory.[5]

A singular (though not unique)[6] exception is John Onians, whose work dramatizes key issues for world art history and thus provides a focus for this paper. Onians has not only pioneered world art studies, but, starting with an essay published in the first issue of *Art History*—of which periodical he was also the first editor—he has often written on the earliest human art.[7] Many of his essays and books constitute a larger project with a vast chronological sweep. Onians has given various names to this project: natural art history[8], biological art history[9], and neuroarthistory,[10] and he has made related forays into the geography of art.[11] His recent comprehensive book on neuroarthistory starts in the remote past with cave painting and ends in the near present. While Onians has repeatedly highlighted the Chauvet cave (he regards its paintings as origins of two-dimensional

2. See for example Cynthia Stokes Brown, *Big History from the Big Bang to the Present* (New York/London, 2007).

3. A prime example is Yuval Noah Harari, *Sapiens: A Brief History of Humankind* (London, 2014). For deep history see comprehensively Andrew Shyrock and David Lord Smail et al., *Deep History: The Architecture of Past and Present* (Berkeley/Los Angeles/London, 2011). The concentration on the past fifty years to the neglect of what occurred before then ironically exemplifies what Shyrock calls 'shallow history.'

4. Daniel Lord Smail and Andrew Shyrock, 'History and the "Pre"', *The American Historical Review* 118, no. 3 (June 2013), pp. 709–737.

5. E.g., Georges Bataille, *Prehistoric Painting: Lascaux or the Birth of Art* (Lausanne, 1955), most recently evoked by Hal Foster, *Brutal Aesthetics: Dubuffet, Bataille, Jorn, Paolozzi, Oldenburg* (Princeton, 2020).

6. E.g., Whitney Davis, 'The Origins of Image Making', *Current Anthropology* 27, no. 3 (June, 1986), pp. 193–215, and *Masking the Blow: The Scene of Representation in Late Prehistoric Egyptian Art* (Berkeley, 1992); David Summers, *Real Spaces: World Art History and the Rise of Western Modernism* (New York/London, 2003).

7. Desmond Collins and John Onians, 'The Origins of Art', *Art History* 1, no. 1 (1978), pp. 1–25.

8. John Onians, 'A Brief Natural History of Art, *Compression and Expression: Containing and Explaining the World's Art*', ed. John Onians (Williamstown, 2006), pp. 235–249.

9. See the discussion in John Onians, 'Art History and Memory, From the Couch to the Scanner: On How the New Art History Woke Up to a Neural Future', *Art History* 40, no. 4 (2017), pp. 707–723.

10. John Onians, *European Art: A Neuroarthistory* (New Haven/London, 2016).

11. John Onians, 'The Biological and Geographical Bases of Cultural Borders: The Case of the Earliest European Prehistoric Art', *Borders in Art: Revisiting Kunstgeographie*, ed. Kartzyna Murawska-Muthesius (Warsaw, 2000), pp. 27–33; John Onians, 'Introduction', and 'Art, Hunting, and Gathering', *Atlas of World Art*, ed. John Onians (London, 2004), pp. 10–15.

12. Onians 2016 (see note 10), p. 13.

13. Davis 1986 (see note 6); Robert Bagley, *Gombrich Among the Egyptians and Other Essays* (Seattle, 2015).

14. John Onians, *Neurohistory from Aristotle to Zeki* (New Haven/London, 2007), pp. 159–177.

representation) and returns to it in this book, he also says that the original impetus for his project came from an encounter with Jasper Johns.[12]

Onians' account of Chauvet is a crux in his argument. Like other scholars, including some who have dealt specifically with prehistoric or ancient art,[13] he takes aim at E.H. Gombrich, whom he has otherwise appraised as a forerunner of neurohistory.[14] He criticizes Gombrich's response to the discovery of Chauvet, wherein Gombrich surmised that the 'complete mastery' of technical means

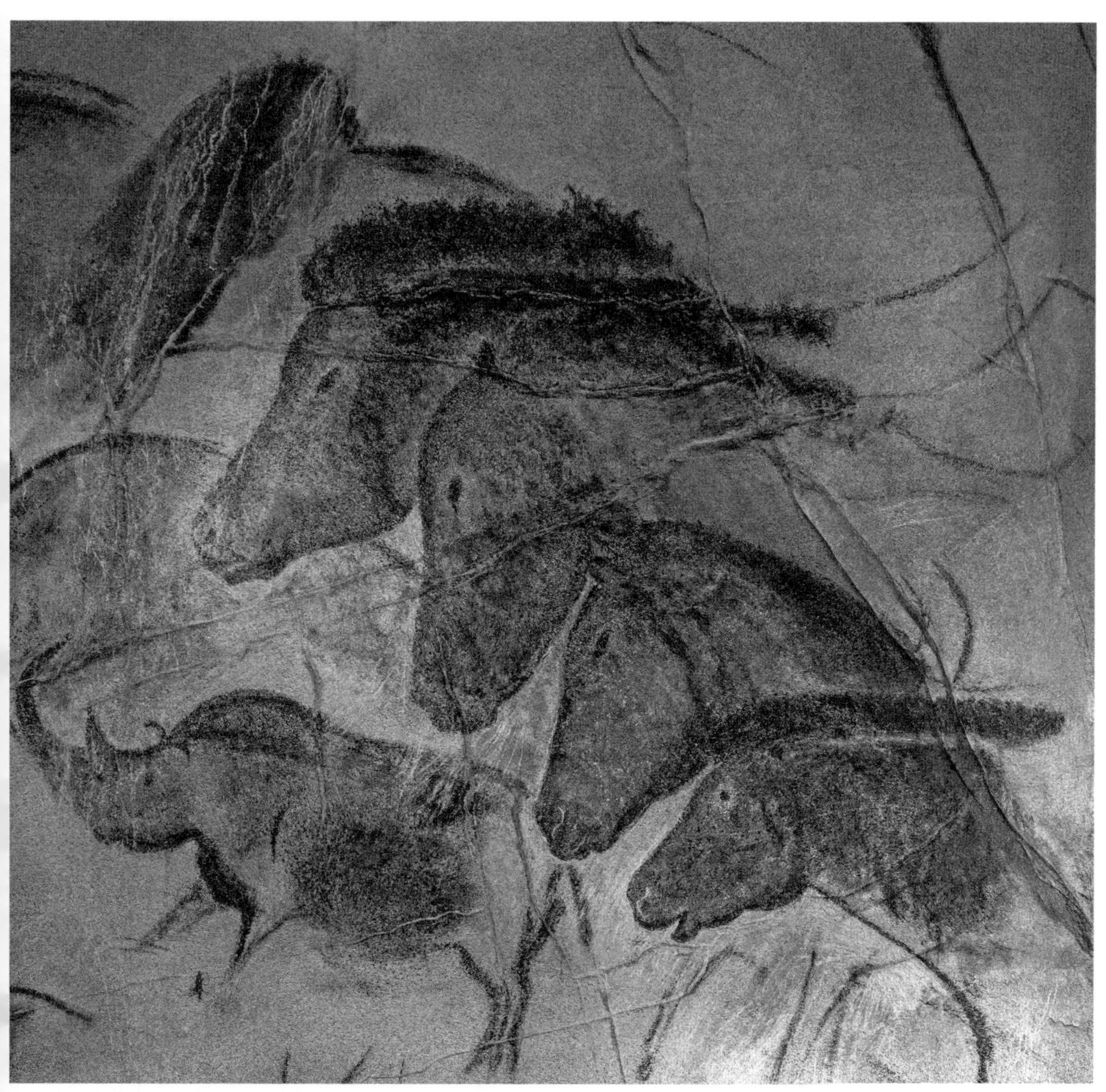

Painting from Chauvet Cave (Image ID: EPMFRP, Arterra Picture Library / Alamy Stock Photo) (Getty Images).

displayed by Chauvet's artists was 'presumably based on a tradition extending much further in the past'.[15] Onians' critique implicitly reacts to Gombrich's famous thesis that the solution to the 'riddle of style' in art (hence its continuing history) lies in a continuing process of making and matching.[16] Onians instead adopts a hypothesis of Michel Lorblanchet, historian of palaeolithic art, that explicitly rejects what Lorblanchet called globalizing approaches by asserting that the cradle of art is found in the brain.[17] In Onians' paraphrase, art originates as 'less a manifestation of culture than a spontaneous response to environmental contingencies'.[18] Onians develops the thesis that art 'does not spread from one or more centers as a shared cultural practice' but has a neurological genesis. Art comes from direct encounter with immediate surroundings and develops as an evolutionary process involving the natural selection of physiologically rooted responses.[19]

Yet the ubiquity of contemporary art and collections should alert us to a major 'Eurocentric' problem in relying exclusively on the European archaeological record.[20] 'Prehistoric' paintings have been discovered in South America, Africa, Australia, and Southeast Asia, many recently. Most significant, a painting of a warty pig and handprints found in 2021 in a cave on Sulawesi has been dated to at least 45,500 years before the present, thousands of years older than the paintings at Chauvet, which are the earliest such works in Europe. This discovery calls into question Onians' thesis that European cave paintings are responses to the climate of the 'Ice Age', physiological reactions to geographical determinants. Kendari (where the cave paintings have been found on Sulawesi) lies approximately four degrees south of the equator and was not located near glaciation.

Onians and other proponents of biological ('natural') rather than cultural explanations for art-making also evoke primate behaviour in their arguments. But there is much more to be said about observations of animals.[21] More recent studies of orangutans—rather than the literature on primates to which Onians refers—come to different conclusions than his. The processes (studied 'in the wild') by which orangutans make tools suggest they are open to influences that are not biologically ('neurologically')

15. E. H. Gombrich, 'The Miracle at Chauvet', *New York Review of Books* (14 November, 1996) pp. 8–12, quotation from p. 12. Cf. Onians 2016 (see note 10), p. 24.

16. As elaborated in E.H. Gombrich, *Art and Illusion: A Study in the Psychology of Pictorial Representation* (New York, 1960).

17. Michel Lorblanchet, *La Naissance de l'art. Genèse de l'art préhistorique* (Paris, 1999), p. 218.

18. Onians 2016 (see note 10), p. 20.

19. Ibid. pp. 23ff. This argument is already encapsulated in his earlier publications, e.g. *Atlas of World Art*, ed. John Onians (London, 2004), pp. 14–15, where geographical determinants are also emphasized.

20. As recognized by Michel Lorblanchet and Paul Bahn, *The First Artists: In Search of the World's Oldest Art* (London/New York, 2017), pp. 266-267. Larissa Mendoza Straffon, 'Evolution and the Origins of Visual Art: An Archaeological Perspective', *Handbook of Evolutionary Research in Archaeology*, ed. Anna Marie Prentiss (Cham, 2019) pp. 407–435, summarizing and expanding on material in her dissertation. Larissa Mendoza Straffon, *Art in the making. The evolutionary origins of visual art as a communication signal.* Ph.D. diss. Leiden University, 2014, provides an excellent introduction to theories of the origins of human art, while pointing to the importance of data from outside Europe.

21. See in general Robert W. Shumaker, Kristina R. Walkup, Benjamin B. Beck, *Animal Tool Behavior: The Use and Manufacture of Tools by Animals* (Baltimore, 2011). One possibly relevant point to consider in regard to what has been seen as the apparently inexplicable creation of sophisticated paintings at Chauvet and the stagnation or decline of cave painting thereafter: the study of bonobo apes indicates that their tool making may be punctuational, i.e. involving periods of slowing down as well as sudden apparent periods of insight and acceleration. Does this provide a suggestive parallel with cave painting? See further W. C. McGee, *Chimpanzee Material Culture:*

determined, including change of habitat and interaction with other orangutans.[22] Orangutans preserve their tools and utilize them as symbolic markers, identifying signs they use to demarcate groups, and such usages spread from one group of orangutans to another. Scholars of orangutans have consequently argued that the geographic variation they have observed indicate that orangutans possess cultures, according to a definition of cultures as entities patterned on innovation and diffusion. Their analysis also has implications for the understanding of how human culture originates.[23] It moreover relates to an independent interpretation of human toolmaking that suggests how art defines cultures.[24]

Contemporary art practices amplify such considerations of 'toolmaking' as art, as they suggest that painting ('two-dimensional representation') offers a very limited notion of what constitutes art. Contemporary art comprises performance, body art, installation, found objects, crocheting, and much more. A similar broad variety exists in very early human art. Lorblanchet's description of the 'irremediably' fragmentary record of the palaeolithic indeed refers not just to gaps in our knowledge of cave paintings, a major problem, but to all those things that have been irretrievably lost: 'the embroideries, the garments, the feathers, the painted and carved wood, paintings on human or animal skins, ephemeral images made on the ground.'[25] Jean-Marie Le Tensorer, whom Lorblanchet holds as a model,[26] in fact asserted that the origins of art, considered as a human creation with an intended purpose containing both aesthetic and symbolic elements as part of its function, lie not in painting, but in toolmaking.[27] Lorblanchet's own account of the first artists follows this line of thinking: he deals with painting only after discussing several other sorts of surviving human artistic artifacts, from tools to *bolas* to jewellery to elements of installation to inscribed blocs, only then to handprints, and finally to paintings on surfaces.

Considering the evolution of early human art, Onians acknowledges that tools evince both an aesthetic impulse and continuing refinement, but asserts that practical reasons related to hunting caused increasing sophistication in toolmaking.[28] However, continuing refinement led

Implications for Human Evolution (Cambridge, 1992).

22. See the comprehensive introductory overview, Carel P. van Schaik, *Among Orangutans: Red Apes and the Rise of Human Culture* (Cambridge, Mass./London 2004).

23. See for example Carel P. van Schaick et al., 'Orangutan Culture and the Evolution of Material Cultures', *Science* 299, no. 5603 (3 January 2003), pp. 102-105; Ellen J. M. Meulman and Carel P. van Schaick, 'Orangutan Tool Use and the Evolution of Technology', *Tool Use in Animals: Cognition and Ecology*, eds. Crickette M. Sanz, Josep Call, and Christophe Boesch (Cambridge, 2013), pp. 176–202.

24. See David Summers, 'Arbitrariness and Authority: How Art Makes Cultures', *Time and Place: The Geohistory of Art*, eds. Thomas DaCosta Kaufmann and Elizabeth Pilliod (Aldershot/Burlington Vt, 2005), pp. 203–213.

25. Michel Lorblanchet and Paul Bahn, *The First Artists: In Search of the World's Oldest Art* (London/New York, 2017), pp. 266–267.

26. Lorblanchet 1999 (see note 17) is dedicated to Le Tensorer.

27. Jean-Marie Le Tensorer, 'Les prémices de la créativité artistique chez Homo erectus', *MILLE FIORI. Festschrift für Ludwig Berger (Forschungen in August 25)* (August 1998), pp. 327–335.

28. Onians 2006 (see note 8), p. 241.

to creating tools that were no longer usable as such—the arrowheads produced in the Neolithic period (Onians refers to the same era as Mesolithic) were much too delicate to be effective weapons, just to mention one example.[29] Highly refined arrowheads and flints were treated much as were beads, objects made 'from a range of raw materials, such as shell, soft stone, mammal teeth, bone, amber, and ostrich eggshell'.[30] They were handled as goods: deposited in graves, used as objects for communication, and traded or exchanged (as were the distinctive stones, amber, and mollusc out of which they were made), which often came from distant sources starting at a very early date.

This leads us back to questions about the role of social and cultural factors in the origins of art and the possible existence of antecedents for Chauvet. While the paintings on Sulawesi also suggest texture and are shown in profile like those in Chauvet, their forms do not overlap, they do not suggest sequences, and they do not have shading. It is possible to regard them not only as antecedent in time to Chauvet but also in stylistic development, as other recent discoveries hint at an even longer process of development of marking techniques. In 2018, the oldest known markings by *Homo sapiens* were found on a small stone flake dated circa 71,000 BP. These consist of six red ochre parallel lines crossed by three diagonals. This flake was discovered in the well-known Blombos cave (South Africa), and its striations may be compared to the lattice pattern scratched in the famed ochre block dated circa 77,000 BP also found there. This supports the idea that the ochre block was used for aesthetic purposes, and both have been convincingly argued as early evidence for drawing and the origins of visual art.[31]

Furthermore, the transport of materials, including the Blombos ochre block itself, ochre found in other pertinent contexts,[32] and very ancient flints,[33] point to involvement of other possible social and cultural factors related to aesthetic questions, also suggesting another way how apparently unconnected finds may be related. Several explanations other than physiological/neurological causes have indeed been raised in discussions of the role of transport in the appearance of forms as well as materials in distant areas. They include spread from a source,

29. Summers 2005 (see note 24), p. 208, also persuasively argues that the development of arrowheads like those found in elite burials were deliberately made to display virtuosity.

30. Shyrock and Smail 2011 (see note 3), pp. 226, 230–232.

31. Straffon 2017 (see note 20), p. 412.

32. Ibid, p. 413.

33. Summers 2005 (see note 24), p. 205.

34. Shyrock and Smail 2011 (see note 3), p. 232.

long-distance networks, and common functions as social ornament, among other factors.[34]

In conclusion, the issues raised by Onians resonate with considerations of global art throughout human history. Much as 'deep historians' have argued that the treatment of objects as goods spans the whole of human existence, many other concerns illuminated by the discussion of 'prehistoric art' pertain to all art history. They involve such questions as: simultaneous invention versus diffusion; geographical versus cultural determinants; innate characteristics versus learned factors; the role of skill (*techne*, art); the importance of exchange; symbolic, communicative, and other purposes in art; migration; refinement.

This essay has emphasized the importance of issues raised by concerns with the distant past for all art historical scholars regardless of their field of expertise, and suggested how insights gained from the study of contemporary art may inform our approach to very early art. In keeping with the intentions of this book, we might also conclude with suggesting that deep art history may also provide a new outlook for the study of contemporary art. The very basic issues with which contemporary artists deal—along with the problems of assessing their work that critics and historians now have—are consistent with the questions that face us when we attempt to understand the earliest human creations. Deep art history not only reminds us of the continuing chain of creation but may provide insight into ways of looking at contemporary art. Finally, the importance of primates for understanding the earliest art at a time when most primates are now endangered species should remind us that the survival of human beings on the planet, like that of our cousins, is becoming increasingly precarious.

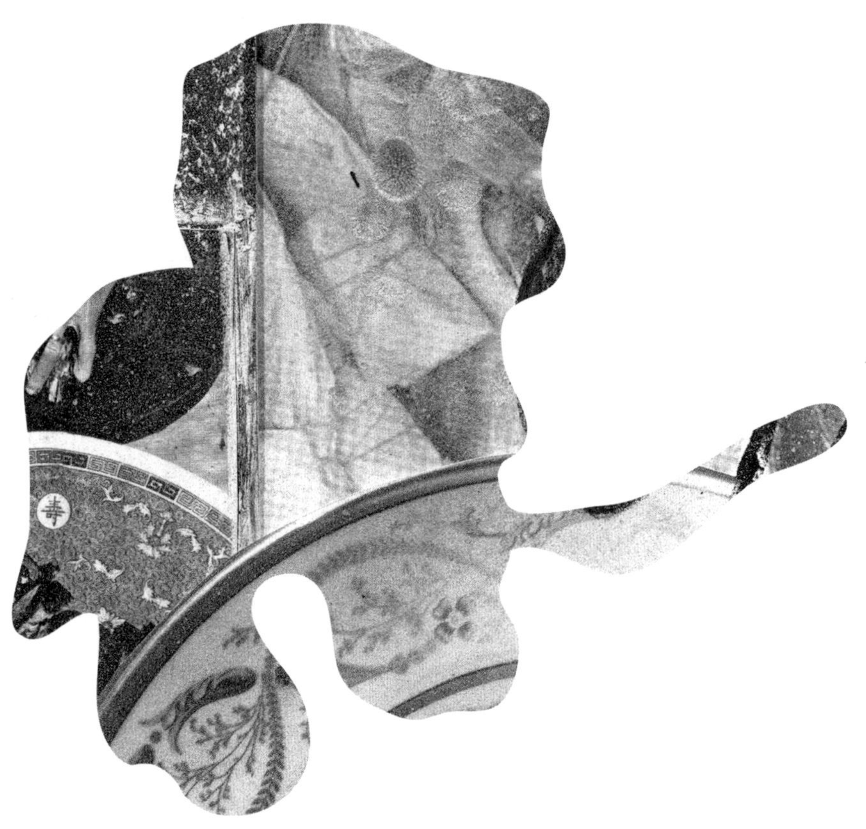

THE FUTURE OF THE PAST
What Comes after World Art History?

Claire Farago

INGREDIENTS

• Study of Planetary Culture
• Intra-Disciplinary Collaboration
• Sociobiological Synthesis (Interrelationship of Biological and Social Processes)
• Evolution as a Rhizomatic Structure
• Nature/Culture as a Cultural Construct

In *The Future We Choose: Surviving the Climate Crisis* (2020), the architects of the 2015 Paris Climate Agreement, Christiana Figueres and Tom Rivett-Carnac, warn that 'we have almost extinguished nature's capacity for self-renewal'. We will not recover everything, but well-planned regenerative practices will restore our ecosystems 'to a new state of regained health with enhanced resilience'.[1] The negative impact of humans as geologic agents is a shared catastrophe we have inherited: it is not simply of our own making or lifetime. Yet here we are, as the doomsday clock is about to strike midnight. I ask myself, what role does art history have in raising awareness and motivating action to mitigate the existential threat that collapse of our planetary ecosystem poses? Can we advance the public's interconnectedness with the planetary life-support system that so urgently needs to be restored? Mitigating the effects of climate disruption, the collapse of ecosystems, and the mass extinction of animal species calls for conversations between disciplines in the same way that the agricultural revolution 10,000 years ago could be explained only through the convergences of archaeology, geology, and history.[2]

. Christiana Figueres and om Rivett-Carnac, *The uture We Choose: Surviving he Climate Crisis* (New York, 020), pp. 71–72.

. Dipesh Chakrabarty, 'he Climate of History: our Theses', *Critical Inquiry* 5, no. 2 (Winter 2009), p. 197–222.

The project of writing a planetary history of culture that is truly non-Eurocentric invites collaboration across various disciplinary platforms, between scientists and humanists working in the shadow of catastrophic climate change.[3] In this spirit, I offer a thought experiment in the form of an intra-disciplinary collaborative project aimed at creating a sense of global citizenship by conceiving a history of planetary culture that all living creatures and their environments share. Not to replace art history, but a complement to ongoing efforts to think about contemporary art in a world/global framework: a new wing added to the existing sprawling house capacious enough to embrace archaeologists, anthropologists, musicologists, scientists, philosophers—in short, all who study cultural artifacts.

Why is such a broadly conceived, inclusive history of planetary culture desirable now? The responsibility of intellectuals to society has shifted in the current era of human-induced climate change. Global capitalism has made the depletion of resources so rapid, convenient, and barrier-free, writes journalist Naomi Klein, that 'earth-human systems' are becoming dangerously unstable in response.[4] In the wake of human-induced environmental disaster, we also witness demographic shifts on an unprecedented scale accompanied by the rise of populism and totalitarianism worldwide. At the centre of theoretical efforts across a wide span of methodologies, subjects, and scales of research for the past quarter century has been whether a global art history inevitably follows the logic of economic globalization, or whether (paraphrasing Monica Juneja) it can provide an alternative conception to effectively theorize relationships of connectivity that encompass disparities as well as contradictions and negotiate the multiple subjectivities of the actors involved?[5]

Whose life is worth recording? Remembering? Whose rights are restricted to 'bare life', treated as disposable? To understand our social responsibilities as intellectuals, we need to take into account how supply chain economics degrades vast numbers of people and the environment. The 1990s were an era of resistance to free trade and US hegemony that foreshadowed the global spread of populisms, writes Martín Arboleda, in *Planetary Mine*.[6] The task of the left today is to grasp the brutal reality of

3. Rob Nixon, *Slow Violence and the Environmentalism of the Poor* (Cambridge/London, 2011).

4. Reporting on a meeting o[f] the American Geophysical Union in 2012, Naomi Klein, 'Why Science Is Telling All o[f] Us to Revolt and Change Ou[r] Lives Before We Destroy the Planet', *Alternet* (30 Octobe[r] 2013), admin.alternet.org/print/environment/naomi-klein-why-science-telling-all-us-revolt-and-change-our-lives-we-destroy-planet, accessed on 28 February 2019.

5. Monica Juneja, '"A very civil idea...": Art History, Transculturation, and World Making: With and Beyond the Nation', *Zeitschrift für Kunstgeschichte*, no. 81 (2018), pp. 461–486.

6. Martín Arboleda, *Planetary Mine: Territories of Extracting under Late Capitalism* (London/New York, 2020).

planetary interdependency *and* its emancipatory possibility. In short, minerals feed the machines and human labour functions as an appendage to the technical apparatus. Shifts in class structure are interrelated across the supply chain network: the reproduction of the Chinese working class hinges on the dispossession of Latin American famers—and along with it come the deforestation, contamination, and cancer epidemics that the extraction of raw minerals and mega-agriculture entail. The flipside of the smooth flow of goods is the relentless precarization of workers.[7]

Not only do workers lose their traditional lifestyles and homelands to extractive capitalism, they lose their cultural identity. De-colonial and transcultural approaches call attention at the local level to the uneven playing field due to different historical circumstances in different places, asking difficult, previously unasked questions of the historical records that survive. It is exactly for this reason that historical understanding belongs in discussions of contemporary global art. As a historian studying objects and texts of the past, the work that I produce is re-writing the history of the past in the present. Understanding of the human by indigenous peoples who hold to an ontology of animism, once a marker distinguishing savages from civilized peoples, is now a useful paradigm for questioning the division between the biological and social realms. The principle of 'affordance', a term coined by perceptual psychologist James Gibson in 1966, refers to the complementarity of the individual animal and the environment.[8] We could start to frame an ecological approach to the history of planetary culture without setting humans in a sovereign position apart from the natural world.

In this short paper, I will identify and de-couple two fundamental, inherited categories of Western/Mediterranean origin that can either prevent or help us imagine a history of planetary culture broadly defined to encompass all artefacts: nature (biology) and culture (society). According to social anthropologist Tim Ingold, instead of re-drawing the opposition between innate capacity (biology) and acquired content (culture), a new 'sociobiological synthesis' is needed to describe the way all creatures learn through processes of growth and discovery forged 'in the crucible of their common life'.[9]

. Thea Riofrancos, 'Seize nd Resist: The Global upply Chain Is up for rabs', *The Baffler*, no. 54 Sept/Oct 2020), p. 16.

. James J. Gibson, *The enses Considered as erceptual Systems* (Boston, 966).

. Tim Ingold, 'Prospect', *iosocial Becomings: ntegrating Social and iological Anthropology*, eds. im Ingold and Gisli Palsson Cambridge, 2011), pp. 1–21. mong other prominent oices arguing along similar nes, see Bruno Latour, *acing Gaia: Eight Lectures n the New Climate Regime*, ansl. Catherina Porter Cambridge, 2017). My nanks to Kitty Zijlmans for nis reference.

Today science understands identity in terms of the molecular structure of DNA shared by all forms of life, which is a very different model from the one built into the foundational texts of art history. Where the nineteenth-century Darwinian model of evolution originally stressed the interconnectedness of life in terms of the anatomy of individual organisms, the current understanding of evolution defines identity at the molecular level of genomes consisting of DNA.[10] The analysis of whole genomes shows that the people who live in a particular place today almost never exclusively descend from the people who lived there in the past.[11] Analyzing biological identity in terms of the complete set of genetic material present in an organism has created the possibility of addressing previously unapproachable questions to write the deep history of human populations, their movements, and their mixing throughout the planet.[12] The estimated date of the earliest skeletal evidence for the spread of humans from Africa to Eurasia is 1.8 million years ago.[13] Scientific concepts of biological identity formulated at the molecular level connect all life forms. The implications of ongoing ancient DNA analysis are far from settled, but the new science of ancient genetics is currently able to demonstrate that we are all blends of past populations. There is no 'pure' lineage of *Homo sapiens*: humans from different populations interbred extensively with each other. Modern humans also bred successfully with Neanderthals, and Neanderthals interbred with other archaic humans, as the 2018 report of an offspring of a Neanderthal mother and a Denisovan father confirms.[14] Darwin's metaphor of a tree that defines the shape of evolutionary development is now re-conceptualized for ancient human evolution as a rhizomatic structure spreading laterally, with increasing evidence of the ways that organisms regulated through environmental forces alter the genetic make-up of future generations. Traits are dynamic and derive from the complex intersection of multiple genes with their natural and cultural environments.[15]

Depending on how culture is defined, there is no conceptual basis to exclude archaic humans and other animals from the planetary history of world culture. There is also extensive artefactual evidence of the deep history of the planet that was not available when the field of art

10. Richard Dawkins, *The Selfish Gene* (Oxford, 1976; 2nd ed., 1989). Dawkins proposed a definition of identity on the molecular level, which I support, but his characterization of memory as transmitting 'memes' of information is untenable. See the blisterin critique by Matthew Rampley, *The Seductions of Darwin: Art, Evolution, Neuroscience* (University Park PA, 2017), pp. 53–58.

11. David Reich, *Who We Are and How We got Here: Ancient DNA and the New Science of the Human Past* (New York, 2018), p. xi, n. 9.

12. Whole genome identifie paternal and maternal lines of descent, whereas older forms of DNA analysis were limited to the maternal DNA known as 'mitochondrial DNA'. The work has progressed rapidly thanks to technological advances in computer analysis and identification of DNA sites in fragments like the petrus bone inside the ear where DNA is highly concentrated

13. Reich 2018 (see note 11), p. 67, dates the spread of *Homo erectus* from Africa, estimating that humans spli at 1.4 million –1.9 million years ago; modern humans separated from Denisovans and Neanderthals ca. 770,000–550,000 years ago; Denisovans split from Neanderthals ca. 470,000–380,000 years ago. These figures derive from estimates of the mutation rate of genes, but the order of the splits and the distinctness of the populations can be determined well from genetics. It is also possible that these splits happened in Eurasia, descending from the original *Homo erectus*. The nomenclature used for archaic humans refers to a loosely related family of highly evolved archaic humans who inhabited a vast region of Eurasia (Ibid, p. 74).

14. Carl Zimmer, 'David Reic Unearths Human History Etched in Bone', *New York Times*, 22 August 2018, nyti.ms/2u2h8gW

15. Citing Stephen Mithen, 'Neanderthals, Denisovans, and Modern Humans', Review of Reich, *London Review of Books* 40/17 (13 September 2018).

6. Ibid.

7. Reich 2018 (see note 1), p. 26, mentions stone ools using the Levalloiis echnique which requires s much cognitive skill nd dexterity as the oolmaking techniques of nodern humans 50,000 ears ago; jewellery made f eagle talons, Krapina avie, Croatia, ca. 130,000 ears ago, a Neanderthal ite; stone circles inside runiquel Cave, France, 80,000 years ago; and a uman style tool known as Châtelperronian, found n midst of Neanderthal emains, 44–39,000 years go.

8. Eyton Avital and Eva ablonka, *Animal Traditions: ehavioral Inheritance in volution* (Cambridge, 000), pp. 10–11. My thanks o Matthew Walsh for this eference.

9. Ibid. Avital and Japlonka ite the important work on nterplay of genetic and ultural factors that uses he mathematical tools f theoretical population enetics, quantitative enetics, and epidemiology, nd applies them to culture, reating cultural practices s if they were transmissible ntities.

history was conceptualized in the nineteenth century. Artefactual material survives in many locations around the world and is not conventionally taught in art history courses, which still claim that cave paintings and mobile objects from European sites dating 30–40,000 years ago are the oldest surviving examples of human 'art'. The DNA evidence that *Homo sapiens* interbred with other humans that produced fertile offspring puts into question modern understanding of the category species used to distinguish *Homo sapiens* from archaic humans.[16] Archaic humans made stone tools, cared for the sick and elderly, made jewellery with symbolic associations 130,000 years ago, constructed stone circles in caves 180,000 years ago, and left other material evidence of their cultural activities before and after they interacted with *Homo sapiens*.[17]

Imagine how an ecological approach to the history of planetary culture that included animal life could benefit the future. With recent developments in animal behavioural science, the importance of social learning—inventiveness, innovation, adaptation, and other patterns of behaviour resulting from interactions between animals and their environment—is once again the focus of evolutionary theory. When studied in detail, many patterns of behaviour are found to be complex products of several types of learning rather than inherited traits. Defining 'culture' to mean social traditions and the transmission of social traditions, Eytan Avital and Eva Jablonka report studies of generations of macaques living on the Japanese island of Koshima who taught each other to wash sweet potatoes after these were introduced into their diet by scientists.[18] They note studies of similar adaptations by raccoons, coyotes, and certain birds. Behavioural scientists today are contributing to genetic theory in studying how learned behaviour has a genetic impact through natural selection. The systematic study of animal and plant behaviour in a non-positivistic framework is in its early stages, but in the coming years, we will certainly learn much more about the intelligence and emotional capacity of animals.[19] What if the ways that animals think, feel, behave, use tools, solve problems, improvise, and so forth were taught in the Humanities as part of the general education curriculum?

Biology can never be used again to posit one-to-one relationships between cultural and biological individuals in isolated specimens, as histories of art based on nineteenth-century ideas of morphology do, because biological identity operates at the molecular level while cultural identity operates at the level of objects located in networks of exchange. Nor does genome sequencing support a teleological explanation of cultural history, as Eurocentric accounts do in insisting on the superior state of European civilization. The deep history of human migration and the circulation of cultural artifacts may look remarkably similar as rhizomatic structures of connectivity, but they operate independently at vastly different scales.

In conclusion, efforts to bring the social and the biological together in numerous fields are moving beyond the inherited dichotomy between nature and culture. It is, in fact, an open research question to investigate how biological and social processes are interrelated. Historians of art and all forms of culture have the expertise to contribute to an unprecedented planetary consciousness of who we are, where we came from, and where we are going in the era of climate and ecosystem emergency. Although the term 'ecology' may be new, the relationship of art to its environment has been a central concern since the discipline of art history was professionalized in the nineteenth century. The critical question has always been *how* to define the relationship between culture and nature or, in the words of Ingold, 'socio-becomings' that bring the social and the biological together into a single frame.

This article is a preview of my book in progress, provisionally titled, *The Future of Cultural Memory in the Era of Climate Disruption*, forthcoming from Routledge Press, 2022.

Remy Jungerman

'The act of creating the works is how I honour my ancestral upbringing on my mum's side; the artworks are the remnants'

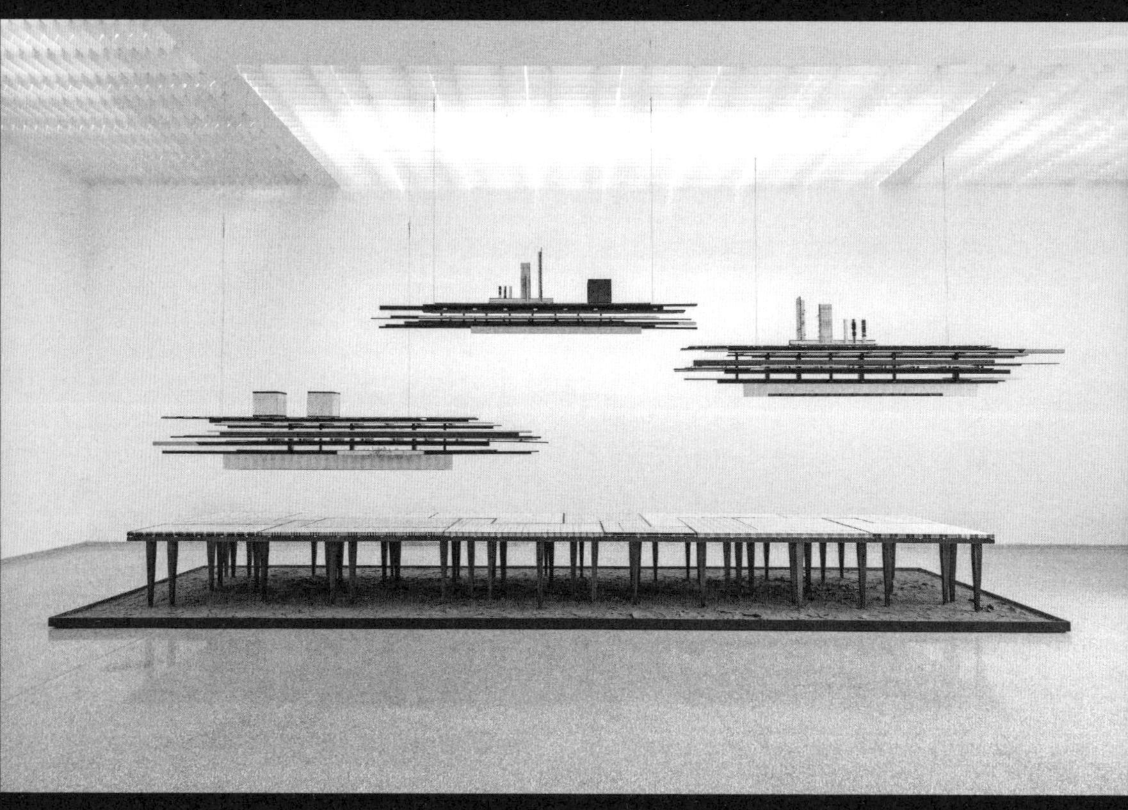

EARTH WATER

Remy Jungerman, *Visiting Deities*, 2018–2019, cotton, textile, kaolin (pimba), painted wood, meranti table legs (58), dry river clay, nails, yarn, mirror, river water samples (Cottica SR, Hudson US, Amstel NL), 975 × 340 × 260 cm. Photo Aatjan Renders.

‘Winti is an Afro Surinamese religion. The textiles you see in my work are the same as worn during various Winti ritual practices...’

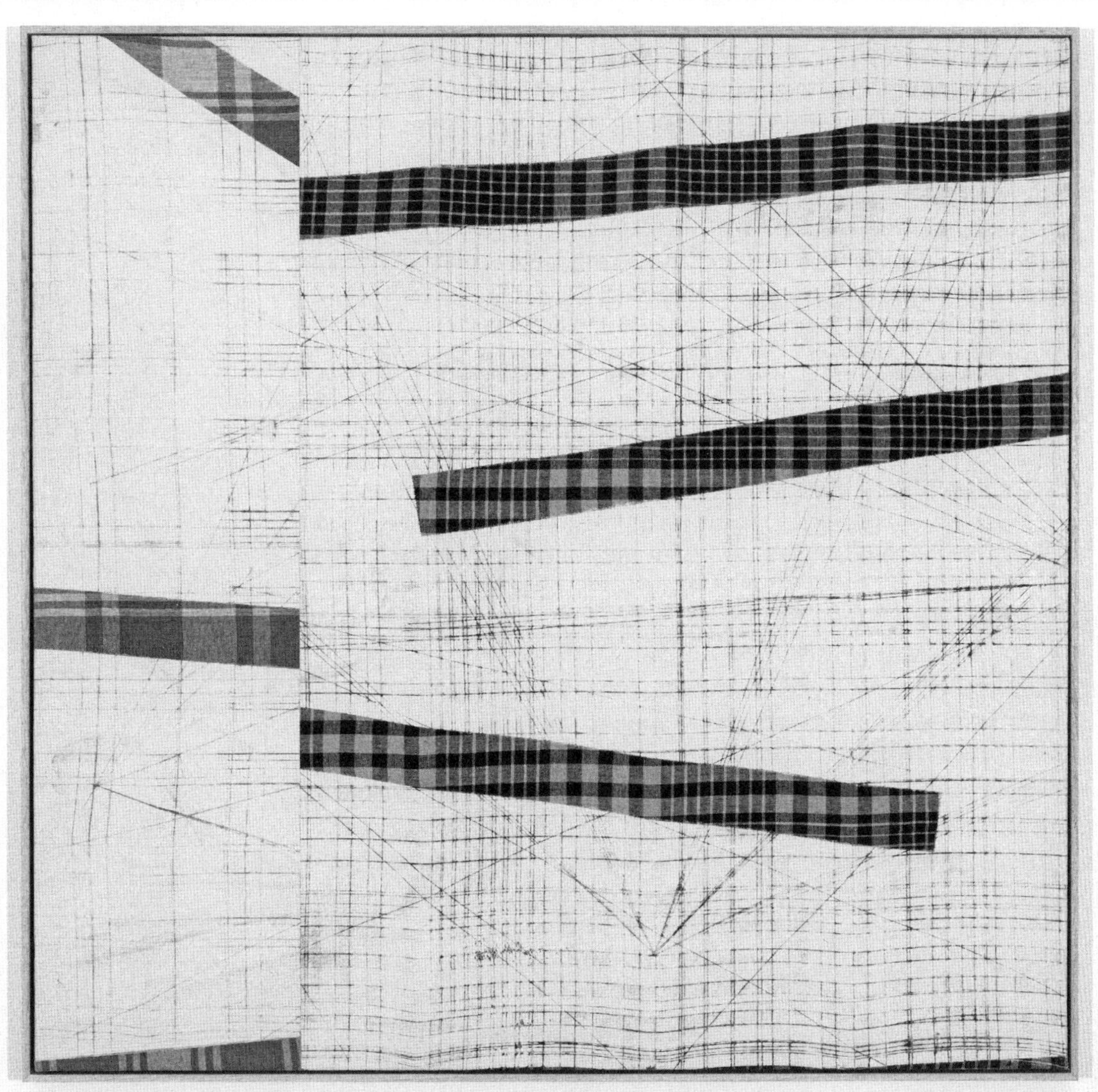

FOREST

SKY

Remy Jungerman, *Pimba AGIDA MADAFO III*, 2020, cotton, textile, kaolin (pimba) on wood panel, 80 × 80 cm. Photo Aatjan Renders.

AFTERS

In the Autumn of 2020, Kitty Zijlmans informed her colleagues at the Department of Art History at Leiden University about her retirement in the Summer of 2021. As her close colleague, I started to think about a 'parting gift' right away. A conversation with Korrie Korevaart, who worked closely with Kitty in the LUCAS Management Team, initiated a brainstorm about an edited volume. We agreed that a thematic collection of interesting and challenging essays would be highly appreciated. The contributors should be selected from the many scholars and artists Kitty collaborated with over the past decades. But where to start? And how? Instead of running this project in secret, I decided to invite Kitty to cooperate in her own 'farewell volume'.

The theme of this book was clear from the start. Kitty's mission of promoting a global perspective to (contemporary) art had to be endorsed by a successor to her seminal volume *World Art Studies*, co-edited by Wilfried van Damme. Knowing that Kitty enjoys cooking as a mental relaxation to compensate the huge academic work-load, and realizing that cooking is a core activity of people anywhere on the world, led me to the idea of the cookery book format.

About fifty invitations were sent out. It can be considered a token of very high appreciation that almost all of the invitees swiftly and positively responded to the call. But the dream of the publication could only become true thanks to the immediate and unconditional commitment of Astrid Vorstermans, publisher and director of Valiz, the 'home' of the predecessor *World Art Studies*.

On behalf of all the contributors to the volume, as well as her colleagues at the Department of Art History, LUCAS and ACPA at Leiden University, I wish Kitty a happy and healthy future, together with her partner Rudi. This volume will act as part of her legacy to future students who will no longer be able to attend her inspiring classes.

Helen Westgeest, co-editor

Cooking is a form of chemistry, in which all cooks blend their local ingredients and traditions, criss-crossing them with those of other parts of the world when using outlandish fare or spices, and by simmering, marinating, boiling, drying, frying, slow-cooking, baking, grilling (etc.) concoct these ingredients into the most delicious dishes. Kitty Zijlmans has been using this chemistry with her students for decades, in making them taste the flavours and variety of visual art forms from all over the world, and by stimulating and understanding learning through all these different 'cooking' or research methods.

As Helen expresses above: this book is an invitation to future students. But there is an intricate network of colleagues, former students (being a Zijlmans' alumna myself), and other art practitioners and scholars who will find new nourishment, savoury, sweet and spicy, to advance thinking, writing, and making art within open, world-wide frameworks.

We invite all of you to take a seat at a large table, to taste and savour the different dishes of this book, exchange together, share the results and bond. With a big thank you to Kitty Zijlmans, and a toast to her future.

Astrid Vorstermans, publisher

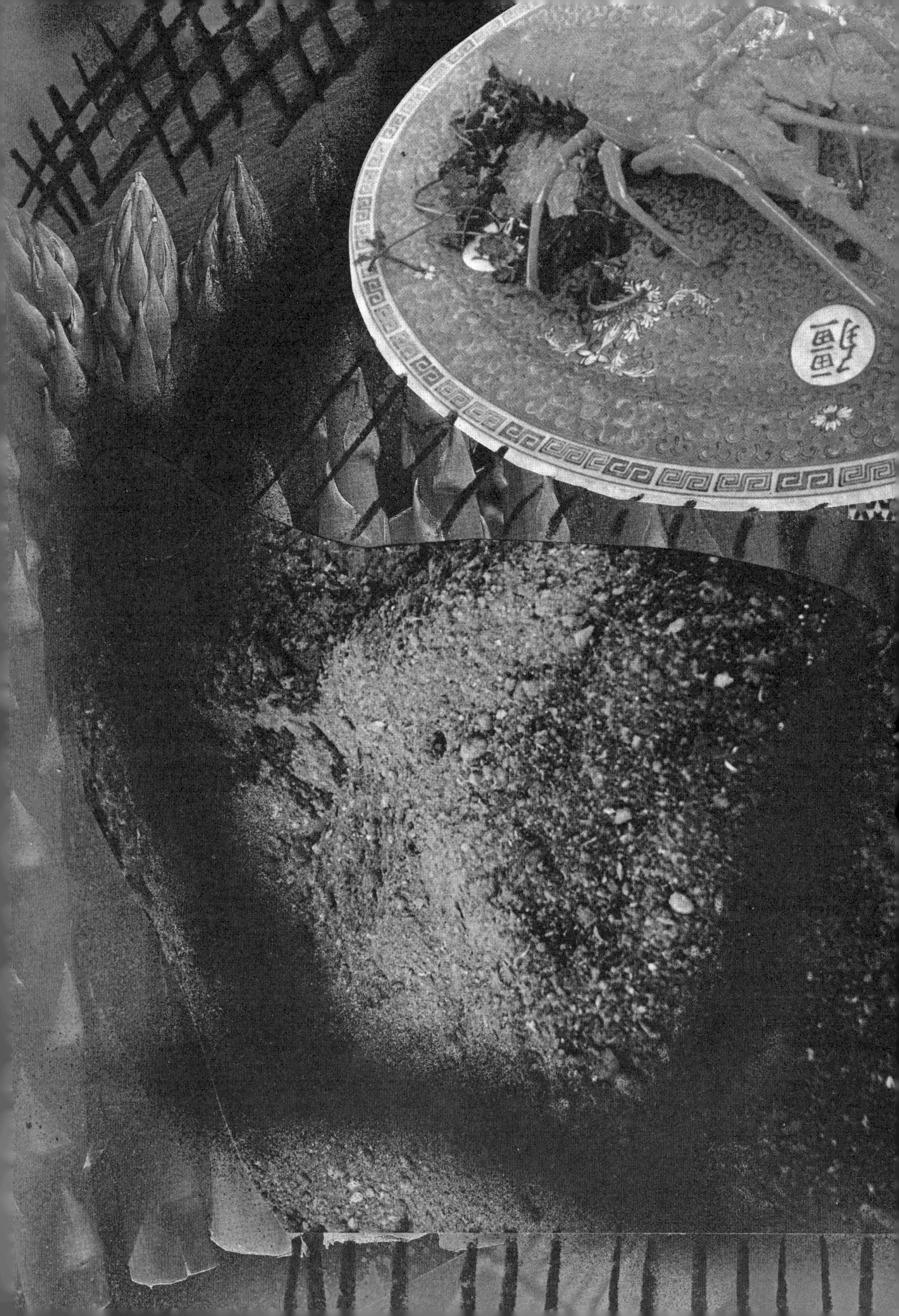

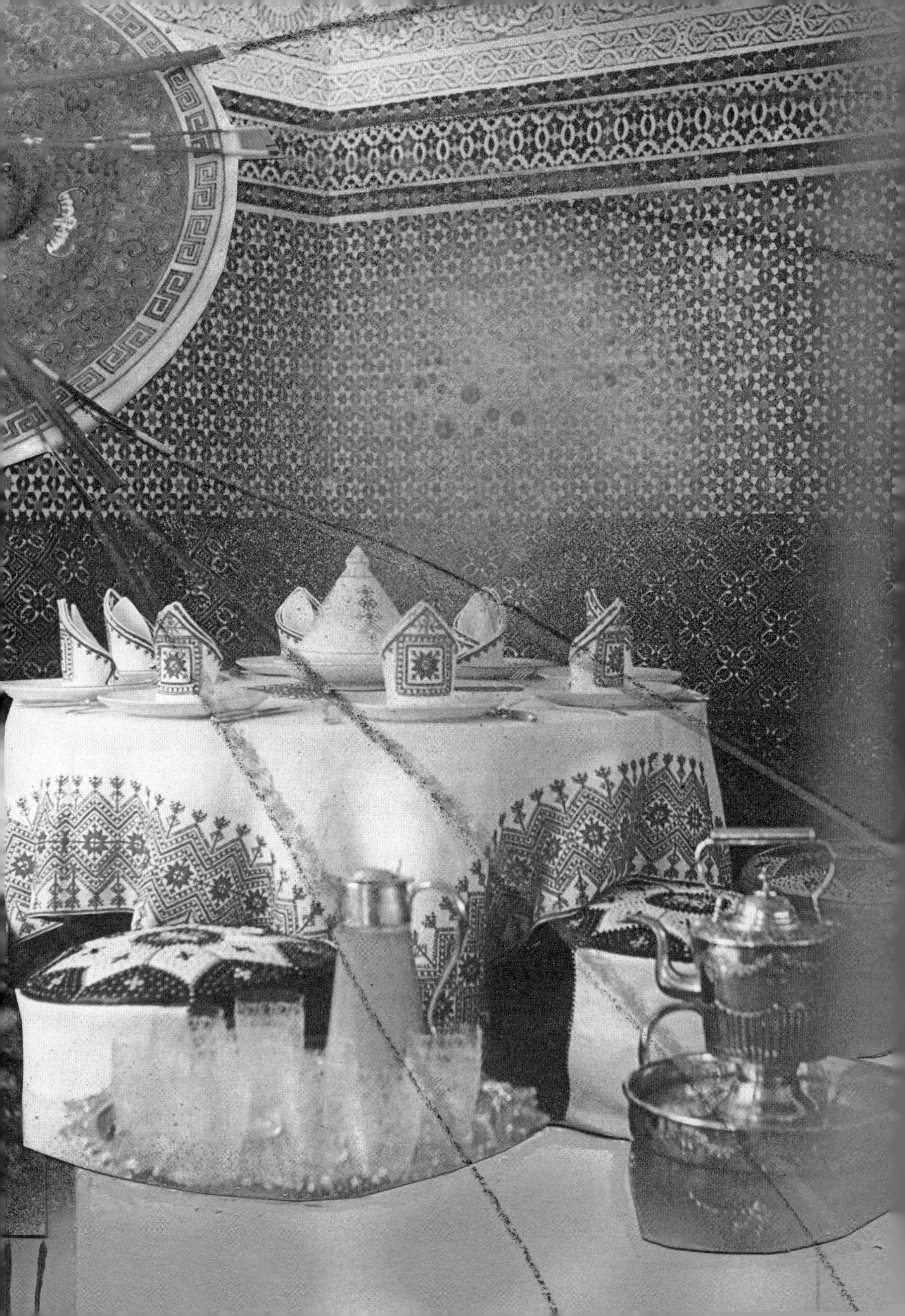

BIOGRAPHIES

Thomas J. Berghuis is a curator and art historian based in Leiden, the Netherlands. A scholar of contemporary art in China and Indonesia, Berghuis previously worked as lecturer in Asian art at the University of Sydney, curator of Chinese art at the Guggenheim Museum in New York and founding director of the museum MACAN in Jakarta. More recently, he worked as a lecturer in contemporary art at the University of Amsterdam and as a consultant for various (inter)national art projects.

Elisabeth de Bièvre studied at Utrecht University and the Courtauld Institute, London. She has taught at the University of East Anglia, University College London, and UCLA and delivered the Baldwin Lectures at Oberlin College, Ohio, and the Gombrich lectures at the China Academy of Art in Hangzhou. Concerned with the arts worldwide she has developed theories on the influence of the physical and cultural environment on art production, particularly in the Netherlandish context. After articles in *Art History* and elsewhere, her most recent publication is: *Dutch Art and Urban Cultures, 1200–1700* (2015).

John Clark is Professor Emeritus in Art History at the University of Sydney where he taught for twenty-two years. He published *Modern Asian Art* (1995), and *Asian Modernities: Chinese and Thai Art of the 1980s and 1990s* (2011). *Modernities of Chinese*

Art (2010) and *Modernities of Japanese* Art (2013) were published by Brill. *The Asian Modern, 1850s–1990s* (2021) was published by the National Gallery of Singapore. Also from 2021 is his *Contemporary Asian Art at Biennials, studies from 2000–2005*.

Thomas DaCosta Kaufmann is Frederick Marquand Professor of Art and Archaeology, Princeton University. The recipient of many fellowships, memberships in academies, and two honorary doctorates, he has published or edited nineteen books and over 250 articles and reviews on art and architecture in Early Modern Central Europe, art and science, the geography of art, and the theory and historiography of art history. Elizabeth Pilliod's and his *Global Visions*, a comprehensive new global art history textbook, is forthcoming (Pearson).

Parisa Damandan (Iran) is a (documentary) photographer, photo journalist, teacher and art historian. Since 1993 Damandan's research aims at preserving endangered photo archives, gathering and classifying numerous archival materials including the early studio photographers of Esfahan, the photographs of the German telegraph engineer Ernst Hoeltzer, and the photography archives of ruined studios in the city of Bam (IR) after the earthquake. She collaborated with the British Library's Endangered Archives project in Iran and organized the photography collection and digital visual data bank of the late poet Ahmad Shamlou. Her work includes documentary films, papers, exhibitions, films and books.

Wilfried van Damme studied Art History, Archaeology, and Cultural Anthropology. He received his PhD in art history from Ghent University in 1993. He has been mainly concerned with developing an intercultural and interdisciplinary approach to aesthetics, in addition to publishing on world art studies and intellectual history. Van Damme has taught African art and world art studies, most recently at Leiden University (2004–2021). Of late, he has been involved in a forthcoming exhibition on African aesthetics at the Art Institute of Chicago.

Sophie Ernst is a Dutch artist based in Berlin and Oxford. In her artistic and theoretical work (PhD Leiden University, 2016) she asks questions about mediated perception in relation to architecture, memory, historical objects, and identity. Her works evolve from conversations and interviews and she sees making art as a response to these encounters. Exhibitions include: Moscow Biennale; Asia Triennial, Manchester; Sharjah Biennial; Johnson Museum, Cornell University; Nasher Museum, Duke University; ZKM Karlsruhe; Kunstverein Heidelberg; Museum de Lakenhal Leiden; Yorkshire Sculpture Park.
– sophieernst.com

Angèle Etoundi Essamba, born in Douala, Cameroon, was educated in France and graduated from the School of Photography of Amsterdam, where she lives. At the intersection of the social, gender, and the artistic field, African women constitute her main subject. Challenging and breaking with stereotypical representations, her portraits reflect strength, pride, and awareness. She exhibits worldwide, and her work has appeared in many publications, including: *Passion* (1989), *Contrasts* (1995), *Symboles* (1999), *Noirs* (2001), *La Métamorphose du sublime* (2003), *Dialogues* (2006), *Voiles & Dévoilements* (2008), *Black & Red* (2012), *Women of the Water* (2013), *Invisible* (2015), *Strength & Pride*, (2016), *Daughters of Life* (2018), and *Renaissance* (2019).

Paul Faber studied Art History at the University of Amsterdam (UvA). After teaching at the University of Amsterdam and the Rietveld Academie, and working as Head of Presentations at the Wereldmuseum Rotterdam, he was Africa curator at the Tropenmuseum Amsterdam for seventeen years. Currently he is an independent curator and author. He realized many exhibitions and publications, mainly on modern and popular art and culture in Africa and Surinam.
– paulfaber.nl

Claire Farago is Professor Emerita at the University of Colorado, Boulder, and Ruth and Clarence Kennedy Professor of Renaissance Studies at Smith College, Northampton, MA (Fall 2021). Her publications include *The Fabrication of Leonardo da Vinci's Trattato della Pittura* (2018), co-authored with a team of Leonardo scholars; *Art is Not What You Think It Is* (co-authored with Donald Preziosi, 2012); *Grasping the World: The Idea of the Museum* (co-edited with Donald Preziosi, 2004); and *Reframing the Renaissance* (1995). She was among the first to shift emphasis in art history toward transcultural studies.
– cfarago.wordpress.com

Anne Gerritsen teaches the History of China at the University of Warwick (UK) and holds the Chair of Asian Art at Leiden University. Her recent work focuses on exchange between Asia and Europe, especially porcelain. Recent publications include *The City of Blue and White: Chinese Porcelain and the Early Modern World* (2020), *Writing Material Culture History* (co-edited with Giorgio Riello), second edition 2021 and *The Global Lives of Things* (co-edited with Giorgio Riello), 2016.

Isabel Hoving is Associate Professor at the Department of Film and Literary Studies at Leiden University, where she teaches postcolonial theory and theories of globalization, gender studies, video game studies and cultural analysis. Her publications include monographs on Caribbean (women's) literature and the intersections of postcolonial theory and ecocriticism. She has co-edited books on Dutch racism, the literatures of (Dutch) migration, Caribbean literatures, African literature and art, and has written a range of essays on the artistic exploration of globalization, climate change, racism, gender, and sexuality. Between 2014–2019, she acted as the first academic (chief) Diversity Officer in the Netherlands.

Stijn Huijts is managing and artistic director of the Bonnefanten museum in Maastricht, the Netherlands. Prior to joining the museum in 2012, he served as founding director of SCHUNCK* Heerlen, and as director of Museum Het Domein in Sittard. He has organized numerous exhibitions and collaborative projects with artists, including the Dutch Pavilion at the 26th São Paulo Biennial. Huijts has served on the board of the International Committee of Modern Art Museums (CIMAM), and the advisory board of the Dutch National Heritage Board. He holds an MA in cultural studies from the University of Amsterdam.

Nancy Jouwe is a cultural historian and freelance researcher, lecturer, and public speaker. She is interested in the (post)colonial past and present, intersectionality, and social and cultural practices. As author and co-editor she published on intersectionality and feminism, gender and colonialism and the Dutch history of slavery. Her most recent publications include *De slavernij in Oost en West. Het Amsterdam onderzoek* (2020); *Slavernij en de stad Utrecht* (2021); and *Slavernij Herbezien* [Revisualizing Slavery] (2021).

Remy Jungerman, Surinam-born Dutch artist, lives and works in Amsterdam. He attended the Academy for Higher Arts and Cultural Studies in Paramaribo, Surinam, before moving to Amsterdam where he studied at the Gerrit Rietveld Academie. In his work, Jungerman explores the intersection of pattern and symbol in Surinamese Maroon culture, the larger African Diaspora, and twentieth-century 'Modernism'. In engaging seemingly disparate visual languages in conversation, Jungerman's work challenges the established art historical canon.
– remyjungerman.com

Sonja van Kerkhoff, of Dutch, Scottish, Isle of Man, Irish, and Cornish descent, was born in Hawera, Taranaki, Aotearoa New Zealand. She is a graduate of the Dunedin School of Art (1982), the Maastricht Institute of Arts (1993), and has an MSc in Media Technology from Leiden University (2008). She was a multimedia designer for Dutch Educational Broadcasting (now NTR) from 1999–2009. Her conceptually driven works of art range from the interactive to sculpture and printmaking. She is a contributor to *Feminist Art Activisms and Artivisms* (2020), makes exhibitions, and writes art reviews.
– sonjavank.com;
– sonjavank.wordpress.com

Meta Knol is director of Leiden European City of Science 2022. She studied Art History at Utrecht University, specializing in modern and contemporary art. From 2009 to 2020 she was director of Museum De Lakenhal in Leiden. She is an advocate of museological innovation, makes exhibitions, likes to write about visual art, preferably thinks and works in an interdisciplinary way and is a co-initiator of various cultural initiatives, including Framer Framed in Amsterdam. Knol holds various board positions in the cultural sector, such as at Kunsten '92 and the Rembrandt Association.

Frans-Willem Korsten holds the chair by special appointment 'Literature and Society' at the Erasmus School of Philosophy in Rotterdam, and is Associate Professor at the Leiden University Centre for the Arts in Society (LUCAS). He published monographs on the Dutch baroque, theatricality, and sovereignty, such as *A Dutch Republican Baroque* (2017), and has written extensively on the relation between literature, art, capitalism, and law. His latest publication is *Art as an Interface of Law and Justice: Affirmation, Disturbance, Disruption* (2021).

Katja Kwastek, et al: Joo Yun Lee, Maryland Institute College of Art (MICA), Baltimore; Katja Kwastek, Vrije Universiteit Amsterdam; Chris Lee, Pratt Institute New York; Virginia MacKenny, University of Cape Town; Kyveli Mavrokordopoulou, École des Hautes Études en Sciences Sociales, Paris; Jacqueline Hoàng Nguyễn, Konstfack University of Arts, Crafts and Design & KTH Royal Institute of Technology, Stockholm; Jennifer Pranolo, Pace University, New York; Lize van Robbroeck, Stellenbosch University; Pippa Skotnes, University of Cape Town; James Webb, artist, Stockholm; Carine Zaayman, Research Center for Material Culture, Leiden & Vrije Universiteit Amsterdam.

Sybille Lammes is Professor of New Media and Digital Culture at Leiden University. She has been a visiting Research Fellow at the University of Manchester, and worked as a researcher at the University of Warwick as well as at several universities in the Netherlands. Her background is in media- and play-studies. She is co-editor of *The Routledge Handbook of Interdisciplinary Research Methods* (2018) and T*he Playful Citizen* (2019). She is the PI of *Playing Politics* (NWO).

Charl Landvreugd, artist / researcher / educator, applies the results of his research to think about citizenship and belonging and how this is expressed in the visual arts in continental Europe. As a Goldsmiths (BA), Fulbright and Columbia University (MA) alumnus he obtained a PhD in Curating Contemporary Art at the Royal College of Art in London. Landvreugd is Head of Research & Curatorial Practice at the Stedelijk Museum Amsterdam.
– landvreugd.com

Gregor Langfeld is Professor of Modern and Contemporary Art History at the Open University (Netherlands) and the University of Amsterdam. Research includes canon formation, collection and exhibition history, and provenance research. Publications include: 'Modernism in Migration: Relocating Artists, Objects, and Ideas, 1910–1970', *Stedelijk Studies* (co-edited with Tessel Bauduin, 2019); *German Art in New York: The Canonization of Modern Art between 1904 and 1957* (2015, also in German); *The Stedelijk Museum and the Second World War* (co-edited with Margriet Schavemaker and Margreeth Soeting, 2015).

Christa-Maria Lerm Hayes is Professor of Modern and Contemporary Art History and Academic Director of the Amsterdam School for Heritage, Memory and Material Culture, University of Amsterdam. Until 2014 she was Professor of Iconology in Belfast, where she led an art research PhD programme. Her books include: *Brian O'Doherty/Patrick Ireland: Word, Image and Institutional Critique* (edited, 2017), *Post-War Germany and 'Objective Chance': W.G. Sebald, Joseph Beuys and Tacita Dean* (2011), *Joyce in Art* (2004), and *James Joyce als Inspirationsquelle für Joseph Beuys* (2001). She has curated art and 'literary art' exhibitions internationally.
- christamarialermhayes.eu

Sarat Maharaj is Professor of Visual Art & Knowledge Systems, Lund University, Sweden. He was Professor of Art History/Theory, Goldsmiths University of London. He was Rudolf Arnheim Professor, Humboldt University, Berlin (2001–2002) and Stedelijk Fellow, Amsterdam (2018). Curatorial projects: 'Documenta 11' (2002); 'Farewell to Postcolonialism', Guangzhou (2008); 'Sao Paolo Biennale' (2010); 'Pandemonium: art in a time of creativity fever', Gothenburg (2011). His publications cover: Marcel Duchamp, James Joyce and Richard Hamilton, Textiles, Cultural Translation, Xeno-Sonics and Xeno-Epistemics. Two current research projects: Sounding the Knowledge Mecca, Bloomsbury, London and The Apartheid-Era Art History Room, Durban, South Africa.

Tirzo Martha is an artist, co-founder, and director of the Instituto Buena Bista in Curacao. His social involvement and the way in which he knows how to involve his audience directly or indirectly in his creative process of making art, form the common thread in his sculptures. His recent exhibitions include: 'Het huis dat nooit af is' [The house that is never finished], CODA Museum, the Netherlands (2020). Recent publication: *I Wonder If They'll Laugh When I'm Dead* (2017). Martha lives and works in Curacao and the Netherlands.

Larissa Mendoza Straffon is a cognitive archaeologist from Mexico City. She currently is a postdoctoral researcher at the Centre for Early Sapiens Behaviour at the University of Bergen (Norway) and the Cognitive Psychology Unit at Leiden University. Her research focuses on the origins of visual art and aesthetics as a means of understanding human cognitive and cultural evolution. She obtained her PhD at Leiden University in 2014 with the dissertation entitled *Art in the Making: The Evolutionary Origins of Visual Art as a Communication Signal.*

Ni Haifeng is an artist, born in Zhoushan, China. He lives and works in Amsterdam and Beijing. He was part of the mid-1980s New Wave movement in China, marking the beginning of Chinese contemporary art. His work has been exhibited internationally, including: 'China Avantgarde', Haus der Kulturen der Welt, Berlin (1993); 'Unpacking Europe', Museum Boijmans Van Beuningen, Rotterdam (2001); '5th Shanghai Biennale', Shanghai Art Museum, Shanghai (2004); 'Global Contemporary', ZKM Center for Art and Media Karlsruhe (2011); 'Manifesta 9—The Deep of the Modern', Genk, Belgium (2012).
– haifeng.home.xs4all.nl

Stéphanie Noach conducts research, writes, teaches, and curates exhibitions. Her current research focuses on the dynamic relations between the dark, opaque, and black in contemporary art, especially in Latin America and the Caribbean. She has curated exhibitions and events at Havana Biennial, Lugar a Dudas (Cali), MUAC (Mexico), Museo de Antioquia (Medellin), Museo de Bellas Artes (Havana), Stedelijk Museum Bureau and Stedelijk Museum Amsterdam. She is a doctoral candidate at Leiden University and currently a fellow at Harvard University.

Anja Novak is an art historian based at the University of Amsterdam. She obtained her PhD in Art History from Leiden University with a dissertation on the spectatorship associated with Installation Art. Her research focuses on artforms that involve a space-time dimension, spectatorship, and embodied-affective responses to art. Recent publications: 'Broken Circle and Spiral Hill: Having Entropy the Dutch Way' (2020), 'On Myths, Social Engineering and Desire' (with Martine van Kampen, in *Land Art Live. The Flevoland Collection*, 2021); 'Affective spaces. Experiencing atmosphere in the visual arts' (in *Archimaera*, 2019).

John Onians is an art historian who studied at the Courtauld and Warburg Institutes. He is now Professor at the China Academy of Art, Hangzhou, having taught for many years at the University of East Anglia, Norwich. Currently he is exploring ways in which neuroscience can help with the solution of art-historical problems. His recent books include *Atlas of World Art* (editor, 2004), *Neuroarthistory from Aristotle and Pliny to Baxandall and Zeki* (2007) and *European Art: A Neuroarthistory* (2016).
– johnonians.com

Rob Perrée studied Dutch Language and Literature and Art History at the University of Amsterdam. He is an independent international writer and curator with a focus on media art and contemporary African-American, African and Caribbean art. Founder and editor in chief of the online magazine www.africanah.org.

Selection of exhibitions: ‘Postcards from Black America’, De Beyerd Breda/Frans Hals Museum Haarlem (1998–1999); ‘The Visitor’, Istanbul, Galerist, with Emre Baykal (2004); ‘Tembe Fu Libi’, Moengo, SU, with Remy Jungerman (2015); ‘Tell Me Your Story. 100 Years of Storytelling in African American Art’, Kunsthal KAdE Amersfoort (2020).

Georges Petitjean is an art historian who wrote his PhD on Western Desert art at La Trobe University, Melbourne. His main field of interest is the transition of Indigenous Australian art from its sites of origin to the wider art world. Currently curator of the Fondation Opale/Collection Bérengère Primat in Switzerland, he has lived and worked in Australia for several years. From 2005 to 2017, he was curator of the Museum for Contemporary Aboriginal Art (AAMU) in Utrecht, Netherlands. Most recently he curated ‘Breath of Life’ at the Fondation Opale.

Rosalien van der Poel is an art historian and works at Leiden University as Institute Manager of the Academy of Creative and Performing Arts. She is a research associate China at Museum Volkenkunde and board member of the Royal Asian Art Society in the Netherlands. Recent publications include ‘Signed *Beijing Zhou Peichun hua*: Images for foreigners’, leidenspecialcollectionsblog.nl (2021); ‘Sensitive plates’ and ‘sentimental keepsakes’. The Social Life of Reverse Glass Paintings: From Canton to Leiden’, *Revista de Cultura* (2019); *Made for Trade—Made in China: Chinese Export Paintings in Dutch collections: art and commodity* (PhD Leiden University 2016).

Henk Slager is Professor of Artistic Research (HKU Utrecht). He has made significant contributions to the debate on the role of research in visual art. In 2006, he co-initiated the European Artistic Research Network (EARN), a network investigating the consequences of artistic research for current art education in symposia, expert meetings, and presentations. Departing from a similar focus on artistic research, he has also produced various curatorial projects, e.g., ‘Timely Meditations’, 5th Guangzhou Triennial (2016); ‘To Seminar’, BAK, Utrecht (2017); ‘Research Ecologies’, Venice (2019); and ‘Farewell to Research’, 9th Bucharest Biennale (2020). He recently published *The Pleasure of Research* (2015).

Rudi Struik moved to Canada with his parents at the age of five. He studied at the Malaspina Art College in Nanaimo, British Columbia, and after returning to the Netherlands in 1978 continued his studies at the Vrije Academie voor Beeldende Kunsten in The Hague. He makes assemblages and installations from a variety of (used) materials and objects weaving them into new stories. The experience of migration is a recurring theme in his work, see for example the international exhibition ‘The Unwanted Land’, Museum Beelden aan Zee, Scheveningen (2010–2011).
– rudi-struik.com

Eva-Maria Troelenberg is Professor of Modern and Contemporary Art History at Utrecht University. She was head of the Max-Planck-Research Group 'Objects in the Contact Zone—The Cross-Cultural Lives of Things' at Kunsthistorisches Institut in Florence—MPI. Her main fields of interest include the modern Mediterranean, the perception of Islamic art in the West, as well as the practice and theory of transcultural art history. Her recent publications include the volume *Reading Objects in the Contact Zone* (co-edited with Felicity Bodenstein and Anna Sophia Messner, 2021).

Leonor Veiga is an art historian, currently associated with the University of Lisbon through the project 'A History of Presence: A Dialogue between Portuguese Collections of Material Culture from Southeast Asia and Southeast Asian Artists'. Her PhD dissertation, entitled 'The Third Avant-Garde: Contemporary Art from Southeast Asia Recalling Tradition' (Leiden University, 2018) was awarded the Humanities Best Dissertation Prize by the International Convention of Asian Scholars (2019). Her writing on the arts (2010–2021) focuses mainly on Southeast Asia, and her curatorial work (2006–2020) includes exhibitions in Indonesia, Mozambique, London, Macau, and Lisbon.

Leon Wainwright is Professor of Art History at The Open University. His research has a transatlantic scope, spanning a range of studies on modern and contemporary art, anthropology, and museums. His books include the single-authored titles *Timed Out: Art and the Transnational Caribbean* (2011) and *Phenomenal Difference: A Philosophy of Black British Art* (2017), and the co-edited volume *Art in Theory: The West in the World* (2021). He is a recipient of the Philip Leverhulme Prize in the History of Art.

Janneke Wesseling is art historian and art critic. The focus of her work is on the field of artistic research and on reception aesthetics. She is Professor in Practice and Theory of Research in the Visual Arts at the Academy of Creative and Performing Arts (ACPA) of Leiden University. Recent publications include: *The Perfect Spectator: The Experience of the Art Work and Reception Aesthetics* (2017); *Of Sponge, Stone and the Intertwinement with the Here and Now: A Methodology of Artistic Research* (2016); *See it Again, Say it Again: The Artist as Researcher* (editor, 2011).
– jannekewesseling.blogspot.com

Helen Westgeest is Associate Professor of Modern and Contemporary Art History at Leiden University. Her research mainly gears towards insights provided by interdisciplinary approaches into the role of visual media in the meaning production of contemporary artworks. Recent publications include: *Slow Painting: Contemplation and Critique in the Digital Age* (2020); *Video Art Theory: A Comparative Approach* (2016); *Photography Theory* *n Historical Perspective: Case Studies 'rom Contemporary Art* (co-authored vith Hilde Van Gelder, 2011, Chinese ranslation 2013).

Kitty Zijlmans was Professor of Contemporary Art History and Theory/World Art Studies at Leiden Jniversity from 2000–2021. In 2010 he was accepted as member of he KNAW, the Royal Netherlands Academy of Arts and Sciences. Her ields of interest are contemporary ırt, art theory, and methodology from a global viewpoint. Her publications nclude *World Art Studies: Exploring Concepts and Approaches* (co-edited vith Wilfried van Damme, 2008); *Sustainable Art Communities: Contemporary Creativity and Policy in he Transnational Caribbean* (co-edited vith Leon Wainwright, 2017).

Robert Zwijnenberg is Professor Emeritus of Art and Science nteractions at Leiden University. In ıis research and writings Zwijnenberg ocuses on the role of contemporary ırt in the academic and public debates on the ethical, societal, political, egal, and cultural implications of biotechnological innovations. He pecifically engages with a growing ıumber of artists, known as bio-artists, vho use the opportunities provided by the life sciences to work with ıew materials: living materials that raditionally do not belong to the ırtistic realm.

Design and Publisher

Lotte Lara Schröder is an artist and graphic designer, interested in ecological and natural phenomena. Her 'free' work consists of drawings, paintings, and collages, often combined with sound or objects. Lotte created the overall book and cover design, and the opening chapter images of this publication. These collages reveal elements of our culinary and food system, embedded in layered cross-cultural visuals. Each chapter opening shows a vegetable that 'travelled the world'. The seven themes—double-page spreads—freely symbolize the topics of these parts of the book. Images from Lotte's personal archive mixed with others sourced online, reveal personal, natural, and sometimes upsetting visuals that represent our current state of being.
—www.termsofcircumstance.org
—www.speculativepress.org

Valiz is an independent international publisher, addressing contemporary developments in art, design, architecture, and urban affairs. Their books provide critical reflection and interdisciplinary inspiration in a broad and imaginative way, often establishing a connection between cultural disciplines and socio-economic questions. Valiz is headed by Astrid Vorstermans and Pia Pol.

www.valiz.nl
@valiz_books_projects

INDEX OF INGREDIENTS

INDEX OF NAMES

M

N

R

COLOPHON

EDITORS
Helen Westgeest, Kitty Zijlmans

CONTRIBUTIONS BY
Thomas J. Berghuis, Elisabeth de Bièvre, John Clark, Thomas DaCosta Kaufmann, Parisa Damandan, Wilfried van Damme, Sophie Ernst, Angèle Etoundi Essamba, Paul Faber, Claire Farago, Anne Gerritsen, Jacqueline Hoàng Nguyễn, Isabel Hoving, Stijn Huijts, Nancy Jouwe, Remy Jungerman, Sonja van Kerkhoff, Meta Knol, Frans-Willem Korsten, Katja Kwastek, Sybille Lammes, Charl Landvreugd, Gregor Langfeld, Chris Lee, Joo Yun Lee, Christa-Maria Lerm Hayes, Virginia MacKenny, Sarat Maharaj, Tirzo Martha, Kyveli Mavrokordopoulou, Larissa Mendoza Straffon, Ni Haifeng, Stéphanie Noach, Anja Novak, John Onians, Rob Perrée, Georges Petitjean, Rosalien van der Poel, Jennifer Pranolo, Lize van Robbroeck, Pippa Skotnes, Henk Slager, Rudi Struik, Eva-Maria Troelenberg, Leonor Veiga, Leon Wainwright, James Webb, Janneke Wesseling, Helen Westgeest, Carine Zaayman, Kitty Zijlmans, Robert Zwijnenberg

TRANSLATION
Janey Tucker (Perrée), Anna Yeadell (Knol, Landvreugd), Susan Pond (Huijts)

COPY-EDITING
Leo Reijnen

PROOFREADING
Elke Stevens

INDEX
Elke Stevens

IMAGE RESEARCH
the authors, Lotte Lara Schröder

GRAPHIC DESIGN
Lotte Lara Schröder
(incl. chapter openings, theme images, cover)

TYPEFACES
Ohno Blazeface by OH No Type Co.
Ginto Normal by Dinamo
Times New Roman MT Std

PAPER
Munken Print White 1.5 100 gr
Fedrigoni Arena Natural Rough 200 gr

LITHOGRAPHY
Mariska Bijl, Wilco Art Books, Amsterdam

PRINTING AND BINDING
Wilco Art Books, Amersfoort

PUBLISHER
Valiz, Amsterdam 2021
Astrid Vorstermans & Pia Pol
www.valiz.nl

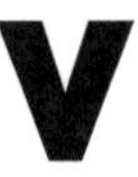

INTERNATIONAL DISTRIBUTION
BE/NL/LU: Centraal Boekhuis, www.centraal.boekhuis.nl
Europe/Asia (except GB/IE): Idea Books, www.ideabooks.nl
GB/IE: Anagram Books, www.anagrambooks.com
USA/Canada/Latin America: D.A.P., www.artbook.com
Australia: Perimeter Books, www.perimeterbooks.com
Individual orders: www.valiz.nl; info@valiz.nl

This publication has been printed on FSC-certified paper by an FSC-certified printer. The FSC, Forest Stewardship Council promotes environmentally appropriate, socially beneficial, and economically viable management of the world's forests. fsc.org

This book has been generously supported by the
• Mondriaan Fund
• Academy of Creative and Performing Arts (ACPA), University of the Arts, The Hague / Faculty of Humanities, Leiden University

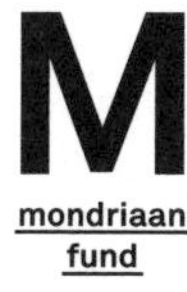

Academie
Academy of
der
Creative and
Kunsten
Performing Arts

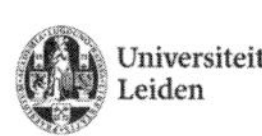

ISBN 978-94-93246-05-8
Printed and bound in the EU, 2021

MY RECIPES

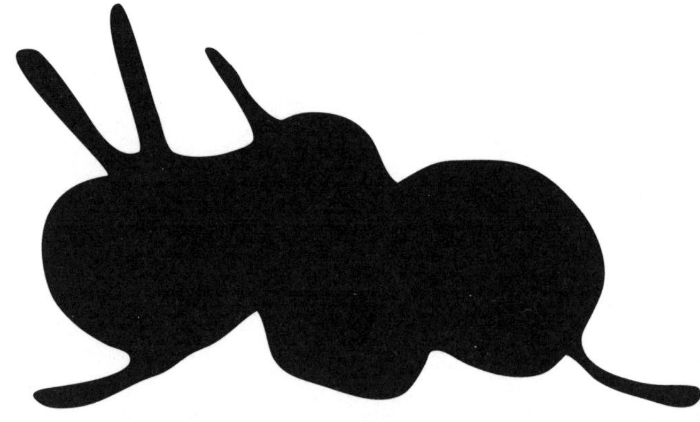

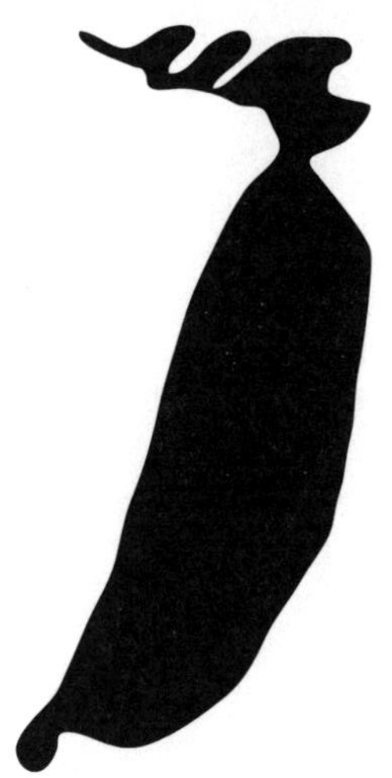

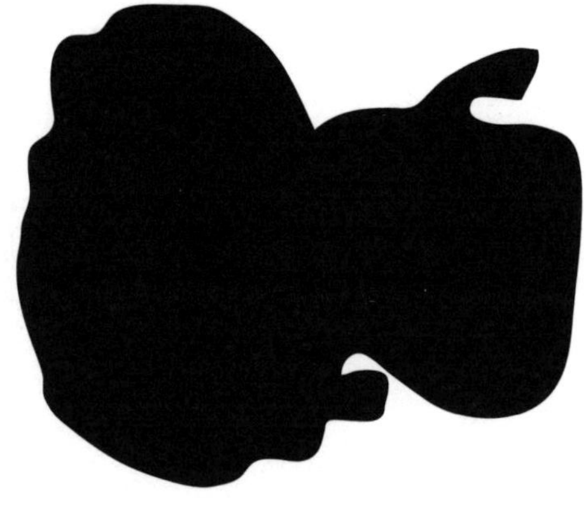

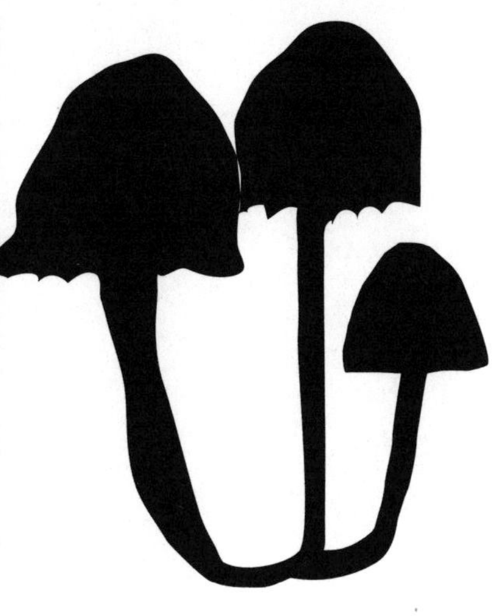

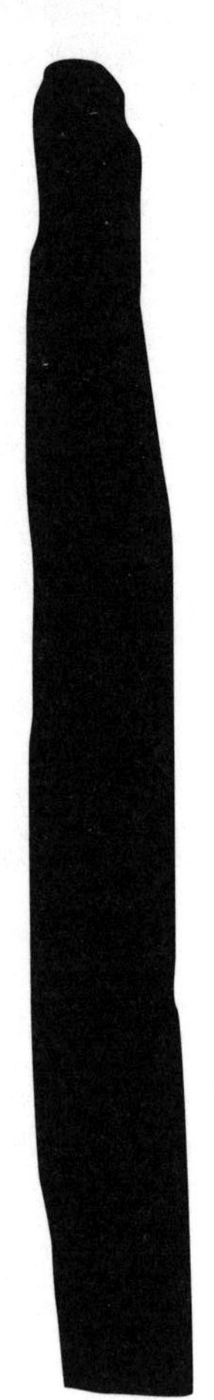

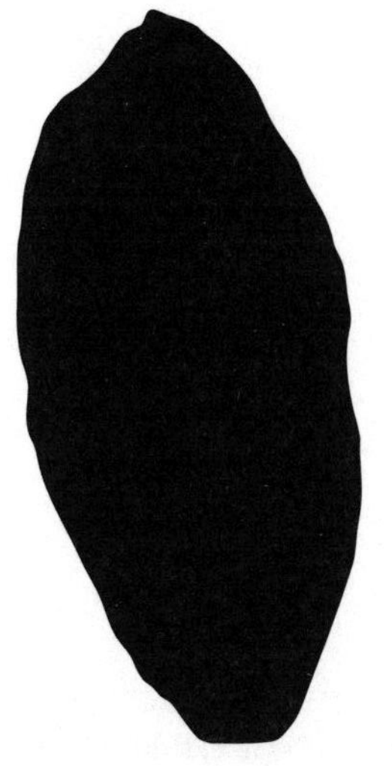

Plural

The PLURAL series focuses on how the intersections between, identity, power, representation and emancipation play out in the arts and in cultural practices. The volumes in this series aim to do justice to the plurality of voices, experiences and perspectives in society and in the arts and to address the history, present and future meaning of these positions and their interrelations. PLURAL brings together new and critical insights from artists, arts professionals, activists, cultural and social researchers, journalists and theorists. Series design by Lotte Lara Schröder.

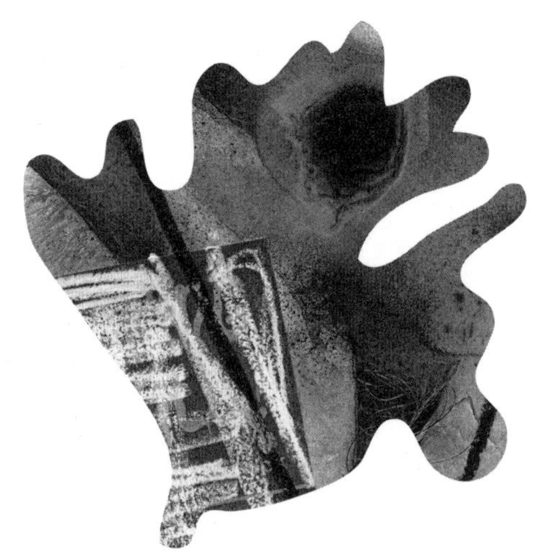

Mix & Stir is the fourth volume in the PLURAL series.

Printed and bound in the EU, 2021

The other three are:

Feminist Art Activisms and Artivisms
ed. Katy Deepwell, ISBN 978-94-92095-72-5

SHAME! and Masculinity
ed. Ernst van Alphen, ISBN 978-94-92095-92-3

DESIGN STRUGGLES
Intersecting Histories, Pedagogies, and Perspectives
eds. Claudia Mareis & Nina Paim
ISBN 978-94-92095-88-6